READING:
A HISTORY

Reading

A HISTORY

JOAN DILS

Reading: a history

Copyright © Joan Dils, 2019

First published in 2019 by
Carnegie Publishing Ltd
Chatsworth Road,
Lancaster LA1 4SL
www.carnegiepublishing.com

British Library Cataloguing-in-Publication data
A catalogue record for this book is available from the British Library

ISBN 978-1-85936-234-1

Designed, typeset and originated by Carnegie Publishing
Printed and bound in the UK by Cambrian Printers

Contents

Foreword

IN 1961 in an article in the *Berkshire Archaeological Journal (BAJ)*, Dr Cecil Slade, lecturer in history at the University of Reading and founder of a new department of Archaeology, called for the publication of edited transcripts (and translations where necessary) of the records of the Corporation and the Abbey and other significant sources relating to the borough as an essential preliminary to a new 'History of Reading'. There had been no scholarly history of the borough since Rev Charles Coates' *History and Antiquities of Reading* in 1802 though the third volume of the *Victoria County History of Berkshire* (1923) included a substantial account of the town, its manors and parishes.[1] Since 1961 other histories have appeared, notably Daphne Phillips' *The Story of Reading* in 1980.

The first transcripts of important medieval texts by Dr Slade and other colleagues appeared in the *Berkshire Archaeological Journal* in 1961 and in a few subsequent volumes. In 1986–7 Professor Brian Kemp's edition of the charters of Reading Abbey was published and together he and Dr Slade summarised (calendared) the contents of the borough's medieval deeds which sadly remain as unpublished transcripts in the Berkshire Record Office.[2] Perhaps Dr Slade's greatest gift to future historians is his edition of the account rolls of Reading's Merchant Gild, published shortly after his death by the Berkshire Record Society (BRS). Founded in 1993, the Society has already produced several volumes of the sources so valued by Cecil and promises many more. Moreover, editions of national records such as the Poll Taxes of 1377–81 and the Compton Religious Census of 1676 containing material relevant to Reading have appeared in print.[3]

I have utilised these and other printed original sources, published accounts of aspects of the town's history, MA and doctoral theses written over the last half century, and many unpublished records held in local and national record offices to produce a work which I hope will begin to realise Cecil's dream of an 'up-to-date history of this ancient and important borough.' Although this is a chronological account, successive periods have each been discussed in terms of their distinctive social, economic and political structures which indicate, I believe, that Reading's history has been shaped in large measure by two factors: primarily its location and secondly the energy and skills of the townspeople, especially the many newcomers the town has attracted over the centuries.

The commission to write a new history was made by Carnegie Publishers at the suggestion of Dr Alan Crosby. I am immensely grateful to both of them for entrusting me with the task and their patience over my many missed deadlines. For its eventual completion I am indebted to the generous help of many amateur and professional local historians. The staff of the Berkshire Record Office and Reading Local Studies Library (RLSL) have patiently answered my requests for documents; Anne Smith (RLSL) and Angela Houghton (Reading Museum) have provided illustrations from the borough and museum collections; David Cliffe, Sidney Gold, Brian Kemp, Margaret Simons, Anne Smith and Margaret Yates read several chapters, saving me from a number of errors and omissions, those remaining being my own. Other colleagues and friends have contributed material from their own researches, noted in my references. My biggest debt is to Clive Brown who has not only drawn the maps but also conjured digital images of remarkable clarity from a variety of sources.

Finally, to my three Rs: my deceased husband, Ray, who always supported and encouraged my work, and my daughters Ruth and Rachael to whom this book is dedicated.

1

Beginnings and the early medieval town to *c*.1350

F ROM a barely visible settlement in the fifth century and a small royal borough in 1086, Reading had acquired a charter, a thriving market, a royal abbey, a Franciscan friary, and had become the second richest town in Berkshire by 1334. Such progress had been fostered by its location and its ability to attract migrants.

Beginnings

Geologists trace the site of Reading to a fortunate combination of rocks and rivers several millennia ago creating a four-mile long, 30 foot high gravel ridge bisected by the river Kennet before it joined the Thames. The ridge is best appreciated today by the way the road to Caversham via Reading Bridge declines steeply under the embanked railway. Archaeologists have found tools and other evidence of early settlers some thousands of years ago attracted by the dry terrace above flood levels, with good water supplies, fertile soil for arable and pasture and access across both rivers by fords.[1] Documentary sources for historians do not appear until comparatively recent times.

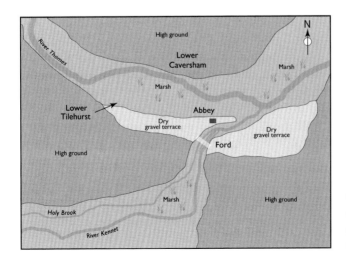

The site of Reading on a gravel terrace above the Kennet (based on a map in M. Hinton, *A History of the Town of Reading*, 1954).

The occasional but frequent finds of coins in the town centre are not yet thought sufficient to indicate a major Roman settlement within the ancient borough though recent archaeological investigations within the post-1887 borough have revealed evidence of rural settlements dating from the Iron Age and Roman periods (first to fourth centuries AD) and at Green Park and Reading Business Park. Finds of coins and pottery excavated prior to housing and other developments in the Whitley area suggest the existence of similar settlements there. More significant may be the excavation of a timber-lined Roman well, a baptismal font and many artefacts at Dean's Farm, Caversham in 1988 and of a hoard of about 300 late Roman coins and possibly a Roman farm at Ridgeway School, Whitley in 2015. The evidence that Reading was the port for Silchester, if it exists, has yet to be found.[2] It is not clear why a site with

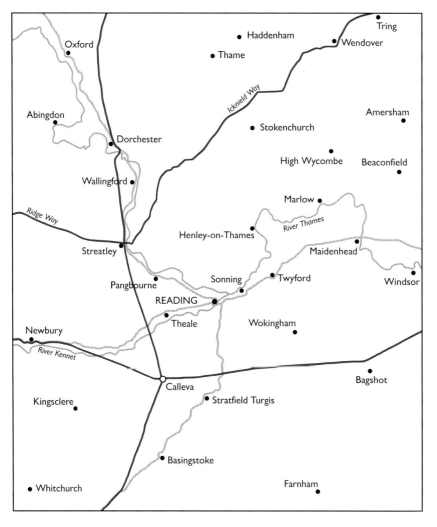

Reading's location: Roman roads converged on Calleva; rivers and Saxon roads on Reading. (CS)

obvious advantages was not more heavily populated, especially given that it had access by water to London, the main town of Roman Britain and by road to the north by an ancient crossing of the Thames at Caversham. The nearest Roman roads ran several miles to the west and south heading for the major town of this period, Silchester, *Calleva Atrebatum*, 'capital' of the Atrebates, about 14 miles south of Reading. Ironically, the finds made there in the 1920s are a major attraction at Reading Museum where a special gallery was created for it.[3]

In the fifth century Silchester gradually became a backwater as Roman administration began to collapse about the time the first Anglo-Saxons arrived in the Reading area. A number of their cemeteries have been discovered including two small ones in Reading, one near the Kennet/ Thames confluence and the other near present-day Cemetery Junction with 50 burials. Some have suggested these indicate Silchester's attempts to defend its territory from incursions by using one Saxon group to repel others, a doomed technique adopted elsewhere. These people soon settled over an area possibly coterminous with the Domesday Hundred of Reading.[4] Margaret Gelling agrees, suggesting that *Readingas* or *Radingas*, is one of a group of place names ending in *-ingas*, denoting areas of early settlement. The name means 'the people of Read(a)', 'the red one'; it did not refer to a confined urban location but to a much wider region, possibly extending for seven miles bounded by the Thames, but these people and their leader gave the future town its name. The nearby village of Sonning (*Sunningas*, Sunna's people) has a similar derivation and was probably a settlement in the neighbouring province. This region which would become part of the county of Berkshire was a disputed zone between Mercia and Wessex until at least the ninth century, and although a number of potential urban sites developed, among them Abingdon with an abbey, Wantage, Cookham and Reading with minsters, there was as yet no single important centre. Consequently, according to Asser's *Life of Alfred*, written in 893, the county derived its name, *Berrocscire*, not from a town but from a natural feature, the abundance of box wood.[5]

Archaeological evidence for early Anglo-Saxon Reading is disappointingly sparse, especially in the area between Broad Street and Minster Street around St Mary's church, considered to have been the heart of the small settlement. A coffin with ninth-century coins has been unearthed in St Mary's churchyard and a few more burials, one of *c*.630–780 in the Forbury and another of the ninth century have been found to the north-west.[6]

In the late sixth and early seventh centuries the Thames valley provided an important corridor between the rich agricultural area around Eynsham/Dorchester and Westminster, and it was here that an exceptional number of minster churches was founded: 25 of them in Berkshire including one in Reading. These were sometimes substantial

The Hundred of
Reading, 1086. (CS)

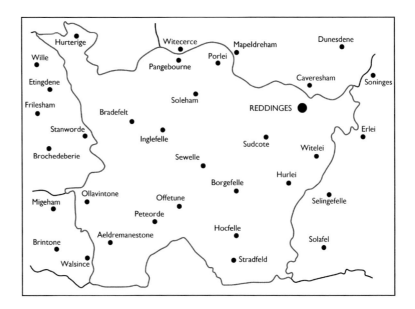

Hurterige
Wille
Etingdene
Frilesham
Stanworde
Brochedeberie
Migeham
Brintone
Walsince
Ollavintone
Aeldremanestone
Peteorde
Offetune
Bradefelt
Inglefelle
Sewelle
Soleham
Witecerce
Pangebourne
Porlei
Mapeldreham
REDDINGES
Sudcote
Witelei
Borgefelle
Hocfelle
Stradfeld
Hurlei
Selingefelle
Solafel
Caveresham
Dunesdene
Soninges
Erlei

The Saxon settlement is thought to have extended from the Kennet to modern Broad Street, and the Danish camp to have occupied the area on which the abbey was built. (CS)

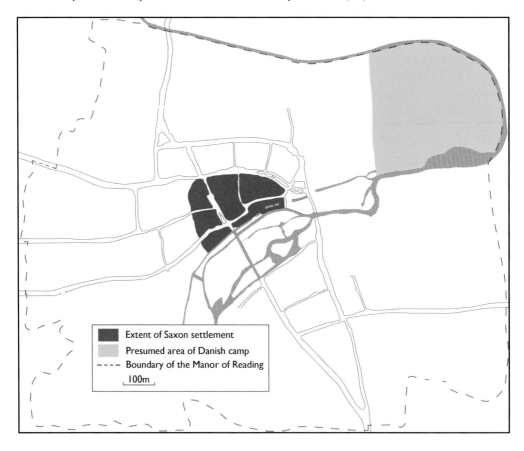

Extent of Saxon settlement
Presumed area of Danish camp
Boundary of the Manor of Reading
100m

stone churches with outbuildings, although Reading's was probably wooden, home to a community of priests who had responsibility for a large parochial area whose population came to the minster for Mass and other church services. (Parishes centred on a parish church were a development of the twelfth century.) Intended to become important centres, the sites of minsters were carefully chosen, often in a royal vill above a waterway with an important road crossing.[7] Reading met all the criteria: it lay on a 'nodal point' where river and road met and Asser called it a royal vill in 871. The precise site chosen has traditionally been located where St Mary's church would later stand, just north of the Holy Brook and the crossing of the Kennet by Seven Bridges. As with most minsters, virtually nothing is known about its early history. However, such institutions became important social and economic as well as religious centres. Market places organically developed outside the west door of the church, as worshippers leaving the service became customers. The street outside what is now St Mary's west door is wide enough for a market place; it was known as Old Street by about 1160 and later

The west front of St Mary's church faced onto the Old Market in Old Street, now a wide street, West Street.

the Old Market. From its northern end a concave-curved street (later Broad Street) marked what is thought to be the northern boundary of the emerging town, the Minster Mill stream forming its southern limit. What would be called Minster Street (the name was not recorded until *c.*1240) emerged at some date at right angles to Old Street; its path would be diverted to the south by a later extension of St Mary's graveyard. So around the minster precinct the Saxon town grew; in Reading as elsewhere, minster preceded town, not vice-versa.[8]

It was this putative urban settlement which was attacked by a Danish Viking army in 871 and where it made camp over the winter. Groups of invaders, driven from their homeland by a combination of overpopulation and political instability, had been plundering monasteries and towns since the 850s but returning home for the winter. However, from 866 large armies, having plundered in summer, found secure bases in England and remained. In 871 fresh from victories over Northumbria, Mercia and the East Angles, they turned westwards. Probably travelling via the Thames, they made Reading their base for an invasion of Wessex. Asser wrote that they fortified their camp with a *vallum*, a rampart, riding out to plunder livestock, especially horses, food and precious objects. Unlike Wallingford which by the 880s was a *burh*, one of a ring of heavily defended settlements to protect the heartland of Wessex, Reading was a soft target given its easy access by water. The camp was set up to the east of the Saxon town, the most likely place being a triangle on the gravel ridge to the west of the Thames/Kennet confluence. It was a good defensive site bounded to the north by water meadows reaching to the Thames and to the south by the Kennet. The name, *Vastern* ('stronghold' in Old English), later applied to the water meadows, seems to confirm the location, added to which a sword dating from the ninth century was discovered in the Vastern in 1831. If the camp housed the whole army, said to number three thousand, it would have occupied most of the space between Broken Brow and the western boundary of the later abbey.

Though the men of Wessex defeated the invaders in battle they could not prevent them retaining their hold on Reading where the following year they were joined by a great army. Alfred, king of Wessex after his brother's death, had little choice but to buy them off, allowing them to find winter quarters in London. Thereafter, during the decades of war against successive Viking raids, the consolidation of royal power in Wessex, the formation of the Danelaw (Danish-occupied eastern England) and the emergence of a kingdom of England, nothing is recorded about Reading.[9]

However, the Danes had not finished with the town. From the 980s a powerful army of professional soldiers began to raid the kingdom of Æthelred the Unready. 'Towards midwinter' in 1006, led by King Swein

ED:WARD REX: VBI:hARO

Part of Reading's
Bayeux
Tapestry:
Edward the
Confessor
enthroned. (RM)

of Denmark from a base they established on the Isle of Wight, they
'took themselves to their prepared depots, out through Hampshire into
Berkshire at Reading; and they did, in their custom, ignite their beacons
as they travelled, and travelled then to Wallingford and scorched it all up
… that year the King paid tribute to the Danes.'[10] Danish raids continued
sporadically for several more years but there is no further record of
attacks on Reading. On the contrary, the town is thought to have enjoyed
modest prosperity; the economy revived as the Danes exchanged raiding
for settlement. Certainly there was a 'minor late Saxon mint' here, the
least of all the mints established by Edward the Confessor (1042–66) since
only two coins have been discovered compared to six from Oxford and
12 from Winchester. Reading was one of 12 new mints set up by the king
early in his reign possibly to strengthen minting facilities around London
at a time when Wallingford was 'in disorder' but whose usefulness waned
as Wallingford recovered. Edward may also have given the settlement the
status of a borough by virtue of its role not as a mint but as a trading
centre. This would have allowed its merchants to acquire personal and
commercial freedom and eventually some local self-government.[11] There
was also a nunnery here, possibly founded in 979 but not present in 1086,
thought to have been located east of the town where the abbey was later
built rather than on the site of St Mary's church.[12]

The Danish attack on Reading

According to the *Anglo-Saxon Chronicle*

[The year] 871. Here the raiding army rode to Reading in Wessex and three days afterwards two jarls [ealdormen] rode up country; then Ealdorman Æthelwulf met them on Englefield and fought against them there and took the victory; and one of the jarls whose name was Sidroc was killed there. Then four days later King Æthelred and Alfred his brother led a great army there to Reading and fought against the raiding army; and great slaughter was made there on either side, and Ealdorman Æthelwulf was killed and the Danes had possession of the place of slaughter.

And after this fight [at Ashdown when Æthelred and Alfred were defeated] a great summer fleet came to Reading. After Easter Æthelred died and Alfred succeeded him and continued the fight.

871. Here the raiding army went from Reading to London and took winter quarters there.

Source: Michael Swanton (ed. and trans.), *The Anglo-Saxon Chronicles* (paperback edn, 2000), 71–2. Swanton sites Englefield as ten miles west of Reading, its name meaning 'the plain of the Angles' as interpreted by Margaret Gelling.

According to Asser's *Life of Alfred*, 893

In the year of Our Lord 871 and in the twenty-third year of Alfred's reign, the army of the pagans of hated memory left the Kingdom of the East Angles and came to the West Saxons. They came to the royal vill which is called *Raedigam* lying south of the River Thames in the county which is called *Beurrocscire*. The third day after their arrival two of their counts with a great number of men rode out to find booty, and others made a *vallum* between the Thames and *Cynetan* [Kennet] Rivers on the right side of the royal vill. Æthelwulf, a count of the country of *Bearrocscire* met

them with his comrades in a place called *Englafeld* in English, in Latin the Field of the English, and there was a battle there fought fiercely by both sides. And when at last both sides stopped, one pagan count was killed and part of the army destroyed. The rest fled, giving victory to the Christians.

When he had been told about this event, King Æthelred and Alfred his brother came to *Raedigam* four days later with an army.

Note: as a monk, Asser saw these events in terms of Christian-pagan wars. *Source*: W. Stephenson (ed. and trans.), *Asser's Life of Alfred* (1904).

The Norman Conquest

1066 is one of those dates which every schoolchild once used to know and perhaps still does. There is no evidence about the Berkshire levies which fought at the Battle of Hastings though doubtless they were there. To commemorate this victory, a great series of pictures was embroidered, probably by English women, which we know as the Bayeux Tapestry. It was displayed in Bayeux cathedral on great occasions and is now housed in a splendid museum in the town. In 1885–86 the Embroiderers' Society of Leek in north Staffordshire made a remarkable facsimile for which there was little commercial interest except in Reading; Arthur Hill saw it at an exhibition, bought it for £300 and gave it to the borough. When the museum was refurbished in 1992 a special room was prepared where it can be seen in all its splendour. It is a monument to the skill of Victorian needlewomen from a county long admired for its artistic skills and a credit to the generosity and foresight of a Reading Mayor.

Part of Reading's Bayeux Tapestry: the Saxon fyrd attacked by Norman cavalry. (RM)

Domesday Reading

William I, having spent twenty years imposing his authority over the English, sent out commissioners to ascertain exactly what he had acquired. The *Anglo-Saxon Chronicle* reported that in 1085 he 'sent men all over England to each shire … to find out … what or how much each landholder held … and what it was worth.' The commissioners summoned juries made up of the sheriff and leading men from the shire to answer their questions, their replies subsequently collected, amended and abridged by royal clerks at Winchester. The English called their work the Domesday Book, a record as final as that at the Last Judgement, intended not only for taxation purposes but also as a 'final authoritative register of rightful possession'.[13]

Domesday Book was organised by shire or county, listing first the lands of the king, followed by that of the abbeys and chief landholders. Heading the Berkshire entries is the borough of Wallingford, demonstrating its superiority as the county town. There are two entries for Reading, one as a manor and one as a borough: the latter status Reading men would later claim to have held before the founding of the abbey. The manor was a Norman construct whose lord had judicial and financial rights over its inhabitants. It could include just one or part of one village or several villages and hamlets. Reading manor occupied the area of the post-1560 borough. It was large: 85 farming households, arable land worked by 56 ploughs, substantial amounts of meadow, pasture and woodland, three fisheries and four mills.[14] It was obviously flourishing: in 1066 and later it was worth £40 but in 1086 it was £48. Both sums probably refer to the amount of revenue the king could expect to collect.

The term 'borough' is ambiguous. Reading was not a fortified *burh*, nor are any specific borough features mentioned, yet it is the only other place in the county given this status. Like Wallingford it was a royal borough and would have been governed by a royal reeve responsible for collecting the king's revenue and had a borough court.[15] However, whereas Wallingford's entry is very detailed, that of Reading affords only 'the vaguest picture'. Listed are twenty-eight *hagae* (plots or sites), thought to be evidence of urban status though the meaning is not entirely clear. A *haga* was not synonymous with a house or workshop, several of which may have occupied one plot.[16] The absence of any reference to plough land, *villani* (villagers) or *bordarii* (smallholders) emphasises the urban nature of the settlement, though there were three acres of meadow which could have been the low-lying land along the Kennet. The meadow was part of the land held by Henry de Ferrers *ad hospitium* 'for a lodging' which, it is suggested, was to entertain visiting officials in Reading, already a stopping place on royal journeys to the west. The borough, then, was a small urban island in a rural sea. The descriptions in the two entries, manor and borough, are needed to complete an admittedly vague picture; even so Reading had fewer properties listed even than Windsor.[17]

Another lord was the abbot of Battle who held a church in Reading, the minster church discussed above, with a considerable estate which in 1066 had been held from King Edward by Leofgifu (Leveva in Latin). It was once thought that she was the abbess of Shaftesbury but more recently it has been suggested that she might have been the last abbess of the former nunnery in Reading. Twenty-nine dwellings (*masurae*) in the manor of Reading belonged to this estate occupied by 17 villagers and smallholders who worked the arable and meadow and grazed pigs in the woodland. Battle Abbey, founded and endowed by William, also drew an income from the fisheries and two mills. The manor, on the western edge of the borough, took its name from Battle Abbey. It had a church with a substantial income, confirming it as a minster and probably the forerunner of St Mary's parish church.[18]

The vagueness of our knowledge of Domesday Reading extends to estimates of its population, possibly 400 in the borough and manor combined, a modest settlement.[19] However, two features of the town, significant contributors to its later economy, were already clear: its location and a plentiful water supply. The rivers powered what were probably only corn mills in 1086; they would later be adapted to serve the cloth industry.

The Berkshire Eyre of 1248

At some time between Monday, 16 June and 27 July 1248 huge crowds of people, mostly men, crowded into Reading to attend the Berkshire Eyre. This was one of the courts held periodically since the time of the Conquest by some of the king's justices or judges who every few years left the royal courts in London where they normally sat and travelled round the country hearing all manner of cases, criminal and civil, from a whole county. The sessions, introduced in 1166, came to be known as 'eyres' and eventually the judges would be called 'justices in eyre' or 'travelling judges' from the Latin *iter* meaning a journey. In the thirteenth century the Berkshire eyres were mainly held in Reading, not Wallingford, so at least once in every decade of the century the town was host to this great assembly. Perhaps the town was chosen because it was more centrally placed for those attending from the county but possibly because the abbey could accommodate the many men, possibly up to a thousand, who were summoned by the sheriff to attend: sheriffs past and present, coroners, barons, knights, freeholders, four men from every vill to say nothing of the litigants and prisoners. Added to the excitement of watching the many grand individuals riding in, townspeople could expect to do good business during the time the courts sat, usually about four days but often up to several weeks, and beyond.

On the first day, after preliminary business, the presenting juries, twelve freemen from each of the county's twenty-two hundreds and the leading vills were chosen by electors selected by the bailiff. The juries swore an oath to be truthful in presenting any breaches of criminal or civil law or infringements of royal rights committed in their hundreds. A jury of the county would determine the verdict. Among the jurors for Reading were Thomas Cissor, perhaps a tailor, Hervy goldsmith, Alan vintner and Walter Fachell. Like Abingdon and Windsor, Reading was called a vill though Wallingford had the title 'honour' with a charter giving its inhabitants the right not to plead except in their own courts.

Reading men and women brought their own criminal and civil suits against others and were in turn accused of wrongdoing. Robert the painter issued a writ of *novel disseisin* (recent dispossession) alleging that John Scot and his wife, Amice, unlawfully held his tenement (property) in the town. Other similar writs throw light on family or social relationships. Stephen's father, another Stephen, died when he was a minor leaving him in the wardship of Thomas the merchant. Now Stephen junior claimed his inheritance, a shop in Reading, occupied by William the goldsmith and his wife, Gunild, daughter of Stephen senior who, she said, had bequeathed it to her. In another case Amice, daughter of Edmund Gentil and widow of Robert de Muncy, said that her husband had demised (sold) her house in Reading. She had been unable to 'contradict' him 'in his lifetime' but now she claimed the property from its present occupiers, John of Woodcote and his wife Gillian; the jury delayed its verdict because

Gillian was a minor. A father had entrusted his young son to the guardianship of a friend or neighbour, and his two daughters inherited property, one of whom when married said she could not prevent her husband disposing of it.

Another case involved strained social relationships. Thomas the tailor who held a freehold in the town said he was prevented from carting his hay and corn to his grange and from attending church by the most direct path because Nicholas of Wallingford had erected a paling across it. The previous owner of a neighbouring property, John the stabler had always used this path to take his cart, horses and cattle to the junction with the king's highway. After John's death, his widow, Christian, held the property as her dower; she let Thomas use the same route for six years but then she married again and the new husband, Nicholas, was not like-minded. What Christian thought about it is not known but like Amice, the decision which was hers as a widow, was not hers to make as a married woman.

Criminal cases also involved women both as accusers and accused. Two cases of alleged rape and one of assault had unsatisfactory outcomes and modern parallels. Edith, daughter of Luke of Basingstoke, failed to attend court to pursue her case. Aline, daughter of Philip the merchant, accused Ralph Lamb of rape and the theft of a silver clasp, both of which he denied. The male jury believed his assertion that she had brought the case out of hatred, abetted by her brother. She lost the case.

An accusation of assault and robbery by Edith, wife of Robert Black, was not upheld, but the jury did agree that she had been beaten, a fine distinction.

Some women and men accused of larceny, potentially a capital offence, escaped by claiming sanctuary in St Mary's church which, like all churches, afforded protection for forty days, after which the unfortunate had to 'abjure the realm', leaving by a pre-determined route. This was the course chosen by both Emma of Whitton and David Anetrol. The alternative was worse, outlawry or, as with Sewal the Uverur, found guilty by the jury of several thefts, hanging. Imprisonment as a punishment was not an option.

Infringements of trading regulations such as the sale of inferior or underweight cloth and wine were also brought to the eyre by the Reading jury, though most of these would have been tried by the abbot's court. He also pocketed a share of the amercements (fines) paid by wrongdoers at the eyre and the goods forfeited by convicted felons. Several guilty offenders were said to be 'in mercy', amerced or fined by the court; some convicted felons or those claiming sanctuary were said to have no chattels so nothing could be confiscated. Judges might preserve the king's peace but they also helped fill his exchequer.

Sources: M.T. Clanchy (ed.), *The Roll and Writ File of the Berkshire Eyre of 1248* (Seldon Society, 1973), *passim*; Helen M. Jewel, *English Local Administration in the Middle Ages* (1972), 62, 139–40.

Topography, c.1350

Within a few decades of the Domesday Survey, the town's status and its topography were dramatically affected by the foundation of Reading Abbey, whose precinct eventually occupied about 30 acres on the eastern boundary of the borough. It was a good half mile from St Mary's church in the Old Market, so-called to distinguish it from a new Market Place which was created by the abbey sometime between its foundation in 1121 and c.1186–1213 at the latest when a deed refers to several stalls in the Market Place, some abutting a wall of the abbey.[20] It seems that some traders were renting stalls in this new space; at least seven are noted including one in the middle. Other traders would eventually follow, though the borough continued to assert the rights of the original market area. By the fourteenth century trade had been drawn to the new site, reducing the wealth of the area round the Old Market. The new Market Place had a more conventional shape, a narrow triangle, its apex on the north side where St Laurence's church overlooked the sloping site. Immediately south of the church, a gateway led into the abbey precinct. The south-eastern exit from the Market Place was High Street. The deed noted above also mentions a messuage in a new street to London. This was London Street, an extension of High Street made by the abbey to create a new route to London bringing trade into the new market and past the abbey gates. Before 1186 a new bridge over the Hallowed Brook, the Hallowed Bridge, was constructed north of the existing High Bridge which was also called the Great Bridge.[21] Near the High Bridge was the town wharf, mentioned in a deed of 1428, but there were quays on the riverbank by 1213. To the west of High Bridge on an island in the Kennet was the Gildhall. South again was Mill Lane and St Giles' Mill.

Cordwainers' Street or Shoemakers' Row formed the east side of the Market Place. On the opposite side *Tothull* or *Tothill*, a Saxon term for a look-out, formed the south-western exit from the market to the junction between High Street (later King Street) where in the fourteenth century the markets for fish and meat, Fish Shambles and Butchers' Shambles were located. The westward continuation of High Street (called Brode/ Broad Street in 1611) was divided by a block of shops forming Cheese or Fish Row on the north and Butcher Row on the south.[22] Further along the street Gutter Lane ran from its north side to New Street. Broad Street then crossed Old Street becoming Pangbourne Lane, another route to the west. The Drapery leading into Minster Street extended from the eastern end of the Butchers' Shambles, continued westwards and crossed Old Street south of St Mary's church where it became Castle Street. This name, recorded about 1250, possibly recalled a temporary fortification built by the Conqueror. Opposite the church and roughly parallel to Castle Street was Lortmer Lane or the Lorimery. Old Street itself continued southwards over the Kennet by a series of bridges known at this date as Seven Bridges, becoming Wood Street, passing the parish church of St Giles and on towards Winchester.

The north-western exit from the Market Place was the New Street, laid out by 1165 when the name first appears; it may have been narrower than at present. It was a major northward extension of the town, a further example of the influence of the abbey on the town's topography. At its western end, Town's End, was Greyfriars, a Franciscan friary established there in 1285 though it did not give its name to the street until the early sixteenth century. St Edmund's Chapel stood at the junction of New Street and the road north to Caversham. Some sources claim it was deconsecrated in 1479 and converted into a barn, but Speed's map of 1611 shows it as a chapel. Some property deeds describe the long, narrow burgage plots on which most properties were built. One in New Street, 127 × by 17 ft (about 42 × 6 metres) in 1270, was typical. No building materials are recorded, although we can safely assume that almost all were of timber with, at first, thatched roofs. North of New Street low-lying meadows through which several brooks flowed extended to the Thames. Reading never was a walled town, though its boundaries were marked by crosses, three still visible in 1552: Coley Cross on Castle Street, Cornish Cross at the end of Broad Street and Fair Cross in London Street.[23] So in the two centuries after 1121, a time of growing prosperity nationally, a street pattern emerged which would remain virtually unchanged for at least six hundred years and whose basic shape would survive all subsequent developments.

Population

Estimating the size of the population of any medieval community is a hazardous enterprise; sources are few and difficult to interpret, but thanks to the exigencies of medieval kings, national direct taxes were occasionally levied, called subsidies after 1207. They can throw some light on aspects of thirteenth- and fourteenth-century Reading.

Few records of the early subsidies survive, but by the 1290s there are more lists of taxpayers available, including those in the tax of 1297, which levied a ninth of the value of moveable goods – household goods, grain, livestock and merchandise. Ninety-seven laymen and five women are listed in the borough, heads of households who had built up sufficient wealth; the tax threshold was nine shillings. To these should be added those with too few taxable goods, those too poor to pay at all and the untaxed regular and secular clergy, possibly making a total population of possibly 1,250, three times the number in 1086. This would be in keeping with what demographers claim were national trends of increasing numbers in the twelfth and thirteenth centuries, possibly as much as three times the Domesday figure. Any growth would have stalled during the years of bad weather and disastrous harvests from 1315 to 1317 and, judging by evidence from elsewhere, would have declined thereafter. Certainly there were death rates of 10–15% in some rural communities in these years but whether or not the population continued to stagnate or decline is very unclear. The returns of the lay subsidy of 1327 would suggest that the borough with 135 taxpayers, suggesting a population of about 1,400–1,500, was holding its own.[24]

Migration

A small number of outsiders occupying, buying, leasing or selling property appear in the abbey's charters from the mid-thirteenth to the early fourteenth century. About half came from Berkshire villages and towns, mostly within a ten-mile radius; the rest were from adjacent counties with a sprinkling from more distant towns – Banbury, Malmesbury and London. The 1297 tax roll lists 25 men and women with locative surnames, such as William of Rotherfield and Matthew of Cirencester; seven were Berkshire men but others came from as far away as Banbury, Cricklade and Croydon and a woman, Alice 'of Romsey'. Others from villages in Berkshire and adjacent counties appear in borough deeds and yet more in the lay subsidy of 1327 from the same areas. Rixon identified 200 immigrants before c.1350, about a quarter from villages and towns within a ten-mile radius, half from Berkshire or neighbouring counties and a fifth from places within five miles of the Great West Road. There were a few Jews in Reading in the mid-twelfth century, useful as money lenders though some charged high interest rates.[25]

Markets and trade

The essential role of a town was as a market for the sale of the produce of its inhabitants and to facilitate the exchange of goods between them and the population of surrounding villages and smaller towns. In Anglo-Saxon England markets grew up on suitable sites leaving no written evidence of their origins; Reading claimed such a prescriptive ('before writing') market. That the borough was a market centre at an early date is evident from a number of Anglo-Saxon terms which occur locally The town had a 'portmoot', a town court which predated the abbey, where in the thirteenth century a number of property transactions were made and witnessed. The Portman Brook and a meadow by the same name lay to the north of the town, the term *port* identifying Reading as a trading place or market.[26] As suggested above, the wide Old Street opposite the west door of St Mary's church was the site of Reading's original market, although it is impossible to date its beginnings. No market is mentioned in the borough's entry in Domesday Book but then very few are for other

St Mary's Butts, 1883, showing the wide street of the medieval Old Market. (RL)

towns. There was no reason to single out the profit the king or lord derived from a market in his borough, even an important one; market tolls and other levies were included in the overall income he enjoyed.[27]

The first written evidence of Reading's market is the use of the name 'Old Market' which occurs frequently in deeds of the early thirteenth century. It was also called the Corn Market in a deed of 1316, presumably the 'customary place' agreed by the gild with the abbey in 1254. In the new market in the Market Place all manner of other commodities were traded, among them corn and iron, recorded as sold there in a deed of 1347, probably on Saturdays as recorded in later documents. In a deed of 1397 the Market Place was called 'le Corn chepynge' or corn market. Obviously by this date the Market Place had become *the* trading area. In the Amyce Survey of 1552 the Flax Market, recorded in 1432, is recorded as Flaxen Lane in the centre of the Market Place. Meat and fish were sold very close by in the Butcher and Fish Markets or Shambles. Easy access to the wharf on the Kennet just to the south of the new Market Place was another boost to the growth of trade in this area which became the commercial hub of the town; significantly there was no wharf near the Old Market.[28] Nothing is known of the role of royal reeves, but regulating marketing would have been the primary concern of whatever local institution predated the later Merchant Gild. Soon after 1121 the abbey, as the new lord of the borough, assumed control of the market, taking all the profits from tolls and fines levied in the portmoot court held by the abbey's steward. At some point a clerk of the market was appointed by the abbot, whose duties included determining the time the market opened and closed and ensuring that regulations concerning quality and correct measurements were obeyed.[29]

Although the records of the portmoot have not survived, some central government documents provide a snapshot of the importance of the corn trade in about 1300. Grain purchased by royal officials for the king in 1295 included 42 quarters of wheat and 419½ quarters of oats bought in Reading, amounting to 30% of the oats but only 2% of the wheat purchased in the upper Thames, Kent and Essex that year. Henley was the main grain market, but Reading was 'a significant supplier of oats to London'. Corn was shipped to the capital by river since transport costs for a quarter of wheat were just over a farthing (¼d.) a mile compared with 3½d. by cart. From Reading the cost was 4½d. a quarter, giving the corn merchant 15% profit though he only ventured so far if he was sure it would repay the effort.[30]

Less frequent than markets though equally important were the three annual fairs, held in the Forbury, the profits also claimed by the abbey. As was customary in the middle ages, the fairs were linked to locally significant feast days, that of St Laurence, whose relics the abbey owned (10 August), St James whose hand was another of the abbey's most precious relics (25 July) and SS Philip and James (1 May). All three lasted for four days.. A fair offered a variety of experiences: perhaps to buy Droitwich salt and East Anglian pottery, to purchase exotic spices and fabrics from foreign merchants, to gawp at jugglers, acrobats and other entertainers or to be tempted by tricksters and slick salesmen. Other traders in the town especially those in the Market Place profited from the influx of customers.[31]

Occupations before 1350

Organisation and control of trade and crafts in medieval boroughs was often in the hands of a Merchant Gild. As a borough with a corporate identity before 1121, it is likely that there was such a gild in Reading before that date for it is unlikely that the abbey would have allowed it to develop afterwards. A lease dated between 1158 and 1165 refers to the 'liberties and customs which a burgess has', the term 'burgess' being synonymous with gild member. These were the leading men of the town though nothing is known of their activities as gildsmen before a charter granted by Henry III in 1253 granting the members of the gild freedom from tolls throughout England, followed by an agreement between the gild and the abbot the following year. There is little further evidence before 1357 when the gild accounts begin.[32]

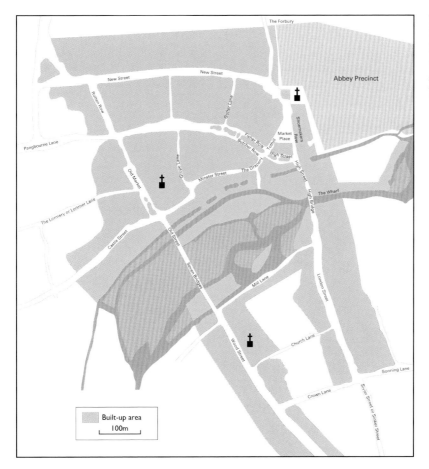

The distinctive V-shape of Reading's streets with their names as recorded before 1350. (CS)

The earliest evidence of how people in early medieval Reading earned a living comes from street names in the charters (property grants and leases) of the abbey. The Drapery (clothmaking) occurs early in the thirteenth century, as does Cordwainers' Street or Shoemakers' Row. The Lormery or Lurtemerelane (Lorimer Lane) indicating makers of metal bits for horses' bridles and Butcher Row appear by the mid-century, Fish Market in 1303 and le Sivekarestret (Sivier Street) in 1311. The latter was called Sinker Street (*le Cymkareestret*) in a deed of *c.*1270. The town must have had its bakers from the earliest times but the first reference to Bread Lane does not occur until 1332. A reference to Potters' Lane in the early thirteenth century may indicate the presence of makers of brass cooking vessels; potters were so called because they made clay moulds to make pots and pans but there may have been others producing domestic ware.[33] However, by the early thirteenth century some streets were home to widely differing trades such as a tailor, a vintner and a goldsmith in Lorimer Lane. The charters sometimes include the occupations of the sellers, purchasers or donors of property, though it would be unwise to suggest that these trades were not present before the date of the charter. Mercers or merchants appear about 1200 and vintners before 1258. Both were retailers, as was Philip the chapman (an itinerant salesman). A deed of 1255 was witnessed by a vintner and a merchant but also by a cordwainer, a draper and a dyer. During the century and a half after 1200 a few other trades appear: bakers, cooks, a brewer, carpenters, coopers, a mason, a tailor, a glover, a tanner, and a miller. For the wealthy townsman and for travellers there was a barber. The presence of four goldsmiths in the town in the mid-thirteenth century suggests a wealthy clientele[34] who would also have patronised the stall of Sampson the Spicer or Grocer recorded in *c*.1255 who may have been the same as the one trading in the Corn Market (the Old Market) about the same time. A few rents were paid in exotic foodstuffs such as a clove or a root of ginger, obtainable from the same source or from a fair. Borough property deeds from the same period confirm the range of trades, adding others including a tiler and a tinker. In 1240 a tannery and a brewhouse stood near together in Minster Street. The collapse of a drain in Friar Street in 2013 led to the discovery of leather artefacts probably dating from this period suggesting substantial leather working took place here, and tanning pits were discovered during excavations at the Oracle. Since the number and sophistication of different crafts is a useful indication of a town's size and importance, we can judge that Reading already had a substantial economic role in the region.[35]

A partial picture of the situation at the end of the century emerges from the returns of the Taxation of Ninths (1297) though occupations are ascribed to only 33 of the 102 taxpayers. Most were in trades processing leather or manufacturing leather goods. Leather was the most versatile and widely used component of objects in everyday use until the last century, for clothing (shoes, gloves, jerkins), household goods (buckets, jugs, mugs), and transport (harness, saddles etc.). For the rest, several sourced or sold foodstuffs: there was a vintner, a brewer, an acatur (a victualler) and a fisherman, though no baker or butcher was listed. There was one goldsmith and a solitary chapman. He may not have been the only retailer since some of those listed paid tax on 'merchandise' (*mercimonium*) with no reference to their having produced it.[36]

The small proportion of taxpayers in the community and the limited evidence of the 1297 tax make it difficult to come to more definite conclusions about the urban economy at this date, in particular about the role of cloth production which would later become so important. The origins of Reading's cloth industry are shadowy; references to property transactions in the abbey cartularies indicate that cloth was being produced by the thirteenth century – a tenter yard on an island near the Gildhall in 1204–15, a fulling mill in St Giles' parish by 1260–90, a rented fulling mill in Pangbourne, 1270–85, a dyer witnessing a deed before 1258, and John the dyer living in High Street about the same time. The Drapers' gild was in existence by mid-century. About the same time two men were accused of breaking the laws governing the sale of cloth. Since at this date many communities produced cloth, there is no certainty that Reading's industry was of more than local significance until the fourteenth century when a rhyme describing towns by their main product referred to 'teule de Radingis' (cloth of Reading).[37]

However, one aspect of the economy is clear: the importance of agriculture. Closeness to the countryside is regarded by historians as the primary feature of the medieval town, many having 'rural outskirts' or 'islands of cultivation within their boundaries'.[38] This was certainly true of Reading. Open fields abutted directly on to New Street and London Street, the latter, and its extension Sivier Street being merely ribbon development through arable land and pasture. Alongside the river Kennet was low-lying pasture and meadow, one meadow said to have been 'within the Seven Bridges'. About 1200 the abbey was receiving tithes of corn, peas, beans and lambs from the parishes of St Mary and St Giles, the latter including the rural hamlet of Whitley. Property deeds from the twelfth to fourteenth centuries refer to pasture land: Nicholas of Coley enjoyed rights of pasture in North Field (*Northfeld*) and Long Marsh (*la Longemerchs*). Caversham Lane ran across the East Mead and The Vastern meadows on a raised causeway, suggesting really wet grassland.[39] So it is not surprising that almost half the taxpayers in 1297 owned some agricultural produce. Thirty-one kept pigs, an animal frequently encountered in towns since they could be housed in the long backside or garden of a property, usually one or two but John of Denmead had six. A single pig would provide the household with salted meat and bacon; keeping six suggests pig-rearing. John also dominated the dairying aspect of Reading's agriculture with his four cows. Fifteen townspeople kept a single animal providing dairy produce for the family and possibly some spare to market. The presence of draught animals, most probably oxen, in twelve households betokens ploughing, though John of Denmead owned a cart as well. Forty-three taxpayers had stores of grain, mainly wheat and barley though a few had maslin (mixed corn of wheat and rye) and one or two dredge (mixed grain of barley and oats) or just oats. The tax was assessed at Michaelmas (29 September), soon after the harvest, which explains why the amounts of one or more types of grain in store were quite substantial.[40] The only other product mentioned was honey. The 1327 subsidy roll does not list goods taxed and the range of occupations noted is narrower though significant. In addition to leather and metal workers were a glazier, a painter, two tilers, and a worker in horn, a product used as 'windows' in lanterns.

Woman workers, single, married or widowed also appear. There were six, probably widows or spinsters, in the 1297 tax return, two of whom were newcomers, from Yateley and Romsey in Hampshire. Alice of Romsey, among the wealthiest in the town, had goods 'in her chamber' as well as tannery goods, corn and a pig. Nine women appear in the 1327 subsidy roll. Except for one widow, their marital state is unknown though all were taxed as individuals, not as wives of named husbands. Katherine Vachel, probably a member of a family important later in the town's history, was the wealthiest and Edith le Deyesti may have owned a dyehouse. Women appear in the abbey cartularies and borough deeds as property owners, several being widows bequeathed a house or shop by their husbands while two were given a messuage (a property) on marriage. Matilda was a brewer, a popular occupation for a married woman. Agilia followed the traditional practice of insuring against poverty in old age by giving property to a manor or religious house, in her case to the abbey, whose almoner would provide her and her son with food and clothing.[41] Unfortunately Reading lacks records which might illuminate the lives of poorer women at this date though the existence of Grope Lane suggests that in Reading as in Windsor some resorted to the oldest profession.[42]

Wealth in 1297

A pyramid of wealth is evident in 1297 as in later tax returns. Historians estimate that only about half of property owners were above the tax threshold of goods worth nine shillings. About a third had crops and animals worth ten shillings, and about the same number 20 shillings or less. About one in five were assessed at less than 30 shillings. The richest were William le Grindar whose tanning enterprise, crops and livestock amounted to 80 shillings, the same as the merchandise of Roger le Dubbar. William Cosyn, another tanner and farmer was assessed at 98 shillings. At the apex was Walter of Reading with crops and livestock taxed at 100 shillings.

Religious life

Although it was not a large town, Reading had three parish churches by c.1200. The oldest, St Mary's, has already been discussed; its parish extended beyond the borough into Coley and Southcote. It has been suggested that St Giles' church was built to enable inhabitants of the small 'suburb' south of the Kennet's many streams to hear Mass. Its boundary stretched southwards, eventually encompassing the hamlet of Whitley. The third, St Laurence, began as a chapel adjoining the abbey precinct to serve a growing community living near the new market. It was a parish church probably by 1197 serving the smallest parish in area. It was wholly urban whereas the others extended into the manor.[43]

The strength of commitment to one's parish, usually strong in medieval towns and expressed in pious offerings, and the depth of religious belief as shown in donations to religious houses is difficult to estimate before will-making became more common in the fifteenth century. Some gifts were made to the abbey almoner for the poor: all Walter Olaf's lands in Reading and the rents from the various properties of Peter of Rotherwick to provide 'an annual pittance' on the anniversary of his death, such donors believing that good deeds would contribute toward their salvation. Others provided for candles or lamps to burn on an altar in the abbey or a church to invoke the intercession of the Virgin or a saint. Alan of Banbury's will of 1311, after conventionally invoking the Virgin Mary and all the saints, made bequests to a hospice at Crowmarsh (Oxon), to the poor in bread at his funeral, to those watching by his coffin the night before and to the friars at Greyfriars. To all the altars of his parish church of St Laurence he gave 3*d*. but to that of Blessed Mary, 12*d*.[44] All three parishes had been given property in the town by pious donors before 1500.

Reading's relative standing by 1350

Over time, national and local developments affect the fortunes of all towns: some flourish and grow, while others decline either absolutely or relatively. The dominant town in Domesday Berkshire and a leading urban centre of the south-east was Wallingford, but later tax returns show how far it had fallen behind its Berkshire neighbours in size and wealth. In 1327 there were only 38 taxpayers in Wallingford compared with 79 in Newbury, 110 in Abingdon and 135 in Reading. However Reading's tax yield was £13 15*s*. 6*d*., compared with Newbury's £23 2*s*. 7¾*d*.* Newbury's higher tax take is explained by the large amounts paid by a few very wealthy townsfolk, whereas Reading had a greater number of small contributors. So although Reading was the largest, it was not yet the richest town in the county.[45]

In the 1334 subsidy Wallingford did not even merit a place in a listing of the 100 highest-taxed towns in England. It was assessed at £96 4*s*. 9*d*. Newbury, still the wealthiest of the Berkshire towns at £421, was ranked 22nd in England with Abingdon (£269) at 46th. Reading came 40th assessed at £293 1*s*. 3*d*.[46] Its economy like that of Newbury would

---

* Before decimalisation in the early 1970s the pound sterling (£, L, from Latin *libra*) was divided into twenty shillings (*s*., from Latin *solidi*, not actually an abbreviation for shilling), which in turn were divided into twelve pennies (*d*., from the Latin *denarii*). From the thirteenth century until 1960 pennies could be quartered into farthings (from the Anglo-Saxon *feorthing*, a fourth part). A frequently used monetary unit was the mark: there was never an English coin of this value, but it was often used in accountancy and law. It equalled 160 pennies, or two-thirds of a pound, i.e. 13*s*. 4*d*.

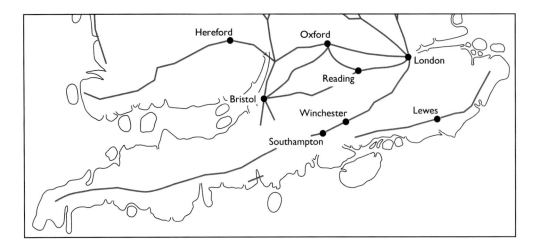

Hereford
Oxford
London
Reading
Bristol
Winchester
Lewes
Southampton

Reading's
location on
a main route
from London
to the west on
the Gough Map
c. 1375.

later be based on the cloth trade though it had other advantages, not least its location, which over time would give it supremacy. Already, although there was no recognised 'county town' in Berkshire, Reading was gaining an equivalent status. The county gaol had moved to the borough from Windsor by the 1330s, and for at least a century the county sessions or eyres, law courts presided over by royal justice, had been held in the town. The large numbers attending the event, often over several days, boosted the town's trade, so much so that when in 1338 the Abbot of Reading was able to exclude the justices, the burgesses complained that they had become too poor to pay their taxes. Exaggerated it may have been, but the complaint did cut some ice with royal officials.[47]

2

Abbey, borough and urban government, 1121–1529

THE arrival of eight monks in Reading on 18 June 1121 was arguably the most significant event in the borough's history, and the monks the most important newcomers in 400 years. Led by Brother Peter, they came from the abbey of Cluny in Burgundy at the request of king Henry I who wished to found an abbey in Reading and favoured the Cluniacs, a reformed Benedictine order known for the splendour of their liturgy and the magnificence of their monastic buildings. Endowing a religious house where daily prayers would be offered for his and his family's eternal salvation was the typical act of a medieval king or lord of this period though his age (he was 50) and the death of his only legitimate son in a shipwreck the previous year may have hastened Henry's decision. The church was intended to be a royal mausoleum where Henry and all future kings would be buried.[1] The choice of Reading was a practical one, conveniently located as it was on the road from Windsor to the west, often travelled by the court, and since the town and the manor belonged to the Crown, the abbey would be built on Crown land. When complete it had sufficient accommodation for the king and some of his entourage, while the chapter house was able to accommodate meetings of whole parliaments, lords and commons.

The eight pioneers were joined by several monks from the Cluniac priory of Lewes, Sussex. Reading was at first like Lewes, a daughter house of Cluny subject to the supervision of its abbot and with only a prior, Brother Peter, as its head. Such a subordinate role was not thought fitting for a major royal foundation and in 1123 Hugh, formerly prior of Lewes, became the first abbot of an independent Cluniac abbey. He was in office in 1125 when Reading was granted its foundation charter. Over the years Reading's connection with Cluny weakened so that by the late thirteenth century, if not before, it had become effectively a Benedictine house though it maintained Cluniac observance. Its head was elevated by the Pope to the status of a mitred abbot in 1191 and from the thirteenth century he attended parliament. The abbey became very wealthy. In addition to Henry's original endowment of the town of Reading, the manors and churches of Reading and Cholsey, the manor of Thatcham and the church of Wargrave came gifts of other manors in Berkshire,

The first modern plan of the abbey by Dr J.B. Hurry in 1896. Modern research has modified the layout of the dormitory area. (WMC)

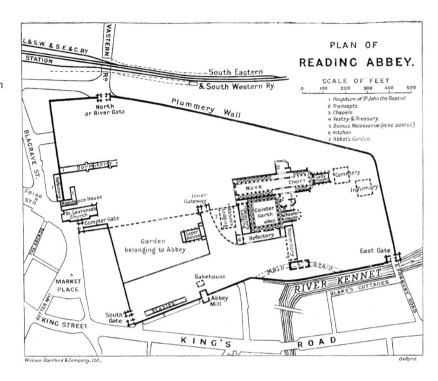

Some surviving capitals from the abbey cloisters now in Reading Museum. (RM)

Reading abbey ruins: the flint core of some of the walls of the warming room/ parlour with the dormitory above. Note the impression in the flint of an arcaded passage to the north of the parlour. (JD)

The font, St James' Roman Catholic church made from a capital from Reading Abbey. (JD)

The text of the thirteenth-century song 'Sumer is icumin in' known as the Reading Rota, once in Reading Abbey library and now in the British Library (Harley 978 f11v). (© The British Library Board)

and in 1139 the manor and church of Leominster (Herefordshire) to support a dependent priory. As other grants by successive kings and queens added to its estates in other counties, Reading became one of the richest and most important abbeys in England, with an income in 1535 of £1,938 14s. ¾d. All grants made before c.1200 were held in free alms, donors expecting no return except the monks' prayers. No expense was spared in constructing the splendid church and conventual buildings in white stone from Caen in Normandy on 30 acres to the east of the borough. The dedication of the abbey church in 1164 was performed by no less a personage than Thomas Becket, Archbishop of Canterbury, by which time Henry had been buried before the high altar for almost 30 years.[2] At this date there were probably about 100 monks but numbers fell thereafter to just 65 in 1305. The Black Death (1348–49) had a catastrophic effect, reducing the community to 35 in 1445 where it remained until 1539.

The monastic community followed the Rule of St Benedict, prescribing a balanced programme of prayer, work and rest. The most important work required of the monks was *Opus Dei,* God's Work or the Divine Office, seven services of psalms and readings in the abbey church, the first before dawn and the last after sunset. In common with other Benedictine houses, Reading interpreted other work as academic study. The abbey acquired by gift, by purchase and by copying borrowed manuscripts, a large library of over 300 volumes, including Bibles, scripture commentaries, the writings of the Church Fathers, histories and classical texts including study aids and a few works in Greek. Monks with expertise in canon law and theology gave daily lectures to the community, probably in the chapter house. During the two silent meals, they listened to readings from volumes kept in the refectory and during the day worked in the cloister using the books kept there.[3]

For the townspeople the abbey was less a house of prayer than their overlord. Reading had become a seigneurial borough, its lord not a distant monarch but the abbot, a very present superior with judicial powers over all his tenants in cases from assault to murder. Fines for breaches of the peace and market regulations were collected in the abbot's portmoot court held in the gild hall.[4] Part of the abbey's income came from rents paid by occupiers of tenements (abbey properties composed of houses, workshops and gardens), by lessees of the town mills and fisheries, and tolls paid by traders in the market. The abbey also received the profits from tolls and rents for stalls at the three fairs granted to it by successive monarchs: St Laurence's fair (10 August) by Henry I; St James' fair (25 July) by Henry II and a fair beginning on the feast of SS Philip and

The built-up area of the borough *c.*1300, the boundaries of the three parishes and the site of the abbey.

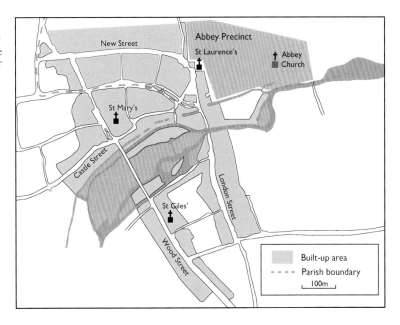

James (1 May) by King John in 1205.[5] All lasted four days and were held in the abbey's outer court, the Forbury. By the fourteenth century weekly markets were held in the new Market Place immediately to the south-west of the gate where the clerk of the market, appointed by the abbot, could more easily regulate trading practices.

However, Reading's market role predated the abbey and the town did not owe its future growth or prosperity solely to the abbey. Undeniably there were economic advantages from the beginning: the king's grant to abbey of freedom from tolls throughout England applied to the townsmen, too. Though merchants attending the fairs and their customers from the local villages patronised the town's hostelries and craftsmen, other visitors came with less worldly intentions. Various royal benefactors and others had donated a large collection of relics to the abbey; 237 were listed in the 1190s, of which the most important was a hand, believed to be that of St James the Great, whose main shrine was and is at Santiago de Compostella in Spain, but who joined the Virgin Mary and St John as one of the abbey's patrons. Large numbers of pilgrims came to Reading drawn by the promise of indulgences to be gained by praying at the shrine and the miracles said to have been worked by the relic. Many were accommodated in the Hospitium, the guest house of St John built by the abbey, partly for poor travellers, but others repaired to the town. For Reading's traders and craftsmen all were welcome customers

The abbey's second seal, 1328, one side showing the Virgin, St James (as a pilgrim) and St John; the other the King with SS Peter and Paul. (Man)

needing rest, refreshment, repairs to shoes and clothing, many eager to
buy souvenirs in the shape of metal cockleshells, St James' symbol which
featured on the abbey's arms and was later incorporated into that of the
university. Nearby shrines, especially that of Our Lady at Caversham,
added to the town's attraction for pilgrims.[6]

The town's hostelries, stables and their workers also profited from
the many courtiers and their servants who accompanied monarchs and
powerful churchmen to Reading on several occasions of national significance. They came in January 1136 for the burial of Henry I in the
abbey church and frequently with King John and Henry III in the next
century. They were here with Edward III when John of Gaunt married
Blanche of Lancaster in 1359 and when Edward IV made public his
secret marriage to Elizabeth Woodville in 1464. In the troubled reign of
Henry VI parliament met in the abbey in 1453, and in Edward's reign
in 1467. Such occasions provided the townsfolk with exciting diversions
from the daily grind, but more important was the boost they gave to the
trade of innkeepers and all manner of victuallers.

From the very beginning the abbey was the town's largest employer,
especially during the forty or so years when hosts of craftsmen and
labourers constructed the great church and abbey itself. Though as was

A painting by Stephen Read, donated to the borough by Dr J.B. Hurry – an imaginative portrayal of the marriage of John of Gaunt to Blanche, heiress to the duchy of Lancaster in the abbey church, 1359. (RM)

customary in Benedictine houses, senior monks known as obedientiaries – the guest master, the almoner (who distributed alms) and the cellarer (in charge of supplying provisions) supervised the administration – most of the physical work was entrusted to laymen. Two abbey bailiffs supervised law and order in the town, and the many conventual buildings required an army of skilled craftsmen and labourers to keep them repaired. The abbey was keen to exploit the borough's waterways. The Hallowed or Holy Brook, a stream of the Kennet, flows past the southern boundary of the abbey, joining the main stream before flushing the Necessarium or toilet block. Within the borough it is now stone- and brick-lined and culverted, the latest archaeological evidence suggesting that the natural channel was re-aligned to serve the abbey mill, constructed before 1200 and leased to a miller. About 1300 an extensive waterfront with wharves was constructed on the main Kennet stream to receive cargoes from London.[7] The abbot, who had his own lodgings, kept almost forty servants to maintain an establishment fitting for such a high-ranking churchman. The keeper of the wine cellar kept the household well supplied with wine; in May 1447 two pipes, each containing 126 gallons were dispatched from Southampton for Abbot John Thorne.[8]

Other townfolk, especially the poor, gained from the presence of the abbey since charity was an essential monastic duty. The name Orts Lane (now Road) derived its name from the word for left-over food distributed to the needy at the abbey gate. The hospital or hospice of St Mary Magdalen for lepers, sufferers from various skin complaints, was built in 1130 and in 1193 an almshouse added to the Hospitium, to house thirteen poor men and women though since the women were widows of burgesses they were certainly not those most in want. Both were dissolved some

The ruins of the abbey mill. Note the 'dog-tooth' work on the arch, typical of Romanesque architecture.

The Holy/ Hallowed Brook and ruins of the abbey mill. (JD)

The second common seal of the abbey, 1328, showing the founder with SS Peter and Paul. (BK)

time after 1479 when the burgesses complained that 'th'abbott take the profytt therof, and dothe no suche almes nor good deds ther with'.[9] If monastic hospitality had its limits, Reading will-makers reciprocated by excluding the abbey from their bequests.

Most abbeys had a school to educate their novices which may have been the purpose at Reading but lay scholars were also admitted and it is even possible that a school pre-dated the abbey; Roger, Bishop of Salisbury (1125–39) forbade anyone to 'teach school' without the abbey's permission. A surviving almoner's account confirms that a school existed in 1345 when he paid for food for ten boys and a mitre for the boy bishop on St Nicholas Day (6 December) and the master's salary. By 1468–69 there were still ten or so scholars, though all but two paid something towards their board and tuition. Sources disagree as to how this institution became Reading Free School. A former theory, based partly on a comment by John Leland, is that during a visit in 1486, the date the modern school celebrates as its foundation, Henry VII ordered that the Hospitium and its endowment be converted into a free grammar school for boys from the borough with a master paid a salary of £10 a year. The more likely version, however, is that king Edward IV ordered John Blyth, Bishop of Salisbury (1499–1505) to reform the administration of the Hospitium, which the abbot obeyed rather tardily by converting it into a free school sometime during Blyth's episcopate, with a master chosen by the abbot, paid ten marks (£6 13s. 4d.) a year. Further confusion has arisen because John Long, schoolmaster, was buried in St Laurence in 1502/3. He is now thought to have been master of the earlier fee-paying school.[10]

The Merchant Gild and the abbey

This was not the first, nor the last, complaint by townspeople against the abbey. As we saw in the previous chapter, a Merchant Gild had almost certainly been in existence before 1121. Such gilds, composed of leading merchants and craftsmen of the town, are known to have acted as early forms of urban government which would have included some regulation of trade and markets, and this seems to have been the case at Reading. Members of the gild were known as burgesses, a privileged status open to a small elite by invitation from existing members and by payment of a fee. Seventy-four members were recorded in 1456, perhaps an unusually large number but still a tiny fraction of the town's workforce. The gild held some property – shops, houses, stables, barns, the meadow called Portmanbrook and its gild hall – which together with entrance fees, payments from outsiders for the right to trade, and fees for the use of the beam to weigh wool produced most of its income. The date at which the game of swans, another useful if small money-spinner, became part of their portfolio is not known. It is first mentioned in 1501, there is a drawing of the gild's swan mark place in their 'minutes' in 1507 and in 1543 Thomas Benwell leased the farm of the eight swans for half a mark (6s. 8d.) a year, providing the mayor with three 'good signettes' a year.

A custom associated with borough status, the right to bequeath property by will, burgage tenure, operated in the town.[11] So despite the absence of a borough custumal or a charter of privileges, Reading was undoubtedly a borough to all intents and purposes. The arrival of an increasingly well-endowed abbey with its great church and monastic buildings towering over the town could put all this at risk. Law and order would in future be enforced by two abbey reeves, later called bailiffs. Two constables were chosen by the gild but sworn in by the abbey steward. Otherwise, it has been suggested, the abbot accepted the status quo.[12] However much the gild felt aggrieved by the new regime, no records survive of any disputes, if indeed any took place, until 1244 when abbey officials of Reading (and St Albans) were accused of killing people in their towns, possibly in connection with demands by the abbeys for contributions to pay off their debts.

Nine years later in a period of months, June 1253 to February 1254, a series of claim and counterclaim by abbot and town culminated in Reading's first borough charter. Following attacks by townsmen on the bailiffs, probably because of further fruitless demands for money, the abbot complained to king Henry III, who summoned the burgesses to justify their refusal and substantiate their claims to long-standing privileges. Unfortunately for them, the absence of proof allowed the king to uphold the abbey's position. Why he later switched his favours from abbey to town is unknown, but in any event on 5 July 1253, in return for a huge fee of £100, Reading was granted its first charter. Compared with the lengthy document listing Wallingford's privileges a century before it is very short, no more than 125 words including the king's titles, the witnesses and the date, and it did not grant them anything more than what they claimed already or enjoyed as living on abbey land. The crucial difference was that their privileges were now enshrined in a royal charter, independent of the abbot's favour: the legality of the Merchant Gild and the right of its burgesses to trade free of tolls throughout England.

Other claims by the burgesses were still outstanding, especially the right not to be tried outside their gild hall, and the restoration of the market to its former location. The abbot in turn complained that the burgesses continued to deny him the use of the gild hall. Eventually in

February 1254 agreement was reached on many issues and confirmed in the king's court in a formal document called a final concord. The abbot agreed that the markets should be held in their customary places, the burgesses should keep their gild hall, the Portmanbrook Meadow (but at an increased rent of 6s. 8d. a year) and their 12 properties and, most important, have their Merchant Gild with all its privileges for ever. All pleas relating to the town would be tried by the abbot's steward at the abbot's court in the gild hall, to which the gild held the key, surrendering it to the official for the duration of the court. The burgesses agreed that on admission to the gild each son of a burgess would pay the abbot a fee of four shillings, while an 'outsider' (*homo forensicus*) would pay him half the fee determined by the gild, which would receive the other half. The abbot would also receive a *chepyngavell* (an Anglo-Saxon term for a trade tax), of 5d. a year from each burgess for the right to trade. Annually the abbot would choose one burgess 'acceptable to them' to be warden of the gild who would take his oath both to gild and abbot. 'Warden' was the new name of the head of the gild, formerly called the steward. Both sides had gained something. For the burgesses the confirmation of their gild and its rights in perpetuity was of great and lasting significance. For the abbot effective control of urban government had been re-asserted. Though the agreement did not give the gild any share in governing the town, which remained firmly in the abbey's hands, it did allow the gild 'great freedom in its internal affairs', and later records show that it had administrative responsibilities for some urban concerns.[13]

For the next two centuries disputes between town and abbey were infrequent, or at least no accounts of them have survived. There is no record of a rising against the abbey during the Peasants' Revolt of 1381 such as occurred at Bury St Edmunds, though Richard II's decision to hold a council here en route from St Albans to London suggests the authorities may have had some concerns. Ten years later, an argument between the steward and the gild over the choice of constable does not seem to have caused more than a temporary breach in abbey–borough relations. Both abbey and gild had vested interests in the stability and good order of the borough and both had a role, though an unequal one, in its adminis-tration. The gild was mostly occupied with its own affairs, discussed by the burgesses in the gild hall on Friday mornings, an occasion called a 'morowe speche' or 'morning speke'. These were important occasions to settle both gild and town business. Absence without permission and failure to arrive on time attracted a fine, 3s. 4d., for lateness in 1528 when the mayor's sergeant had been ordered to ring the bell to remind tardy burgesses of the meeting. The gild had a common seal, proof of its ability to act as a legally corporate body (though the abbey disputed this), and a chest in which to keep its important documents and those of some townsfolk who used it as a secure repository.[14]

Of particular concern to the gild was the title and status of its head. In 1301 a royal writ ordering the election of two MPs was addressed to the mayor and bailiffs, a title the abbot refused to accept but which the burgesses used thereafter. It is not known why a Chancery official should use the term,'mayor', but in all its accounts, which survive from 1364/5, the gild used no other term. To meet the expenses of his office, the mayor was granted an allowance by the gild. He could also dispense patronage, albeit limited: the right during his year of office to admit one man to the gild without a fee. His disputed title made no change in the way he was chosen, at first solely by the abbot. An improvement was achieved by 1486, if not before, when the burgesses presented three of their number to him from whom he selected one. All burgesses were obliged to attend, being fined for failure to do so; ten shillings at the selection of the three candidates, and ten marks (£6 13s. 4d.) when the abbot made his choice. It was to the burgesses as well as to the abbot that the new mayor swore his oath. Yet he still lacked any outward display of his status, so important in an age when symbols of authority carried great weight. The abbot's superiority was obvious since his steward was preceded by men carrying tipped staffs. Then, on a visit to the town in 1453 Henry VI inexplicably granted the mayor the right to have a mace carried before him. On 3 November 1458 a mace costing 3s. 4d. and said in 1523 to be 'garnished with sylver' was brought to the gild meeting. This demonstration of insubordination seems to have prompted the abbey to claim it was an 'infringement of its privileges', the king agreeing and ordering the mayor to forbear its use. The matter was not settled in favour of the borough until 1487, when a clause in a new charter gave the mayor the right to have two sergeants at mace, a practice which continued thereafter. He was also allowed a small sum by the gild for expenses incurred in entertaining important visitors.[15]

Burgesses were always a small, self-selecting elite, with wealth and lifestyles beyond the reach of ordinary townsfolk and, like burgesses elsewhere, increasingly determined to display their aloofness from the commonalty, at least in the later middle ages when records appear. They certainly seemed to grow in confidence, especially towards the end of the period when their administration became more formalised. The oath of a new burgess was first recorded in 1456: to uphold the common good of gild members, to prefer this to his own, and to keep secret their 'common counsel'. An unspecified offence by a former cofferer, Robert Farle, against the gild resulted in his expulsion in 1463, and in 1535 they agreed that any conflict between gildsmen would be settled by four senior burgesses appointed by the mayor. Corporate solidarity was reinforced by formal meals variously called breakfast (*jantaculum*) or lunch (*prandium*), though part of the entrance fee to the gild, 3s. 4d. supposedly for a breakfast, was simply a device to keep more of the fee from the abbot.[16] When gildsmen rode out to escort the king into the town in 1454, they were provided with gowns, ensuring they presented the gild as a substantial and wealthy body. In their hall, three silver and silver-gilt cups were the modest beginnings of a collection of town plate. They displayed their superior status to the rest of the town by a practice which is recorded from 1477 of accompanying the body of a deceased burgess from his house to the church where he was buried, and attending the 30 Masses said for his soul's salvation. For a mayor or former mayor they would attend both the ceremony (the dirge) on the eve and the funeral Mass itself. Further confirmation of the mayor's authority and status was the temporary expulsion of William Lendall from the gild for disobeying him in 1513.[17]

Apart from the mayor, the most important gild officers were the ones who kept the accounts, the two cofferers elected annually by the burgesses. They were responsible for collecting the rents from gild properties and fees for the use of gild equipment such as the beam to weigh wool, and for making any necessary payments for goods, repairs to property, and gifts to the abbot and other influential visitors. The accounting year ran from Michaelmas (29 September) to Michaelmas, one of the two most important quarter days and the one frequently used to begin a contract, especially a lease. Later in the year, sometimes very much later, they presented their accounts to the gild meeting. The editor of their accounts believes that there was no 'system' in the way the accounts were presented and that the 'gild's financial practices were ... complicated'. Nevertheless they show that by the fifteenth century the gild administered and collected the fees for some economic activities in the town: the use of the beam to weigh wool, increasingly important in the economy, and loading and storing goods at the wharf. In 1519/20 the task of collecting rents and tolls was divided between the cofferers: one responsible for the charges for using the wharf and the wool beam, the other for collecting various rents including the use of the beam to weigh yarn. Though the income from the use of the beam more than doubled over the century, it is not possible to say with certainty that this was because of expanding trade since nothing is known of the scale of charges. Another source of income found in almost all borough accounts were the fines paid by townspeople who allowed their pigs to stray, a very frequent occurrence judging from the 6s. 8d. a year which John Hastyng was willing to pay in 1473 for rounding them up and collecting the fines. The regulations controlling pigs were made by the abbot but control of the animals and maintenance of a pound were the responsibility of the gild which kept the fines though little seems to have been spent on cleaning the inevitable mess from the streets.[18]

Extension of the gild's supervision of the borough economy came with the charter of 1487 granted by Henry VII, possibly for financial reasons though more likely to secure support for his tenuous hold on the throne following his victory over Richard III at Bosworth two years earlier. It contained only three clauses, one concerning the mace discussed above. Another freed the burgesses from serving on juries outside the borough. By far the most important economically was the one granting the mayor and burgesses 'supervision and correction of all men in the said Town engaged in the working and making of cloths, to correct the same … for the reformation of defects and bad work if there be any'. The fact that the abbot received any fines imposed was really less important; the town had control over the quality of what had become the basis of its growing prosperity. Taken together, the earlier regulations and the charter show the gild acting like the majority of English borough authorities, protecting the quality of its manufacture and the fairness of its trading practices.[19]

Beyond economic affairs, the gild shared in keeping law and order in the borough. The abbot's steward and his two bailiffs were in overall

Medieval Wards (coloured lines) and parishes (coloured strips). (CS)

charge but at street level were other officials. Two constables, probably chosen solely by the gild, had responsibility for law and order. By the mid-thirteenth century the borough was divided into five wards cutting across parish boundaries: High, London, Minster, Old and New, each with two wardens chosen annually by the burgesses to keep order on their streets. Even more local was the frankpledge or tithing, a custom dating from the Anglo-Saxon period by which groups of families, originally ten, were responsible in law for each others' good behaviour. After the Dissolution, when the town was a corporate borough, better record survival shows that all males over twelve attended the bi-annual court leet and demonstrated their membership of a frankpledge; presumably it was the same when the court was held by the abbey's steward. According to another ancient custom, communities were expected to provide men and arms for the king in times of war or rebellion. In Reading the gild had custody of the town's 'harnayse' or armour including four brigantines (coats of mail), sallets (head pieces) and bills (long, stout staffs).

Though impossible to prove, it may be that the wealth generated by an expanding cloth-making industry in the fifteenth century gave the body of burgesses the confidence to respond to any challenge by an abbot to their status and even to initiate a contest. Relations had been strained since the 1430s when successive abbots contested the gild's right to the rent paid by non-Reading butchers for their stalls (the Out Butchery), claiming that they stood on abbey freehold. After much expensive legal wrangling, abbot John Thorne I's (1446–86) challenge was successful and the rents disappeared from the gild accounts after 1447/8, although it is obvious from later evidence that the burgesses had not accepted this as a *fait accompli*. As we have seen, there were rumblings over the title of mayor and his right to the mace, a situation not improved by the powers given to the gild in the 1487 charter. Complaints were raised with Edward IV in 1479/80 about the abbey's neglect of its charitable work in the borough, notably its chapels and almshouses; reforms were promised but not made.

The emergence of more combative personalities at the end of the century, Abbot John Thorne II (1486–1519) and Richard Cleche, a newcomer to the town and gild, may have been significant in the escalation of the quarrels, probably about 1500. Much of what had obtained since 1254 was now in question. The burgesses' claim to be a corporate body and their right to the Out Butchery rents were both strenuously denied by the abbot, who also said they held the gild hall only on sufferance. He also restated his sole right to choose the constables to keep law and order in the borough and to punish offenders. He also rejected the gild's claim to present three candidates for keeper of the gild ('mayor' was a title he would not use), insisting on his free choice. At its most serious, the abbot refused to choose a mayor for several years, the burgesses illegally choosing their own, and, when Richard Cleche was warden/mayor in 1499, dismissing the constables chosen by the abbot. It was not until 1507 that all matters in contention were resolved by four judges including Bishop Richard Fox, Henry VII's Lord Privy Seal. Reading's corporate borough status was confirmed; the gild's right to present three candidates from whom the abbot chose the keeper of the gild was restored; the mayor could use the mace; the gild would appoint constables and wardens of the five wards but they would be admitted and sworn in by the abbot's steward. The customary payments by new burgesses and the *chepyngavell* were also confirmed. The question of ownership of the Out Butchery was referred to Bishop Fox and the Lord Chamberlain, to be settled finally in 1525 with the gild keeping the land but paying rent to the abbot. Despite one or two disputes in 1509–10, no further conflicts were recorded.[20]

One significant aspect of the borough's affairs which remained firmly in the burgesses' hands was the choice of its MPs. Until the mid-thirteenth century, the king sought counsel from his Great Council, his major barons; occasionally and then more frequently, the commons – knights of the shire (county representatives) and burgesses (from some boroughs) – were also summoned. The king and his councillors began to bring important judicial matters and government policy to these assemblies, which came to be known as parliaments. By the mid-fourteenth century great lords, both laymen (lords temporal) and bishops and abbots, including the abbot of Reading (lords spiritual) had secured the right to be summoned. After 1339 no true parliament excluded the commons. They became particularly important since taxes could only be raised with the consent of parliament, taxes which would be paid by counties and boroughs.

The first assembly to which burgesses were summoned met in 1265. Thirty years later Reading sent its first two MPs to parliament; thereafter (except in 1653, the Barebones' Parliament) two burgesses represented the borough at Westminster until 1884. In 1295 the writ for the election was sent to the bailiffs, the abbot's officials, but that for 1301 to the 'mayor and bailiffs' of the borough and later to the mayor and the community. At some date thereafter the choice came to rest with the burgesses alone, though of those MPs elected between 1386 and 1421, five served as bailiffs, four of them later chosen as mayor by the abbot. The electorate was small, never more than 50. An inner circle of about 20 burgesses could have controlled the election, and the abbot had some indirect influence through his choice of mayor.[21]

Borough MPs had to be burgesses, achieved by admitting outside candidates to the gild without a fee. There was usually little need for this because for the most part Reading was represented by its burgesses, among them clothiers and merchants, some of them mayors or future mayors, bailiffs and cofferers. They need not neglect their borough responsibilities for long since parliaments rarely sat for more than a few weeks, and contacts made there could prove useful. The borough was responsible for paying their expenses, a small price in return for the influence they would have in protecting the town's interests. Social and political change in the fifteenth century saw county gentry, a growing social group, eager to find seats in parliament (Thomas Beke of Whiteknights sat in 1478), and embattled royal houses looking to place supporters there. For a short period between 1483 and 1504, five of Reading's nine MPs were royal servants, though this might not mean they had no local loyalties. One, Richard Smythe, served in the royal household as Yeoman of the Robes to Queen Elizabeth, wife of Henry VII and thereafter to Henry VIII. He received various grants from the Crown including the posts of Keeper of Swallowfield and Steward of Caversham. Elected the town's MP to the parliaments of 1497, 1504 and 1512 he 'adopted' the town. He was among a group of Reading men who in 1505 obtained a royal licence to acquire lands in mortmain with an annual value of twelve marks to sustain the Jesus Mass in St Laurence's church, being one of the ten 'maynteners' of that gild in 1493. In his will he gave all his property in the borough to the Jesus Mass on condition that an annual obit was held for his and his family's souls. He was a generous donor to the parish and town: to the parish luxury fabrics to be made into vestments and money for the making; to twelve poor men of Reading money, gowns and bread at his funeral; to forty poor maids half a mark each at marriage and 3s. 4d. every Friday for a year to the neediest in the borough.[22] After 1504 burgesses again represented the town, including those who sat in the Reformation Parliament.

3

Prosperity and piety,
*c.*1350–1540

URING the two centuries after the Black Death, a period nationally of political instability and uneven economic growth, Reading acquired a self-confidence from the wealth resulting from its expanding industry and trade. It avoided the decline suffered by many less fortunate towns, and was acknowledged as the premier urban centre in Berkshire both in size and wealth.

Population

By 1348 Reading had a population of about 1,500. Then came the epidemic of 1348–39, the Black Death. If the impact was as severe here as elsewhere, then between a third and a half of the townspeople died then or when plague returned in 1361–62.[1]

Those who survived were subjected to one of the best known of medieval impositions, the poll tax of 1377, 1379 and 1381, frequently used by historians attempting to estimate the population of a local community. For Reading only a damaged list of names survives for the 1381 tax, levied at 12*d.* a head on all adults, i.e. those aged over 15. The government determined the amount to be collected from each community, equal to 12*d.* from every resident, man and woman, but the amount paid by each individual was to be decided locally based on his/her ability to pay. Reading's assessment was £29 3*s.* 0*d.*, equivalent to a shilling (12*d.*) from 583 taxpayers. Assuming that young people under the age of 15 represented at least a third of the population, Reading was home to at least 875 people. However, it is known that tax evasion was widespread; possibly as many as 40% of the population escaped. If true, then Reading's population could have numbered over 1,200. This was not quite a return to pre-plague levels but, even so, Reading was the largest of the county's towns for which tax returns survive.[2]

It retained this position at the end of the middle ages. The next useful tax for historians is the Lay Subsidy of 1524–25, almost a century and a half later. What happened to Reading in the interim is unknown though frequent epidemics and low replacement rates in will-making

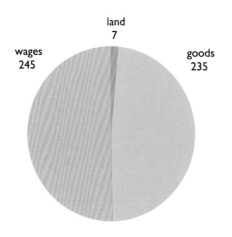

wages
245

land
7

goods
235

Reading
taxpayers,
1524.

families suggests that the population was slow to expand. The 1524–25 subsidy, efficiently levied to pay for Henry VIII's wars, was based on a new assessment of the laity's wealth. Clergy were taxed separately. Since for much of England, lists of taxpayers' names survive, it has been quarried for studies of the size and wealth structure of many communities. Equal halves of the tax were paid in each of these years on whichever assessment criteria gave the Crown the biggest return: landowners paid one shilling in the £ of rental income; those with little or no land paid a progressive tax on the capital value of their goods (personal property) starting at 6d. in £; those with few or no taxable goods paid at least 4d. in £ on wages. The returns for Reading's three parishes show 523 taxpayers in 1525. Attempting to estimate total population based on these returns is problematic. A very tentative estimate might suggest a population of about 3,400. This would take account of the number of those under the tax threshold of £1 a year in wages or £2 in goods; if Reading resembled other towns then these would number between a quarter and a third of the townspeople.[3]

Migration

The increase in the town's population between 1381 and 1524 suggests that it was not entirely caused by natural increase (i.e. more births than deaths). Nationally the population barely rose during these years, remaining stubbornly at between 2.3 and 2.5 million.[4] Some towns and villages even shrank as people moved to find work. Evidence for immigration into Reading, all from tax records, is slight but convincing. Surnames of a few who paid the 1381 poll tax suggest they were incomers, or descendants of incomers, some from nearby, Caversham and Hurley, but most from as far away as Cricklade, Gloucester and Northampton. Fifteenth-century kings levied taxes on foreigners, called 'aliens' in the documents, who came from beyond the lands claimed by the English king; 11 first-generation immigrants living in Reading, one a weaver and five of them married, paid this tax in 1440. The Tudors charged foreigners double the basic tax rate; 11 of them, one from France, eight from the Low Countries and two others are identified as 'aliens' in the 1524–25 subsidy. Some men applying to enter the Merchant Gild were probably non-residents, especially those paying higher entry fees, since the gild had the right to set differential rates. These ranged from 3s. 4d. to 11s. 8d. in the 1440s. Occasionally there are indications in a will that the deceased was not originally from the town. In 1536 John Kent bequeathed 6*s*. 8*d*. to churches of Thatcham where he held land and where his namesake and godson lived and where he was probably born. A generous gift of £10 by William Justice was to his birthplace but other donors gave no explanation: Thomas Carpenter left 40*d*. to the parish church of Streatley and Thomas Coxwell 8*d*. to the repair of Coxwell church.[5]

The Merchant Gild and the borough economy

The right to earn a living in most medieval boroughs was controlled by groups of traders and craftsmen organised into gilds. Some, as in York, could trace their origins to the early twelfth century, and many more made such claims without firm evidence. Among them was Reading. The first written confirmation for its Merchant Gild appears in its 1253 charter giving all burgesses, a term synonymous with gild membership, the right to trade throughout England free from tolls. Such a right was a normal part of borough charters, but this one also gave explicit royal recognition of the gild's existence. It was followed in 1254 by an agreement between the abbey and the gild which confirmed the right of the burgesses to have a gild with a warden chosen by the abbot to whom all members paid an annual fee for the right to trade.[6] As with most negotiated settlements, there were losses as well as gains but on balance the borough had cause to be satisfied if not pleased with the result.

In particular the abbey retained its control as lord of the borough, exercised through its two bailiffs. The abbey remained clerk of the market, its officials determining the time it was to open and regulating buying and selling. The abbey was later given the right to set the assize of bread (to determine its price in the market in line with the price of wheat) and the assize of ale based on the price of barley.[7] Breaches of market rules and other bye-laws would have been judged by his bailiffs in the abbot's annual portmoot or borough court. The absence of court records leaves us with little information about marketing except for a document called the *Puncta Gilde* or Ordinances of the Gild which regulated trade, especially by outsiders. As the name indicates, these rules were made by the gild, not the abbey, but since the document was lodged with the abbey's charters, it seems likely it was drawn up with its approval.[8] Among the terms was a regulation that all goods must be sold in the lawful, customary place; cloth brought for sale must contain no coarse wool mixed with the good; if a butcher sold meat from an animal which had died suddenly, the carcass was to be burned; only gild members could sell by retail old cheese, oil, suet or wax. All offenders would be 'in mercy', that is liable to be amerced (fined) by the bailiff and the fines were paid to the abbey, not the gild.

Rules concerning hours of work and trading practices, commonplace in medieval towns, appear in the gild's records in the fifteenth century, although theoretically only the abbot could make bye-laws. In 1443, for example, the gild ruled that barbers' shops must not open after 10 p.m. between Easter and Michaelmas (29 September) and 9 p.m. at other times except for 'eny straunger or eny worthy man of the towne that hath need'. Two years later it imposed a fine of 4d. on anyone who took a merchant into his house to buy corn before the merchant had traded in the market. The quality of manufactures was normally the responsibility of wardens of craft gilds, but those supervising some essential goods were elected by the Merchant Gild in the mid-fifteenth century; in 1444 and in 1464 two wardens each were appointed to supervise the crafts of the shoemakers, merchants and fullers. Certain activities were carried out on property owned by the gild, the Scleyinge or Slaughter House, Portmanbrook meadow and the wharf. In 1464 the gild ruled that no burgess was to buy meat from a butcher unless the animal had been slaughtered in the 'Scleyinge house'. Grazing on the meadow was for burgesses' cattle only, one milch cow apiece between May (refined in 1505 to the Monday before Corpus Christi) and 1 November. In 1481 William Lynacre, a draper, leased a house the wharf for seven years, possibly used as one means of exporting his cloth.[9]

William would have recouped his rent by charging fees for storing goods at the wharf or loading and unloading, called at other times 'customs of the wharf'. The amount of trade by river is not known but it was important enough to be the subject of an agreement between the borough and the abbey in 1405: the abbot granted passage between sunrise and sunset for boats and showtes (flat-bottomed boats) carrying merchandise or foodstuffs on payment of one penny per showte by a Reading man and two pennies by others. Craft had to wait at Broken Brow while someone from the abbey was sent for to open the lock. Increasing trade in the following century caused the gild to give one of the two cofferers or treasurers the sole duty of supervising the wharf and the wool beam, and in 1535 to split the control of the wool beam from that of the wharf. At certain times, especially around fair days, the wharf was busy; in 1506–07 wharfage for the period around May Day and St James Fair amounted to 12s. but only 5s. 5d. for the rest of the year.[10]

The three fairs attracted traders from outside the borough, including tanners who were only allowed to sell goods on these days. Other outsiders were more restricted: they could not retail cloth or iron or iron tools at any time, and tailors were limited to what they could carry on their backs. Foreign fishmongers could only trade with the bailiff's permission provided that no gildsman had fish to sell. Such regulations limiting outsiders' trade ensured they did not threaten the livelihoods of the borough's artisans but did come when the town needed the goods they brought. The tolls the abbey levied on outsiders gave another advantage to the inhabitants who traded freely in the market. Giving townspeople preference in buying essential foods was another concern of many urban authorities. In Reading no 'foreyn' (outsider) could buy corn before 'la tierce', which possibly meant 9.00 a.m. This would ensure that residents were able to purchase all they needed.[11]

Occupations

It has been claimed that cloth was the 'economic mainstay' of the town by c.1400; certainly two Reading MPs were involved in exporting cloths in 1394–95, years when the county was sharing in the great expansion in English cloth exports. Other cloth producers were leading townsmen. Three of 18 borough MPs between 1386 and 1421 with known occupations were involved in the cloth trade: two weavers, William Stapper (1386) and John Clerk (1414), and a dyer, William Derby (1404).[12] However, the evidence is confused. In the admittedly incomplete poll tax return of 1381, only three dyers, three kempsters (wool workers) and two shearmen were recorded, a total of eight clothworkers of a total of 102 identifiable craftsmen and 13 'callemakers', possibly cappers. It seems more likely that it was during the fifteenth century that cloth came to dominate Reading's economy, despite the general economic depression of the middle years. From the accounts of the Merchant Gild in occasional years between 1414 and 1489 we know the occupation of 25 new gild members, over a third of whom were in the cloth industry as drapers, dyers, weavers and fullers, and another 14 in similar occupations were non-members. A record of entrants to the gild from 1435–64 has 12 clothworkers, a quarter of those mentioned.[13] In 1510 when burgesses were named and their trades given, 14 of the 45 were engaged in cloth production or sale as drapers, weavers, fullers and dyers, about a third of the town's workforce, a proportion which would obtain throughout the century and beyond.[14] A fullers' craft gild was in existence by 1464 when the burgesses appointed two wardens; a similar gild of weavers was in place by 1520 if not before. 'Guardians' or wardens of both the fullers' and the weavers' crafts are mentioned in an agreement of this date.

Firm evidence of Reading's increasing importance in production for an overseas market appears only in the mid- to late fifteenth century when a small number of Reading men begin to feature in the aulnage accounts (national records of those paying a tax on woollen cloth for sale) and on a scale which suggests that this was not a new feature of the town's economy. Five burgesses are listed between 1468 and 1482, one or two dealing in substantial amounts: Robert Farley, draper, paid on 95 cloths in 1468–69 and William Linacre on 200 over two years, 1468–70. William was one of a number of eminent burgesses who were

Reading's woollen cloth industry

In contrast with Newbury and west Berkshire where production of narrow, ribbed cloths called kerseys predominated, Reading dealt overwhelmingly in white and coloured broadcloth which required a large variety of skilled craftsmen and women.* High-quality wool from sheep pastured on the Berkshire Downs was purchased by clothmakers, also called clothiers or drapers as whole fleeces either from the grower or in the town's wool hall. From 1430 to 1511 it appears that wool was weighed on the common beam ('common' being the normal word meaning 'for common use'). What happened previously is unknown and from 1511 there was a separate beam solely for wool, an indication of its expanding and increasingly important role in the economy. Wool would first be sorted since the quality of the wool varied according to whether it came from the sheep's back (the finest) or belly (the coarsest) and any burrs and twigs removed. It was then washed and some wool dyed if it was used to make coloured cloths giving us the phrase 'dyed in the wool'.

Next the wool was oiled (using butter, goose fat or imported olive oil) combed using cards or stockards, oblongs of wood embedded with nails which aligned the wool fibres ready for spinners. This could be done by men or women but the next process, spinning to make the yarn, stronger and well twisted for the warp and less so for the weft, was exclusively women's work. Spinners rarely appear in documents though women carrying distaffs appear in many illuminated texts. Where cloth was produced commercially, as in Reading, most yarn would have been spun on a wheel probably at home as part-time work. Elizabeth Kent (died 1549) who was carrying on her husband's business had cards but only one spinning wheel in the wool house. Spinning was a slow process: it took fourteen spinners a week to produce enough yarn to make one broadcloth, 48 lbs of warp yarn and 65 lbs of weft according to an agreement made between clothmakers, weavers and fullers in 1520. Craft gilds of fullers and weavers had been in existence since the fourteenth century but little is known about them.†

Weaving was man's work. A narrow kersey cloth, 36 inches wide was woven on a narrow loom by one man but a broadcloth required two. The same agreement specified that a Reading broadcloth should measure 3¼ yards (297 cms) in width and 30 ells (32½ yards or 29.29 metres) in length before final processing. The work, involving setting up the loom as well as the actual weaving, would take over a week for which the weavers would be paid ten shillings for 'livery' cloth and 13s. 4d. for fine cloth between them, a good wage. The cloth was then checked for knots and other intrusions, a process called burling, then sent to be fulled or thickened. Both Minster and St Giles' Mills had wheels used

* The description of cloth production is based on Christine A. Jackson, 'The Berkshire Woollen Industry, 1500–1650', unpublished Ph.D. thesis, University of Reading (1993), 50–63. At this period drapers produced cloth; later they merely sold it; Richard Aman, draper, leased a dyehouse. TNA, Will of Richard Aman PROB 11/27/29.
† BRO, Will and inventory of Elizabeth Kent, widow, 1550 D/A1/88/10; BRO, Agreement between clothiers, weavers, fullers and tuckers of Reading, 17 February, 11 Henry VIII, 1520. R/1C 2/1; Slade, 'Reading', 5.

to turn hammers which pounded the cloth while the soap and fuller's earth in the water helped clean and matt the fibres, and it is likely that even at this early date, mills at Caversham and Burghfield were used. Since the abbey had its own mills, it is probable that cloth was fulled there, too, either on its own account or by fullers who leased it. Fulled cloth was restored to shape, 2 yards wide and 26 yards long, by being attached to tenter hooks and gently stretched on a rack, hence the phrase 'to be on tenter hooks'. What malevolent spirit realised that this useful implement could be put to more malign purposes? Finally a skilful process called dressing involved first raising the nap of the cloth, using teasles set on to wooden 'handles' then shearing it with huge shears to create a smooth surface. Finer cloths required one or more repeats of the process. Any flaws produced at this or earlier stages would be removed by a drawer before the cloth was pressed and packed. All cloths made in Reading had to carry a seal kept by three burgesses 'so as to be known for a Reading cloth'. The settlement of a dispute between the clothmakers and the weavers and fullers in 1520 determined that if the workmanship were not 'true' as determined by two men from each of the trades – clothmakers, weavers and fullers – then the clothmaker would be 'recompensed'. It may be significant that this occurred during a trade depression, one of several which affected the industry in the 1520s and 1530s.

Some coloured cloths were dyed after weaving and others sold as undyed or white cloths to be finished in Flanders and elsewhere in Europe. Materials including oil, woad and alum were imported via Southampton in substantial quantities by 1439. The total amount of woad obtained from the port between 1443 and 1489 was at least 495 balets, each weighing between 224 and 280 lbs with small quantities of madder and oil, which suggests that Reading produced more blue-coloured cloths than yellow, though later probate evidence shows the dyers' ingenuity in mixing dyes to produce a variety of colours. Though Reading imported materials for cloth production through Southampton, there is only one record of cloth being exported by this route: in December 1527, Walter Payne sent 40 kerseys carried by four horses to the port.* It would seem that Reading exported its cloth through London as it did later, though evidence to confirm this is still to be found.

Unfortunately no inventories for men in the cloth industry survive for this period though will evidence shows that many, even weavers and fullers, became prosperous enough to enjoy a pleasant lifestyle. William Knight's will of 1525 does not state his occupation but he mentions two broadlooms and a kersey loom; he leased property in Colthrop and Crookham, owned silver spoons, dressed in furred gowns and satin doublets and gave about £20 to various monks, priests and parish gilds for prayers.†

*   B. Bunyard (ed.), *The Brokage Book of Southampton* vol. 1, 1439–40 (Southampton Record Society (1941), appendix C; Olive Coleman (ed.), *The Brokage Book of Southampton, 1443–44* (University of Southampton, 1961), 322. Winifred A. Harwood, *The Southampton Brokage Book, 1447–48* (University of Southampton, 2008).
†   TNA, Will of William Knight of Reading made 5 May 1525, PROB 11/26/1.

The upper lights of a window in the church of Notre Dame, Semur, Burgundy, showing processes in making broadcloth: sorting wool, carding, washing spun yarn, weaving. (JD)

The lower lights of the window: fulling or dyeing, burling, shearing, raising the nap. (JD)

clothiers; he was mayor in 1463–64, as were Thomas Beke and William Pernecote, drapers, who were also paying aulnage in these years. By this date Reading had increased its role in the Berkshire cloth industry from less than 2% of the county's cloth exports in 1394–95 to 20% in 1468–70, the town's best years in this period.[15] Maintaining the quality of a product of such importance to the town was granted by the charter of 1487, the mayor supervising cloth production 'for the reformation of defects and bad work'. The growing significance of the clothing interest in urban politics as well as the urban economy is obvious from the number who held high borough office at the end of the period, including drapers Richard Cleche, mayor three times between 1487 and 1502 and also the borough MP in 1510, and John Pownsar, mayor and MP in 1514–15.[16] Unfortunately no inventories for men in the cloth industry survive for this period, although will evidence shows that many, even weavers and fullers, became prosperous enough to enjoy a pleasant lifestyle. William Knight's will of 1525 does not state his occupation but he mentions two broadlooms and a kersey loom; he leased property in Colthrop and Crookham, owned silver spoons, dressed in furred gowns and satin doublets and gave about £20 to various monks, priests and parish gilds for prayers.[17]

As cloth production grew in importance in Reading's economy, the significance of leather relative to cloth declined. Of about 176 individuals with recognisable occupations in the poll tax returns, 28 were either manufacturing leather or using it to produce goods such as shoes and saddles. Over the next century the trade employed about one in five of those entering the gild, proof of its continuing value both in the town's economy and in the day-to-day needs of the community. Excavation on the site of the Oracle shopping centre has produced evidence of a substantial fifteenth-century tannery.

More important than leather both in numerical and practical terms was the provision of food and drink, whose practitioners dominated the trade structure in 1381, bakers, butchers, maltsters, innkeepers and others forming over a third of the named traders. There were even two cooks either working for the abbey or providing fast food to eat in or take away; 'an elaborate stone building' near the Minster Stream may have been a public cook shop. In the next half century more butchers, bakers, fishmongers and a lone spicer joined the gild and were among the burgesses named in 1510.[18] While such trades were numerous in any medieval town, what distinguishes Reading is the large numbers of inn or tavern keepers, eight, named in the poll tax, though very few joined the gild. They provided hospitality for the retainers of important visitors to the abbey and also for the many travellers who passed through the town. The 15 tailors recorded in 1381 may also have found customers among such visitors as well as among wealthy townsfolk; another seven applied to become burgesses in the mid-fifteenth century. Four other craftsmen were gildsmen by 1510, two carpenters, John and Henry Hawthorne (relationship unknown), a cutler Robert Boyfield and a pewterer, William Melvyn alias Staunford. Farming continued in the fields and meadows close to the built-up area; cows still grazed on the Portmanbrook meadow; and pigs, found in most backsides (gardens), frequently roamed the streets until confined to the pound.

Among the wealthiest burgesses were the mercers or merchants. Though only two were named in 1381, at least seven entered the gild between 1448 and 1464 and there were six in 1510. Using probate inventories from later in the century we can hazard a guess that they dealt in a variety of mainly imported goods, especially luxury fabrics such as silks and satins. Grocers sold spices and dried fruits from abroad, and vintners retailed wine. No grocer or vintner occurs in Reading's records in this period, although oranges, raisins, 'fruit' and wine were among the goods sent by Southampton merchants to the borough. In 1447–48 fruit

A reconstruction of Le Kychene, a late fourteenth-century cookshop. It probably belonged to the abbey and served a large clientele with hot food to take away or eat in. (Under the Oracle)

was traded in 'pieces', some to Simon Kent, who appears in gild records as a fishmonger. The amounts of wine were substantial: ten pipes, in 1443–44 each containing 126 gallons; 17 pipes in 1447–49 in addition to specific orders for the abbey, plus two pipes for the George Inn and two pipes each for local gentlemen, Richard Drew of Southcote and William Vachell of Coley.[19]

Three members of the royal household belonged to the gild in 1510: Richard Smythe, valet of the king's wardrobe, Richard Meredith, servant of the king and Richard Justice (also called mercer), groom of Queen Katherine's wardrobe. Richard Smythe, elected the town's MP to the parliaments of 1497, 1504 and 1512, 'adopted' the town and became a burgess in 1509. While it is understandable that Richard Smythe should feel an affinity with the borough, the case of Meredith is unclear but both men are examples of the close connections between Reading and the capital.

Gild membership is an imperfect guide to the town's occupational structure, however, since it was composed of a select group, never more than 40 to 50 at any one time, obviously only a fraction of the workforce. Suitably qualified non-members were able to trade by paying an annual fee. For a short period in the mid-fifteenth century they appear in the gild accounts as 'outsiders' who hired stalls possibly permanently or just for market days. These have been identified as Reading men, outside the Merchant Gild, possibly members of the shadowy craft gilds. They should probably be distinguished from 'foreigners' who did not belong to the town but who also purchased the right to trade at certain times. At certain periods between 1373 and 1446 the occupations of 62 'outsiders' are known of whom 14 were in the cloth industry, all except two being weavers or fullers. Equal numbers were in the leather trades, but bakers, butchers and fishmongers were almost as numerous as cloth and leather workers combined.[20]

Gild records also underestimate the role of women in family and urban economies. Women were not gild members and though it seems that some widows could continue their husbands' businesses, it is not clear for how long. Part of an agreement

Brass of an unknown woman *c.*1530, in St Mary's church in 1802. (Coates)

between the abbey and the gild in 1507 stated that widows of burgesses should pay a *chepyngavel* of 2¼d., allowing them to buy and sell freely in their houses or shops. The work they did at home as spinners was essential for cloth making, though it rarely merits a mention. There was a washing place by the gild hall which is only recorded because the gild received rent for it, not because housewives and servants washed clothes there. A traditional role for women, though not professionally, was as midwives; two paid the poll tax in 1381. Two more were callemakers and another a kempster, a wool worker. The 1381 returns also provide the best indication that in Reading as in other medieval towns, women known as ale-wives or brewsters brewed and sold ale. At least seven are named in the poll tax, one a married woman trading independently, the others most probably widows since the authorities frowned on single women living alone. Two were rich enough to pay double the basic rate of tax. The *Puncta Gilde* ruled that foreign (non-gild) brewsters could not put up the sign that new ale was on sale until its quality had been proven. A few women appear as servants in the poll tax and others in wills, usually bequeathed a few shillings which may have been their wages since these were usually paid at the end of a service contract. Some bequests were simple acts of generosity: Thomas Glover gave each of his maidservants, Agnes and Cecily, a pot, a pan, six dishes, a candlestick and a basin of pewter; Alys Adams' servant, Jane Bulkeley, received spoons, platters, table cloths and a pot, a useful 'bottom drawer'. Alice Catour's father could afford to provide something better for her: she was apprenticed to a London embroiderer, giving her a trade much in demand, not least for church vestments.[21]

Wealth and social structure

Reading's was a hierarchical community based on wealth and status: a small elite at the top, many families of modest means below them, then those just getting by and an unknown number who lived on or below the poverty line. The 1381 poll tax confirms the evidence of the 1297 tax list. Richest of the 418 taxpayers were 11 men and women who paid between four shillings and 3s. 6d. each. Just over two in five paid the standard rate of a shilling, about one in three paid a little less, and about another one in three paid a little more. At the other end of the wealth spectrum was a large group paying sixpence each, with others, including some apprentices and women servants, contributing just four pence (a groat) and the poorest two or three pence. Just how fairly or accurately the tax burden was shared in Reading is not known, but for some any amount was more than they could afford and many avoided paying anything.[22]

A valuable feature of many poll tax returns is the grouping of taxpayers into something resembling households. A husband's and wife's tax is noted as a single payment. Paying separately were young people spending their teenage years and their early twenties in their masters' houses as apprentices and 'servants', that is domestic servants and resident employees. Nationally they made up about one in five of the urban population. In the tax lists of towns such as Oxford, older children, servants and apprentices appear next to the name of the master and his wife. In those of Berkshire villages and towns, all or most servants were grouped together at the end of the lists. The end of the Reading list is damaged; of the last 34 fully legible names, 21 are servants of the abbey (married and single), 7 are undifferentiated servants, 2 the daughters of men listed earlier, and 4 with no attribution. The end section containing 141 names is completely missing. If the Reading return followed the order of that of other Berkshire communities, then many of the missing names would be those of servants, some of them women domestics. Analysis of the surviving part of the document reveals a social structure in Reading so different from that of other English towns as to be unlikely: only 28 servants (21 of them servants of the abbey) about 6% of the population. With the addition of some or all the missing names, the proportion could be up to 28%, a more acceptable figure.[23]

The wealth and social structure revealed in the 1524/5 lay subsidy returns is much more sharply defined.[24] The richest men were parishioners of St Laurence, the smallest parish by area but with the largest number (245) of taxpayers. It was also the richest parish paying more than £265 of the borough total of £422 over two years. From St Mary's

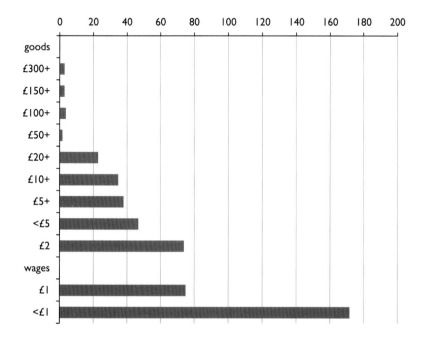

Reading wealth, 1524.

parish 164 men and women paid almost £128, but 123 from St Giles and Whitley account for a mere £25. Almost half taxpayers (45%) paid 4*d*. or 6*d*. on wages, a proportion also found in other cloth-making towns such as Newbury. Since they did not possess taxable goods to the value of £2, they had little protection against unemployment or sickness. Above them stretched a hierarchy based on possessions, from the roughly 20% assessed at the lowest rate of £2, through master craftsmen like Henry Hawthorn, a carpenter assessed at £30, to the elite 2% or 3% of the population whose wealth was very substantial and whose payments raised the average tax take: Thomas Beke (assessed wealth £60), Thomas Everard, draper (£320) and Richard Turner, mercer (£200). At the very bottom were the poor whose numbers are unknown, but if Reading followed the pattern of other towns would not have amounted to less than 25% of the population. Even so, based on its subsidy payment, Reading was the tenth richest provincial town in England.

For the period between the poll tax and the lay subsidy, some wills begin to appear which, though not as useful as probate inventories, can add to our understanding of the richer families in the town and their lifestyles. Few will-makers stated their occupations but among those who did, clothiers and drapers predominate along with a few mercers. Some of the bequests in the will of William Justice, a gild member in 1510, indicate the wealth a successful mercer could amass. His bequests to relatives and friends alone amounted to 135 ounces of silver plate and about £160 in money. The home of Thomas Everard, chandler, was furnished with hangings on the walls of the hall (main living room), parlour and chamber (bedroom). He left his wife, Marie, £200 and all his jewels and at least another £150 to friends, relatives, servants and the church. William Knight's success in the cloth trade was visible whenever he was seen in the street. He owned several gowns, two fur-lined, satin doublets and two coats, one violet in colour. Among gifts to his daughter, Margery, were four yards of cloth to make a gown and 40 yards to the poor 'to make them coates against the wynter'.[25] Compare these amounts with craftsmen's wages of a few pounds a year.

Some of this wealth was invested in property, either in the borough or elsewhere. Christian Nicholas, the first of three generations of burgesses, owned a property in Old Street and four tenements (house and/or workshop and land) in High Street and London Street. Robert Bennett, a clothier, added to his four Reading properties land in South Stoke and Caversham, Oxfordshire. Nicholas Hyde, mercer, lived in a tenement in the Market Place but owned others in New Street, Shoemaker Row and Flaxen Lane. Walter Barton had leased land and rights in the parsonage in South Stoke, had a farm where over 360 sheep grazed and other land at Streatley. Those unable to buy property invested in leases from the abbey, the borough or the parish. All these they could leave to their

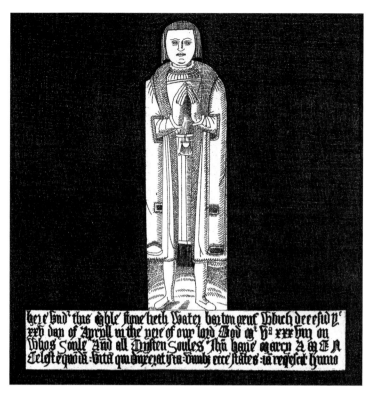

A brass of Walter Barton in St Laurence's church 1538. Here under this table stone lieth Water barton gent Which decesid ye xxv day of Apryll in the yere of our lord God MVXXXVIII on whos Soule And all Crysten Soules Jhesu have mercy AMEN.

chosen legatees, Reading being a borough where property could be bequeathed by will.[26]

Property deeds provide some evidence that London merchants traded and owned property in the borough in the fifteenth century but more detail comes from wills in the early Tudor period. Thomas Glover was one of several men with contacts in both Reading and London. Thomas wished to be buried in St Margaret's church, Westminster, but his bequests were to St Giles in Reading where Thomas Harding owed him money and where one of his executors lived. The will of William Wrottesley, gentleman, states he was 'of Reading' but his burial place and the object of several bequests was St Olaf's parish in the City. He owned property in Reading and left money to several townsfolk and for tapers to burn at the shrines of Our Lady of Caversham and Our Lady of Reading in St Mary's church. George Hyde was also buried in a City parish, St Peter, East Cheap, but had silver plate in Reading gildhall and a house in the Market Place. He may have been a son of Nicholas Hyde and inherited the house after the death of his father and then his mother. If so, then he is one of many young men who found employment in London. Nicholas Parker seems to have been employed by a London pewterer, Thomas Mason. Nicholas was unmarried and had some connection with Reading where half his pewterer's moulds were.[27]

Late medieval parish and religious life

The late medieval parish and its church provided the focus of people's religious and, to some extent, social life; the abbey was not of great significance for the daily devotions of the townspeople. Reading's parochial structure, established before 1200, was largely unchanged until the 1860s. All three parishes were served by vicars, king Henry I having made the abbey the rector and patron of two ancient parishes. Thereby the incumbent lost the great tithes of corn and hay to the new rector but retained small tithes on other produce and on wages, and enjoyed the profits from fees and offerings. When the abbey founded the third parish, St Laurence, it did not provide the vicar with glebe land and he could not collect tithes from his parishioners. Instead his was a corrody vicarage, his income being paid by the abbey though he also received traditional offerings and fees for baptisms and other services. Despite modest incomes, none above £15 a year, all three parishes were served by Oxford graduates in the early sixteenth century and perhaps before.[28]

Each parish developed institutions similar to those found all over England. By the fourteenth century parishioners had been given responsibility for the upkeep of the nave, the main part of the church, while that of the chancel lay with the rector. They also had to provide all that was needed for celebrating Mass and the sacraments. The income to meet these charges came from parish (as opposed to the incumbent's) property, from burial fees and from collections at parochial festivities. It became customary for a parish meeting to choose churchwardens, usually two, to carry out these and other responsibilities and give an account at the end of their year of office of money received and spent: the churchwardens' accounts. Very few such records survive for this early date, though fortunately those for St Laurence and St Giles do. They contain invaluable information about the importance of the parish in the life of the town.[29]

The church of St Giles, a print drawn and engraved by C. Tomkins c.1790. (Coates)

S.ᵗ GILESS CHURCH ⁄⁄ READING

Every day the streets resounded to the clamour of bells, summoning parishioners to church, sounding knells for the dying and tolling at burials, greeting feast days and royal visitors. No wonder they so often needed repair. Each Sunday parishioners assembled for Mass which at St Laurence was a splendid affair, with priests resplendent in vestments of satin, damask and cloth of gold, accompanied by singing from a choir of men and boys. Very wealthy parishioners like Richard Smythe and Julian Bye bequeathed rich fabrics to the church for vestments, believing this would give them a share in the blessings gained at the altar. Thomas Glover gave his best diaper table cloth to St Giles for an altar cloth. Benches had been installed where seating for women on their side of the nave could be purchased, the more expensive ones near the front for burgesses and their wives. There were not enough seats for everyone; poorer parishioners probably stood at the back. Whether everyone was attentive is doubtful. All the prayers were in Latin, but they could always look at the great crucifix flanked by statues of the Virgin and St John on the rood screen, which separated them from the chancel, or at the wall paintings and statues of the saints, Our Lady of Pity, St Catherine, or St George resplendent on his horse. Some people had a favourite saint and left money in their wills for candles to burn before the statue. Nicholas Niclas bequeathed £40 to St Giles' church to make an image of the Visitation of the Virgin. With the bishop's permission, divine service could also be celebrated in private houses, two inns in Reading with their own chapels being given this privilege in 1411 and 1412.[30]

Brass in St Laurence's church of John Andrews, priest, vested for Mass who died 3 March 1428. He asks passersby to pray for him for he was what they are and they will be what he is. (Coates)

Saints were revered as intercessors able to help believers attain heaven, the most powerful of them being the Virgin Mary. During the fifteenth century devotion to her and to the Name of Jesus became popular, richer members of all three parishes forming parish gilds or fraternities with these as patrons. Gild members prayed for living and dead associates at a special altar at which Mass was said once a week by a gild priest. Some chose to be buried there: William Justice 'before the altar of Jesus' in St Mary's. Rent from property bequeathed by members, such as Richard Smythe's two tenements in London Street, provided an income for a gild chaplain. Others donated money. Some gild members seem to have become close associates or friends: Richard Smythe bequeathed a gold ring to each of the 12 'sisters' of St Laurence's Jesus Mass a gild founded by Henry Kelsall before 1493. The gilds were sometimes called chantries, though only Colney's Chantry in St Mary, founded in the fourteenth century, with an endowment and a permanent chaplain could genuinely claim the title.[31]

Whether or not they belonged to the gild, many pious men and women made bequests to provide for prayers for their souls, especially Masses. Some of these bequests were substantial, ensuring intercession would continue for long periods or occasionally for ever. The most common gift was for a priest to say a Mass a month after death, the month's mind, and on the anniversary, the year's mind. Some asked for a Mass on thirty consecutive days, a trental. Some wills were very explicit. Thomas Everard's specified an 'honest priest' to say Mass three times a week for two years and a yearly obit (Mass for the Dead) for ten years; Christian Nicholas' ten marks (£6 13s. 4d.) for a priest to say Mass in St Giles' church for a year and his two sons to pay the vicar five shillings to celebrate all the 'obsequiis mortuorum' (rites of the dead) on 31 January and an obit the day after. Churchwardens often paid for an obit for benefactors of the parish. An unusual bequest was made by William Justice: 100 nobles to be given to 100 poor maids or widows at their marriage on condition that at their wedding Mass they should say a *Pater Noster*, *Ave*, and Creed for his soul and 'for all soules whome I have trespaced or offended', and £10 for ten trentals to be sung in St Mary's for the same intention.[32]

Will-makers often requested that donations be made to the poor at their funerals, at once demonstrating their social status and ensuring a

Engraving by
Charles Tomkins
of St Mary and
the churchyard.
(Coates)

St Laurence's
Church. (JD)

good number of people to pray for them. John Love gave a black gown
each to 20 poor men, a smock to 20 poor women and 40 shillings to the
poor 'having need, to pray for the helthe of my soul'; Thomas Pantry £4
to be distributed at his funeral, £3 at his month's mind and £2 at his
year's mind. William Knyght gave two pieces of white (undyed) cloth to
be given to the poor 'to make them coates against the wynter'.[33]

More permanent provision was made by endowing schools and
almshouses as chantries where the recipients of charity would daily offer
prayers for the founder. Somewhat cynically, but not without some justification, such provision has been called 'the purchase of Paradise'. Only
one is known in Reading in this period. John Leche or John a Larder's
will made on 10 February 1476 included a bequest of his capital messuage
(his main home) and five small tenements in Old Street next to them
near St Mary's churchyard as almshouses, plus several other tenements
and land. His executors were also to use the proceeds from debts owed
him to purchase three houses for three more poor people, and to buy
land to provide an income to give the almsmen and women 13s. 4d. (a
mark) a year.[34] Such bequests were small in proportion to those given to
relatives and friends and, though welcome to those receiving them, did
little to relieve poverty in the town, which was exacerbated in the early
1520s by bad harvests and a trade depression. In 1531 the first of many
inadequate government initiatives allowed JPs and borough authorities to
license beggars.

A few will-makers put their trust in the prayers of Reading's monks
and friars, the latter being more popular at this period. In 1508 Christian
Nicholas gave them 6s. 8d. for prayers not only for himself but for all
Christian souls, a common practice at the time. William Trewe (1512)

bequeathed half a quarter of wheat. One or two others chose to be buried in the friary church, including Edith Chester (1534). John Stanshawe, esquire (1516) buried in the chapel of St Francis, gave 12*d.* to maintain the rood (cross) in another chapel, 20*s.* to the friars for prayers, 12*d.* to every friar priest and 8*d.* to those not priests. Perhaps it was his obvious affection for the place which prompted his son, Robert, to buy it after the Dissolution, live in and finally die there.[35] In contrast there was only one bequest to the abbey from a townsman: William Knight gave £6 13*s.* 4*d.* (ten marks) to the abbot, 12*d.* to every ordained monk and 8*d.* to those not priests. His will was dated May 1535, when the fate of the abbey may have been already decided.[36]

Most parishioners would have made contributions to the parish during their lifetimes. In preparation for some great feasts such as Christmas and All Hallows (All Saints whose vigil was Hallowe'en) collections were made for wax to keep lights on the rood screen. At Easter all who received communion made a small donation to the priest. Now in death the parish provided. Since only the wealthy could afford their own coffin, most people were buried in a shroud but housed in the parish coffin which, covered by a parish pall, stood on a parish bier the night before the funeral during a service called the dirge or *dirige* and during the Requiem Mass the next day. They would then be buried in the churchyard. There does not seem to have been a charge for this, but if relatives wanted to hire great candles to burn around the coffin, have the bells tolled, or if the deceased was buried in the church, the combined fee was substantial.

It is impossible to know how committed parishioners were to their beliefs. Few would have grasped the finer points of theology, and we do not know how often sermons were preached in Reading's churches; St Laurence certainly had a pulpit. What is clear is that as early as 1412, the Bishop of Salisbury was concerned that some of his flock had rejected traditional teaching, influenced by itinerant preachers; they and their adherents were called 'Lollards' or 'babblers'. Lollard beliefs were based on the teachings of John Wycliffe, an Oxford scholar and priest, but varied from person to person. Most commonly they believed that the Scriptures should be translated into English so that all could understand the word of God; possession of 'lollard' books was often taken as a proof of heresy. Many denied the value of the Mass and such pious works as pilgrimages, veneration of images and relics. Though they were critical of the power and wealth of the clergy and religious orders, many historians do not regard them as anti-clerical. However, given that Church and State were so closely allied, an attack on one threatened the stability of the other. In 1401 a statute *De Heretico Comburendo* ('concerning the burning of a heretic') decreed that anyone convicted by a church court of heresy and refusing to abjure (repent), or having abjured again lapsed into heresy, should be handed to the State to be burned alive, the first time in English history such a law was enacted.

Lollardy was widespread in north Berkshire and the Chilterns, preachers being active in many towns and villages. In 1412 Thomas Punche of St Giles appeared before the officials of Bishop Hallam accused of possessing manuscript books in English containing heretical teaching. No verdict was given; perhaps there was insufficient evidence. In 1499, however, in one of his campaigns against Lollardy, Bishop Blyth's enquiries uncovered seven heretics in Reading in St Giles' and St Laurence's parishes, including a tanner and his wife, a weaver, a tailor and a cooper. All were brought before the bishop at his court at Sonning, abjured and were sentenced to the normal penance. On Saturday 23 March they were to walk barefoot into the Market Place with a bundle of faggots on one shoulder and carrying a torch, both signifying the fate of a relapsed heretic. There they would publicly abjure their beliefs in a traditional formula. On Palm Sunday, 24 March, they were to walk barefoot in their respective parish processions. Two women from St Giles also abjured and did penance.[37]

The majority of the townsfolk, meanwhile, though suitably cowed by the spectacle, were doubtless cheered by the thought that their Lenten fast would soon end. The whole of Lent, Fridays throughout the year and the eve of great feasts were meatless days, hence the importance of the regulations in the *Puncta Gilde* on fish sales. Fresh fish was caught in local rivers, and preserved fish, especially salted (red) herring, was transported in barrels, possibly from London but certainly from Southampton. On 20 February 1449, just in time for Ash Wednesday, John Scharpe's cart left for Reading carrying 250 hake and three casks of white, unsalted herring. Even the elite observed the rule: at a gild feast on Friday, 21 September 1498, St Matthew's Day, the menu included bread, salt fish, conger, eels, pike, perch, trout, haddock, and oysters accompanied by tasty sauces made from spices, mustard, vinegar and sugar, with pears and nuts as another course.[38] With suitable quantities of ale and wine a meatless day need not be without its pleasures.

Untrammelled enjoyment, however, was reserved for Sundays and for the many saints' days and festivals, holy days, which were the holidays of medieval England, especially the long work-less time between Christmas and Twelfth Night (the feast of the Epiphany), the most suitable period, with its short days and poor light, to down tools. Some feast days were marked by social gatherings since the parish, after the alehouse, was the major provider of entertainment. Most occurred in spring and summer, starting with the week after Low Sunday, seven days after Easter Day. Monday was Hock Monday followed by Hock Tuesday when on successive days women and men captured a member of the opposite sex and asked for a forfeit or a small coin. The money collected was given to the churchwardens who then returned some of it to provide bread, ale, flesh (meat), a capon and spices for a supper. May Day, the feast of SS Philip and James, followed soon after. This was traditionally a festival when the young people collected greenery from gardens or the woods, often staying out through the night to do so, followed by a day of jollity. Reading was no exception. St Laurence churchwardens' accounts record receipts from the gatherings of the bachelors in 1504, called 'young men' in 1515. The bell ringers drank their way through two gallons of ale on May Day 1507, and doubtless the morris dancers were similarly refreshed. The 'bow' felled, brought home and set up in the Market Place in 1503–04 sounds like a maypole. To add to the festivities, and because being a fair day, the large crowds would pay good money to be entertained, on a few occasions in the early sixteenth century the parish organised a play. Its theme was sometimes Robin Hood and Maid Marion, players occasionally travelling from other towns. The parishes paid a drummer, minstrels and morris dancers.

Traditionally Whitsuntide was the time for a parish feast, a 'church ale'. All three Reading parishes held one, St Laurence in the church since there was no church house, the more usual venue. The churchwardens collected wheat and malt from parishioners to make bread, pastry and ale, and paid for meat and spices and the baking of pasties. They also provided a drummer, for after the feast came dancing. The feast of Corpus Christi (Body of Christ), established in 1264, was everywhere celebrated with church services and processions and much bell ringing. St Laurence's parish performed a play. Little is known about it though it was probably the story of Creation and the Fall, costumes being provided for Adam and Eve.[39]

Such descriptions of happy occasions should not create an impression of 'Merrie England'. Alongside the tales of merriment should be put the sheer grind of physical labour in kitchen or workplace, widespread insecurity bred of under-employment and the threat of having no work at all, and near or actual poverty. The period ended with the beginnings of inflation, some bad harvests and epidemics of sweating sickness and bubonic plague. And in religion, the whole world was about to be turned upside down.

4

The years of crisis, 1529–1600

T HE religious and political turbulence of the Tudor age brought dangers to be avoided and opportunities to be grasped. The loss of the abbey and the twists and turns of confessional allegiance were the context in which astute local politicians weathered early financial problems and gained incorporated status for the borough.

In 1529, the year Henry's rejected queen Catherine of Aragon visited Reading, two townsmen were in London attending the first session of the Reformation Parliament which during its long life would pass a series of statutes declaring Henry Supreme Head of the Church in England, compelling allegiance to the children of Henry and Anne Boleyn and creating new heresy offences. One of the MPs, Thomas Vachell, would play a powerful role in the town's fortunes in the coming decade. Proximity to London and the presence of several Reading men in the royal household ensured that the leading burgesses were aware of the king's 'great matter' and the significance of this parliament.

Meanwhile townsfolk had other concerns. Difficulties in the cloth industry, the mainstay of the economy, continued as trade with the Low Countries was disrupted by war. The cycle of depressions was nothing new though the effects of this one were exacerbated by the high price of bread caused by a run of bad harvests from 1527 to 1529. There were still positive sides to town life: parishioners celebrated parish feast days as before and villagers frequented the weekly market. The bells of St Laurence rang to welcome the king on three occasions between 1531 and 1535 when some of the royal entourage would have been guests of the abbot, Hugh Cook, who was in good standing with the Crown, exchanging New Year's gifts with the king and entrusted by Lord Lisle, an illegitimate son of Edward IV, with the education of his stepson, James Bassett.[1] However, Abbot Hugh was also aware of the power and intentions of Thomas Cromwell, the king's vice-gerent in ecclesiastical matters and sought to keep on good terms by making him steward of the abbey in 1536 with a fee of £23 6s. 8d. a year.

Photograph of Greyfriars Church c.1860–69, once the church of Greyfriars Friary. (RL)

The dissolution of the friary and the abbey

The first intimation of things to come was a visit from royal commissioners in 1535 travelling the country valuing all ecclesiastical properties. The result was the *Valor Ecclesiasticus*. The friary's income is not recorded but the abbey's was £1,938 14*s*. ¾*d*., making Reading one of the richest monasteries in England.[2] The following year an Act dissolving all religious houses with an annual income of less than £200, judging them *ipso facto* guilty of 'manifest sin, vicious and carnal living' spelled the end of Greyfriars. In August 1538 Dr John London, one of the most ruthless of the commissioners, effected his task with typical efficiency, finding time to destroy several shrines in Caversham, including one to the Virgin, removing their relics and sending their valuable plate to his superiors. Within a month of his arrival he had dissolved the friary, sent away the mostly aged friars in secular dress with small amounts of cash and set a guard to prevent pillaging. Dr London complained that Reading had many poor people and 'all things that might be had they stole away'; but for the support of Thomas Vachell and the Mayor 'they wolde have made no litell spoyle'. The burgesses too had an eye to the main chance, complaining to Cromwell that 'ther town-hall ys a very small house and stondith upon the river wher ys the comyn washing place of the most part of the town'. The noise of the battledores beating the clothes, they claimed, was such that they could not hear themselves speak at gild meetings, and asked for Greyfriars church as their gild hall. They were given it, at a rent confirmed in 1542 as a half-penny a year. Their existing hall, soon known as the Old Yeld (Gild) Hall, was divided into separate premises for workshops, stables and such. The rest of the friary site was granted as a residence to Robert Stanshawe, a groom of the king's chamber who died there in 1549.[3] This was the first of a series of grants by which friary and abbey property was leased not for the upkeep of the borough but to profit royal servants and others who wasted no time in profiting from the bonanza of confiscated church possessions.[4]

A print showing Abbot Hugh at prayer with other images including an early version
of the Corporation seal. (Coates)

Cromwell could not use the excuse of reforming the great abbeys to seize their wealth, so tempting to a cash-strapped monarchy; the 1536 Act had praised their religious zeal. Cromwell's own commissioners had reported that at Reading 'they have a good lecture in Scripture read daily in the Chapter House and the abbot is at it himself'. Instead, pressure was put on abbots with promises of good pensions and property in return for a quick surrender; Abingdon succumbed but Reading, like Glastonbury and Colchester, resisted and all three paid the price for opposing Henry's wishes. Abbot Hugh was accused of denying the Royal Supremacy, a treasonable offence. After imprisonment in the Tower, he was returned to Reading for 'trial', a note in Cromwell's hand ensuring the outcome was not in doubt: 'the Abbot of Reading to be sent down to be tried and executed at Reading with his accomplices. ... See that the evidence be well sorted and the indictments well drawn.' His 'accomplices' were John Rugge, a monk and John Eynon, former vicar of St Giles. The penalty for treason, hanging, drawing and quartering, was carried out on 14 November 1539 before the abbey. The site of the abbey and all its possessions including all its properties in Reading and the advowsons of its parishes were forfeit to the Crown as the property of a convicted traitor, though the abbey, not the abbot, was the owner. Choice items of furnishings, vestments and plate were entrusted to Thomas Vachell to be sent to the king. He and Sir William Penizon took control of abbey lands, Vachell as overseer of its Reading property and bailiff of the town, and Penizon in the more lucrative post of chief steward of Reading and overseer of all its Berkshire lands.[5]

The Borough Charter of 1542

For a group of powerful burgesses the dissolution of the abbey provided an opportunity to gain more than a new town hall, namely long desired corporate borough status. Putting aside conflicting religious beliefs, a small group of Catholic and Reformist burgesses worked together to obtain a charter in 1542, giving them the local self-government they had failed to wrest from the abbey. Reading was thus one of the earliest monastic boroughs to become incorporated though the Crown retained the lordship. The charter made the burgesses of the Merchant Gild a 'corporate community' or corporation with 'perpetual succession'. Effectively they were an oligarchy empowered to choose new members and elect the mayor (also a justice of the peace), from the ranks of the aldermen. This was a new title given to seven of the 'more discreet and sufficient' burgesses, among whom were those who had led the successful drive to obtain the charter. The mayor chose two sergeants at mace to serve warrants enforcing the judgements of his weekly court of record, a small claims court. The corporation had the usual rights of a corporate body: a common seal, the right to acquire and own property in common and to sue in the courts. Some former customs barely changed, notably that burgesses still chose new entrants to the gild though half the entry fine now went to the Crown as did the yearly *chepyngavell* payable by every burgess. Oversight of markets and fairs was the borough's responsibility though the profits were the king's and leased to Penizon.[6] No new property was granted to the borough other than what the gild had owned, and no provision was made for the upkeep of bridges, so vital for the town's commerce, or the school. Incorporation had come at a price. Income to administer the borough was inadequate and in 1546 the corporation borrowed £6 from St Laurence churchwardens and two years later cut the mayor's expense allowance by a third. By the early 1550s the cofferers were recording large deficits in the accounts, worsened by expenses incurred by suitably entertaining young King Edward in 1552 and Philip and Mary in 1554, expenses which were met by contributions from the burgesses. An attempt to make the corporation more exclusive by limiting the number of burgesses to 30 was abandoned; instead an additional fee of 20 shillings was added to the usual entry fine.[7] An influx of new gild members helped to push the accounts into surplus by 1555.

Map based on an original by S. Peyton from Roger Amyce's survey, 1552, with additional research as published in Joan Dils (ed), *Redding 1540–1640*.

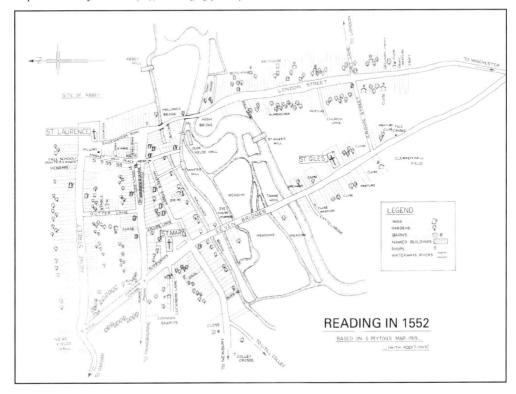

READING IN 1552

BASED ON S PEYTON'S MAP, 1919
(WITH ADDITIONS)

LEGEND

INNS	
GARDENS	
BARNS	B
NAMED BUILDINGS	
SHOPS	S
WATERWAYS, RIVERS	

The sale of abbey lands and the demolition of its buildings

Others had a mind to profit from the dissolution of the abbey. To survey and manage the vast amounts of property which had fallen to the Crown, a new ministry, the Court of Augmentations, was set up and though the wisest course was for the Crown to retain the land, living on the income, only sales would produce enough ready money to finance the king's wars. Purchasers were eager and waiting. Among the gentlemen, merchants and royal officials wishing to add to their estates or acquire enough to become landed gentry was William Gray or Grey, who had made his somewhat unsavoury reputation in Thomas Cromwell's service. In 1545 when land sales were at their peak he paid the huge sum of £2,133 3s. 0d. for 179 messuages (houses and their outbuildings), the George and the Crown inns, St Giles' and Minster mills and various gardens, stables and barns in the borough, effectively half of it. The Court of Augmentation survey of former abbey possessions in the town in 1552 revealed just how wealthy Gray had become. Other royal servants and local gentry acquired borough property though in total less than a tenth of what Gray owned.[8]

For most of this time the abbey site, the church and the conventual buildings remained essentially unchanged. Unlike some other monastic boroughs, such as Tewkesbury, Reading had no need of another church and no one willing to buy one, though some saw the value of its building materials. In 1547 when Edward VI, Henry's nine-year-old son became king, his uncle, Edward Seymour, future Duke of Somerset, seized power as Protector. A man greedy for power and the wealth it could bring, he acquired the site of Glastonbury and then in 1548 persuaded his nephew to grant him not only the site of Reading Abbey but also the lordship of the borough and manor, Whitley Park, and the profits of two fairs. Informed by Roger Amyce of the amount of valuable lead on the roofs, about 450 tons, he ordered its removal and the demolition of the buildings.[9] The work was entrusted to George Hynde, a minor royal official and a lead worker by trade, who kept detailed accounts of the process, no doubt in case he was accused of peculation. Between 10 February and 29 May 1549 local craftsmen and labourers worked on the site, enjoying an income at a time when many who had been employed by the abbey had lost their jobs. At least 11 carpenters paid 9d. a day assisted by labourers at 6d. a day dismantled the roofs; 16 other labourers pulled down the lead and carried it to plumbers to melt down for ease of transport. Among other workers were sawyers, a tiler, three gatekeepers and 16 men who watched at night to prevent 'stealing and imbeseling'. Someone had learned the lesson of Greyfriars. The total cost of dismantling buildings, refining and transporting the lead amounted to £193 9s. 10¾d.[10]

There were ready purchasers for the dressed stone, thousands of floor and roof tiles and wooden furnishings. A London ironmonger bought all the stained glass, the images at the high altar and a huge load of iron; a Reading carpenter acquired a hundred laths. Even the monks' 'commen Jakeses' and 'jakes stools' from the toilet block at the southern end of the dorter (dormitory) were sold. St Mary's churchwardens bought the monks' choir stalls and other building materials which they used in a major rebuilding of the church. Total receipts were £206 3s. 8d., so the Crown made little profit. The ones who did were Somerset and Sir Richard Sackville, Chancellor of the Court of Augmentations, the former acquiring most of the lead and the latter the rest plus 18 tons of stone and 7,000 house tiles for which neither paid a penny.

One of the floor tiles recovered from the abbey church by modern excavations. (RM)

After Somerset's execution, the abbey site reverted to the Crown. There were still a few buildings on the site including three houses, stables and the abbey guest house, the Hospitium. Some were used by royal visitors, Edward VI in 1552 and Philip and Mary in 1554. Mary, like her father, appointed a royal servant as Keeper in the person of Sir Francis Englefield, who was also high steward of Reading, posts which he held until 1559. More stone was removed from the abbey for new buildings at Windsor Castle during this period.[11]

The Reformation in the parishes

Even before the abbey was looted, the churchwardens of all three parishes had begun to dispose of some of their church plate, anticipating, as did many others, that otherwise it would shortly be seized to swell the royal coffers. In the years 1537–38, 1544–45 and 1547–48 St Laurence's churchwardens sold candlesticks, chalices and other sacred vessels of gilt and silver for more than £113, giving some of the proceeds to the town to improve the roads. Better the community should profit than strangers. Soon after, St Giles raised £26 in the same way. The first years of St Mary's accounts are undated, but it seems likely that there too the sale of £85 12s. worth of plate before 1553 was early enough to thwart the royal commissioners.

Some of the proceeds were needed to pay for the building work, church furnishings and goods required by the new forms of worship, imposed piecemeal by Henry but more thoroughly by his successors. Henry dallied with aspects of the teachings of Luther and other reformers, imposing changes through injunctions issued by right of his supreme headship of the Church of England. Parishes varied in the speed and enthusiasm with which they responded. Reading was no exception, St Giles being the most conservative and St Laurence the most radical. Even so, with the Crown as lord of the borough and until 1546 patron of all three livings, compliance was wise. In 1538 St Laurence obeyed the injunction to purchase a Bible within months; there is no evidence that St Giles obeyed until 1546. St Laurence was also the first to buy copies of the earliest service in English, Thomas Cranmer's *Litany*, soon after its publication in 1544, and sometime in 1547–48 had a copy of a whole English service sung at Windsor that year as well as nine psalm books for the choir. It was another two years before St Giles' churchwardens bought anything. The slow response of St Giles may have been reinforced by Sir Francis Englefield's acquisition both the rectory and advowson of this parish and of St Mary in 1546 for the huge sum of £1,676 2s. 10½d. Englefield held to the old faith.[12]

Soon more radical changes to church services and the appearance of the churches themselves were ordered. On Edward VI's accession in 1547, evangelical reformers including the Duke of Somerset and the future Duke of Northumberland dominated the royal council and Archbishop Cranmer introduced a complete and radical Protestant theology expressed in an English liturgy.[13] Again St Laurence was the more compliant or enthusiastic, providing the full range of service books, the first and second *Books of Common Prayer*, a *Book of Homilies* (sermons) and Erasmus' *Paraphrases* (of the New Testament). The Prayer Book contained the text of the Communion Service, the celebration of a sacred meal, rejecting the sacrificial aspects of the Catholic Mass. A sacrifice requires an altar; a meal needs only a table. Within two years stone and marble altars were torn down and replaced by wooden tables. The reformers also rejected devotion to the saints and prayers for the dead, hence Edward's Injunctions to remove all statues, cover wall paintings with whitewash and destroy stained glass windows which had representations of the saints. By July 1553 when Edward died St Giles' and St Laurence's churches had been thoroughly 'reformed'. Gone were the rood lofts with their lights and images, the Easter sepulchres, even the gild altars since the gilds which supported them were suppressed in 1549, their property confiscated and their priests deprived of both post and income. St Mary's churchwardens' accounts of the church restoration mention a pulpit but no rood screen, no gild altars, no sepulchre. Vestments, copes and altar frontals of satin, velvet and damask found new uses in the furnishings and wardrobes of wealthy townsfolk.

Some of them may not have been wholly unsympathetic to the changes. As early as 1540 fewer Reading will makers were making bequests to parish gilds or leaving money for Masses. In some cases this indicated changed religious allegiance but in others perhaps an unwillingness to invest in an institution with an uncertain future. A growing number chose (or the will writer chose for them) an ambiguous opening sentence such as, 'I bequeath my soul to almighty God', avoiding any clearer declaration of faith. Few at this date were willing to commit to such an unambiguous reformist will as did Stephen Cawet, a former church-warden of St Laurence in 1543.[14] There was no decline in the popularity of parish festivities in the early 1540s, yet they came to an abrupt end soon after 1547. May Day and Whitsuntide celebrations, and even Hocktide ended by 1548, the loss of a whole tradition of popular culture.

Then everything went into reverse. In July 1553 Mary Tudor, daughter of Henry VIII and Catherine of Aragon, became queen. She was determined to restore the Catholic faith and papal authority. The churchwardens' accounts betray something of their problems when in a single accounting year (between July and 29 September 1553 in the case of St Laurence) they sold the last of their images then restored those on the rood screen, replaced communion tables with altars, bought Mass books and rapidly returned to the old forms of worship. The conservative parish of St Giles led the way though St Laurence could not but follow given the influence of Sir Francis Englefield.[15] Easter 1554 was celebrated in full Catholic ceremonial and within a year Hocktide, church ales and Whitsun feasts were again part of parish life. The speed of this restoration suggests many retained an ingrained loyalty to the old ways but things were not quite the same. People's faith had been shaken, or perhaps they no longer trusted their legacies would be honoured. Very few invoked the saints or the Virgin in their wills and almost no one left money for prayers. Parishes seem to have bought only the essentials needed for Catholic liturgy, though they may not have needed to. Edward's reign had been too short for everyone to have embraced the new ways and some parishioners may have taken away church goods in hope for better times to come. In 1556 a very wealthy, devout clothier, John Hethe, bequeathed a crimson velvet canopy (over the altar), a white damask altar cloth, white silk curtains and part of a satin cloth for the Easter Sepulchre to St Mary; some Latin service books quickly re-appeared at St Laurence and St Giles. In any event priorities had to be set since parish finances had been strained by the outlay incurred in conforming with previous changes, so providing essentials was perhaps the only choice at first. What further adornments may have been added had Mary reigned longer than a mere five and a half years must remain a mystery.

For convinced Reformers this was a dangerous period, but in Reading they seem to have conformed at least openly and only one man suffered for his beliefs: Julins Palmer, a former master of Reading School, burned as a heretic in Newbury in July 1555.[16] Too late for Palmer, the accession of Elizabeth I in November 1558 was soon followed by another about-turn in state religion. Beginning the following year, a series of parliamentary statutes and royal injunctions re-imposed Protestantism but of a more moderate kind. All the restored altars in Reading, so recently hallowed for the celebration of Mass, were again pulled down (within months at St Laurence), the Easter Sepulchres and the tops of the rood screens with their images sold by 1562. Communion tables were speedily set up, although the purchase of the required books, *Homilies*, Erasmus' *Paraphrases* and the new *Book of Common Prayer* (the Prayer Book) came piecemeal over the next few years. St Mary's churchwardens did not record the last purchase until 1564. Perhaps, chastened by their experience of obeying previous government orders, only to have them reversed by a new administration with all the associated financial implications, parishes were proceeding cautiously. Yet Elizabeth's was a lasting religious settlement and, as it was consolidated, those aspects of popular culture associated with traditional religion died out. Hocktide, Whitsun ales and other festivals ended in St Laurence in 1559, though in St Mary's Hocktide clung on until 1563 and the Whitsun feast until 1566. With the flight into exile of Sir Francis Englefield in 1559, powerful local support for the old religion ended.

Evidence suggests that within a few years only a very few remained faithful to Rome, although how far written records reveal people's true beliefs is open to doubt. Only one, William Boxwell in 1573, made a Catholic will, calling on the Virgin and all the holy company of heaven for prayers, although 40 parishioners of St Lawrence were said to have attended Mass in 1583.[17] Most townsfolk and councillors, to judge by their wills, were conforming but moderate Protestants by the 1570s, leaving money for funeral sermons, some reading the Bible at home and all generally accepting Elizabeth's compromise settlement. Especially in St Laurence parish, however, there was a growing number of more fervent, some would say more extreme 'godly' Protestants, nicknamed Puritans. They had the support of Robert Dudley, Earl of Leicester, high steward of the borough from at least 1566 until his death in 1588 and his successor, Sir Henry Neville. One or two councillors, notably Thomas Aldworth (four times mayor and twice a borough MP) and Edward Butler had puritan sympathies. The patronage of Leicester, Neville and the Knollys family ensured that a number of Reading MPs shared their beliefs.[18] They rejected any survivals they regarded as 'Romish' or 'papist'; George Baron, possibly a curate, administered communion on Easter Tuesday behind locked doors, a wise precaution since he did not wear the surplice as required by the Prayer Book. The four times mayor, Richard Watlington, another puritan, helped John Smith to become master of Reading School. Smith later became vicar of St Laurence. Another schoolmaster, Thomas Charlton (1591–1612), was also a Puritan. Godly influence spread. Some lay folk bought puritan books: John Richer of St Laurence had several Bibles, a *Geneva New Testament*, and Calvin's *Instructions* as well as the popular *Book of Martyrs* by John Foxe, most bequeathed to his wife. William Burton, St Giles' puritan vicar from 1591 to 1612, had a running battle with his conservative parish since he refused to wear a surplice, use the words of the Prayer Book or give communion to communicants kneeling.[19] By the 1590s Reading was religiously divided and though Puritans did not have the same influence in the corporation or the town as did they did in Newbury, it was nevertheless significant.

To add to religious uncertainties, the years between 1547 and 1558 (the reigns of Edward VI and Mary) experienced the worst series of harvests of the century, creating steep rises in food prices. Then in 1558 came a virulent form of influenza which struck Reading as badly as any other community. In that year burials in St Mary's parish totalled 46 and the next year 28, more than double the norm; payments to St Laurence's churchwardens for ringing knells and burials in church also rose significantly, and more than half of all the wills for the whole decade were proved in the church courts in the two years 1558–59. Superstitious townsfolk may have wondered if this was a judgement from God on what was being done in his name.

The boundaries of the borough as fixed by the 1560 charter which were unchanged until 1887.

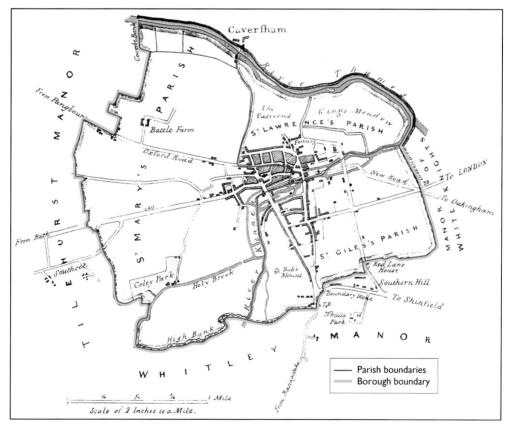

As we have seen, the reigns of Edward and Mary were not easy ones for the new corporation. Though the accounts were in surplus by 1555 there was little to spare and repairs mounted. The Crown was an absentee lord, with little concern for the town's infrastructure, especially the bridges and wharves on which its economy depended. So it was with relief that after 18 years of penury Reading secured a new charter from Elizabeth which with only minor amendments would remain the basis of its government until 1835. Among those named as burgesses in this 1560 charter were two of those elected aldermen in 1542, Robert Bowyer and Thomas Aldworth.[20]

It was in many respects a more generous grant than that of 1542, giving Reading wider boundaries and full independent borough status. As with all newly created corporate boroughs of the period, Reading's corporation was a self-perpetuating oligarchy. Nine capital burgesses, one of whom was mayor, were named in the charter; they would choose 12 or more secondary burgesses.[21] The capital burgesses would select one of the secondary burgesses to fill any gaps in their ranks, and replace him with 'one of the better sort' of the town. On 1 September each year the nine nominated three of their number, one of whom was elected mayor by the whole corporation.[22] The mayor and corporation could make and enforce bye laws, a major motive for seeking a new charter since it enabled the town to control its economy. In addition to his weekly court of record, the mayor could now hold a bi-annual court leet to deal with breaches of the bye-laws. Officials nominated in the charter included the steward, later called a recorder, and two cofferers or treasurers. The latter would in future be appointed annually by the new mayor from among the secondary burgesses. They held office for two years, first as junior, then as senior, ensuring continuity of experience. Appointed at the same time were two salaried constables whose responsibilities were to keep law and order and later to enforce the poor laws, and unpaid wardens for each of the five wards. Two salaried sergeants at mace elected by the capital burgesses served the mayor's writs and arrested offenders; one of them had charge of the Counter, the town gaol.

The financial clauses of the charter explain both the Crown's reasons for granting it and the borough's for seeking it. The profits of the town's weekly Saturday market, of which the mayor was the clerk, and of four fairs, each of three days centred on 1 May, 25 July, 21 September and 2 February, went into the borough coffers, called the Hall, as did fines imposed in borough courts and the chattels of convicted felons. More important was the right to acquire land worth up to £100 a year and the grant by the Crown of over 200 borough properties, most of those not purchased by William Gray. The houses and gardens, shops, inns and

Reading Borough's coat of arms 1566. It is thought the figure in the centre represents Elizabeth I. (RL)

other former abbey property ensured a substantial income for the future. However, the Crown took the opportunity to rid itself of all its financial liabilities in Reading. The borough was now responsible for all 19 bridges, 'ruinous' after years of royal neglect, with only a grant of 200 loads of stone from the ruined abbey for immediate repairs, the maintenance of the Free School, the appointment of the master and the payment of his annual salary of £10. After 1578 when they set up a house of correction in the former Greyfriars church, the corporation held its meetings in part of the school house, the refectory of the former guest house of the abbey, the school retaining the other half.[23]

The mayors in 1559 and 1560 were Edward Butler and Thomas Turner, also MP for the borough in 1559, who had become burgesses in 1550. Though Turner died in 1570, Butler survived until 1584. Both were typical of the long-serving governing elite of Reading, since the office of burgess was held for life. Seven of the nine capital burgesses of 1560 served for at least ten years, two until after 1580. Secondary burgesses, waiting to fill dead men's shoes, needed patience. Of the cohort of 1560, only two would be elevated by 1570, others never moving up the ranks. A similar pattern prevailed for the next two decades, but because five capital burgesses died between 1590 and 1600 a substantially changed corporation was in place at the end of the century.[24]

Some surnames, especially Aldworth and Turner, recur in the *Diary* throughout the decades following incorporation. These and a few other families dominated borough government. The Aldworths, brothers Thomas and Richard, were mayors in six years and members of the Turner family in 17 years between 1523 and 1630. Burgess families intermarried: Richard Johnson's daughter, Rebecca, married an Aldworth and his sister

Some personalities of Reformation Reading

Hugh Cook alias **Faringdon** was the last abbot of Reading, elected in 1520. He frequently attended the House of Lords, was a county JP and served on several government commissions. He seems to have been interested in the new learning, although he remained conservative in belief. He was favoured by Henry VIII, being appointed a royal chaplain and chosen to sing the Requiem Mass for Jane Seymour in 1537, although he believed the Pope had the power to allow marriage with a brother's widow, which Henry disputed. He took several steps in the hope of saving his abbey from dissolution including taking the Oath of Supremacy (acknowledging Henry as Head on earth of the Church in England) and giving a pension to Thomas Cromwell. To no avail. In 1539 he was imprisoned in the Tower on a charge of treason. On 14 November after a travesty of a 'trial' he and two others were hanged, drawn and quartered before the abbey gateway. He was beatified by Pope Leo XIII in 1895.

Thomas Vachell, a gentleman of Coley, Reading, was born before 1500. His Reading house was later called Lady Vachell's almshouses. His father was Thomas Vachell of Coley and his mother Agnes, daughter of William Justice of Reading. Either he or his father was one of the commissioners to administer the 1524–25 lay subsidy for the borough. He served as borough MP from 1529 to 1547 and again in the 1540s. In 1533 he was appointed by Thomas Cromwell as a 'local watchdog', becoming deputy high steward and then bailiff of the borough. He was active in forwarding the dissolution of both of Reading's religious houses, helping John London to dissolve Greyfriars in 1538 and taking part in the trial and execution of the abbot the following year. For these services he was appointed overseer of abbey lands and bailiff of Reading, and in 1543 acquired abbey lands in Southcote and Tilehurst near his Coley property. His political activities were driven more by ambition than conviction; he seems to have been conservative in religion. He died in 1552 and asked to be buried without any great pomp in St Mary's church. His eldest son, another Thomas, sat in Mary's parliaments.

John Bourne, a wealthy clothier of St Mary's parish, was one of first aldermen chosen in 1542 and one of leading men who obtained the first charter. He served as mayor in 1544–45, 1552–53 and from September 1558 to his death on 13 December 1558. His will, dated 24 November 1558, was that of a traditional Catholic with requests for Masses, substantial gifts to the church and the poor as well as over £390 to his children.

Sir Francis Englefield (1522–96), the eldest son of Sir Thomas Englefield and Elizabeth Throckmorton, inherited the family estates in Berkshire and elsewhere in 1543, was knighted in 1547 and joined the household of Princess Mary two years later. He remained her loyal supporter and a fervent Catholic. He derived a large income from his posts including master of the Court of Wards and constable of Windsor Castle. In Reading he purchased the rectories of St Mary and St Giles and served as Berkshire MP from 1555 to 1557. On Elizabeth's accession in 1558 he had to resign all his appointments and left the country. He never accepted Elizabeth's religious settlement, and eventually lost all his property except what he conveyed to his nephew. He died blind and in comparative poverty in Valladolid.

William Gray or **Grey**'s name is not as well known as that of Blagrave. Gray, an evangelical, made his dubious reputation in the service of Thomas Cromwell and the Duke of Somerset, among other ways as the writer of anti-papal ballads. In 1545 he purchased almost half of the former abbey properties in the borough and the manor of Bulmershe. He served as Reading's MP from 1547 to 1552. His marriage to widow, Anne Blagrave, was childless, so it was her son, John, by her first husband who inherited Gray's property including that in the borough. A bust of his step-grandson, John Blagrave, mathematician, is in St Laurence's church.

Edward Butler was born about 1512 and lived through some of the most dramatic changes in the town's history. A successful mercer, he also owned a dyehouse and had bought or purchased leases of land in Berkshire, Oxfordshire and Surrey. He was a member of the corporation for many years and elected mayor four times. His will is that of a Protestant who has taken to heart the doctrine of justification by faith alone; he bequeathed £20 to the poor of Reading 'not because yt shall profit me anything at all towards the work of my salvation but because yt will relieve them'. He left his wife of 42 years, Alice, and three married daughters, Alice, Mary and Elizabeth. He and they were commemorated on a brass on a grey marble tomb in St Laurence church which once stood in the chancel. All that remains of it is a small section of the brass showing Edward and one of his daughters. Since a recent refurbishment and reorganisation of the church interior it has apparently been mislaid.

Sources: DNB; TNA, Wills of John Bourne, 1558, Edward Butler, 1584 and Thomas Vachell 1552 PROB 11/42/19, 67/17 and 36/25; Aspinall, 36–7; S.T. Bindoff (ed.), *History of Parliament: The Commons, 1509–1558* (1982), i, 510–11.

was the wife of Bernard Harrison; John Hethe's wife, Elizabeth, was the daughter of John Bourne, three times mayor; Thomas Turner's daughter married William Edmunds. Not only were certain families but certain trades were powerful. Two of the first nine capital burgesses of 1560 were clothiers, three were mercers and two were tanners. In 1570 the upper ranks of the corporation still included three mercers, three clothiers, a draper and two tanners. A decade later clothiers became even more dominant, occupying five places to the mercers three. In fact the change mattered little since all were men of substance with similar entrepreneurial flair though it reflects the prosperity of the cloth industry in the closing decades of the century. Wealth, and the status it conferred, was a necessary qualification for holding office which was demanding of time, money and the ability to govern.[25]

It is not possible to judge how well the corporation managed the borough's finances in the early years since no accounts of the Merchant Gild survive after 1516 and those of the borough are lost before 1584. Thereafter, surviving records for eight of the years to 1600 show that rents from the properties granted in 1560 were the financial mainstay, providing an average of 80% of the revenue, the rest coming from the farm of the tolls of the market and fairs, and the lease of the Wool Hall and beam. Over the period, income dropped from a peak of £118 19s. 2d. in 1585–86 to £83 18s. 4d. in 1599–1600. However, the accounts balanced in five of the eight years with a modest surplus. Fees and salaries absorbed about £30 a year, just over a third of expenditure. Small amounts went to provide luxury items such as sugar and wine for visiting magistrates and judges at assizes and quarter sessions, and to the high steward when he came to town. Both the winter and summer assizes were generally held in Reading until about 1689 with occasional sittings at Abingdon. Expenses in 1588–89 included 7s. 2d. for 'wine and cakes about the bonfire', a celebration, no doubt, of the defeat of the Armada and a custom which would be repeated in later centuries as beer and bonfire became the accepted way to mark an occasion of national rejoicing. Bridges required constant repair and major reconstruction, such as the 'new makinge' of the High Bridge in 1592/3 that pushed the town into serious deficit. Such expenditure would loom large in later accounts.[26]

As for the townsfolk, some enjoyed a modest prosperity during Elizabeth's reign, despite increasing rents and higher food prices, especially in the 1590s. In the absence of major epidemics after an outbreak of plague in 1564 the population began to rise. Then in the 1590s came a repeat of the 1550s: cold, wet summers resulting in poor harvests, rising food prices and higher death rates, experiences shared with the rest of the country and immortalised in *A Midsummer Night's Dream* where foul weather and crop failure were attributed to a quarrel in Fairyland.[27]

Population and the appearance of the borough

Though by far the largest in the county, Reading was a small town. In 1547 a survey was made by royal commissioners of property belonging to parish gilds in preparation for seizing it, recorded as chantry certificates. They include an estimate of the number of 'houseling folk', those over 16 and eligible to receive communion: 1,000 in the parish of St Laurence and 500 in each of the other two, giving an estimate of about 3,000 for the total population. They lived in an area surveyed by Roger Amyce in 1552 for the Court of Augmentations of the whole borough and manor. His detailed description street by street and property by property, giving owners, identifying mills, inns, shops and even wells is almost as good as a map of the town.[28]

The first contemporary map was not made until 1611 when John Speed published his *Theatre of the Empire of Great Britain*. In contrast to Amyce whose object was to identify and record individual properties, Speed's aim was to portray the kingdom in a series of county maps, each with an inset of the county town, as a gift for king James I. Reading's pre-eminence in Berkshire ensured that it alone of the county's towns was included in his atlas. It was, he said, 'one of the most ancient and cheifest in the county'. He could not find space for it on the county map since it was essential to include there a magnificent perspective of royal Windsor Castle so he included it on the Buckinghamshire page.[29]

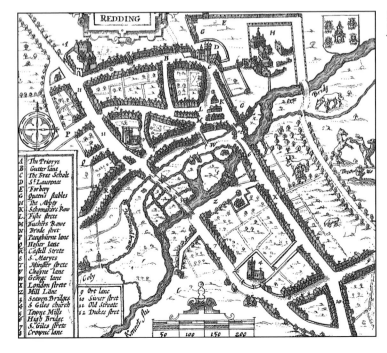

Map of Reading by John Speed, 1611.

Together the work of Amyce and Speed provide a vivid portrait of the borough in the Tudor period and beyond though they were too early to include a prestigious development of 1620, a covered walk called the Piazza, a gift from John Blagrave, the celebrated mathematician, adjoining the south wall of St Laurence's church. Reading was typical of towns at this time, islands in the countryside which permeated them. Speed used conventional symbols to denote these rural areas reaching right up to the first buildings. Amyce had identified them as pasture and meadow. Much of St Giles' parish to the south was farmland, including the area east of London Street called the Orts, and St Mary's parish to the west included countryside. With St Laurence in the north, the three parish churches stand in the outer areas of the town.

A striking feature of the map is the distinctive elongated triangular shape of Reading's streets, still traceable today. The population was concentrated north of the Kennet's streams, with ribbon development along roads running south and west through the fields. The county gaol was situated in Castle Street, the main west road towards Newbury, Bath and Bristol. There were no town walls, although two crosses marked the western boundary: Coley Cross in Castle Street, Cornish Cross in Broad Street. On the east side of the town was the Market Place, with a communal well, the pillory and the stocks. This triangular space had long since been filled with houses and shops with Flax or

Print *c*.1850 showing the south facade of St Laurence with the Blagrave Piazza and the cobbled Market Square (artist unknown). (RL)

Flexen Lane at the southern end. It was paved, probably with flint cobbles, at the borough's expense. The east side, called Shoemaker Row, was mainly occupied by these craftsmen but otherwise there was little industry here or in the nearby streets, home to wealthy merchants and traders. The opposite side was still called Tothill.

Immediately to the south in what he called High Street (modern King Street), Amyce located buildings he called '*una domus de novo edificata vocata the newe shambles*' (a newly built house called the New Shambles), ten individual shops or workshops with storerooms above. In 1585–86 these storerooms would be converted into the Woolhall. Leases in the next century explain that it was approached by stairs at the west end of the block.[30] Its westward extension Speed called Broad Street, long since divided into lanes called Cheese Row/ Fisher Street and Butcher Row by a block of shops with the Round House

An engraving of the memorial in St Laurence church to John Blagrave, mathematician holding a globe and sextant with figures denoting geometric shapes. (Man)

at one end and the Corner House at the other. The Weighing House for yarn in Cheese/Fish Row was described as newly built in 1534.[31] Further west on the north side was the Shambles, the official slaughter house at the corner of Gutter Lane, and west again on the south was the opening into Grope, later Chain Lane.

The Common (communal) Wharf stood on the bank of the Kennet just east of High Bridge on the other side of which on an island was the former gild hall, the Old Yield Hall. After the borough gained a new town hall in the 1530s, the old one was divided into individual units, leased as workshops and stables. Beyond the Kennet to the south were meadows and pasture, the northern outskirts of St Giles' parish which was traversed by a road south (London Street) and then east (Ort Lane) to London, and another (Wood Street) to Southampton. At the apex of the triangle of streets, beyond the borough boundary but within St Giles' parish, was the rural hamlet of Whitley, whose inhabitants were mainly farmers.

To the north of the Market Place was a gateway next to St Laurence's church giving access to the Forbury, formerly the outer precinct of the abbey. Over it was the small town gaol, the Compter, used to detain petty

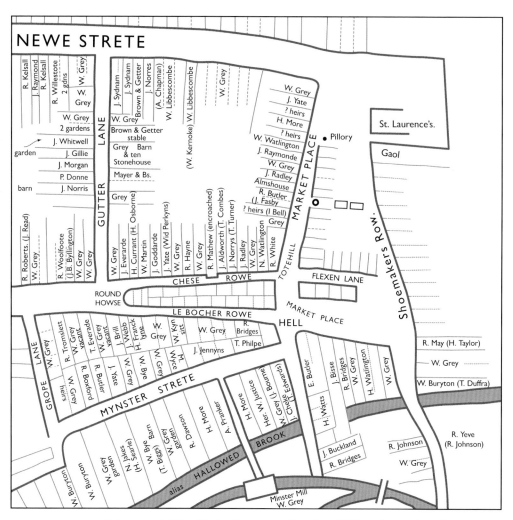

Enlargement of the Market Square area based on S. Peyton's map from Roger Amyce's survey 1552. The common well of the town is shown as a circle in the Square. The correct name for what Peyton calls the Gaol was the Compter, the borough prison.

offenders awaiting trial in the borough court. Beyond the church was the former refectory of the abbey guest house, part occupied in Speed's day by the free school and part used as the town hall. Some bridges appear on the map, as do two of the mills, one called Town Mills, more often St Giles' Mill; Amyce identified the other as Minster Mill and called the bridge north of High Bridge the Hallowed Bridge, spanning the stream of the same name. Neither mentioned Abbey Mills on the Hallowed or Holy Brook to the east, though both show the gardens or 'backsides' as they were known attached to the majority of the tenements, a term embracing properties which were both homes and workshops, and sometimes retail shops. These were tightly packed, mostly gable-end to the street on a narrow frontage of 20 or so feet but had long gardens. Wealthy townsmen occupied houses fronting the street, some with an entry at the side. The universal building material was wood and plaster but anyone inserting a chimney, an increasingly popular practice, had to use brick or stone. As a further guard against fire, buildings had to be roofed with tiles, as did any 'hovels' or sheds erected in the backsides. In these green areas townsfolk stored their trade goods, stabled their horses, grew vegetables and fruit, and kept pigs and poultry, the resulting smells being one of the less attractive features of town life.[32] Scattered through the town according to Amyce were twelve inns and taverns though a survey twenty years five later recorded only seven and three respectively.[33] Some, like the Bear where important visitors stayed and the Cardinal's Hat in Minster Street were large and well appointed; others such as the Holly Bush opposite St Laurence were more modest establishments.

What neither map nor survey can portray is the state of the streets and the watercourses. Though the council paid a paviour and a scavenger to maintain the Market Place and 'market streets', court leet records show a profound disregard, even by burgesses, of the many bye laws issued in a futile attempt to keep other streets clean and unobstructed.

This substantial seventeenth-century house in Castle St would have belonged to a wealthy merchant or clothier. It is now a solicitor's office. The wide entry once opened onto a long garden, now a yard.

Saint Mary Butts west side

An imaginative drawing of St Mary's Butts based on surviving buildings on the
south-west corner. (Vanda Morton in *Redding, 1540–1640*, 1980)

In addition to paving the frontage, hanging a lantern outside on autumn
and winter nights and keeping clear the gutter running down the middle
of the road, householders were required to remove heaps of animal and
household refuse from the front of their properties to the town dung heap
in the Forbury within 24 hours. All these orders were routinely flouted.
Wardens of the five wards reported foul muddy rainwater flooding the
streets when gutters were blocked with bits of carcases thrown out by
butchers or dirt from housewives' sweeping, pigs hunting through the
debris, traffic held up by parked carts, heaps of firewood or timber, illegal
extensions (encroachments) to house fronts and even an occasional sawpit.
Broad Street posed a particular challenge to passers-by on market days
when sheep pens were erected on the south side. The Holy Brook, a major
source of Reading's domestic water, was almost permanently polluted by
effluent from domestic privies, pigsties, stables and dye-houses, and
sometimes by housewives and cloth workers using it for washing. In
1575 Reading became subject to the Commission of Sewers, obliging the
council to enforce the upkeep of the Holy Brook and the purity of its
water by lessees of the mills and property owners on its banks, for which
they used the mechanism of the court leet, with little success if repeat
offences are a guide.[34]

5

Borough society and economy, *c*.1540–1640

D ESPITE epidemics and trade depressions, this was a time of
population growth and of prosperity for many Reading people. The
cloth industry remained the main source of the town's wealth, although
it faced severe pressure in the 1620s and 1630s.

Population

The town's population, about 3,000 in 1540, doubled over the century,
the same increase as in the English population as a whole. In Reading's
case, natural increase accounts for about 2,000 extra people; the rest
came from immigration. Growth was not even, being halted by periodic
epidemics: the sweating sickness in the 1540s, influenza in 1557–59 and
thereafter most commonly bubonic plague, but overall all three parishes
saw increasing numbers, especially after 1580.[1]

Migrants formed a significant group in all towns at this date, most
moving within a few miles, others venturing further afield. About half
of those in Reading came from within ten miles of the town. They have
been categorised as 'betterment' and 'subsistence' migrants, the former
in search of work and prosperity, most often as apprentices; the latter at
best seeking whatever temporary job they could find, at worst hoping for
alms or poor relief. Some undoubtedly were looking for easy pickings
through theft or deception. Whatever their intentions, poor migrants
were not welcome. Betterment migrants usually found employment and
some prospered.[2]

They joined a highly structured society where status was determined
by rank and wealth but where men could rise through education, success in
business or marriage, or fall through misfortune or profligacy. Status was
recognised by modes of address: wealthy burgesses and other prominent
townsmen were called Master, their wives Mistress, titles normally
reserved for the gentry with whom such families were often connected.
The 'middling sort', respectable craftsmen and their wives, were known
as Goodman and Goodwife, everyone else by their Christian names
only. Even where worshippers sat in church was socially determined. In

This seventeenth-century woodcut shows a typical family of the 'middling sort'. The husband smokes a long-stemmed pipe; the wife cares for the children.

the chancel of St Laurence's church sat the mayor and the schoolmaster. On the front row of the nave, where seat rents cost a shilling, sat the burgesses. Behind, where rents fell from 8*d*. to 2*d*., were the male parishioners. Wives of more affluent men occupied the south aisle, others sat at the back of the nave where seats cost a penny, a fee beyond the reach of poorer folk who presumably stood.[3]

The social mix of some of St Giles' parishioners in 1634–35 is suggested by a list of those paying poor rate, the amount paid dependent on wealth. The richest of the 126 ratepayers were ten individuals who paid from 4*d*. to a shilling a week. About two in three of the others paid from one to three pennies, another one in three just a halfpenny. The rest of the parishioners were either too poor to contribute or themselves received parish relief.[4]

Craft gilds

About the time when the Elizabethan charter was granted, five 'books' containing the rules of Reading's craft companies or gilds with lists of their members were compiled on the orders of the mayor and corporation.[5] Trade gilds had certainly existed in medieval Reading but little is known about their organisation. Perhaps, confident in their corporate status, the town's rulers wished to give authority to customary agreements.

Significantly the first 'book' related to the Company of Clothiers and Clothworkers, whose members made up at least a quarter of the male workforce, to say nothing of the many women spinners and carders. When John Leland visited the town in the 1540s, what drew his attention was the many-streamed Kennet whose 'very commodious' waters washed the clothiers' wool, filled the dyers' vats and drove the fulling mills. 'The toune,' he said, 'chiefly stondith by clothyng.' The list of members of the company is headed by 28 clothiers (plus a mercer and a draper), followed by 3 dyers, 30 weavers, 29 shearmen, a shuttlemaker and an ashburner.[6] Entry to the gild and the freedom to practise a craft was by a fine or fee payable to the 'use of the hall', that is for the benefit of the borough; for clothiers, dyers and weavers it was at least 40 shillings. In an attempt either to facilitate inspection or to prevent over-production, the gild rules, enforced by two wardens, limited each clothier to two broad looms, although all could put out weaving to freemen weavers of the town who had served an apprenticeship. As was common in all contemporary trades, work was to be kept within the gild and within the town boundary to the exclusion of all non-Reading craftsmen. In addition there were strict demarcation lines within the gild: only clothiers and dyers could dye cloth or wool, a rule further refined in a Privy Council judgement of 1589 allowing clothiers to dye wool but limiting the dyeing of cloth to dyers; finishing processes (dressing) such as shearing and burling were not to be entrusted to fullers.[7]

Though narrow cloths, kersies, were manufactured, the traditional product of Reading was broadcloth, defined by statute in 1552/3 as 28 to 30 yards long, seven quarters (1¾ yards) wide and weighing 90 lbs when dry. Making such cloths was very labour intensive; it took craftsmen with a variety of skills about seven and a half working days to produce one un-dyed cloth. Many undyed and undressed cloths were exported but increasingly Reading manufactured dyed, finished cloth

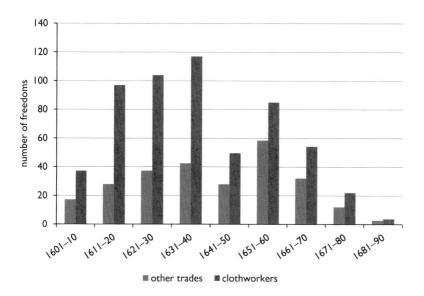

Reading trades, 1601–1700.

which commanded a higher return. Both products were very expensive.[8] By the early seventeenth century some clothiers were making a new high-quality product, Spanish cloth, lighter than broadcloth and dyed in a variety of colours – sky-colour, beggar's grey, 'fezant' and many others. In the early sixteenth century most clothiers were entrepreneurs who used a 'putting-out' system providing independent craftsmen with yarn, and marketing the final product, but in later years most took the whole operation in house, owning fulling mills and even dye-houses.[9]

Clothiers and dyers were wealthy men; the enterprise required a great deal of working capital invested in both equipment and materials with a long pay-back interval. When Walter Bye died in 1579 he left a twelve-room dwelling house, comfortably furnished, two well-equipped workshops for finishing cloth and two for dyeing. In stock were at least 82 partly finished broad cloths and yarn for over 150 kersies, most already dyed in a range of colours – azure, sky-colour, red, tawny, green and russet among them – with large amounts of expensive dyestuffs ready for use. His property was worth £2,125 18s. 2d., of which the vast majority was tied up in working capital. He had £65 in cash, and owed £240. Some independent cloth workers or cloth finishers still operated. William Laud, father of the future Archbishop of Canterbury, was one. In his garden he had racks to stretch fulled cloth back to its original size, teasels and shears in the workroom for the finishing processes, and accommodation in his house for his employees.[10] The gild rule that a master could employ only as many unmarried journeymen as he could accommodate in his house applied only to weavers, but many others, Laud included, seems to have conformed.

The first six clothiers listed were described as burgesses, members of the corporation, and so were nine members of the Mercers' and Drapers' Company.[11] Together they dominated the borough's politics as they did its economy; the mercers' and drapers' gild entry fee of £4 reflected the wealth they could hope to accumulate. When Richard Johnson, mercer, died early in 1628, his estate was valued at almost £700. The gild also included other retailers, wealthy haberdashers as well as lowlier chapmen (travelling salesmen), 36 tailors and two apothecaries. All were retailers more or less, each limited to his own sphere: no mercer or tailor could sell woollen cloth or women's hose, and only haberdashers could retail woollen hats and caps. Mercers seem to have sold a wide range of goods. In John Beele's shop in 1638 were reams of paper, quills, silk and thread buttons, points, garters, thread, varieties of ribbons and lace, fabrics such as lawn, fine linen, silk and fustian, waistcoats and much more, valued at over £190. By 1633 seven apothecaries and eight grocers were licensed to sell tobacco. Obviously smoking was becoming popular.[12]

Some of Beele's stock came from the pinners, members of the Cutlers' and Bellfounders' Company. This gild encompassed a motley range of

Portrait of Archbishop William Laud (date unknown) dressed as a wealthy cleric. (Man)

crafts including substantial numbers of workers in brass, pewter, lead and iron, smiths being the most numerous. They, like the majority of craftsmen other than cloth workers and merchants, provided for the every-day needs of the townsfolk. There were also several carpenters, joiners and bricklayers, with a few turners (highly skilled woodworkers), painters and glaziers. William Knight, bellfounder, was a member; he cast the great bell of St Mary's in 1584 but probably turned his hand to making cooking pots between commissions. His son, Henry, certainly did. He was owed over £100 from parishes in several counties, which may explain why he needed a steadier income nearer home.[13] Inexplicably, five barbers belonged to this company. One of its rules was that non-resident tooth-drawers should use only barbers' shops for their painful operations.

Often neglected by historians yet essential to the urban economy was the production of leather and leather goods, based on the products of the livestock farming of the county especially the hides and pelts of beasts slaughtered by the town's butchers and the bark from its plentiful woodland. Leather producers, tanners and curriers, and leather workers, mainly shoemakers, saddlers, glovers, cobblers and others belonged to the Tanners' and Leather-sellers' Company. Tanners, with a large amount of capital tied up in raw materials processed over many months, had the potential to become wealthy; three of those listed in 1570 were burgesses.

William Laud, senior, father of William Laud, Archbishop of Canterbury

William Laud lived in St Laurence's parish. Traditionally his address has been given as the north side of Broad Street. This cannot be confirmed, but it would correspond to the other evidence; in 1584 he was living in the High Ward of the borough of which this street was part. In about 1570 he appears in the list of members of the Clothiers' and Clothworkers' Company as a shearman, a skilled cloth finisher. The only borough office he held was as warden of the High Ward in 1572. Unfortunately since the parish register of St Laurence does not survive for the period and William did not make a will, it is not possible to determine very much about his family apart from the name of his wife, Lucy, the administrator of his estate, and of his son, William. William junior, born in October 1573, was awarded a Thomas White scholarship to Oxford University in 1589 and graduated in 1594. Even young William's grandmother for whom St Laurence's bells tolled in 1578–79 is not named. William senior died a few days before the inventory of his household and trade goods was made on 25 April 1594. He was buried in a coffin in St Laurence church, both expensive options for the well-to-do; most corpses were clothed in a shroud and interred in the churchyard. He owned a 'service book', perhaps a copy of the *Book of Common Prayer* from which he could follow the church services, but not a Bible. His administrators gave two shillings to the poor at his funeral and afterwards spent five shillings on food and drink for his neighbours, perhaps reflecting what they believed were his wishes.

He may have been ill for a time since the physician's fee was ten shillings, a substantial amount, and there were no cloths either finished or being processed in his workshops. His illness may also account for his modest estate, valued at just £52 17s. 2d. He died in debt to several tradesmen, a butcher, a baker, a fishmonger, a brewer, a tallow chandler and a shoemaker as well as two clothworkers who may have been his employees. Such debts were not unusual since accounts were rarely settled immediately and employees were paid at the end of the year or of a contract. The huge amount of £28 he owed to a Richard Lawde pushed his estate into deficit.

His inventory shows the comfortable home and large workplace of a master craftsman of the period. There were two living rooms, a hall and an old hall, both with fireplaces, good quality joined tables, stools and a two or three chairs. Cushions, a carpet for a table and wall hangings called stained cloths gave a modicum of comfort, though not all windows were glazed; the others would have had wooden shutters. His parlour, also heated and hung with stained cloths, was part-living, part-bedroom and may have been where he slept. It was furnished with tables, a settle and three chests containing a substantial quantity of table and bed linen as well as his 'wearing clothes' which included two hats, three cloaks, three doublets, a couple of leather jerkins and two old shirts, not a lavish wardrobe. He had a larger collection of weapons than he was required by law to possess – swords, a dagger, a stout bill, a fire-arm called a caliver and head armour, perhaps explained by fears of Spanish aggression. The equipment in the buttery (kitchen) was more than adequate for feeding a large household: spits, kettles (cauldrons), skillets and brass pots for cooking, with a quantity of pewter dishes for the table.

Over the hall and the buttery were the two family bedrooms called chambers, each with two bedsteads, comfortable feather mattresses and pillows. Pewter chamber pots were an additional luxury. The chamber over the hall with a settle in front of the fire, wall hangings, a table and chairs was particularly well furnished in contrast to the third 'chamber wheare the men[employees] lye' sparsely equipped with three old bedsteads, flock beds and bed linen.

In his workshops were many sets of tools for cloth finishing: teasels, shears and burling irons (for removing knots). In one garden were racks to stretch cloth back into shape after fulling, along with peas and beans and in another, more racks and a few poultry.

Sources: Admon. Bond, inventory and accounts of William Lawde, 1594, D/A1/201/188; St Laurence's churchwardens' accounts, D/P97/5/2; Reading Court Leet, September 1584, R/JL1/1/10; *Dictionary of National Biography*.

John Sharpe, chosen burgess later, had almost £270 of leather, bark and calf skins in tan vats in his backside, three employees, a well-furnished house, silver plate and ready money in his purse at his death in 1591. Glovers produced a variety of goods: in Francis Duke's shop were gloves, purses and satchels ready-made, and calf leather, white leather and sheep skins in various stages of processing in alum and lime, as well as a substantial amount of wool. Unlike glovers who used both white leather for elegant gloves and tougher, tanned leather for working gloves, shoemakers worked only in tanned leather. They produced a range of ready-made footwear: Richard Blackman made boots, children's shoes, high shoes, three-soled shoes and shoes in all sizes from 4 to 13, although exactly what that meant in terms of foot size is not known.[14]

The rules and members' list of the Victuallers' and Innholders' Company were already missing in 1816 when John Man wrote his history of the borough but he recorded the list of trades and their entry fines, details of which had survived. They included butchers and fishmongers, bakers and brewers, food processors such as maltsters and salters, and vintners who were essentially retailers, along with chandlers (candle-makers) who used the fat residue from carcasses to make candles.[15]

Regulation of trade

Each gild had its own rules, some of which applied to all, especially those restricting work to freemen of the borough. Demarcation lines were set: cobblers not shoemakers were to mend shoes; carpenters and joiners must keep to their own trades; no mercer could sell woollen cloth. A master craftsman's employees, journeymen, had to reside with him if they were unmarried. Sunday was a rest day; not even bear-baiting, a prerogative of the tanners, was allowed though one butcher's shop could open. In addition to gild rules, the corporation also made provision to protect the quality of some essential products by appointing 'searchers' of meat, fish and leather. Bye-laws regulated the quantity of beer sold in officially 'sealed' pots according to the price of malting barley, and the weight of loaves according to their quality and the price of wheat.[16]

Gild membership, the freedom to practise a craft, depended, not only on paying a fee but having served an apprenticeship in the borough or elsewhere, although it is clear that gild members were at liberty to change occupation or take on a second. As was common at this period, apprenticeship was regulated by the borough's council, not by individual gilds. Apprentices lived with their masters while training, a period of between seven and nine years and continued to do so as unmarried employees. So much is clear from a listing in September 1584 of men over the age of twelve from the High Ward required to attend the court leet. After a successful apprenticeship a young man became 'free' of the town, able to practise his trade. After several years of steady employment, a fortunate few were able to become master craftsmen, take on apprentices and employ journeymen. Properties occupied by master craftsmen were at once their homes and that of their workmen and servants, male and female, their workshops, and the shops where they sold their products direct to their customers which they were required to do. Their probate inventories describe some or all the rooms of their houses: the shop/workshop, the hall (main living room), kitchen and buttery or store room and chambers (bedrooms for the family), and men's or maids' or servants' (the usual term for an employee) chambers. In some cases it is clear that these were at the top of the house and were shared by two or more servants of the same gender.[17]

A shoemaker and his employees (journeymen) produced ready-made shoes in various styles and sizes. (J. Amman and H. Sachs, *The Book of Trades*, 1973)

Mention has been made of shoemakers mainly living in one street, Shoemaker Row. There seems no obvious reason for this example of 'occupational zoning' but with other trades such concentration arose from the demands made by production methods. Leather producers and brewers were congregated near the Kennet utilising its ample water supply; dyers and fullers were found in similar locations, although cloth finishers, needing no such provision, could be found almost anywhere. Butchers sold in and around the Market Place, although the slaughtering place was the Shambles in nearby Gutter Lane, and fishmongers traded in Fish Street with its easy access to the Wharf where barges, including those from London unloaded. Many retail shops and homes of mercers, drapers, chapmen, were situated in the High Ward, in and near the Market Place, undoubtedly a prime location, close to the Forbury where fairs attracted lucrative custom. Some barbers and apothecaries settled there too.

Reading in its hinterland

Despite its many crafts, Reading was above all a market town. Though its craftsmen traded daily with the townsfolk, its Saturday market attracted outsiders. Farmers from nearby villages would naturally bring their produce to sell, but producers and purchasers at the periphery of its market area had a choice and exercised it. The four fairs had the potential to draw in local gentry, and tradesmen and merchants from further afield. To attract them it was important to improve the infrastructure by repairing bridges, and paving and cleaning the Market Place, and also

A German
barber-surgeon's
shop *c*.1568. The
equipment in
this shop shows
that a barber-
surgeon not
only cut hair
and trimmed
beards but also
bled patients and
provided some
medical services.
(Amman and
Sachs, *The Book
of Trades*)

to guarantee fair trading conditions, regulating the quality of goods sold and ensuring good measure. The mechanism for this was contained in the 1560 charter: a court leet. Meeting only twice a year, it still managed to prosecute offenders against the borough's trading bye laws who used weights and vessels not 'sealed' to ensure they gave good measure, sold under-sized loaves or poor-quality meat and fish, and mercers, clothiers and others accused of cheating their customers. A small claims court, a court of record, met weekly to adjudicate on debts. Both were chaired by the mayor.[18]

Reading with its natural geographical advantages and the measures it took to provide good marketing conditions had an impact on its hinterland far in excess of its size. Much of the raw wool for its cloth industry came from the Berkshire Downs, bark for tanning leather from the Forest area in the east and elsewhere, and barley for ale and beer from the county's rich arable areas. Edward Symons' licence in 1639 to collect tolls from 'foreigners' crossing the town's bridges or passing under the Reading side of Caversham Bridge specifically excluded those bringing in corn, hay, wool or wood to sell in the market. He paid £16 a year for the privilege. Barges paid 4*d.* toll, loaded wains, wagons and carts 2*d.* and a laden packhorse ½*d.* so he would make a profit if at least 2,000 crossings were made, an indication of the traffic to the town's markets and fairs. Farmers such as Robert Loder were attracted to the Saturday corn market, and to its fairs came leather producers from Newbury and Wokingham. Their profit could be spent on luxury items such as sugar and raisins sold by the town's mercers.[19] Local gentry and their wives would come for the spices, mace, ginger, cloves, and exotic fabrics on sale in a number of shops. More humble purchasers came from many local villages and towns smaller than Reading or were visited by travelling chapmen. Twenty of John Beele's customers lived in Berkshire villages and towns from as far away as Binfield and Wallingford as well as Henley and Goring in south Oxfordshire and Tadley and Stratfield Saye in Hampshire. One such was 'Abigail at Walter Fyllemore's' who owed him two shillings, perhaps a servant girl spending some of her hard-earned pennies on pretty lace or a few fancy buttons. The quantity of ready-made shoes produced in the town was far in excess of the town's needs and was destined for this wider market. Professionals, lawyers, scriveners, apothecaries and barbers or barber-surgeons, also provided services that were available only in an urban setting.

Reading men owned land in many Berkshire parishes from Binfield and Hurst in the east to Thatcham and Kintbury in the west. Some retained property they inherited in their native communities; others bought or leased land as the soundest form of investment, and one easily accessible given the active land market of the period. A favoured few owned London properties.[20]

London was by far the most important point of contact for Reading trade, accounting for about 20% of the debts recorded in tradesmen's probate documents. A weekly service by carrier's cart and by barge via Kennet and Thames carried passengers and freight to and fro, traffic by water probably the more significant. Reading bargemen had a part share in their boats: Abraham Edwards' one-eighth share was valued at £40.[21] From London came oil (for the cloth trade), soap, sea coal, luxury fabrics and spices which Reading mercers and drapers sold to local gentry who attended quarter sessions and assizes or patronised fairs. One of the most useful imports was fish since the ban on eating meat on Fridays survived the Reformation. When John Sone, fishmonger, died in 1593, he owed three London fishmongers over £50 for barrels of fish. In 1597 Benjamin Turner had in stock salmon, red (salted) herrings, stock fish (dried cod), ling and Newland (Newfoundland) fish, probably bought from the nine London tradesmen to whom he was indebted. Others imported Berwick and Scots salmon and herring, mostly salted or dried. Downstream went malt and timber loaded at the several wharves at or near Reading; Robert Johnson's estate owed for the carriage of 40 quarters of malt to London in 1608.[22] The collection of tolls at the town wharf by High Bridge was farmed by the council. The farmer or lessee paid a fee to take over the lease for an agreed time, and a fixed annual rent. He made his profit from the excess of tolls paid over the rent charge. In the 1590s the rent was £3 6s. 8d.; in 1638 it was £6 with a fee of £80 to take on the lease.

Trade was not the only link with London, although it was the one which gave rise to the others. Whereas most Reading fathers apprenticed their sons in the borough, the more affluent or more ambitious, such as Nicholas Gunter, four times mayor, and Robert Johnson's administrators, placed them with London merchants and tradesmen, probably those with whom they had made contact through trade. Networks of men with similar interests seemingly developed: John Gateley made his will in the shop of Thomas Browne of Bowchurch in 1575 with two Reading men as witnesses. Others invested in London property, notably Thomas Aldworth who had a house in Watlington Street in the City.[23]

Richard Tench,
his family and friends

The family was the bedrock of society, the place where, with the husband in charge supported by his wife, their children learned to be good Christians and productive, obedient members of society. Home was where people spent much of their leisure time, sometimes with friends invited for a meal, for conversation, for entertainment. A rare glimpse of how such friendships arose and flourished is provided by the evidence of witnesses called by both sides when the will of Richard Tench was contested in the court of the archdeacon of Berkshire in December 1600.

Richard was born in Ditton, Shropshire, about 1531 and came to Reading when he was 22 or thereabouts to work in the cloth industry as a journeyman. In the Gild Ordinances of c.1560 he was listed among the shearmen of the Clothiers' Company. By 1559 he had moved to London Street in St Giles' parish where from 1581 to 1583 he served as churchwarden. In a survey of 1577 he was recorded as one of Reading's seven innkeepers, leasing a substantial establishment, the Hind Head, with at least four guest rooms called chambers called Hall, London, Brystowe (Bristol) and Steyrehead (Stairhead) chambers. He leased a well-equipped cloth finishing

workshop next door, describing himself as a clothworker in his will, though most of his wealth was tied up in the inn. His inventory, drawn up after his burial in June 1599 amounted to £111 16s. 3d., a sizeable sum. He married twice and had a grandson before 1597. His wife, Annis (Agnes), died in 1581 but at what date he married his second wife, Alice, is not known. Alice and Richard had three surviving children under 21.

John Astell, a weaver born in High Wycombe, Buckinghamshire, lived with the family from about 1582 and possibly helped to run the inn; he certainly did after Richard's death. He was in the house when in April 1599 Richard was discussing his affairs with an acquaintance. Richard asked him to bring from a cupboard in the parlour a paper whose significance John, unable to read, did not at first realise.

The acquaintance was Thomas Purcell, a lawyer at the Court of King's Bench, a gentleman way above Richard socially. He had known Richard for about six years, partly 'because they two were countrymen', meaning they both came from the same county, Shropshire, and partly because he stayed at the inn on his way through the town. He had lived in Wokefield, about seven miles to the east of Reading for about eight years but previously had spent 12 years in London. He was aged about 60, a little younger than Richard but the same age as John. On this spring day, Richard explained that he needed to change his will, leaving less to his wife to bring up the children than he had hoped because his assets had 'somewhat decayed' during his long illness. Thomas duly made the amendments to which John put his mark.

So did William Dibley, a Reading man who had known Richard for about 40 years, meeting him when they were both journeymen in the town; they were about the same age. On one of his frequent visits during Richard's illness, Richard had become very tearful, confiding that his son, young Richard, had behaved badly towards 'his gossip' (friend) at Wokingham and he was minded to reduce his inheritance. William had a good opinion of Richard senior, 'a good, sensible and wise man' despite his inability to read or write.

The gossip who had been 'abused' was Thomas Kenton, another man in his early sixties who had come from Henley-on-Thames as a teenager and had come to know Richard. He too had married and had six children. They both lived in St Giles' parish and 'had delt together in divers bargains and matters'. Since Thomas was a baker, it is likely that he had supplied the inn with bread. He was still providing Richard's

widow with horse bread and hay. Richard had trusted him to keep the first will 'fast bound and sealed up' until a year before when Richard had asked for it. Thomas was a wise choice; he could both read and write.

This will had been written by another acquaintance, a professional scrivener, William Ockham, who had known Richard for over 30 years, having met him 'by reason they were young men and lived near together'. He, too, held Richard in high esteem as one who was 'able to deal and trade in this world well and sufficiently'.

What other men and women had been part of Richard's circle during his long life in Reading is not known. He would have met neighbours walking down the long street to the church where he would have been a familiar figure. Others he would have engaged in conversation as they relaxed at the inn or supplied him with beer and produce. They remain shadowy figures compared with the few whom a chance record of a court case has brought into the light.

Sources: BRO, Archdeaconry of Berkshire deposition book; St Giles' parish register, 1564–99, D/P96/1/1; Will and inventory of Richard Tench, 1599 D/A1/126/202; L. Harman, *The Parish of St Giles-in-Reading* (Reading, 1946), 93. At this date all matters concerning wills were determined by courts held by the bishop, the archdeacon or their officials.

As in earlier periods, London men lived in the borough or had property there: John Wapulls (d. 1580), a yeoman of the royal household and William Westley (d. 1623), a lawyer at the Court of Common Pleas, had houses in Reading.

While some Reading men sought prosperity by leaving the borough, others from its market area were attracted to it as apprentices or craftsmen. Some prospered. Humphrey Dewell, a yeoman's son from White Waltham, about five miles east of Reading, took over the running of a large inn, the Cardinal's Hat in Minster Street, in the 1550s after the death of his mother-in-law, Margaret Wyer. Humphrey's son, Francis, was the innkeeper until his death in 1616. Not so fortunate was William, son of Turnor Sampson, gentleman of Binfield, a village in the same district, who died before completing his apprenticeship.[24] Hugh Tew came from Binfield to Reading to be a glover's apprentice, entered the trade and died a wealthy man. One of the more distant migrants was Walter Bateman born in Kendal, Cumbria, who came to Reading in his late thirties. By the time he died in 1630 he had built up a large cloth-making enterprise and had served as mayor. Another prosperous clothier and mayor, Thomas Aldworth, came from the Berkshire town of Wantage and like many newcomers boosted the town's economy. About one in eight of those recorded in the register of freemen between 1603 and 1642 was not a townsman and almost a quarter of those listed in the *Diary* of the corporation from 1606 to 1637.[25]

Women in society and economy

Not all migrants were men. Women came, sometimes as maidservants, sometimes to marry. Neither Margaret Hawnch nor her servant, Edith Elborne, witnesses in the church court in 1573, was born in Reading; Margaret came from Hambleden, Buckinghamshire, as a child and Edith from Purse Candle near Sherborne, Dorset, as a teenager.[26] Whether Reading-born or incomers, women were essential to the social and economic well-being of the town. The substantial households of master craftsmen and merchants were demanding of food, clean linen and other basic necessities supplied by the women of the house. Wives, daughters and servants worked together. There was nothing of the 'upstairs, downstairs' culture of Victorian England, although servants could expect to sleep in a frugal maids' chamber, sharing a bed as well as a room with their fellows. Good servants were encouraged. John Blagrave's charity (1611) provided ten marks (£6 13s. 4d.) to be awarded each Good Friday to one poor maidservant chosen from three candidates, one from each parish, who had served one employer well for at least five years. John Kendrick's will (1624) provided 40 shillings on marriage to one woman who had served seven years, and rent from Archbishop Laud's bequest of land in Bray (1640) was partly used to give a marriage portion every three years to five servant girls with three years' service. Occasionally servants appear in the formal record. Ellyn Paise hung out the washing in her master's orchard about 8 or 9 o'clock on 6 February 1622: linen sheets, shirts, pillow cases, a shirt, and a smock. Three hours later she found that it had been stolen.[27]

The contribution made by a wife was sometimes acknowledged in her husband's will. Richard Reve commended his 'wellbeloved' wife 'who hath laboured hard with me through hir Youthe for the getting of all myne estate'. The wife of Goodman Brackston, possibly Anthony Brackston, butcher, gave him more questionable support. She withheld one of his lead weights which borough officials suspected was too light, preventing the court leet jury from examining it. When they eventually did, Brackston was fined 3s. 4d. Some wives learned enough about their husband's business to continue it as widows. Alice Tench retained the lease of the Hind Head in London Street, employing a tapster to assist her. More unusual was Elizabeth Kent who carried on her husband's cloth-making trade, employing women as spinners and putting out the yarn they produced to weavers to make kerseys. For several years in the early seventeenth century Widow Malthus and Widow Stephens leased the right to collect tolls for weighing wool on the wool beam.[28]

Inns, alehouses and leisure activities

Alehouses were the places where newcomers gathered, honest men in hope of hearing about work and scoundrels in expectation of easy pickings. For the council such places were threats to a stable society since they lured men into drinking and gambling instead of working and attending church. For these and other reasons, all inns and alehouses were required to hold a licence from the borough justices; unlicensed houses, especially those where serious disorder or opening during service time was reported by the constables, were suppressed. Taverns and inns were also required to forego the sale of meat in Lent and on fish days. However, they were the only public places where townsmen could escape from what were often cramped conditions at home, drink being an anaesthetic against a generally tough existence. The authorities, especially the more fervent Protestants disapproved of gambling in alehouses and inns on such games as bowls, cards and shove-groat, although the habit was ingrained at all levels of society; Bulstrode Whitelocke, a puritan gentleman from Fawley Court near Henley enjoyed cards. Playing tables and packs of playing cards could be found among the laces, buttons and spices in mercers' and chapmen's shops by those wishing to indulge at home away from the prying eyes of the authorities. Cheating at cards or dice by professional cheats known as coneycatchers was rife; a number were caught and brought before the borough magistrates in the 1620s.[29]

Some were found to have played at the card tables provided at several inns in the town. These were larger establishments providing food and accommodation as well as beer and wine; some had bowling alleys, and all provided a place for gossip and smoking; tobacco was widely available in the town, from 15 outlets within the borough by the 1630s. Occasionally there was music from professional players. It does not appear that Reading had official town waits though there were two groups of musicians allowed to play in the borough. James Shylard who played a 'winde instrumente' led a 'company' of six instrumentalists; Matthew Jackson and his two sons played fiddles and a viol. Inns provided them with a captive audience. A few more affluent townsmen and women made music at home, usually on the virginals, although Thomas Gatley, a dyer, also owned a lute and a cittern. There is no evidence of their repertoire other than a 'pavyn booke', possibly a collection of dances called pavanes, though their instruments would have allowed them to play and accompany madrigals.[30] This was the world of 'polite culture' shared by gentlemen and the aspiring 'middling sort', wealthy merchants and professionals in the towns but in one respect it was open to a wider social group if they could read.

A seventeenth-century woodcut. An innkeeper invites a pair of musicians to entertain his clients. Reading had several such groups who played in the town's inns and taverns.

Print from an original painting of Sir Thomas White. Born in Reading, he became a merchant in London, Sheriff and Lord Mayor. He founded St John's College, Oxford to which he endowed scholarships. Two of these were given to boys from Reading School. (Man)

Books appear more frequently after about 1580; by the 1630s one in three inventories recorded books though they are almost always Bibles with an occasional copy of Foxe's *Book of Martyrs*. Merchants, professionals and clergymen might own a more varied collection of law books or sermons and Alexander King (d. 1577) owned eight English books; unfortunately neither his occupation nor the book titles are not known. Henry Welsh, curate, was unique in the county in possessing a library of 159 religious, medical and classical texts. He and others probably purchased books in Oxford or London since Reading had no bookshop. Such men were educated in the growing number of grammar schools, of which Reading's was typical in that it was a re-foundation of a medieval establishment. It occupied the ground floor of the former refectory of the abbey guest house, which frequently needed repair. The master, usually an Oxford graduate, was appointed and paid £10 a year by the corporation; there is no evidence for an assistant master, an usher as at Abingdon; nor do we know the number of pupils. Some went on to university, facilitated by the will of Sir Thomas White which provided

A seventeenth-century woodcut showing revellers, one of whom seems to be a woman at an inn or tavern.

that every four years the corporation should choose one scholar to enter St John's College, Oxford, which he had founded; William Laud was one of these. Another William, son of Thomas Turner, was an Oxford MA by 1570. More men and even a few women could read, a skill which enabled them to study the Bible. Moreover, a significant number of men could write, at least enough to put a signature rather than a mark on a legal document. About one in three signed their depositions in the church courts between c.1558 and 1620, although no woman did. About two-thirds of the men in St Laurence's parish were able to sign the 1642 Protestation Oath.[31]

Occasionally groups of travelling players, as featured in *Hamlet*, would visit the town. They were usually paid by the cofferer, which suggests they performed in the council chamber for a select audience. To avoid being accused of vagrancy, players had the patronage of the Crown or a nobleman: before 1600 those visiting Reading wore the livery of the queen or the earls of Leicester and Essex, patrons connected to the borough. Payments to at least five groups of 'revellers' and players were made in the first decades of the seventeenth century, including the Countess of Rutland's jester, but changing attitudes caused the King's players to be given 20 shillings in April 1628 'to forbeare their playing', the same amount to another troupe at Christmas the next year and to Lady Elizabeth's servants in August 1631 not to play at the town hall. Perhaps such levity was not thought fitting in a period of economic hardship, but more likely a puritan element was gaining influence in the council chamber. The solitary dancing teacher visiting the town in 1632 also got short shrift but his dismissal was one of the less serious decisions facing the corporation in these decades.[32]

6

A troubled and divided community, 1600–1660

S CARCELY had the town begun to recover from the effects of the poor harvests of the 1590s than it faced challenges lasting at intervals for several decades: epidemics, trade depressions leading to poverty and unemployment, civil war, and a divided, bankrupt corporation and community.

Plague

Bubonic plague periodically threatened urban communities throughout the first decades of the seventeenth century. It came to Reading and other riverside towns such as Henley-on-Thames mainly with traders and travellers from the capital though the disease was widespread locally. To provide the corporation with a speedy confirmation of its presence, bodies of suspected victims were examined by widows like Mary Holt, 'sworn to be a searcher' in 1625. Her positive diagnosis would result in the rest of the deceased's household being isolated in the home or in special pest houses for several weeks. Searchers were well paid; in 1639, Widow Lovejoy received 40 shillings, a kirtle, a waistcoat and freedom for her two sons-in-law, 'foreigners', to practise their craft in the town.

Plague was usually most active in the summer causing an increased number of burials to be recorded in those months. All three Reading clergy noted plague deaths between 1603 (an horrendous year for London) and 1607. An epidemic caused 128 of the 165 deaths in St Giles' parish in 1608, burials following the classic plague pattern, starting in August, peaking in September and not relenting until the cold of February 1609. The vicar wrote 'pla' and eventually just 'p' by the names in the parish register. The disease did not spread far, almost half the deaths occurring in 28 families, one losing six members.

When 'the visitation' hit London again in 1625, Reading hoped to profit 'in regard of the great busyness like to ensue' when the central law courts were transferred to the town, the authorities apparently unaware of an epidemic in St Laurence which had begun in June 1624. Precautions taken by the corporation to limit access to the town – setting

Burials in a plague year at St Giles, 1608.

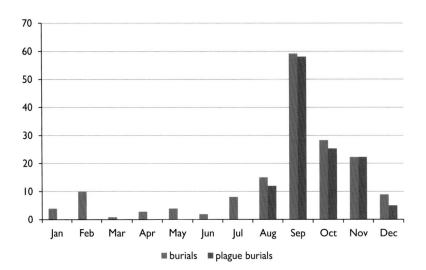

watchmen to prevent known and suspected victims leaving their houses and potential plague carriers entering the town – seem to have succeeded. The death rate in St Laurence's parish had stabilised by August 1625, moving the vicar to write in the register, '*Laus deo pro ejus presidio in tanto periculo*' – 'Praise be to God for his aid in such great danger.'[1]

To isolate the 'visited people' (plague being seen as a visitation from God as punishment for society's sins), the corporation built pest houses on the edge of the borough in 1625. Another severe epidemic between 1637 and 1640 which also affected other parts of England was partly responsible for the town's 297 burials in the year 1639. To meet the cost of a daily allowance to each member of a quarantined household and to build eight more pest houses, additional poor rates were levied as they had been in previous epidemic years, assessed at so many extra weeks' contribution. Nearly 70 extra weekly rates were collected.[2]

Food prices and shortages

This social disruption and added tax burden exacerbated problems already confronting the borough. Some were common to all urban communities. A series of poor harvests in the 1620s and 1630s pushed up the price of wheat and barley by about 20%, causing a similar rise in the cost of bread and beer, staple foods. Wage-earners found it difficult to make ends meet since wages did not rise with prices, if at all, and many families who were on the margins fell into poverty. Hunger could and did provoke unrest, an eventuality to be avoided at all costs. When a mob prevented a cart leaving Newbury with corn in November 1630, the Privy Council ordered Berkshire JPs to imprison the rioters, keep prices down and restrict the amount corn merchants could buy in a single purchase in all Thames valley towns. In Reading the magistrates and corporation ordered corn merchants to hand over a sack of corn from every load to be sold to the poor at less than market price. Even so, an unruly crowd in Reading's Market Place in April 1631 was probably protesting against the export of corn for profit, exacerbating the shortage and raising local prices.[3] The corporation promptly issued a warrant for the arrest of 'covetous and greedy people' who were intercepting farmers coming to market with poultry, butter, eggs and 'other victuals', buying up their goods and selling them in the market at inflated prices, a practice called forestalling and engrossing. Four years later the Privy Council requested a list of maltsters in Berkshire whose numbers were causing a shortage of bread corn partly because farmers preferred to grow barley for brewing and partly because maltsters were buying up corn before it reached the market.[4]

Trade, unemployment and poverty

These problems only partly explain the decline in trade in the town in the 1630s, reflected in the rent which men were willing to pay to farm the market tolls 'untill it shall appeare … that the Markettes are amended'. In 1636 Simon Dee offered only 75% of the corporation's asking price.[5] As important was the state of the cloth export trade. Recessions followed by short-lived booms were typical of the cloth industry. In the late sixteenth and early seventeenth centuries Reading shared in a long period of prosperity for English clothiers, driven by European demand for high-quality dyed broadcloth. Nationally this ended in 'a series of severe depressions … [in] the generation or so after 1614', partly a result of the Thirty Years' War and partly from ill-conceived government trade restrictions. In 1623 the corporation petitioned the Privy Council complaining that 'a sudden decay of clothinge' had caused 'want of worke … [and] greate miserye'. They could not assist the unemployed because cloth sales had fallen, due, they claimed, to unfair competition from northern merchants fraudulently marketing their cloth as made in Reading. The situation was exacerbated during the severe plague of 1625 in London when markets in the capital closed as merchants fled. Cloth production in the borough declined from about 150 broadcloths a week in the first decade of the century to 100 in the early 1620s and a catastrophic 40 or fewer by 1640. Some clothiers were effectively bankrupt: Walter Bateman's debts at his death in 1631 amounted to £468 11s. 8d., exceeding his considerable assets by £87 7s. 8d. In addition he had mortgaged his house and its lease for £300. Despite these gloomy statistics, 40% of those granted freedom to trade in the town were cloth producers, although by 1640 Reading had ceased to be an important producer of cloth for export.[6]

Reading's ability to attract migrants was now a problem, with too few jobs for even native workers. In the early autumn of 1623 the corporation ordered two clothiers from each parish to meet at 8 a.m. each Monday to assign work to some who lacked it, one of several attempts to relieve unemployment. It met with little success. In 1630 the corporation *Diary* recorded a 'great clamour of divers poor people lacking work and employment in spinning and carding', but weavers, cloth finishers and other craftsmen such as butchers and shoemakers were also suffering from the 'hardness of the times'.[7]

They added to the more traditional ranks of the poor, the old, sick, orphans and widows, the latter making up at least half of about 150 people on weekly poor relief in the late 1630s. Very few asked for or were given help so the actual number of those in need was possibly as much as a quarter or a third of the population. In addition casual payments to the poor 'in their need' were given: to the sick, to bury paupers and to apprentice poor children. The substantial sum of 5s. was given to Robert Smithson 'when hee went to London to bee cured of his Majestie for the evill [scrofula]', Charles I being a firm believer in his power to perform this near miracle.[8]

Such payments were made by the parish in accordance with a scheme to provide poor relief introduced in 1598. The connection between poverty, vagrancy and unrest had concerned the authorities nationally since at least the 1530s. An Act of 1576 ordered towns to provide raw materials such as wool, flax or hemp for the unemployed poor to process. In Reading the former priory of Greyfriars became a 'Hospital', a poor house for the old and orphans by 1578. A more comprehensive Act for the Relief of the Poor (1598, amended 1601) distinguished between categories of poor people: 'worthy poor' – the old, sick, orphans – would be given relief; 'masterless men', the able-bodied whether unemployed or just idle (no distinction between the two categories was made) were to be taught 'habits of industry' in 'houses of correction'; 'incorrigible rogues', vagrants, assumed to be avoiding honest labour, would be punished, then put to work. Children of poor parents were to be apprenticed. All this was to be done by the parish through the collection and distribution of a compulsory poor rate by unpaid officials called overseers of the poor. This law, with modifications, remained the basis on which the poor were treated until 1834. In 1614 Reading's burgesses agreed to convert part of the hospital into a house of correction 'for the better government of the sturdye, idle and disorderlye persones ... whiche cause and move much trouble'. William Clayton and his wife were appointed to oversee the work of boys, 'wenches' and 'charwomen' sent to them by the corporation or parish overseers to work on dressing hemp and flax. Vagrants and beggars in the streets were whipped in the Market Place before being sent to the House.[9]

Poor box at the west door of St Mary's church, 1627, Remember the poore and God will bles [*sic*] thee and thy store. (JD)

Like many other communities, Reading did not immediately see the need for a poor rate. All three parishes had a 'poor man's box' by the 1570s or earlier; St Mary's box, at the west end of the church was mended in 1627 and bore the inscription, 'Remember the poor and God will bless thy store'. The borough gave the poor the proceeds from fines for producing faulty cloth, maintaining unlicensed alehouses and other breaches of trading regulations and, especially in the 1630s and 1640s, swearing. However, by 1623 if not earlier levying a parish poor rate had become necessary. All three parishes appointed overseers of the poor who assessed, collected and distributed the poor rate but accounted for it, and any charitable gifts, to the corporation. The total poor-rate levied in 1637–38 in the three parishes amounted to £225 10s. 8½d.[10]

Private charity, the traditional way to relieve poverty, continued to be important. Many will-makers, especially in later years, made bequests to provide money, penny loaves or clothing to be distributed at their funerals or annually on a specified feast day by the churchwardens or

the cofferers. Most bequests were administered by the corporation as the account for Charitable Uses: income from rents on property either bequeathed, or purchased by the borough with cash bequests. This was recorded in a separate account from borough revenues, the Hall accounts. In the early seventeenth century the mayor accounted for

The poor box at the west door of St Mary's church. Charity remained a Christian duty despite the introduction of parochial poor relief. (JD)

charity revenues; later they became the responsibility of one of the cofferers. Increasingly gifts were targeted at the deserving poor or at social improvement: Joan Dewell 'to the most needy working poor'; Richard Johnson to apprentice four fatherless children; Thomas Deane 'wholesome and well sized bread' each Christmas Eve, Good Friday and Ascension Day to St Giles' poor. William Brackstone's bequest of £60 in 1634 was invested to provide 180 poor women and 29 poor men with 4*d*. and 12*d*. respectively; more women than men usually needed help. Some donors provided almshouses: Bernard Harrison (1616), four tenements for men with wives over 50 years of age; William Kendrick (1634), five tenements in Silver Street; Sir Thomas Vachell (1635), a brick house for six sick, old widowers.[11] Significantly, Harrison's and Kendrick's small almshouses were in St Giles, the parish with the greatest poverty: 'the number of poor is so great there and the givers so few.' In 1640 William Laud, Archbishop of Canterbury, gave his home town a magnificent gift of land in the parish of Bray, the income from which would each year pay the apprenticeship fees for ten poor boys from Reading and one from Wokingham, his mother's birthplace.

Bequests and parish poor relief pale beside the greatest gift ever made to the borough. It came in 1624 from John Kendrick, a member of a Reading clothier family; his brother, William, was a clothier and

Copy of a portrait of John Kendrick from the original then in the Council Chamber. (Man)

a burgess. John, a member of the Company of Merchant Adventurers, lived in London and became wealthy by exporting Reading cloth to the Low Countries. He never married. Among the beneficiaries of his will were the boroughs of Newbury and Reading, the mayor and burgesses of the latter receiving the huge sum of £7,600 for several purposes including the building of a brick workhouse to be stocked with raw materials for 'the employment of poore' in producing cloth and other manufactures. Called the Oracle, it consisted of William Kendrick's house and workshop purchased by the corporation at an exorbitant price and extended southwards to provide a number of rooms round a grassed quadrangle. With an imposing entrance from Minster Street, it was completed in 1628 at

An engraving by Charles Tomkins of the entrance to John Kendrick's workhouse, the Oracle *c*.1800. (Coates)

a cost of £1,846. Of the remaining monies, £3,600 was to be loaned to twelve clothiers with free accommodation and equipment in the Oracle to employ clothworkers. The first to benefit were William Kendrick's son, Thomas, his nephew, William Gandy, and John Kendrick's uncle, William Bye. Though strict conditions were laid down about the number of cloths to be produced and the returns expected, the enterprise never fulfilled its purpose. Some weavers and cloth finishers were set on in 1628 but in the depression of the early 1630s it proved difficult to sell the cloths they made, production declined, some clothiers defaulted, and others withdrew from the project.

In 1631 the Privy Council, possibly prompted by critics in the borough, ordered an enquiry by a commission of Berkshire magistrates into the way the charity was being administered, especially the failure of the corporation to provide work for unemployed cloth workers. This was serious since Kendrick's will stipulated that failure to observe his intentions would result in the loss of the entire bequest to Christ's Hospital, London.

Despite the corporation's failings (excessive expenditure on the building, inadequate guarantees for the repayment of loans, and partiality in the clothiers favoured, many being burgesses or related to the Kendricks), the bequest stayed in Reading. As the economic situation worsened, Archbishop Laud began an investigation in 1637 into a complaint by poorer Reading clothiers against unfair competition from the Oracle. The corporation acting on Laud's recommendation contained in an Exchequer decree, invested the remainder of the bequest in property, purchasing land at Sulhampstead, Grimmer's Farm, Goring and Crown Fields, Reading, whose rents would provide interest-free loans to young clothiers and apprentice poor boys. The Oracle would be used to teach orphan children a trade. Kendrick's plans for a cloth workhouse failed partly because the industry was already in decline but more through corporate inefficiency, mismanagement and peculation. Much better managed was his £500 fund to lend £50 each to poor clothiers interest-free for three years, £250 to purchase land whose rent would support morning service in St Mary's and £100 each year as a marriage gift of 40s. each to seven long-serving maidservants.[12]

Kendrick desired the borough to 'preferre the poore of the said town … before others'. Unemployment or under-employment fuelled a wariness of outsiders into suspicion and occasional hostility, feelings not confined to Reading but typical of townspeople everywhere. A prospective craftsman from outside paid a higher fee for his freedom than a Reading man and was only admitted with the corporation's consent, yet complaints against 'foreigners', strangers, were frequently made, particularly in the 1620s, the main one being that their presence damaged the trade of resident workers. Beadles were appointed to arrest able-bodied beggars, have them whipped and sent to the house of correction. Unfamiliar individuals were often the first suspects when a crime was committed, usually theft from people, shops or houses. Between 1623 and 1640 'foreigners' appearing before the borough's courts on suspicion of criminal behaviour on the evidence of eyewitnesses, and being unable to provide sureties, were sent to the house of correction. They included men from as far away as Ireland and as near as Oxford. Two Irishmen were among a group of tricksters who 'cosened and deceyved' a visitor from Suffolk in a gambling game at the Bull Inn in 1625; even worse, one had a pair of rosary beads with a cross. They claimed to be seeking work. During these difficult years the corporation introduced a number of measures to remove unwanted interlopers: each parish was to appoint two men to seek out newly arrived strangers; anyone not given the freedom to practise a craft was to leave; and newcomers with families were required to provide sureties they would not become a burden on the town's poor rate. Giving lodgings to a newcomer could lose a freeman his right to trade.[13]

Politics national and local, 1625–1640

To this saga of social and economic worries was added the troubled political situation created by disagreements between Charles I and parliament over religion, foreign policy and taxation. Many royal policies seemed to threaten the established church, especially his marriage to a Catholic, Henrietta Maria, and his choice of ministers and bishops. Having failed to persuade parliament to grant him taxes, he imposed a 'Free Gift', actually a forced loan, in 1626. Reading's view of the 'gift' was quite clear. The corporation and most of the 'Subsidye men' (those liable to pay tax), meeting in the presence of Sir Francis Knollys of Rotherfield Greys and Sir Thomas Vachell of Coley, agreed that 'his majestie's want [need] of money should be supplyed, but not in manner as it is required; and desire there maybe a Parlyament for then all men should be bound to paye a parte.' Two years later, 90 soldiers en route to Portsmouth for Charles' attack on France were billeted in Reading for a month costing the town about £84, a tax which some refused to pay. To meet the expense of a visit by the king and queen the following year, which included giving each a gilt cup, the cofferers had to borrow £50. The borough had no cash reserves.[14]

After 1629 Charles did not call another parliament for 11 years, a period known to historians as the 'Personal Rule' and to the King's opponents as 'the Eleven Years' Tyranny'. His various means of raising money were legal, revivals of obsolete laws, but politically unwise. In 1631 all men, including some in Reading with an income of £40 a year or more were ordered to 'compound' (pay a fee) for not having received a knighthood. The most controversial was a tax called Ship Money, originally imposed on maritime counties to support ships in wartime. From 1634, when England was at peace, it was imposed annually on the whole country. Reading paid £220, the largest share of Berkshire's assessment of £4,000.[15] At the meeting of the sheriff and county magistrates in December 1636 to decide the amount of the third assessment payable by each borough, Sir Francis Knollys, senior, objected. Sir Francis (1553–1648), whose views were echoed by some townsmen, belonged to an important south Oxfordshire family which had powerful influence on Reading. The tax due was collected but the following year as resistance grew the corporation distrained the goods of those refusing to pay. Even so there remained a shortfall of at least £40, met from borough funds. In 1638 when nationally more than a third of the tax was unpaid, Reading Corporation ordered the sale of all distrained goods to meet the assessment, although it seems sales were slow and eventually goods were returned to their owners. In March 1640 the sheriff of Berkshire complained that opposition to payment in the county was widespread, especially from all the corporate towns, including Reading, which had sent him 'neither money nor certain answer'. Of the £4,000 due in 1639, he had collected a mere £129.[16]

The corporation itself was familiar with straitened finances. Between 1607 and 1640 the total income paid to the Hall account, mostly in rents for property, averaged over £230 a year, a three-fold increase over that of the 1590s. Rents included those for the lease of the tolls of the market, the Wool Hall and four fairs as well as for houses, shops and other property. Smaller sums came from entry fines (fees) for apprentices and strangers to become freemen and fines for breaches of market rules and borough byelaws.[17] The accounts were precariously balanced. About half the income was needed to meet 'ordinary charges', salaries and allowances for the mayor and officers which varied very little from year to year. Extraordinary expenses covered everything else – repairs to borough property, street cleaning, entertainment for visiting judges and magistrates and so on. If most rents were paid, then in two years out of three outgoings were manageable and the accounts showed a small surplus. Substantial arrears of rent as in 1624–25 and 1634–35 created a deficit, as did two major repairs to High Bridge, but otherwise the cause of the shortfall is unknown since only the total of extraordinary expenses was usually recorded. On the other hand, references to 'old debts', 'debt by bond', 'debt to the Cofferer' abound. Any surplus was immediately used to liquidate accumulated debt and in 1638 for the new charter.[18]

Caversham Bridge c.1800. Oxfordshire was responsible for maintaining the northern half (the stone and brick arches) and Reading for the southern (a wooden drawbridge). (Man)

In the accounting year Michaelmas 1641/2 rent arrears on borough property reached a record £90 13s. 1d., though the cofferer distrained plate worth £20 for non-payment of the market toll rent. Extraordinary expenses were over £314, putting the corporation over £254 in debt, in excess of a year's income.

The decade did see some positive developments. William Laud, already a member of the Privy Council, became Archbishop of Canterbury in 1633. He used his influence at court to obtain a new charter for the borough in 1638. It defined the governing body, the corporation, as the mayor, twelve aldermen and twelve assistants, but gave it few extra powers and little extra income. Members of the corporation were named in the

Reading's charter of 1638 with a portrayal of Charles I forming an elaborate first letter. (BRO R/ICI/10)

charter and held office for life. Aldermen filled vacancies in their ranks from the assistants and they in turn from the body of freemen. On the last Monday of August the aldermen selected three of their number of whom one, chosen as the next mayor by the whole body, took his oath on the Monday after Michaelmas (29 September). On the death or resignation of the steward, Sir Edward Clarke, the aldermen would choose a replacement. They also appointed the coroners and annually the two chamberlains (formerly called cofferers). The mayor chose his sergeants at mace. The mayor and his deputy were JPs, giving judgement in the borough's own quarter sessions and granting licences to sell beer. The mayor was clerk of the market and held the assize of bread. The borough could charge pontage of 2d. from carts or waggons and ½d. from laden packhorses crossing the borough's bridges and 4d. for barges going under Caversham Bridge. Two clauses reflect the corporation's immediate worries: no buildings were to be roofed in thatch (to prevent fire), and no tenement was to be subdivided into multiple dwellings, which might attract poor tenants.[19]

Nationally concern was growing over religious divisions. Since the Elizabethan settlement of 1559 the Crown had attempted to sustain a form of worship acceptable to as many as possible, although from the beginning a strong puritan ('godly') element had argued for more radical reform. This moderate Protestantism was challenged by churchmen who thought ceremonial and sacramental worship more important than sermons. William Laud, Charles I and some bishops embraced these Arminian beliefs, which favoured the use of candles and music in worship, displaying 'the beauty of holiness'. To this end Laud ordered that altars, with altar rails, should be placed at the east end of the chancel. St Mary's churchwardens certainly conformed but St Giles' did not. Some townspeople, especially a number of the 'godly' in town and corporation, thought this too near papist practices. A leading opponent was Theophilus Taylor, vicar of St Laurence from 1618 to 1640, which not surprisingly was the most 'enthusiastic' ('godly') parish. Even so the churchwardens spent large sums in the 1630s beautifying the chancel though in 1641 the altar rails were removed. The incumbents of the other parishes, Thomas Bunbury and Hugh Dicus, were either moderates or Arminians.[20] Some parishioners found too infrequent and unsatisfying the sermons preached at church, at certain civic events and on Sundays organised by the corporation from 1625 and delivered by 'neighbouring ministers'. Three years later partly due to the influence of the steward, Sir Edward Clarke, a puritan in the service of the Knollys family, a 'lectureship' was set up: sermons on Tuesdays, given by visiting preachers. The corporation came in their robes, and one member from each household was expected to attend.[21] Thereafter godly members of the corporation seem to have become more influential. In 1629 and 1631 the King's players were refused permission to perform in the town hall, and in 1633 seven butchers were prosecuted for selling meat in Lent. Similar views prompted the Scots to defend their Presbyterian Church against an attempt by Charles to impose the English *Book of Common Prayer* on their country, culminating in a Scots invasion of England in 1639. By 1640 the king was forced to call a parliament to vote taxes needed to equip an army to repel the invaders.

Parliament and the drift to war, 1640–1642

Although the corporation elected the borough's two MPs, in the early seventeenth century the choice was influenced by the Knollys family, a typical case of local gentry involvement in borough politics. Throughout the 1620s the high steward, Sir William Knollys of Caversham, nominated one candidate and the corporation the other. Elections were always contested, the Knollys family never having a monopoly. After 1631 with his great nephew, Lord Holland the borough's high steward, Sir Francis Knollys senior, his brother holding land in the borough and the manor of Battle, and his son, the younger Sir Francis at Abbey House, the family's influence was complete. Young Sir Francis served as one of the borough's MPs from 1624 to 1628. Both father and son were opponents of Charles' policies, their links to like-minded gentry strengthened by the marriage of Sir Francis senior's daughter to John Hampden, a fierce opponent of Ship Money. In the fraught situation of 1640, contested elections were almost inevitable: the king needed a compliant Commons; his critics wanted an opportunity to bring about change. In Reading, Archbishop Laud attempted to provide one loyal member by nominating Sir Francis Herbert, a known prosecutor of puritan pamphleteers but though both he and Lord Holland's nominee, Sir John Berkeley, were elected to the Short Parliament they chose to sit for other constituencies, forcing a bye-election.

The corporation now chose Sir Francis Knollys, father and son, a decision approved by a 'great number of the Cominaltye of the Boroughe' assembled outside the hall determined to have a voice.[22] Later that year another election was needed since the king dissolved parliament within a month without any settlement of his financial problems. This time Laud did not intervene, the Knollys, father and son, being elected to what became the Long Parliament (it sat until 1653) 'by free and general consent of all' first in the 'counsell-chamber' and then in the 'open hall'. The community's voice had again been heard, and it supported the king's critics.

The hope that calling parliament might solve the nation's problems proved unfounded. By 1641 growing distrust of the king and radical measures introduced by the House of Commons on one side and concern to preserve the church and the monarchy on the other combined to divide the country into two parties which drifted into a war which began officially in August 1642. Reading, both corporation and community, was divided. In 1642 parliament ordered all adult males to swear the Protestation Oath to support the 'true Protestant religion', the liberty of the subject and the 'privileges of Parliaments'. Only about half the townsmen seem to have taken it and in February 1643 it was reported that at least 600 men had sworn to attack a future royal garrison in the event of a parliamentary siege.[23] Whatever their allegiance, during the autumn fear of the marauding troops being assembled by both sides prompted the corporation to take defensive measures, erecting posts and chains at town approaches, ordering the trained bands, the local militia, to muster in the Forbury, levying a tax to pay scouts to warn against 'Cavillers abroad', and setting up a continuous watch by householders. No security could be guaranteed by the county gentry who were even more divided in allegiance than was the borough. Even families were split: Anthony Blagrave of Bulmershe for the king, his younger son, Daniel of Southcote, for parliament; Thomas Vachell of Coley a royalist, Tanfield, his nephew, a parliamentarian.

Control of Reading's strategic position and the access it provided to the rich agricultural lands of Berkshire was vitally important to both sides. The town like the county was uneasily placed between Windsor

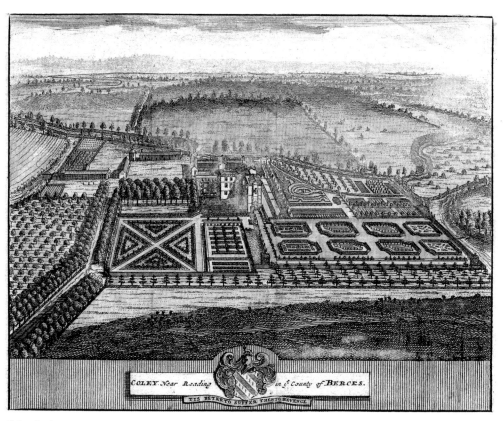

COLEY Near Reading in ye County of BERCES.
TIS BETTER TO SUFFER THEN TO REVENGE.

Coley Park, home of the Vachell family. (JD)

garrisoned by parliament and pro–parliament London, and Oxford where the king set up headquarters when he failed to take the capital. Reading would change hands four times, the first when a short-lived occupation for parliament by Henry Marten of Longworth, county MP, republican and future regicide, was abandoned on 1 November 1642 as the royalist army approached, leaving the town open to royalist occupation.[24] Each side proved equally determined to exploit communities they occupied. The royalist commander of Reading, Sir Arthur Aston, was ruthless both in his physical treatment of opponents and in demands for money. The latter included two 'loans', the first for £2,000 demanded by the king in November and never repaid despite his promises. The corporation raised this from loans secured by pressurising individuals: £1,000 from Mr John Struggill at 5% interest on security of the market tolls and certain rents; £600 from Thomas Harrison, and £200 from William Gandy, brewers, and by a weekly tax on poor-rate payers at 15s. a week for every penny normally paid, equivalent to £500 a week. In January 1643 Sir Arthur Aston demanded another 'loan' which the corporation said could not be raised but eventually was. Demands for uniforms and supplies for the army put further strains on the town's resources, to say nothing of

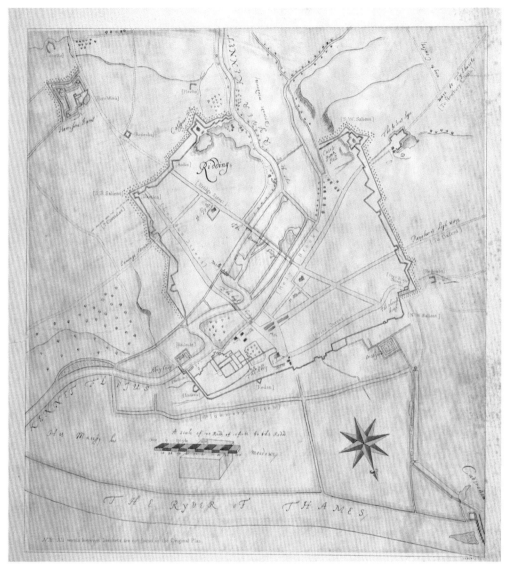

Map of
Reading's civil
war defences,
1643–44. North
is to the bottom
right. (RM)

supporting a garrison of 2,000 foot and 300 horse billeted in the house of
correction and private houses. The school was requisitioned for use as an
arsenal. Defences constructed by forced labour were soon tested by the
Earl of Essex, who laid siege to the town on 16 April 1643 with artillery
and a parliamentary army of 19,000. Three days later, reinforcements
allowed Essex's troops to encircle the town. When the king and Prince
Rupert failed to raise the siege from a base in Caversham, the commander,
Sir Richard Fielding, who had replaced the injured Aston, felt obliged to
surrender on 26 April. His garrison marched out with its baggage but
not its artillery.

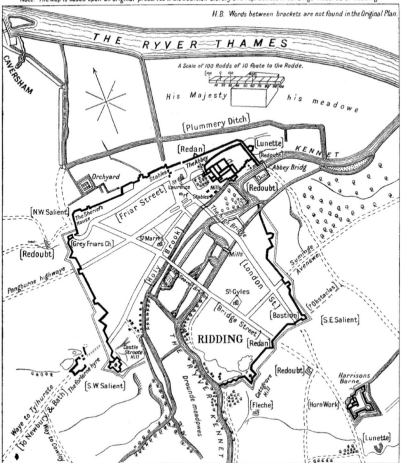

MAP OF READING DURING THE SIEGE OF 1643.

Note. The Map is based upon an original preserved in the Bodleian Library and reproduced in Guilding's "Records of Reading".

N.B. Words between brackets are not found in the Original Plan.

A plan of Reading's civil war defences, based on the original and reproduced in W.M. Childs, *The Story of the Town of Reading* (1905)

William Stanford & Company, Ltd.,   Oxford.

St Giles burials, 1590-1650

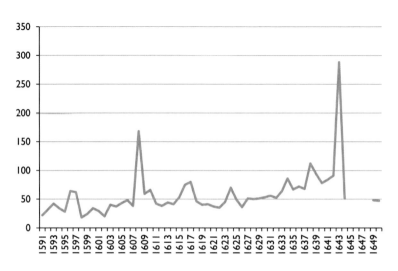

Sketch of Sir Arthur Aston, Royalist Governor of Reading, November 1642–April 1643. (RM)

Sir Arthur Aston.

Sir Jacob Astley, Royalist commander of Reading, 1643–44. (RM)

The town had new masters but this did nothing to improve the lot of its inhabitants. A parliamentary garrison which remained until September 1643 began by plundering houses, ostensibly those of 'delinquents' (royalists), but in practice everyone was at risk. Worse still, an epidemic of 'gaol fever' or typhus, spread from Essex's force to the town and the surrounding villages. Typhus, spread by lice, flourished in crowded, unhygienic conditions such as army camps. Burials in the three Reading parishes in the months following the siege rose dramatically to more than three times the norm and far higher in the countryside. Some of the dead were soldiers wounded in the fight but the vast majority were town and village people.[25] Royalist sympathisers including two vicars fled during the six weeks' grace allowed by the new masters of the town, leaving the corporation depleted; at least five members failed to attend meetings, others refused promotion to alderman, and some preferred to pay a fine or go to prison rather than serve at all. Parliamentary troops withdrew after the Battle of Newbury in September 1643, but the return of a royalist garrison brought no relief. Determined to improve the defences, the governor Sir Jacob Astley, gave householders the option of forced labour or a fine of 12*d.* a day, and from October 1643 taxes of about £200 a month were imposed by the corporation to support the occupying force.

In May 1644 the town changed hands for the fourth and final time as the garrison left to reinforce the royalist army in the South West; until the end of the war parliament held the town which became the headquarters of the Berkshire County Committee. This was a new body set up in every county as parliamentary forces gained control. Composed of their adherents among the gentry and later from the boroughs, the committee replaced the magistrates who in Berkshire and other counties had previously formed the county administration. Boroughs also came under its authority. Among its members were Daniel Blagrave and Tanfield Vachel. In August six members of the committee attended a meeting of the corporation, from which three aldermen and two assistants were ejected as being 'notoriously disaffected to the State', that is royalists. Others were removed in the following years as the committee secured a 'loyal' corporation. Daniel Blagrave joined the corporation in December 1644 and later became borough steward.

Taxation had become far more oppressive than ever it had under Charles. In November 1642 a Committee for the Advancement of Money was set up by parliament to raise money from loans and impositions. The next year weekly (later monthly) assessments (ironically based on ship money assessment) and the excise, a purchase tax on a wide range of goods, were levied and continued throughout the war and after; the excise was retained at the Restoration of 1660. Petitions for relief, including those from the borough, were ignored. In addition, although Reading was controlled by parliamentary troops after 1644, demands for a contribution to support

An extract from a draft petition from Reading to Parliament
c. December 1644

... that since the time the two armyes came into this towne your petitioners have had their sufferings so multiplied upon them, the souldiers growing to that height of insolency that they break down our houses and burne them, take away our goods and sell them, rob our markets and spoile them, threaten our magistrates and beate them, so that without a speedy redress we shalbe constrained, though to our utter undoing yet for the preservation of our lives, to forsake our goods and habitation and leave the towne to the will of the souldiers.

Source: BRO, R/Z3/51

the royalist garrison at Wallingford continued. In June the mayor, William Brackstone, was kidnapped and although he was released within weeks there is no evidence that the corporation made any concession other than a 'submissive letter' pleading inability to pay. Recurring outbreaks of plague in late 1645 and 1646 meant more expenditure as did repairs to Caversham Bridge, damaged during the siege.

Although the war ended with the surrender of Oxford on 24 June 1646, there was no real peace. Risings against Parliament, a rebellion in Ireland and an invasion by a Scots army in support of the future Charles II prolonged hostilities until September 1651. During these years divisions grew in the parliamentary ranks with army officers and moderates in parliament (political Presbyterians) wishing to restore the traditional political and social order, and some radical elements in the army rank and file and in London (political Independents) demanding greater political and religious freedom. Reading became the focus of national events in July 1647 when an army council met here to debate terms to be offered to the king, the basis of Oliver Cromwell's negotiations with Charles at Caversham. All came to nothing. Until hostilities ended, troops remained in Reading supported by taxes or 'loans' though latterly billeted in inns and taverns, not dwelling houses.

Political opinion both within the corporation and the community remained divided throughout and after the war, 'producing bitter political controversy' seen during wartime elections when the conservative corporation, presbyterian in religion and politics and supported by ratepayers (established householders who owned or leased property) was challenged by the more radical body of freemen, many of whom were resident employees of master craftsmen and merchants. The right of 'the commonalty' to a voice in elections had been demonstrated in 1640, but the composition of the electorate, ratepayers or freemen was consistently challenged.[26]

On 30 January 1649 Charles I was executed and England became a republic ruled by parliament and a council of state. The corporation *Diary* ceased to mention regnal years. Of more concern to the people of Reading was the destruction caused by the siege and after, the dire state of the local economy, and the price of basic foodstuffs. If petitions from Reading are truthful, damage to property was considerable, some from gun and cannon fire but more from damage and theft by soldiers. 'They break down our houses and burn them, take away our goods and sell them, rob our markets and spoile them,' complained the borough to parliament. In St Laurence's church seats were broken where soldiers were billeted and Elizabeth Kenton, an old widow with children, had seen her house torn down and burned.[27] The whole economy was badly affected, all trade said to be greatly 'decayed'. Markets still functioned though at a slower pace; the rent charged for the lease of the market tolls let for at least £75 a year in the 1630s raised only £38 in 1645 and £44 in 1647. In 1645–46 income, albeit reduced, was received from fairs. Rent from charity lands and property was frequently in arrears and many requests for reductions submitted, often with taxation and pillaging given in explanation. Some was paid, but income from Kendrick charity land fell by about 70% in 1642–43. At all events, the leases of town property had all been mortgaged for loans from Struggill and others. The cloth industry, already troubled before hostilities began, suffered from the downturn in trade, demands by troops for protection money from those transporting cloth to London and occasional seizures of goods. Harvests had been good during the war years but successive crop failures from 1646 to 1650 pushed food prices up by nearly 50% in five years.[28]

The possessions of royalists or those believed to be sympathetic to the cause were particularly at risk as they lost ground to their opponents. To raise money for the war parliament had set up a Sequestration Committee in 1643 to confiscate and administer the estates of 'delinquents', that is royalists and Catholics. When it failed to raise sufficient income, another organisation, the Committee for Compounding, was established in 1645 to restore confiscated property in return for a fine, a procedure called compounding. Two Reading parish clergy, Hugh Dicus (St Giles) and Thomas Bunbury (St Mary), who had fled to Oxford in 1644, compounded in 1646 paying £60 and £117 10s. respectively. They had also lost the income from their livings and neither was reinstated in the parish.[29]

In 1645 parliament took the first steps towards establishing a national church with puritan beliefs and practice by abolishing the *Book of Common Prayer* in favour of a presbyterian *Directory of Worship*, a guide to the form of service but with no set forms of prayer. The Church of England became presbyterian and although a full structure as existed in Scotland was never achieved, bishoprics were abolished and their lands sold. Celebration of the festivals of Christmas and Easter was made a criminal offence. About 2,000 ministers whose politics, theology or lifestyles were no longer acceptable were ejected, among them Thomas Tuer of St Laurence in 1646. Ejected ministers were often replaced by ones chosen by a Parliamentary Committee for Plundered Ministers. In Reading Christopher Fowler was installed at St Mary in 1646 and John Jemmatt (and after his death his brother William) at St Giles in 1648, both notable preachers and presbyterians. At St Laurence the radical John Pordage officiated for a time but, being too extreme even for a godly parish, was replaced by Thomas Gilbert, an independent and then by Simon Ford, another presbyterian. William Laud would have been horrified to learn that Pordage received money from his charity to supplement the annual income of the vicar of St Laurence. The parish set up a presbyterian form of church government; in July 1646 Daniel Blagrave, John Pordage and parishioners chose Mayor George Wooldridge and three future mayors, 'to be Ruling Elders of the parochiall & Congregationall Eldershipp', perhaps predictably the first borough parish to attempt a presbyterian system as ordered by parliament. The influence of these preachers gradually extended into the council chamber, presbyterians gaining control during the 1650s. Whether the allegation that Fowler and Ford 'have the swaye of the Towne in point of government' in the 1650s was justified, they certainly had considerable influence over co-religionists and led prayer meetings before important corporation decisions.[30]

The choice of master of the Free School was also dominated by confessional beliefs, allegedly to the detriment of effective education. In 1644 the school was sequestered and the master, William Page, was ousted by the County Committee in favour of Thomas Pocock whose teaching abilities and learning, it was claimed, were inferior to his religious fervour. Whatever his qualities, his appointment rode roughshod over the corporation's right to appoint, enshrined in their charter. It was typical of how county committees usurped urban privileges. Following a delayed triennial visitation in 1648 by academics from St John's College, Oxford, Pocock was persuaded to leave with the £20 supplement to his salary from Laud's charity previously denied him. His replacement, the 'civil, godly and learned' Mr Waddon, was the first of several short-lived appointments, the post becoming 'the sport of political and sectarian vicissitude' as power struggles in the corporation and the intervention of presbyterian clergy determined who educated the town's youth.[31]

Otherwise, as far as income from charity lands allowed, the corporation honoured the wishes of benefactors throughout the period. The Blagrave charity gifts to a long-serving maidservant were always made, the corporation finding the money when tenants of charity land failed to pay the rent on time, and some young men were apprenticed with income from Laud's charity lands despite reduced rental income. Several clothing, bread and other charities continued, but no loans to tradesmen from the Kendrick bequest were made between 1642 and 1651, and for a time troops were quartered in the Oracle.

The ending of domestic conflict in 1651 did not lead to stability nationally or locally. Divisions between presbyterians and Cromwell's supporters who dominated town politics during the 1650s and the many townsmen who were either hostile or indifferent to the regime were most evident at election times. When Cromwell's soldiers drove out the 'Rump' of surviving MPs in 1653, finally ending the Long Parliament, there was no general election. Instead a nominated body, nicknamed the 'Barebones' Parliament' was chosen in 1653 from county lists supplied by ministers and church elders; Reading was not directly represented. Following the dissolution of this body, Cromwell was proclaimed Lord Protector. In the first election of the Protectorate in 1654, Reading, reduced to a single-member constituency, was represented by its governor and high steward, Colonel Robert Hammond, who had the support of the presbyterian mayor, Henry Frewen, and the aldermen. An attempt by the townsmen to have Captain Castle elected was stridently put down to the satisfaction of the local clergy, confirming popular fears of growing authoritarianism. Ironically Hammond died before he could take his seat in this short-lived parliament.[32]

The right to the franchise was still not settled for the next two elections. In 1656 the mayor, Thomas Cope, and the presbyterian majority on the corporation supported Sir John Barkstead, a Cromwellian, a regicide and a major general. Major generals, universally unpopular, were appointed in 1655 to bring about 'moral order' by enforcing the laws against drunkenness, swearing, play-going and Sabbath-breaking. Daniel Blagrave, another regicide, a supporter of the independents and an opponent of Reading's presbyterian corporation, was the townsmen's choice. No poll was taken, and the corporation returned Barkstead. Though he lost the election, Blagrave became MP when Barkstead chose to represent Middlesex which he had also won. Blagrave was not left to enjoy his success; the corporation removed him from the office of recorder and sued him for a trifling debt of £20.

Two significant developments affected the outcome of the election of 1658: nationally the growing numbers of republicans and radical sects opposed to Cromwell, and on the borough corporation the emergence of a strong republican minority. Joel Stephens, a republican, was elected mayor in August 1658. In the confused state of national politics following the death of Oliver Cromwell in September and the succession of his son, Richard, Stephens and the republican faction on the corporation were strongly placed to decide the election which they threw open to the public. The candidates were Daniel Blagrave and Henry Neville of Billingbear, another republican opposed to the Protectorate. To prevent their election, Henry Frewin and several councillors attempted to take control of the corporation, declaring the mayor deposed and electing Frewin in his place. After the departure of their opponents, they seized the mace and the borough seal (which would allow them to make the election return), broke open cupboards, took away borough documents and returned William Thornhill and William Whitelocke, two Cromwellians as Reading's MPs. The attempted coup d'etat was over in a fortnight. The rightful councillors held an open election on 30 December when 'neere 1000' voted in the Market Place for the 'official' choice of Blagrave and Neville. They then recruited new councillors and re-elected Blagrave as recorder. The quarrel between the two factions rumbled on into 1659, the rebels, faced with a claim for damages of £5,000, struggling but failing to regain their places in the council chamber. The survivors agreed to resign in May 1660 paying in 1662 a fraction of the damages claimed. More significant was a House of Commons ruling that future parliamentary elections for the borough would be decided by all householders. This applied for half a century.[33]

Records show that despite the factional struggles, corporation members continued to manage the town's trade which revived in the 1650s. Market tolls were let for increasing rents, reaching £100 a year in 1658. The court leet met, fining brewers, unlicensed alehouses, producers of poor quality leather, and cloth finishers working on the Sabbath. Sheep pens reappeared in Broad Street and fairs in the Forbury. The price of beer was again fixed according to the price of barley: in 1654 (or perhaps earlier) a penny bought a quart of best and two quarts of small (weaker) beer. Regulations were enforced concerning lanterns outside houses and cleaning water courses, parish surveyors were warned to repair the highways and overseers submitted their accounts. Large entry fines to lease borough properties such as Portmanbrook Meadow and the Butchers' Shambles were levied, rents collected and debts for non-payment pursued.[34]

Much energy was spent in the 1650s on three matters which originated during the war: settling the claims by John Struggill and Thomas Harrison's widow for money borrowed in 1643 for 'loans' to the king; securing the legacy of £4,000 to the borough made in Richard Aldworth's will to found a school, and the post of master of the Free School. The Struggill and Harrison law suits were finally settled in 1657 partly by further loans guaranteed by members of the corporation. In 1646 Richard

Aldworth had bequeathed £4,000 to the borough to board and educate 20 boys, the capital and interest finally reaching Reading in two instalments (partly for security) in November 1659. The money was used to buy an estate in Sherfield on Loddon, Hampshire. William Head of Earley was appointed master and the first scholars chosen early the following year, dressed in their blue uniforms and installed in The Talbot in Silver Street, formerly an inn. The school was soon called the Blue School and later the Bluecoat School.[35]

Settling the headship of the Free School was equally protracted. Several men had come and gone, usually appointed or dismissed for factional reasons. A contest in January 1656 ended with an order from the Lord Protector, overriding the corporation's right to choose and appointing a new master, Thomas Garrard, though William Page, in post in 1643 when the school was sequestered, still lived.[36] In October 1659 when Richard Cromwell's Protectorate was collapsing, the corporation unanimously removed Garrard, restored Robert Jennings (whom a majority of councillors had preferred to Garrard in 1656) and blocked his access to the school, declaring that Cromwell's appointment had been illegal. Garrard proved stubborn, hanging on until threatened in October 1660 with prosecution at the next assizes and bribed with half a year's salary, though the following April he claimed £15 arrears of salary so he could pay legal expenses incurred in defending his post. By then Charles II was restored to the throne and many corporation members had more to worry about than a recalcitrant schoolmaster.

7

A changed economy and society, 1660–1740

T HE Restoration of Charles II in May 1660 saw the continuation of insecure and fractious national and local politics, with religion as divisive an issue as ever at first. After 1690 council business returned to normal. As the economy continued to revive, the manufacture of malt increased as that of cloth declined. Reading's role as a route town, river port and market was enhanced by improvement to transport links.

Population

Reading's population was smaller in Charles II's reign than in his father's, numbering perhaps 5,500 or possibly even 6,000 by his later years. By 1740 it had recovered to reach about 7,500.[1] Some of this increase was undoubtedly caused by immigration. In 1716 in the context of a disputed parliamentary election, 226 men who had served an apprenticeship for seven years were granted their freedom. Of these, 94 were incomers: 39 from London, 24 from Berkshire, 27 from Oxfordshire, and the rest from Surrey, Wiltshire and Buckinghamshire. One in six newcomers to St Mary's parish between 1698 and about 1750 came from a Berkshire village or town, and about one in eight from elsewhere, most from neighbouring counties but a few from as far away as Worcestershire and Gloucestershire.[2]

The great plague of 1665 which had such dire effects on other towns, including Henley, had little impact on Reading. Two parishes recorded lower than average mortality, none from plague; only in St Giles were plague deaths recorded and there only 23, of which six were in one family. The explanation probably lies in early intervention by the council in preventing coaches from bringing passengers and goods from London and appointing searchers to examine suspect victims and confining them in pest houses in St Giles' parish. Indeed, this was to be plague's last appearance in the borough.

In future the main scourge was smallpox, possibly the cause of a severe epidemic in St Giles in 1675. Everywhere it became more virulent and endemic, dreaded because even if it were not fatal it wreaked havoc

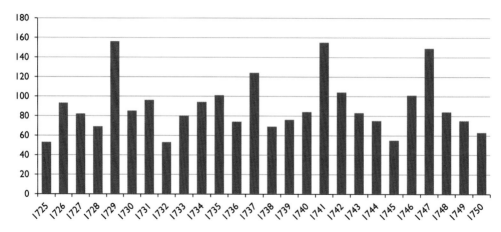

St Mary's burials,
1725–1750.

on the sufferer's skin. In the later eighteenth century teenage lads and maidservants seeking work often included 'have had the smallpox' in their newspaper advertisements. Until about 1750 a series of epidemics which also included influenza and new strains of typhus nullified national and local population growth. Smallpox was prevalent in some south-east counties throughout the 1720s, notably 1727–29 and 1735–39, hitting Reading in 1729. John Loveday of Caversham wrote in August that year, ''tis a very sickly time about us; several are down with the Small-Pox and Fever,' the latter probably typhus or influenza. St Giles' parish register noted that smallpox caused 136 deaths between 2 April and October, 54% of the parish total. St Mary with 156 burials was also affected. Many children died during an epidemic in 1737 in St Laurence and St Giles; infant and childhood deaths were all too frequent at this period. In 1717 Edward Belson, a Quaker and a distiller, noted the death of his daughter, Rachel, aged ten days and ten hours, and two-thirds of the victims of the smallpox epidemic of 1747 in St Laurence were children. The freezing winter of 1739–40, and the cold, wet summer of 1740 heralded another period of high mortality, especially in 1741, possibly from smallpox, influenza and typhus, and in 1747 in St Giles 54% of burials were attributed solely to smallpox.[3]

In periods of food shortages and high prices, the death rate tended to increase, especially during the 'Little Ice Age', the decades before and after 1700 when the climate became colder and wetter. Harvests were increasingly poor from 1657, the worst in 1661 when corn prices rose by nearly 60%. In London a quarter loaf (about 4 lbs weight) cost more than at any time between 1620 and 1760. Other runs of bad harvests occurred in 1695–98 and 1708–11 when London bread prices several times exceeded 8d. a loaf. In 1709 the price of a gallon loaf (8 lbs) 'of the 2nd sort' in Reading rose from 18d. in July to 19½d. in September. There were several disastrous harvest failures in the 1730s and dearth in 1740.[4]

Society in the 1660s and after

A limited view of the town's social structure at the beginning of the period can be gained from the records of a new national tax, first imposed in 1662, the Hearth Tax. Apart from a few exempt trades and certain poor individuals, an annual tax of two shillings, payable half yearly, was imposed on occupiers of properties for each hearth or chimney. It was collected by the local constable who sent the money and the returns via the sheriff to the Exchequer except for 1666–69.[5] The number of hearths in a house can provide a rough estimate of wealth and social status, with ownership of three usually denoting craftsmen, the 'middling sort', and more than three, the 'better sort', gentry, merchants and wealthy master craftsmen. The table shows hearths and households in Reading in the early 1660s.

Number of taxpayers in each parish	Number of hearths						Total households
	10+	6+	4/5	3	2	1	
St Giles	3	17	28	12	30	6	96
St Laurence	7	24	53	41	55	12	192
St Mary	4	15	33	26	40	7	125
Total	14	56	114	79	125	25	413

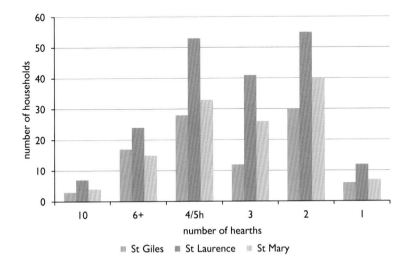

Hearth Tax, 1662–64.

The Reading returns seem to be seriously defective and therefore not a complete reflection of society. We would expect to find over 1,200 households in a population of 5,500, yet only 413 taxpaying households were listed with another seven in St Laurence returned as 'poore and noe distresse [distraint] to be had'. The other 800 or so households with possibly two out of three townspeople were not recorded, the most plausible explanation being that they were too poor to be taxed because they did not pay church or poor rate. Massive tax evasion is possible, though unlikely.[6] If the returns are accurate, and Reading may have been one of the many communities which did not record those exempt from payment, they suggest that two-thirds of its households may have been in poverty. If so, Reading's wealth was even more unequally distributed in the 1660s than in the 1520s.

At the top end of the social scale, the houses with many hearths belonged to the wealthy. Fifty-eight men and two women, Lady Vachell and Lady Knollys occupied houses with six hearths or more; borough steward, Edward Dalby's house had ten. Seven members of the 1660 corporation also had six or more hearths and none had fewer than three. The vicarages of St Giles and St Laurence had four and eight hearths respectively. One or two buildings with many hearths, such as that belonging to Humphrey Maston, were inns; the Free School had seven. The occupations of the heads of some households with four or five fireplaces can be identified, most being clothiers, retailers (mercers, drapers, grocers) and victuallers including at least five maltsters. St Laurence's parish housed the largest number of professionals so far identified: the borough steward, the schoolmaster, two apothecaries, a surgeon and eight other gentlemen.

A changing economy

The tax also reflects the changing economy of the borough as Reading slowly evolved from a town reliant on cloth manufacture to one noted for processing and trading in corn. The cloth industry was still significant; despite the vicissitudes of the 1620s and 1630s and the destruction caused by war, loans were made to cloth workers, and boys were apprenticed to the trade into the 1690s. Clothiers as mayor and five of the twelve aldermen dominated the corporation in 1660. The Hearth Tax returns show that more clothiers (seven) occupied houses with six or more hearths than did other tradesmen. One, Peter Horne (died 1663) had fully equipped workshops with dyed and white wool and completed cloths worth over £360 and a total estate of over £577. Stephen Attwater had purchased land and the lease of the wharf and warehouses at High Bridge and Richard James' leases, credits, workshops, wool and household goods amounted to over £783 in addition to his freehold property.[7] Despite the

The garden side of Watlington House, built in 1688 for Samuel Watlington, clothier and alderman. (JD)

council's petition to the House of Commons in 1698 to take measures to encourage woollen manufacturing trades, however, the decline of the cloth industry continued inexorably as fashions changed. Before 1700 about 20% of the workforce was employed producing cloth (the last broadweaver having been enrolled as a freeman in 1694), 14% before 1730 and a mere 6.5% by the middle of the eighteenth century. Modest amounts of other fabrics, felt and linen, were produced and some weavers turned to rug making. A short-lived sail-cloth industry established by Sir Owen Buckingham in rooms at the Oracle provided employment for some former cloth workers.[8] In 1724 Defoe noted only a 'remnant' of the cloth industry but a great trade in malt.

There had been maltsters in the borough before the Civil War if only to supply the buoyant brewing trade, and St Giles' Mill was grinding malt in Elizabeth's reign. In the first four decades after the Restoration, however, some became important in town politics and increasingly wealthy; two were aldermen in 1660 and four made bequests worth over £1,000 between 1675 and 1698.[9] Reading was not alone in experiencing a flourishing malting industry; the same was true of other riverside towns, especially Abingdon, Henley and Newbury. They had access to the wheat and barley produced by the rich arable lands of Berkshire and the adjacent counties, and to the Thames which provided a highway to London, whose expanding population (possibly 575,000 in 1700) had an insatiable appetite for foodstuffs and fuel from the English regions. In exchange there were ready markets in the borough's hinterland for the capital's exports: sea-coal, imported luxuries and the products of its skilled craftsmen. Reading's location had always made it an important inland port and as its cloth industry decayed, its trading role became relatively more important.

Not for the first or the last time the town survived and eventually prospered by adapting to changing circumstances. The growth in the river trade boosted the income from tolls on barge traffic and made the lease of Reading's wharf and its warehouses increasingly profitable for the corporation and lessees. By 1715 purchase of the lease of the wharves cost £150 and produced £150 a year income for the lessee. Over the same period the rent due from the lessee of the tolls on corn and malt sold in the Market Place remained static: £110 per annum for seven years in 1665, and the same for three years in 1695 with a token £10 entry fine. The rent was unchanged in 1702 and 1720 though the fine was £45. It was not increased until 1741, to £210. The explanation may lie in the growing practice of trading by sample. Four fairs were still held in the Forbury with an unchanging income of £4 for the borough's coffers.[10]

The retail sector began to diversify as mercers, grocers and drapers were joined by cheesemongers, mealmen and corn chandlers. The sale of farm produce, especially corn, was increasingly taken over by these middlemen, many of whom traded comfortably by sample in several large, well-appointed hostelries instead of in the open market. However, traditional trades catering for the every-day needs of the community remained strong, with food and drink employing about 18% of the town's workers and the production of leather and leather goods still an important factor in the economy.

Further evidence of how developments in manufacture, consumer goods and transport were beginning to affect the town's economy appears in 1715. The corporation Diary for that year lists 226 men who had served an apprenticeship and applied for admission to the freedom of the borough in order to vote in a contested parliamentary election. Locally sourced agricultural products remained the raw materials of almost all crafts especially for the leading trade, leather, especially its 28 shoemakers, but also curriers, tanners and glovers. Textiles were still important, but only 24 craftsmen were producing broadcloth. Another 18 were described as 'weaver', and nine more produced fabrics to meet changing tastes – serge, plush (used to make men's coats and breeches) and stuff. Joiners who produced more elegant 'joined' furniture outnumbered carpenters two to one.[11]

Employment for the three bargemasters, the boat builder and the coachbuilder on the list increased as a result of two developments

The Kennet
& Avon Canal
approaching
High Bridge
from the east.
(JD)

in transport from which Reading's whole economy would later profit: the canalisation of the Kennet and improvements to the Great West Road. Proposals in a private bill introduced into parliament in 1708 to straighten the winding Kennet making it navigable from Reading Wharf to Newbury were supported by towns upstream but opposed by the borough as a threat to its economy since Newbury would become a serious competitor in the London trade. Others including millers also objected. Their opposition during the Bill's tortuous passage through parliament was persistent. In January 1710 the corporation gave the freedom of the borough to Berkshire MP, Sir John Stonehouse, for his 'great service' in supporting their cause in the House, and a series of payments to Simon Finch and others to oppose the measure, amounting to over £87. Despite this, the Bill allowing its promoters to make cuts reducing the length of the winding Kennet between the towns by half, build bridges and make locks and towpaths became law on 21 September 1715. When legal means failed Reading continued its opposition with brute force. In 1720 a mob, including the mayor, destroyed some of the canal structures; in 1725 another mob of about 300 attacked a barge in Reading loaded with flour and cheese and another smaller group held up barges at Sheffield Mills near Theale. Death threats were made

Turnpike roads enhanced Reading's importance as a route centre.

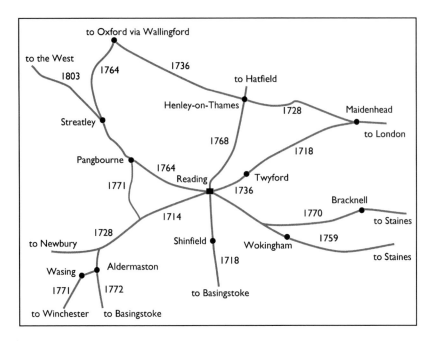

against a barge owner of Maidenhead should he attempt to trade with Newbury. Meanwhile, the canal proprietors began constructing the cuts and building the turf-sided locks, weirs and towpaths and despite the attacks the canal was completed in 1723. Eventually, as trade through the borough's waterways increased, Reading came to see the enterprise as a benefit rather than a threat. Between 1731 and 1760 about 9% of will-makers were engaged in the river trade.[12]

While the Kennet bill was being contested, major improvements to the county's roads were underway with which the corporation had no complaint. Repairs to major roads were still being carried out under the terms of an Act of 1556 requiring parishes to keep the highways in repair using labour and equipment supplied by parishioners. The system was never really satisfactory and completely failed to meet the demands of a growing economy. As with the waterways, improvements were initiated by private investors and achieved by private Acts of Parliament, beginning in the 1660s, allowing groups of concerned individuals to set up trusts to improve a stretch a road, charge travellers a fee at toll gates called turnpikes, and use the proceeds for road repairs, salaries and dividends to investors.

Between 1707 and 1743 a series of Acts was passed for the improving sections of the Great West Road; those for the section westward from Reading to Puntfield (Theale) and eastward to Twyford were passed in 1714 and 1736 respectively. By the latter date the process was complete from Hyde Park Corner to Marlborough, Wiltshire. Other

Map of Reading by John Rocque, 1761.

highways, the Forest Road through Windsor to London, and the north–south roads through the borough, were also 'turnpiked'. Inevitably the developments affected the town's employment patterns. In addition to twelve blacksmiths, seven wheelwrights and three coach makers at work in 1715, will evidence shows that other trades dependent on coach travel, including innkeeping, grew albeit slowly between 1701 and 1760, while those providing food, including food for travellers, doubled.[13] In 1700 only three coachmen operated in the town but stage coaches were operating by about 1750.

National and urban politics and the work of the corporation

Two elements, continuity and insecurity, categorise the work of the corporation before about 1689. Its traditional role – keeping order, collecting rents, leasing and maintaining borough property, repairing bridges, controlling markets, administering urban charities including schools and almshouses, and ensuring that the poor were treated according to their perceived desserts – dominate the minutes of its meetings. However, occasional entries reveal the effects of unstable national politics on a local community. As in the past, political affiliation and religious allegiance were inseparable, but to treat them separately will make for greater clarity.

Despite the presbyterian character of the corporation, royalist sentiment dominated the town, as the country, in 1660. Together an electorate of about 1,100 unanimously elected John Blagrave (Daniel's uncle) of Bulmershe and Southcote and Thomas Rich of Sonning, two royalists, to represent the borough in the Convention Parliament, summoned to determine the political settlement. Then and for the next century Reading was a 'barometer constituency', its MPs always on the 'winning side' although as yet there were no party labels.[14]

The king's accession was proclaimed 'with greate solemnity and rejoicing' on 10 May 1660 on a stage specially erected in the Market Place, his coronation the following April being marked by a bonfire and supplies of beer for the townsfolk. Wisely, the borough sent him a 'voluntary gift' of £50. Whether or not they shared the general rejoicing at the king's return or were reassured by his declarations of 'liberty to tender consciences' and pardon for most of his father's opponents, nine of the corporation swore the oath of allegiance and supremacy. The royal arms, removed from the mace during the Commonwealth, were restored, and Daniel Blagrave was replaced as steward by royalist Edward Dalby. In 1661, elections for the so-called Cavalier Parliament also returned two royalists, Sir Thomas Dolman of Shaw House and Richard Aldworth of Ruscombe. Otherwise it was business as usual with the school, the poor and borough charities on the agenda.[15] The calm did not last.

In tandem with its determination to restore a pure Anglican Church of England, the Cavalier Parliament's Corporation Act set up commissions to evict all town officials who would not swear an oath of allegiance, declare the Solemn League and Covenant invalid and take the Anglican sacrament. In Reading on 27 May 1662 the newly elected mayor, Samuel Jemmatt, seven aldermen and six assistants were removed. George Thorne was installed as mayor, 'loyal' assistants were promoted to aldermen, and wealthy men appointed to the council.[16]

It was this purged corporation that welcomed Charles to Reading on 27 August 1663, meeting the royal party in Ort Lane and presenting the king with £50 in gold coins, another £30 to the queen, and £37 6s. demanded by royal servants. Almost half of this was borrowed. The same year the corporation judiciously asked Bulstrode Whitelocke to resign and chose as high steward George Monck, Duke of Albemarle, one of the king's most loyal supporters and a privy councillor. Soon the regime demonstrated its determination to ensure the loyalty of the boroughs. In Reading Sir William Armorer, a ruthless persecutor of dissent, was imposed on the borough as magistrate and in attendance at council meetings. Corporations were expected to apply for a new charter, Reading finally succumbing to pressure in May 1667, borrowing again to meet the £229 17s. 9d. fee. The borough's gains were small, the Crown's considerable: all borough officials had to take the oath of supremacy, and the appointment of future stewards needed royal approval. The corporation soon commissioned the making of an 'effigy' of Archbishop Laud, later set up with his portrait in the council chamber. Many years later they bought a copy of his autobiography. With commendable efficiency they had all their archives listed, including earlier charters and counterparts of leases, some dating from the time of the abbey, had a bushel measure

A portrait of Archbishop Laud presented to the borough by Dr Peter Mews, vicar of St Mary, 1667.
Artist unknown.
(RM)

sealed 'according to the standard of Winchester' from which another was made to be the market bushel for Reading, and ruled that any unpaid loans from a borough charity to a craftsman would be recovered from his guarantors.[17]

Although such practical matters remained their major concern, religious divisions were never far below the surface. On 30 July 1670 all ten aldermen voted to remove Samuel Howse, a prominent dissenter, from the council. Fear of the return of popery, especially given the prospect of Charles' Catholic brother James succeeding him, dominated national politics in the 1670s and early 1680s. Between 1679 and 1681 attempts were made in parliament to exclude James from the succession in favour of the king's illegitimate son, the Duke of Monmouth, the so-called Exclusion Crisis. Nationally and locally, men driven by deep religious differences had begun to take sides, forming unstable groups, nicknamed Tories and Whigs. Tories supported the Established Church and traditional monarchical government; Whigs (Exclusionists) tolerated dissenters, and defended the role of parliament in government. Reading Corporation included men from both groups, Tories forming the majority. However, the 'patriotic and Protestant zeal' of the borough electorate secured the return of two 'Exclusionist' MPs, John Blagrave and Nathan Knight, in three elections between 1679 and 1681. After the attempt at exclusion failed, support for the king nationally increased; the Tory majority on the council sent him a fulsome loyal address in 1683.[18]

In February 1685 James II succeeded his brother. Reading duly mirrored the national mood by sending two Tories to his first parliament. Later that year, the corporation applied for a new charter, granted in 1686. It was almost identical to that of 1667 except that the mayor had a casting vote in the event of a tie, and, more important, the Crown reserved the right to remove the steward, now called the recorder, and any member of the corporation. In 1687 James commanded that 'unreliable' councillors in all boroughs should resign or be dismissed, to be replaced by more biddable men. Reading's new Corporation included at least one Catholic.[19]

On 30 July 1688 the chamberlains paid for wine drunk, loyally or otherwise, by the corporation at the Ship Inn 'at the day of rejoicing for the birth on 10 June of the Prince of Wales', the future Prince Charles Edward, the 'Old Pretender', which opened the possibility of a Catholic succession and provoked a political crisis. To thwart James' religious policies, a small group of national politicians invited the king's son-in-law, William of Orange to invade. He landed at Torbay on 5 November and marched eastwards. James sent a large force including many Irish to Reading to hold the town against William's advance. Rumours that the Irish would massacre them drove some townspeople to send a request for help from the invaders who on 10 December routed James' troops in what was called 'The Reading Skirmish', leaving six

Richard Aldworth, founder of the Bluecoat School, 1646; an engraving from an original formerly in the council chamber. (Man)

Irish including their captain and two of William's men to be buried in St Giles' churchyard. Many others died following their flight towards Twyford. James himself fled to France allowing a new parliament, to which Reading's voters sent two Whig members, to offer the throne to William (and his wife Mary). England's 'Glorious Revolution' had produced a profound change in government. Some borough politicians found the new regime unacceptable and it was several years before the full complement of Reading aldermen took office but, bowing to the inevitable, the remnant belatedly proclaimed the new king and queen in June, 1689. When William came through Reading in September the following year, he was greeted by the corporation in traditional style and presented with a purse containing 40 gold pieces.[20]

After 1690 more mundane activities, of equal if not more importance for the townspeople, took precedence. Mention was made in the last chapter of the opening of the Blue School in 1660, at first called 'Mr Aldworth's Hospital'. The following year the first boys to leave

The Thames Highway

Print, drawn and engraved by Charles Tomkins, 1791,
of the view through the inner gateway of the abbey towards the Thames with a barge

Reading, a very large and wealthy town, handsomely built, the inhabitants rich, and driving a very great trade. … Their chief trade is by this water-navigation to and from London, though they have necessarily a great trade into the country [i.e. county], for the consumption of the goods they bring by their barges from London, and particularly coals, salt, grocery wares [imported luxuries], tobacco, oils, and all heavy goods. They send from thence to London by these barges, very great quantities of malt, and meal, and these are the two principal articles of their loadings, of which, so large are those barges, that some of them, as I was told, bring a thousand or twelve hundred quarters of malt at a time. … They also send very great quantities of timber … for building merchant ships …'

Source: Daniel Defoe, A Tour Through the Whole Island of Great Britain, 1724–26 (Everyman edn, 1974), 291–2.

were apprenticed to two clothiers, their blue coats handed down to newcomers. A further endowment from Sir Thomas Rich, Reading's MP in 1666, supported six more boys, three each from Sonning and Reading. Bequests by William Malthus in 1700 provided for ten scholars and John West in 1723 six more, all monies being invested in land. In 1723 the school was rebuilt and the corporation opened another smaller school in converted houses in Chain Lane, supported by a bequest from John Hall, an apothecary and former townsman.[21]

Of greater significance was the corporation's success in fighting off yet another claim by the governors of Christ's Hospital in October 1689 to secure the remaining capital of the Kendrick endowment. Complaints about its misuse had already surfaced in 1673 because the Oracle was occupied by practitioners of many trades, not all of whom used loans from the charity to employ the poor, although councillors made some effort over the next decades to ensure that more did so. More serious peculation involved large, apparently unsecured, loans granted to councillors and their associates, especially one of £500 to David Webb and Ralph Avelin repayable at six months' notice to be used to employ clothworkers in the Oracle. (Webb's son was chosen as a White scholar in 1677, more favouritism.) Concerns about the security of the loan culminated in the corporation's demand for repayment by 1 May 1682. The debt was still outstanding when Webb died insolvent in April 1690 owing the borough £600 13s. 10d. of which the corporation eventually recovered just £204 7s. 8d. In the face of this evidence, the borough did not deserve the reprieve it gained against Christ's Hospital, although its records show a wish to improve, including a scheme in 1693 to set the poor to work on different fabrics, linen, sacking, straw hats or 'what is best'. The following February they gave tradesmen of each parish £20 to apprentice poor boys and in 1695 £200 each to the parishes to employ those poor receiving relief. They also installed looms in the Oracle.[22]

Corruption was all the more serious given the extent of poverty in the town. The corporation's belated attempts in the 1690s to use the Kendrick bequest as intended may have been as much a reaction to the misery caused by the poor harvests, harsh weather and industrial depression of this decade as fear of losing the endowment. They regularly petitioned the government to introduce measures to help the declining cloth industry as unemployment caused the poor rate to soar. It was his willingness to provide employment by setting up a sailcloth factory in Reading that 'virtually guaranteed' Sir Owen Buckingham's election as borough MP in 1698.[23]

In addition to managing the lands purchased with the remaining capital of the Kendrick charity and the Bray property bequeathed by Archbishop Laud, the corporation eventually acquired responsibility for all the Blue School endowments. The charities' rental income, excluding about £360 from Kendrick lands, was almost £600 in 1701–02, rising to almost £900 by the end of the period, from which the demands of the various charities and the school had to be met. Borough rents, when they can be distinguished from those of the charities, rarely exceeded £480 though during the 1660s this was sufficient to generate a small surplus.[24]

Councillors had shown more foresight in purchasing early in 1665 two 'engines' or 'Instrumentes to convey water upon howses in case of any danger … by fire', followed three years later by the appointment of Daniel Quirke, provided with a leather coat, an iron hat and two assistants, as the town's first fire fighter. However, it was the 'great diligence of many poor men' quenching the flames which stopped the spread of a conflagration that broke out on 5 November 1681 when celebrations commemorating the Gunpowder Plot in the Market Place included fireworks, one of which fell on a thatched stable and spread to several properties. The church-wardens organised a collection to reward the labourers and watchmen and to repair the damage, and the corporation purchased hooks and chains to pull down burning buildings in future.[25] No mention is made of the source of the water for fire fighting but on 13 March 1695 the corporation authorised a scheme to provide domestic water. Eventually on 13 July 1697 part of Mill Orchard adjoining St Giles' Mill was leased for 1,000 years by George Blagrave of Bulmershe to Ambrose Crowley, ironmonger of Stonebridge, Gloucestershire and four others. They were to build a structure to house an 'engine' driven by water from the Mill Stream to pump water from the Kennet through pipes made from elm along Mill Lane, Horn Street and London Street to a cistern on Browne's Hill. This was to be the only piped water supply for the townspeople until the 1850s.[26]

Less praiseworthy is the role of the corporation in the parliamentary elections of the period, one of 'flagrant corruption and sharp practice'. As returning officer, the mayor could favour one side, councillors were open to bribery, the electors were courted with feasts and prodigious amounts of cash, and both sides used various means to ensure a supportive electorate. In 1708 the House of Commons determined that freemen and householders, numbering about 1,500, could vote. The 'wholesale bribery' of the electorate which followed caused the Commons to reduce this to the 500 or so householders who paid scot and lot (effectively ratepayers). Even so, national political rivalries and the ambition of local gentry sufficed to make corrupt practices, though less blatant, essential for success in the polls.[27]

Anglicanism and the birth of nonconformity

The return of the monarchy brought with it a determination by the majority of royalist MPs in the Cavalier Parliament (1661–64) to restore the Anglican Church of England and force out those who did not accept its teaching and authority, called nonconformists or dissenters.[28] A series of Acts, referred by historians as the Clarendon Code, not only reversed the religious changes of the previous twenty years but reserved all secular and religious offices to conformists. An Act of Uniformity required all teachers in schools and universities and all clergy to take the oath of supremacy and allegiance and receive communion in the Anglican rite; those refusing were ejected from their posts or livings. Clergy were also required to use in worship only the *Book of Common Prayer* as revised in 1662. Some who had been ministers in the State Church when it was presbyterian refused to take the oath or agree to use the Prayer Book but since only one in five clergy nationally and 30 of 150 in Berkshire were ejected, it seems most either did not have strong convictions or had served parishes during the Commonwealth period which had preserved something of the old ways. Reading's clergy were typical: Christopher Fowler was ejected from St Mary; Thomas Tuer was restored to St Laurence (Simon Ford having resigned in 1659) and William Jemmatt was installed in St Giles, in 1649, taking the oath of allegiance and living until 1678.

Fowler was a Presbyterian. With the Independents (later called Congregationalists), Presbyterians formed the largest nonconformist group nationally, both Calvinist in belief, though Presbyterians had a structured church and the Congregationalists autonomous congregations. At first in Reading they formed a single, congregation led by Fowler. Under the Conventicle Act of 1664 any dissenting meeting for worship (a 'conventicle') attended by more than five people was illegal if not conducted according to the *Book of Common Prayer*; those attending risked fines or imprisonment. Whether the Presbyterians had a meeting place in Broad Street in 1662 is impossible to verify, although Fowler seems to have stayed in Reading until the Five Mile Act of 1665 made it illegal for ejected ministers to come within five miles of their former parishes, and those who had not taken the necessary oaths to come within five miles of any town. Baptists, who did not believe in infant baptism, had been present in the borough, it is claimed, since about 1640 though the first written record dates from 1656. In the 1660s they appear to have worshipped in a meeting house in Pigney (Pinkneys) Lane.

Sources differ about the strength of this nonconformity. Churchwardens of the three parishes reported very little dissent, absentees from Sunday service never reaching double figures. Perhaps they were unwilling to inform on their neighbours or draw the attention of the authorities to

Broad Street
Independent
Chapel, 1880–91,
before additions
to the entrance.
(RL)

their parishes. Three conventicles were reported in a survey of 1669 ordered by Gilbert Selden, Archbishop of Canterbury: at Katesgrove, St Giles' parish, hundreds 'of severall sorts and conditions, Some of good fashion' heard sermons by 'poore men' from London and elsewhere. The other two, attended by tradesmen and their families, were held in private houses, one preacher being John Pordage. Another ecclesiastical census of 1676 named after Henry Compton, Bishop of London, reported 40 nonconformists in the parish of St Mary and 100 in St Laurence, suspiciously round numbers. No return for St Giles survives. It has been suggested that this census underestimated the strength of nonconformity.[29]

Dissenters were still worshipping illegally in the borough into the next decade. At the 1682 Epiphany quarter sessions 46 men were found guilty of 'unlawful assembly', possibly a conventicle, and fined far more than the law required. The following October and again in January 1683, 'divers persons' were convicted of attending 'seditious conventicles'. Those named were merchants, craftsmen and professionals. Several, including Charles Calverley, mercer, Thomas Chesterman, clothworker, and John Browne, mealman, were imprisoned for refusing to pay. Others had their corn distrained (confiscated) though sympathisers prevented it being sold in the Market Place saying it was 'Stollen goods'.[30]

The Toleration Act of 1689 allowed dissenters, except Baptists and Roman Catholics, to apply to the magistrates in quarter sessions or to the bishop for a licence to worship legally. Unfortunately very few licensing records for the borough survive although a Mr Duce is said to have preached to a very large congregation in the town in the 1690s and the Presbyterians had two chapels before 1729.[31]

Quakers, or the Society of Friends, had worshipped in Reading since 1654 despite severe persecution. Their goods were often distrained because they refused to pay tithes but in the 1660s greater suffering was inflicted by Sir William Armorer, county and borough JP, who seems to have taken fiendish delight in tormenting them physically and psychologically, even assaulting and imprisoning children and young women. The Friends were a sober, respectable people of the 'middling sort', tradesmen and craftsmen like William Coale, carpenter and John Boult, shoemaker. More prosperous was Thomas Curtis, woollen draper who occupied a ten-hearthed house in Sun Lane which accommodated large numbers of worshippers. In 1660 he leased from the corporation a plot in the Orts for a burial ground and in 1673 helped finance the building of a meeting house in Back Lane. A setback came in 1681 when a challenge to the leadership of George Fox developed into a schism among the Friends lasting well over three decades. The orthodox (Fox) meeting had a licensed meeting house in London Street by 1692 though the first surviving licence for worship in their permanent home on land bought in Church Lane in 1714 dates from 1728.[32]

Poverty, vagrancy and crime

Although they are almost invisible in the Hearth Tax returns, the poor were highly visible in the town. Like other communities, Reading removed any poor who were not entitled to relief, and in 1677 ordering those receiving poor relief to wear badges 'that they may be better distinguished from other poor'. Very few records of the overseers of the poor survive, but enough to suggest that the system operated as it had before 1642. Parishioners and property owners paid according to their means; there is a strong correlation between the highest ratepayers and those with three- to six-hearth houses. Many paid just a few shillings a year. In St Giles the overseers collected as much as was needed, varying from nearly £220 in 1663–64 to over £358 in 1680–81. 'Pensioners' on permanent relief received a small weekly sum and those in sudden urgent need a 'casual payment'. Each year the overseers also distributed the parish share of the Kendrick charity, amounting in 1663 to £15 15s. 6d., mostly at 6d. or a shilling each to 240 poor men and women, and in 1676 a few pounds from other endowments and bequests on 'Ester morn' to 64 widows, and 44 mainly old men.[33]

Each parish had its own overseers, but the borough had overall responsibility for dealing with the poor. It continued to maintain the house of correction, appointing and paying the keeper to set the able-bodied idle, vagrants and 'lewd' people' and unmarried mothers on work including grinding corn with a quern. Paupers without legal settlement in the borough were removed by the 'cripple carrier', who provided straw beds and lodging for homeless, sick poor. Begging poor were rounded up by the bellman, sent to the Oracle and put to work with materials provided from the Kendrick charity. A growing number of charitable bequests to the borough were used to apprentice poor boys or send them to the Blue School, reward faithful servant girls, distribute doles of money and clothes to the aged poor, and fill places in the almshouses.[34]

The needy sometimes resorted to crime: if apprehended they would be tried by the judges at the assizes. One such was Ambrose Strange, a farm worker aged 23, who in the course of a robbery committed murder and was sentenced to be hanged on Saturday, 11 March 1738. As was customary, his body was left hanging in chains. This was not a squeamish age. The records do not say why at the Reading spring assizes in 1720 a 'blackmoor' and three others were condemned and publicly hanged. Many of these unfortunates were buried in St Mary's churchyard.[35]

A changing culture: 'consumer revolution'?

Luxury goods, which were already appearing in many urban households, suggest that in common with other larger towns Reading already enjoyed what has been called a 'consumer revolution' well before 1700.[36] Feather mattresses, 'joined' furniture and pewter chamber pots, which had been symbols of an affluent lifestyle in the borough before 1640, were commonplace among the 'middling sort' in Restoration Reading, as were a set of leather chairs or a chest of drawers. The richer 'better sort' had higher aspirations: to own a looking glass, a clock, a smoothing iron, a jack to turn the spit and a fireplace to burn coal. Jewellers in the town stocked silver watches, gilt snuff boxes, pairs of silver shoe buckles and amber necklaces for rich customers such as the maltster, James Cowdrey. Some men owned books, available from John Chandler's bookshop, which stocked 'books of all sorts'. Francis Tassell, milliner, sold fashionable lightweight fabrics such as dimity which were beginning to supersede wool, and waistcoats, trousers and breeches for men and boys. At least two tobacconists and four apothecaries in the 1680s and 1690s sold tobacco, now cheap enough to import in huge quantities and frequently consumed as snuff.[37]

Some joiners worked in walnut, now the fashionable wood. Edward Belson's second-hand bed was made of walnut, as perhaps was the swing frame which held his looking glass, although there is no record of a craftsman who could have hung the 'printed paper to hang our best room' which he bought in 1710. Changing fashions in fabrics and furniture were

matched by new modes of dress. In 1715 there was just one maker each of periwigs, stays and bodices, but more would follow. They and the two watch- and two clock-makers, and the bookbinder catered for growing numbers of the upwardly mobile 'middling sort'.

Their interest in national and international news had been satisfied by the London press before Reading gained its first newspaper in 1723, late compared with towns such as Worcester and Stamford, but way ahead of other Berkshire towns, and 30 years ahead of Oxford. William Parkes and David Kinner first published *The Reading Mercury and Weekly Entertainer* on Monday 8 July 1723. They intended to provide for 'Three-Half-Pence per Week' useful information from London, the price of corn in local market towns and news items. Truly local reporting only appeared after about 1750 and even then advertisements, being more profitable, occupied most of the space.[38]

Before the arrival of *The Reading Mercury*, London newspapers were provided in coffee houses. The first recorded in Reading seems to have been the Bear Coffee House, probably in the inn of that name in 1681. By the time Edward Belson came to write his diary, there were at least two, John Paise's and Will's. In his bachelor days Belson found the coffee house a congenial place to socialise and catch up with the news.

Print and engraving by Charles Tomkins of the inner gateway of the abbey, 1791. The present structure dates from 1862, when the Gateway was reconstructed after it had collapsed. (RL)

Entrance side to Watlington House, remodelled *c.*1720. (JD)

Facsimile of No. 1, July 8th, 1723

VOL. I.   Numb. 1.

THE
Reading Mercury
OR
Weekly Entertainer.

Monday *July* 8, 1723.   (*To be continued Weekly.*)

READING:

Printed by W. PARKS, and D. KINNIER, next Door to the *Saracen's-Head*, in *High-street*: Where all manner of Printing Buſineſs is handſomely done, as Books, Advertiſements, Summons, Subpœnas, Funeral-Tickets, &c. Shop keepers Bills are done here after the beſt manner, with the Prints of their Signs, or other proper Ornaments. Alſo Gentlemen may have their Coats of Arms, or other Fanſies curiouſly cut in Wood, or engrav'd in Mettal.
[*Price of this Paper, Three-Half-Pence per Week*]

Front page of *The Reading Mercury* first edition, 1723.

He recorded in July 1708 'at coffee house to read … the great victory obtained by the Duke of Marlborough in the Netherlands'. Thereafter he usually spent two pence at each visit, a penny for a dish of coffee and another for 'reading the Mercury', a London paper. John Loveday wrote of going to the coffee house in 1729. Others followed, usually set up in reputable inns. On 18 March 1745 a 'coffee room' opened at the George where coffee, tea or punch could be drunk, the London newspapers read, and good conversation enjoyed. The Mitre followed suit becoming the preferred meeting place of a number of the Reading intelligentsia, including Loveday and his acquaintances: James Merrick a biblical scholar and writer, Robert Bolton, vicar of St Mary, a notable theologian, bibliophile and dean of Carlisle, as well as country gentry in town for sessions or assizes. However, coffee houses were few, far outnumbered by the traditional alehouses with no claim to elegance or demands on literacy: 73 were recorded in 1661.[39]

John Loveday was one of a number of country gentlemen who frequented the town. They in turn gave some credence to its pretension to gentility, echoed in the increasing number of councillors described in their wills as 'gentleman'. They and their ladies favoured an entertainment which began in this period, the assembly, an evening of polite conversation, music, dancing and refreshments which in Reading was occasionally held in the town hall from at least 1727 when Loveday was present. An order of the corporation in 1726 forbidding the letting of the hall to strolling players and puppet shows, ostensibly to prevent corruption of youth and damage to property, was more likely an attempt to preserve this genteel image.[40] It was an image which would strengthen over the following decades.

High Bridge
approached on the
Kennet from the
west. This bridge
has connected the
Market Place and
London Street
since 1787.

An 1840 print
of St Mary's
Episcopal Chapel,
Castle Street.

8

Politics, commerce and improvement, 1740–1835

A FTER the turbulence of the Stuart era, Reading in the eighteenth century settled into a more settled, even moribund political mode. There was little industrial progress, but commercially the infrastructure for prosperity in the following decades was being developed, allowing the borough to capitalise on its location. Meanwhile, something of the fashionable culture and religious enthusiasm of the age rubbed off on Reading, attracting local gentry and erudite preachers. However, poverty and squalor remained intractable problems throughout the period.

Population

The borough's population in 1740 was about 7,500; the national total is estimated as 5.97 million. The first national census of 1801 provides a better estimate. Reading, with 9,742, had grown faster than the national average and by 1831 had grown to 16,048. The increase was greatest in St Mary's parish where the population more than doubled, St Giles' rose by almost 40% and St Laurence's by 27%. Though still a minnow compared with the great cities of the Midlands and the North, Reading

View of Reading from St Peter's Hill, *c.*1790–99. (Print published J. & J. Boydell, 'An History of the River Thames', 1794–96) (RL)

was already more than a modest-sized market town and towered over the other Berkshire boroughs, being described in 1761 as 'the Shire Town'.[1] Some of this growth was the result of migration, of which there is some evidence, although a systematic study of this is not possible until the 1851 census.

Both in the borough and the nation, population expansion came in what is called 'a period of sustained growth' after the mid-eighteenth century and continued into and throughout the nineteenth century, although smallpox long remained a recurring problem. An outbreak in the autumn and spring of 1774–75 in St Giles seems to have prompted the corporation to have 1,000 handbills printed threatening to prosecute anyone inoculating strangers, spreading the infection, or providing lodgings for vagrants.[2]

Borough government

'Moribund' is probably not a wholly unfair description of the corporation for most of the period, discussions at its meetings being similar to those of the sixteenth century, though after about 1785 they were galvanised into a spate of activity. The Corporation Diary shows that the critical comments made of their stewardship in 1833 by the commission on the reform of the boroughs are valid for most of the period, though in this respect Reading was not unlike many towns, large and small. Political control was still in the hands of those with economic power, most councillors belonging to the town's leading trades, especially brewing and retail, although several styled themselves 'gentleman'. A few family names, senior and junior appear frequently making nepotism a strong possibility in this self-perpetuating oligarchy with lifelong council membership – on average councillors served over 23 years – tending to create a gerontocracy.[3]

The corporation's powers and duties were those relevant to the needs of an earlier age, not to a town with growing commercial and cultural aspirations. Like other boroughs, Reading was not entitled by its charters to undertake those urban improvements which by the early nineteenth century were patently necessary. It certainly did not meet often enough to do so, settling down for much of the period to about one meeting a month, including one on the last Monday of August to elect the new mayor and another at the beginning of October for his inauguration. For the most part, the burgesses confined themselves to leasing town properties, repairing them as necessary, insuring important buildings including the schools and the town hall; appointing and paying masters to Reading School and the Bluecoat School; administering the various educational and almshouse charities, ensuring the judges at the Epiphany assizes (the July assizes went to Abingdon) received generous amounts

The new
schoolhouse of
Reading School
(including
the master's
residence
and the boys'
accommodation).
Valpy's new
schoolroom is
hidden behind
the schoolhouse.
Edmund Havell
print, 1816. (RL)

of cake and wine and were comfortably housed in a good inn or the home of a burgess.[4] In general these matters were dealt with effectively. New leases of houses and shops, farming of tolls of the market and the wharf, appear regularly in the Diary. Town and charity lands in Bray and Engelfield were also leased, rent arrears followed up, sales of timber carefully controlled and enclosure supported. Repairs and partial rebuilding of bridges was still a perennial task, and occasionally a major undertaking, especially repairs to High Bridge in 1742 and 1756, Seven Bridges in 1771 and to Caversham Bridge and the causeway leading to it from Town End across marshy land in the 1770s and 1780s. Part of this causeway may have included a 'new bridge built in 1821 on Caversham Road', otherwise evocatively called Watery Lane.

Schools

Robert Aldworth's foundation, always called the Blue School in the Diary and corporation accounts, caused few problems after it was rebuilt in 1723 at a cost of £675 17s. 0d. The same year a bequest of £1,200 from John West enabled another six boys to attend and later be apprenticed, a further fourteen being supported by bequests from William Malthus and John Pottinger. The burgesses took their duties to the school seriously. Boys were replaced as in turn they were apprenticed or dismissed; payments were made for sheets and towels, insurance, repairs, hymn books; headmasters, John and Francis Barnard, Richard Smith and Joseph Church, none of great note, were appointed and most stayed until they died. The school never had the kudos of the Free School but it did a useful job, equipping boys for crafts rather than the professions.[5]

The Free School attracted some eminent teachers and under two talented headmasters, Haviland John Hiley (1716–50) and Richard Valpy (1781–1830), began to acquire a scholastic reputation, although the provision of a suitable house for the headmaster and an adequate schoolroom troubled the corporation for many years. The borough had always provided a house but it satisfied neither Hiley who could afford to build his own nor Valpy who could not. To improve the school's finances Hiley admitted fee-paying pupils who boarded with him, exacerbating the problem. Various strategies were tried and though the corporation baulked at paying £1,000 for a house, in 1786 they added 100 guineas to the £250 raised by public subscription to purchase a property which the corporation held as trustee. Arguments between master and corporation about the schoolroom followed the building of the new town hall in 1786, solved only when Valpy built a new schoolroom himself. Whether reluctance to provide adequately for both master and pupils derived from lack of funds (there was certainly little to spare) or failure to appreciate the value of education is not clear.[6]

Corporation business and finances

The installation of a new mayor was always followed by a feast, though custom demanded a sermon in St Laurence's church first. Peace treaties, royal coronations and birthdays, merited private festivities for councillors and sometimes a treat for the townspeople. Typical were those for the birthday of George II reported in the *Reading Mercury* on 4 November 1745, demonstrating Reading's loyalty as England faced the threat of the Jacobite Rising. Church bells rang, three troops of dragoons fired three volleys, and in the evening all the houses were 'illuminated'. In the Market Place there was a large bonfire, the mayor and corporation appearing to drink the king's health. George III's golden jubilee in 1810 was more soberly marked by a service in St Laurence's church attended by the corporation and other worthies, and Sunday school teachers and children worshipping at other churches and chapels. Collections were taken for celebrations for the less fortunate. The élite were treated to a public dinner at the town hall from which the riff-raff were excluded by the ticket price of 7s. 6d. In 1814 Napoleon's defeat and exile to Elba was marked by the purchase of a barrel of beer from W.B. Simonds who the previous Christmas had supplied half a dozen bottles of old port and two bottles of sherry.[7]

Until about 1800 overall income was normally sufficient to meet these and more important expenses. Two chamberlains, the senior for hall revenues and the junior for charitable uses, were elected annually and continued to administer borough finances. From 1737 to 1822 there was a separate office, the receiver of rents, for both funds, who held office for several years at a time. The last was Martin Annesley who died in post aged 82. The receiver collected rents from property and tolls, as well as other dues such as dividends, met any charges such as his salary (unchanged throughout at £20 a year) and taxes, and gave the chamberlains moneys to meet their commitments. These were the annual payments which remained unchanged for decades (the mayor's allowance, £60 a year by the 1780s, and the salaries of borough officials), varying incidental payments including tradesmen's bills for repairs or building work, and the expenses of the charities, the Blue Coat School and the Laud apprenticeships. The result is two sets of accounts, receiver's and chamberlains', or three counting the receiver's rent rolls. Throughout the period rental income from charity lands exceeded that from borough properties and tolls, although there were equally greater calls upon it. In the last decade of the century both borough and charity rentals showed a modest rise followed by a paper gain after 1808, possibly the work of the committee for leases (see below). There were always rent arrears, sometimes substantial particularly after about 1800, and especially for land in rural parishes owned by the charities. Drawing up a year-on-year comparison is difficult but there is no proof that assets, apart from those of the Kendrick charity, were not prudently managed though it seems possible that charity money was borrowed from time to time when borough expenditure exceeded income from borough rents.[8] However, the corporation built up reserves for such eventualities. The proceeds of the sale of the Golden Lyon to the county magistrates for an extension to the county gaol in 1765, plus cash in hand, a total of £1,073 8s. 9d., was invested in South Sea Annuities as were future credit balances. Most reserves were liquidated in 1787–88 to fund the new High Bridge. Later, surplus cash was invested in government stock, the interest providing useful additional income; cash for more immediate use was deposited in local banks.[9]

By the beginning of the new century, high expenditure on new building and repairs became an increasing drain on borough finances. Other large commitments included buying out liability for the Land Tax in 1799 (over £1,908) and the borough's share of the costs of enclosure in Bray and Englefield. Despite borrowing £1,000, selling large amounts of timber and raising the income of both Hall and Charity accounts, the end of year balances remained slim. In November 1804 members of the corporation were sufficiently concerned to set up a committee to discuss Hall revenue and in 1808 one for leasing corporation property.[10] No report was recorded but in 1809 the full Hall income and expense account for 1807–08 was copied into the Diary; it showed a surplus of just £32 6s. 8d. from an income of £1,799. Most came from rents, £1,463 5s.

od., mostly from charity lands. Another £185 came from the Town Hall being made 'an object of revenue', energetic collection of small tolls, and the New Market rents. Interest on loans cost the corporation over £162. A debt to Alderman Blandy from the previous year had been met only by the sale of timber from borough land, the equivalent of the family silver. Although the corporation needed to show the 'utmost Economy', the new bridge on Caversham Road cost almost £317 to build in 1821, met by borrowing from the Kendrick Charity. The next year the chamberlains took full financial control, producing a small surplus in the Hall accounts until 1825 when debts mounted inexorably. Rebuilding or major repairs were the greatest drain – a new Compter prison in 1825–26 (£317), an iron bridge over the Kennet (over £1,097) and a timber replacement for Caversham Bridge (£1,534) in 1829–30. These were mainly financed by loans totalling £4,000. Law suits over market tolls, a new charter and the Kendrick Charity added to the problem. Much needed repairs to the Oracle costing over £1,000 were out of the question when the annual deficit was never less than £900. Between 1833 and 1835 sales by auction of leases of property in St Mary's Butts, and land at Boulter's Wharf and in the Orts realising almost £7,900 was sufficient to liquidate the debt, pay legal and other costs and hand over a balance of just £600 to the new corporation.[11]

Parliamentary elections

Though the corporation did not elect Reading's two MPs, it might influence the choice. Most MPs were local gentry, though with connections to Reading as befitted a town so economically linked to local agriculture. The 'bustling, demanding, politically astute' and politically independent electorate, those paying poor rate in the six months before an election, numbered between 500 and 600 and since, apart from the corporation, there was no single dominant influence, almost all elections in the period were contested. Until the terms became redundant in the 1780s, either Whig or Tory members might be returned depending on the depth of their pockets, Reading gaining 'the reputation of one of the most corrupt boroughs' in England. Elections became horrendously expensive, partly because money changed hands (30–40 guineas was offered for a vote in 1754) but also because the electors expected to be entertained. Edward Simeon helped his brother John, the borough recorder, to parliament in 1806 and 1810 with various bribes including low interest loans to tradesmen and a ham for each supporting vote. In 1818 one candidate claimed, 'A quantity of ale was actually broached in the town … and the populace reduced in open day to a disgraceful state of intoxication.' No wonder the 1826 election cost £10,000.[12]

Commerce and industry

Arguably the most important development for Reading's future prosperity was the provision of a transport infrastructure, a prerequisite for the transformation of Reading from a traditional market town into vibrant industrial centre. Most was the work of individual entrepreneurs and local individuals, but however complacent the burgesses were as a corporation, as a group and as individual business men in matters concerning Reading's role as river port, route town and market centre, they were proactive both in defending the town's interests and promoting opportunities for its advancement. Repairs to bridges, essential routes into the town by road, should be seen in this light, as should repairs to paving in the Market Place in 1752. So should a complaint to the House of Commons in 1757 at a time of high corn prices that some corn dealers were selling at farmhouses or village markets, depriving Reading of tolls.[13]

Earlier fears that the Kennet Navigation would damage Reading's trade had proved unfounded; improved access to the west contributed to Reading's growing importance as an inland port. By 1806 it had become a 'place of great trade', exporting annually 20,000 sacks of corn, flour, wool, hoops and bark to London from wharves on the Kennet. In 1802 the corporation further improved navigation by straightening and

Looking north across King's Meadow towards the Thames with a horse-drawn barge and Caversham. The town was still an island in the countryside in 1800. (RL)

Navigable
waterways
accessible
from Reading
by *c*.1810:
Kennet and
Avon Canal
and canalised
River Thames.
(WMC)

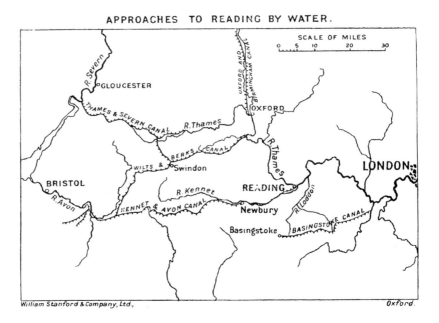

deepening the Kennet from High Bridge to the Thames, Rennie's Cut. A
plan of the cut shows two wharves by Seven Bridges and two on either
side of the new section by High Bridge. By an extension westwards from
Newbury the modest Kennet Navigation became the Kennet and Avon
Canal from Reading to Bristol in 1810, transporting Somerset coal, Bath
building stone and Welsh slates at half the cost of transport by road. A
second wharf was needed by 1828 to cope with the increased traffic.[14]

Improved navigation on the Thames further extended the canal
network. In 1769 the corporation gave practical and financial support for a
private Act of Parliament to construct a cut from the Thames at Sonning
to Monkey Island near Maidenhead enabling barges to avoid a great loop
of the river.[15] The scheme was rejected in favour of a proposal which
became in 1771 an Act 'for improving and completing the Navigation of
the Rivers Thames and Isis from the City of London to Cricklade'. This
established a body, the Thames Commission, with powers to replace
inefficient and dangerous flash locks with pound locks and improve the
tow paths, effectively turning the river into a canal. By 1780 pound locks
had been constructed from Caversham to Maidenhead and by 1790 to
Oxford. With the construction of the Oxford Canal, Reading was linked
to the Midlands by waterway. Further improvements below Maidenhead
after 1795 created a trunk route for the carriage of heavy goods by water
from London to Bristol via Reading and from the borough itself to the
capital, transport cost being 40% of those by road. Coal from the North
East came into or through the town via London. From the Midlands
came coal and pottery, from the Vale of White Horse cheese and corn and

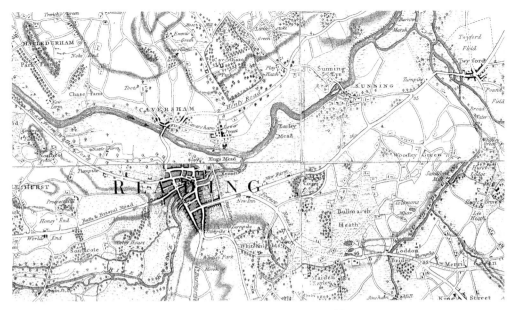

Part of a *Topographical Map of the Town of Reading & the Country Adjacent to an extent of Ten Miles* by Thomas Pride, 1810. The turnpikes on the Bath, Basingstoke and Forest Roads and some of the local estates are shown. (RL)

from Oxfordshire timber. Employment opportunities increased: between 6% and 9% of Reading will makers between 1731 and 1800 worked on the river with both master and men living on the barges plying between High Bridge and Queenhithe, London, even when in 'port'.[16]

Though the roads were not yet metalled, the work of the turnpike trusts was soon producing dividends for the borough. Improved surfaces allowed fast coach services to operate to and from Reading and London by the Great West and the Forest roads. Direct services increased in frequency: Joseph Young operated a thrice-weekly 'flying machine' in the 1760s; Steven Thorne offered a daily summer service in 1775. In 1785 Smith and Weale's 'flying machine' and two post-coaches left daily at 5.00 a.m., 7.00 a.m. and 1.30 p.m. The first reached London at 11.00 a.m. and returned to Reading an hour later. By the late 1790s at least four coaches left every morning all year round and more in summer. Fares were expensive. From six shillings in 1762, they rose to ten shillings inside, half price outside by the 1790s. To meet rising demand, William Hone's company began an 'omnibus' service with fares at eight and five shillings. Four mail coaches and 19 passenger coaches from London to Bath were passing through the town daily. Heavy goods took several days to reach Oxford and Birmingham by waggon; even to London took two days. Freight was expensive at two shillings a hundredweight (112 lbs) and passenger fares were 2s. 6d.[17]

Hone's General Coach Office
KING-STREET READING.

(Adjoining the George Inn.)

Reduced Fares to LONDON
BY THE
OMNIBUS.
Inside 8s. Outside 5s.

Mornings at 10 o'Clock.

TO LONDON
THE TELEGRAPH FAST COACH,

Through MAIDENHEAD and SLOUGH, every day at Twelve (except Sunday,) to *Nelson's* Black Bear, Piccadilly, and Blossom's Inn, Lawrence Lane, Cheapside; from whence it returns every Morning at 11; and Black Bear, Piccadilly at a quarter before 12.

——— ooo ———

"STAR" Coach to BATH and BRISTOL,

Through MARLBOROUGH, DEVIZES, and MELKSHAM, every Morning (except Sunday) at a quarter before Nine o'Clock to the York House Bath, and White Lion, BRISTOL.

TO LONDON.--The ZEPHYR, through WINDSOR,
Every day at half past One.

——— ooo ———

COACHES DAILY TO

Oxford	Brighton	Marlow	Portsmouth	Windsor
Wallingford	Guildford	Bath	Basingstoke	Wantage
Maidenhead	Petersfield	Bristol	Newbury	Faringdon
Winchester	Odiham	Horsham	Marlborough	Cirencester
Alton	Horndean	Southampton	Monmouth	Gloucester &
Farnham	Wycombe	Gosport	Hereford	Worthing.

Wm. HONE & Co. Proprietors.

	£	s.	d.
PAID OUT......			
CARRIAGE......			
BOOKING ...			
PORTERAGE...			

SOCIABLES to Streatley, Newbury, Basingstoke, Windsor, Wallingford, Henley and Maidenhead, daily

---

White, Printer & Binder, Reading.

Handbill advertising coach travel from Reading, late eighteenth century with signed payment by St Giles' overseers of the poor. (BRO D/P96/18/15)

Departures, arrivals and frequent stops to change horses created the coaching inn with its attendant occupations. Between 1731 and 1760 about 6.5% of will makers worked in inns or coaching and about 10% in victualling trades, an imperfect picture given the limitations of probate evidence. A century later, trade directories are a little more revealing. In 1826 there were at least eleven coaching inns, eight coach services, four waggon proprietors, four coach builders, seven farriers and four wheelwrights, the latter two groups serving the general population as well as the coach trade. Hungry and thirsty passengers were customers for bakers, brewers and confectioners.

Its location ensured that Reading became 'above all else, a collecting and processing centre of barley [malt] and wheat [flour]' from its hinterland for export to London with corn-factors and mealmen prominent in the records.[18] John Sutton came to Reading from London about 1800, setting up in King Street in 1806 dealing in corn and seeds. The extent of the trade and its impact on the overall prosperity of the town's market is difficult to assess until the end of the century. The rent paid by the lessees of the farm of the market tolls, usually for three or more years was often subsumed into 'rents' in the accounts. When it was itemised, the amount paid was stable at £100 *per annum* except in 1761 when it was £126. Not until 1806 did the rent rise to £225, by which time over 40,000 quarters of corn and over 9,000 quarters of peas and beans worth over £120,000 were traded each year yielding over £450 in tolls. In 1800 a new 'spacious and convenient' covered market for goods other than grain with 24 stalls was constructed to meet a request from some townspeople. Stall rentals brought in £120 in 1810, declining to £69 by 1813; repaying the loans which had partly funded the outlay of £1,388 10s. 0d. would be slow.[19] Rent for the tolls for the Wool Hall remained at about £11 *per annum*. However, the establishment of a Monday cattle market in Broad Street in 1779 and from about 1800 an extra market on Wednesdays for meat, vegetables and fruit (Saturday being for corn), suggest trade was buoyant. Certainly pictures of the Market Place show it was very busy on market days. Man claimed that 200 waggons a day arrived at Michaelmas, the busiest time. Samples of corn were taken to the Market Place for buyers to inspect and the whole load sold for an agreed price before the market closed at lunchtime.[20] The markets did not have a monopoly on trade. Retail shops, often called 'warehouses', were appearing alongside the shops and workshops of traditional craftsmen; retailing in its many forms was the largest occupational group by 1796.

About 1800 there were four fairs a year held in the Forbury: for horses at Candlemas (2 February), cows and horses on May Day and St James' feast day (25 July). St Matthew's Fair (21 September) was a hiring fair but more significantly was one of the most important cheese fairs in England. In September 1795 the *Reading Mercury* reported the sale of

The George Hotel, King Street, claims to date from 1506. It was an important coaching inn.

An engraving of London Road by W.H. Tims, published 1823. A coach is about to depart from the Saracen's Head. (RL)

Engraving by W.H. Tims of the Market Place, published 1823, with the Simeon Monument, surviving medieval houses on the right and refronted shops and houses on the left. Corn was being sold in the open. (RL)

1,200 tons of cheese from the Vale of White Horse and counties to the west, its export eastwards doubling the value of tolls taken at the Loddon Bridge turnpike.[21]

The industries of the period, as yet less significant than commerce, evolved from the changes already underway in 1660. The transformation was complete when about 1796 the *Universal Directory* described the town's economy. Cloth making of unknown quality survived to about 1750 then vanished, replaced by the manufacture of sailcloth. Traditional craftsmen, butchers, bakers, shoemakers and other leather workers providing for day-to-day needs were as important as ever, but as with so many market towns Reading's main trades involved processing local agricultural produce, some later becoming nationally significant. Based on the good malting barley grown in Berkshire, the town's traditional malting industry built on the expansion of the previous century; a single shipment sent on a Reading barge by five maltsters in January 1769 totalled 364 quarters. Brewing, another traditional occupation, had expanded into large-scale commercial industry by the end of the century. Of the seven firms named in 1796, the largest, that of John Stephens, was said to have produced 25,000 barrels of beer annually. Simonds, which would become Reading's most famous brewery, was founded by William Blackall Simonds in 1789. His father, a yeoman farmer, came from Arborfield to begin malting, a nice example of the close connection between the trades. Another brewer, John Deane, was a partner in a bank founded in 1788, Stephens and Simonds in another in 1791, putting to good use the large sums of money which they sometimes held. Banks in other Berkshire towns had similar origins.[22]

Corn milling, another centuries-old craft, grew in significance, millers appearing throughout the century. Local flour was used in small baking enterprises, including biscuit making; Joseph Huntley, another newcomer, opened his biscuit shop in 1822. Brewing and biscuit making would become the basis of Reading's industrial wealth within a few decades, as would another local product, James Cock's Reading Sauce, invented in 1802, predating Worcester sauce by several decades. Using local clay, bricks had been made in the borough for centuries but now more kilns in Katesgrove and elsewhere were set up; Reading's new houses were almost entirely brick-built. Printing businesses were established. Robert Snare printed John Man's history of Reading, numerous other books and ephemera such as election addresses, J. Rusher published guides to the town, and both set up bookshops. A second newspaper, *The Berkshire Chronicle*, printed by William Drysdale, appeared in 1825.[23]

What little evidence survives suggests that craftsmen's daily wages were adequate but many had no guarantee of permanent work. Carpenters working for Joseph Collier in 1767/8 were paid 2*s.* 3*d.* a day, labourers half that; neither seems to have had regular employment. Few would have had any savings in case of sickness or lack of work.[24]

Poverty and poor relief

Responsibility for the poor was shared. Each parish retained its own overseers of the poor who collected and disbursed the poor rate and by 1732 had established a work- or poor-house where they effectively curbed both 'lavish' outdoor relief and 'idleness and sloth'.[25] Another of the overseers' tasks was to ensure the parish provided poor relief only for those eligible, who had acquired settlement by birth, residence or apprenticeship. However, the borough administered the house of correction and dealt with settlement in the borough quarter sessions. Only about ten years of the proceedings survive (1768–77) but they paint a sober portrait of the poor with doubtful settlement rights. Of about 150 men and 21 women claiming relief (excluding any wives or children), fewer than one in four were originally from Reading and fewer than 50 from Berkshire and surrounding counties. Most men claimed to have a trade, mainly as cordwainers (shoemakers) and bargemen. Two were highly skilled clockmakers and two more had been cabinet makers. One in three men was married with children. Over two-thirds of the men and about half the women could sign their names, a remarkable improvement over the numbers in previous centuries. Several had once made an honest living for a time but employment was very insecure: Ann Rose was a servant to Captain Pearce of St Laurence 'to part on a month's wages or a month's warning' and John Chasworth lost his job as a plasterer in Marylebone when his master's business failed. Others had failed to complete apprenticeships or had served in the militia. The most unfortunate were Scotsmen, some married with children, who came to the borough to work in a new 'very considerable silk manufactory' in St Laurence, said to employ a hundred of them. Thirty-six claimed poor relief between May and November 1774. As no Scot had legal settlement in England, any wives they married in the town and any children fathered there would become a burden on the parish as would women abandoned by soldier-husbands. As in earlier centuries, migrants were often among the most marginalised.[26]

The authorities were concerned, especially as food prices continued to rise during the war against France and the poor harvests after 1794. The amount of poor rate collected in the three parishes in 1776 was over £600 in St Giles, £710 in St Laurence and £947 in St Mary, a total of £2,288 10s. 2d. By 1803 it had risen to over £1,358, £1,550 and £1,401 in the respective parishes, a total of £4,309 13s. 5d. Even so it failed to match expenditure. In 1803 outdoor relief to the poor in their homes and to those in the three parochial workhouses amounted to £4,841 14s. 8d., leaving a deficit of £532 1s. 3d. Reading was not alone. In Berkshire, one of the poorest counties in England, 21% of the population was on poor relief in the year Easter 1802–03 costing over £82,000. A major reason was that the amount of relief was related to the price of bread and the size of the family; with successive poor harvests, bread prices and poor relief rose in tandem.[27] Thereafter poverty and the cost of poor relief remained stubbornly high locally and nationally; from 1817 to 1832 St Giles' poor rate ranged from 3s. 0d. to 4s. 9d. in £ on land and property. Wheat prices from 1800 to 1819 remained at almost double those of the 1780s. In Reading, fear of disorder from vagrants and beggars resulted in the formation of the Society for the Suppression of Mendacity, uniformed beadles being empowered to arrest beggars in the street and enforce a maximum one-night stay.[28] Government concern resulted in the establishment of a royal commission in 1833 and a wholesale reform of the poor laws in 1834.

The corporation administered various borough charities, passing some of the proceeds to parish overseers to distribute, though in times of great need they adopted special measures such as setting up a subscription in January 1757, pump-primed with £21 from borough funds, to buy bread to sell to the poor at well below market price. As food prices rose in the freezing winter of 1766–67, payment of £7 was made to each parish 'in this severe season for the poor'.[29] Charities were well intentioned but obviously insufficient to meet need. Almshouses including those of John a Larder, William Kendrick, Vachell and Harrison continued to receive new inmates selected by the corporation, at most 27 at any one time, and poor boys were still chosen to be apprenticed. These and other endowments from the previous century were supplemented by gifts of property or money to invest to provide an annual income including Mrs Mary Kendrick's for the poor of three parishes not receiving alms and John West's for the blind poor of St Mary's. Mrs Mary Love and Edward Simeon gave large sums to provide bread at reduced prices, Edward Simeon and Alderman Austwick for blankets, clothes and coal.[30]

Prisons, crime and immorality

The house of correction, the Bridewell, established in 1578 (see chapter 6) was still used to house vagrants and petty offenders from borough and county. Deemed unsafe in 1784 the corporation offered to spend no more than £200 on improvements, a sum deemed inadequate by the county magistrates. Exactly what work was eventually carried out is not clear from the records, perhaps the construction of four new cells and repairs to the roof. Certainly in 1790 the corporation borrowed £400 to meet the cost. Not that the building housed many offenders or that very much was spent on them; £12 4s. 6½d. sufficed for their subsistence from 21 December 1813 to the following 25 March. The next year Henry Simpson, the keeper, paid £10 annually, supervised just ten prisoners, four women, one with a child, and six men. Two women stayed for six months, one for a month and one for two. By contrast the six men left

Interior of Greyfriars' Church used as the borough's Bridewell or House of Correction. (Man)

A print of the Forbury with St Laurence's graveyard *c.*1805, in the background the new Town Hall. (RL)

after less than five weeks. Food was adequate, costing 5½d. a day per inmate, as much as a labourer could afford, and straw for bedding.[31]

The county gaol in Castle Street was not one of the borough's responsibilities. The county justices, supported by a rate from every parish in Berkshire had controlled it for centuries. It was a small building, used mainly to house debtors or prisoners awaiting trial at quarter sessions or assizes. Between 1773 and 1775, two women and six men, convicted of fraud or petty larceny were transported to the American colonies for seven years in the ships of London merchants. In order to enlarge the gaol, the county justices purchased the neighbouring property, the Golden Lyon, in September 1763 for £200. The enlarged gaol sufficed, albeit providing worsening conditions for the inmates, until in 1793 a new house of correction, opened seven years before in the Forbury, was enlarged to become a gaol as well. The borough had its own tiny prison, the Compter.[32]

Immorality was the concern of the parishes especially since resulting illegitimate children might become a charge on the poor rate. 'We have Adulters [sic], fornications and too many Common Swearers & drunkards,' reported the churchwardens of St Laurence in 1746; three soldiers and four others were cohabiting with local women in St Giles in 1819 and St Mary's churchyard 'was often at night the scene of gross immoralities'. The religious revival had not penetrated the whole of the borough.[33]

Religion, charities and charity schools

The turbulent religious history of the Stuart century was followed in Reading by a period of calm before further changes in the confessional landscape after about 1760.[34] Little has been written about the Church of England in the borough before the 1760s, making it unsafe to generalise about the local situation though we can say that some Reading clergy were, like Dr Bolton, vicar of St Mary from 1738 to the 1760s, highly educated men able to mix with the local gentry on equal terms. Others, notably Charles Coates, had antiquarian interests; his history of Reading occupied him throughout the 1790s. Their learned sermons did not necessarily improve their parishioners' morals or the churchwardens' concern for the church fabric. There is a disarming honesty about the admission that in 1736 St Laurence was 'not without Common Swearers, Fornicators & Absenters from Church as usual', and in 1788 the archdeacon listed the many repairs and replacements to be carried out.[35]

This calm was disturbed by what is known as the Evangelical Revival, an essentially Anglican phenomenon, the first signs of which appeared nationally in the 1730s. Evangelical clergy were active in good works, indefatigable preachers of the word, and passionate about bringing an awareness of sin and salvation to their hearers. Two exponents in Reading were vicars of St Giles, William Talbot (1768–74) and the Hon. William Cadogan (1775–97). Talbot was noted for his kindness to the poor and those in prison, a man 'baptised with the Holy Ghost and with fire – fervent in spirit'. Cadogan was an extremely successful preacher, making St Giles 'the centre of a strong and vital evangelical witness'. So great was the congregation at his thrice-weekly sermons that a new gallery was constructed in 1784.[36]

Events following his death resulted in the founding of a new congregation. His successor, Joseph Eyre, a critic of evangelical beliefs, so disheartened his parishioners that a number left to worship in a disused chapel in St Mary's Butts. In 1798 they bought the site of the county goal in Castle Street, redundant since 1794. The architect of their simple but elegant chapel of St Mary was Richard Billing who lived in the same street. Later additions to the entrance included a classical façade, still a feature of the streetscape.

Print of Castle Street with the chapel of St Mary (right) and Congregational chapel (left), 1860–69. (RL)

Castle Street

Old Dissent (nonconformist sects existing before 1689) was content to consolidate until the latter part of the century. Membership was transient, small groups of dissenters hiving off to form new churches or joining with like-minded evangelicals of a different sect. Presbyterians, the most numerous of the dissenters in the 1660s had disappeared by 1830. Separated from them, the Independents or Congregationalists later registered for worship a house in the St Mary's Butts. In Broad Street two charismatic pastors, Thomas Noon from 1764 and Archibald Douglas from 1796 evangelised an already growing Independent congregation. Douglas also founded the Reading Evangelical Society in 1797 and served as secretary to the Reading and Foreign Bible Society. During his ministry the old chapel was pulled down

Broad Street Independent Chapel with dates of building (now Waterstones). (JD)

and the existing building constructed in 1800 at a cost of £3,200. By 1807 the congregation in the chapel on the south side of Castle Street had been joined by members from other Independent congregations. A new Baptist meeting house was registered in Hosier Lane in 1754, where a fervent preacher, Thomas Davies, inspired a growing congregation. Other Baptist places of worship were registered in St Giles' and St Mary's parishes in 1818 and 1830 and finally a purpose-built chapel in King's Road opened in 1837. Meanwhile Strict Baptists, more Calvinist in their beliefs, had separated, setting up their own chapels between 1798 and 1830. Quakers did not share the revival but rather declined in number.[37]

New Dissent, Methodism, came to Reading in 1739 with the visit of Charles Wesley. He returned, en route from London to Salisbury or Bristol, over 20 times between 1739 and 1780 to challenge, with some success, a generally indifferent and sometimes hostile town. By the 1770s his journal described large rooms filled by his eager listeners, no longer the 'stupid oxen' he had previously encountered, though true believers were probably few. However there is no recorded licence for a Wesleyan Methodist place of worship until 1813, the 'Inkpot Chapel' in London Street.[38]

The tentative revival of pre-Reformation Catholicism was delayed until the 1790s. In 1791 parliament passed the Catholic Relief Act allowing Mass to be celebrated legally in registered chapels provided these did

Interior of St Mary's Episcopal Chapel, Castle Street by Richard Billing, 1798. (JD)

not have either steeples or bells. In Reading a small community heard Mass illegally in a building in Minster Street rented by Mrs Anna-Maria Smart, née Carman, from about 1760 though in about 1790 they moved to a chapel in Finch's Buildings in Hosier Street served by four French priests who had fled the Revolution. Over the next 12 years over 300 refugee priests came to Reading and were housed in the King's Arms Hotel in Castle Street. Most returned home as the French political scene stabilised under Napoleon, though Abbé de la Balardiere remained until 1833 as chaplain to the Wheble family of Woodley Lodge, Bulmershe.[39]

Philanthropy was one of the fruits of the Evangelical Revival, providing educational opportunities for the poor, though limited in scope and extent. St Giles' parish had a Sunday School by 1786 funded by subscriptions from richer parishioners with four teachers. By 1802, partly through Cadogan's efforts, there were four such schools, attended by 120 children. The other parishes and several nonconformist congregations also founded Sunday schools. They all taught reading (writing might encourage ambitions beyond the pupils' station) and moral behaviour. The formation nationally of the British and Foreign Schools Society (Nonconformist) in 1808 and of the National Society (Church of England) in 1811 provided the impetus for the establishment in the town of two British Schools, one with 280 boys and another for 178 girls and two National Schools. Cadogan and his fellow vicars, Charles Sturgess and Dr John Nicholls supported by evangelicals and others founded a boarding school for girls, the Green School, so-called from the colour of the uniform, which opened in 1782. It provided a practical education for future servant girls. Chosen from all three parishes they received training in basic housewifery and sewing, in the principles of the Christian religion – virtue, modesty, honesty, truth, decency, humility, civility, and kindness and in all, due subordination. At age 14 they learned to write and cast accounts before being sent into service or apprenticed the following year.[40]

Map of Reading, 1813, published in Man, 1816. A tentative expansion of the built-up area has begun towards the east.

A fashionable town

Although there were tentative beginnings before 1700, it was not until later in the eighteenth century that Reading shared fully in the 'urban renaissance', a term for a range of cultural, intellectual and architectural changes which spread from London to larger provincial towns to a greater or lesser extent between the Restoration and the Napoleonic wars. Architectural features derived from classical models transformed the façades of timber-framed and brick houses. There were cultural activities and 'polite' entertainment where the local gentry were joined by urban gentlemen and an emerging urban middle class of professionals and business men who had time for leisure and income to finance it. *The Universal Directory* listed 24 gentlemen, 14 clergy, eight attorneys and 13 medical men.*

By the 1740s, if not before, monthly assemblies were held on Tuesdays during the 'winter season' (October to May) on nights of the full or near-full moon.† The occasional presence of the military, such as General Mordaung's regiment of dragoons, quartered in the town for the winter in 1769–70, doubtless added a spice of excitement to the events, at least for the young ladies.

Assemblies were an important part of the entertainment in many county towns timed to coincide with the assizes but as the summer assizes were held in Abingdon, assemblies in the borough were held on the evenings of Race Week with lamps lit in the Market Place and on the new High Bridge since a full moon could not be guaranteed. London hairdressers and perfumers advertised their wares and local shopkeepers supplied fashionable headdresses with 'crimped feathers and flowers'. Races were held on Bulmershe Heath, just over two miles from Reading from Tuesday to Thursday in the last week of August. So popular was the event that it expanded from three races in the week in the 1740s to three each day in the 1770s. They were run over two miles on Wednesday and four miles on the other days with prizes of £50. The stewards were sometimes local gentry, Sir Henry Englefield of Whiteknights in the 1770s and the more famous Lord Barrymore 20 years later.‡

Among the gentry visitors was Caroline Lybbe Powys of Hardwick House, Oxfordshire. She and her husband, Philip, attended at least one major social event in Reading Race Week. She wrote in her diary for 29 August 1786: 'Went to my mother's for the races at Reading.' In 1794 her family stayed at 'Mrs Micklems'.§ Other visitors also stayed in town, renting an apartment. On 8 August 1785 a first floor 'Genteel Apartment' in the Market Place was advertised with a dining room, kitchen, two bedrooms and servants' quarters.

Townspeople could acquire the requisite skills to enjoy dancing, part of the assembly's

---

* The largest percentage increase in Reading occupations was in craftsmen who built and furnished houses – bricklayers, plasterers, and furniture makers, 17% of wills recorded 1760–1800. P.N. Borsay, *The English Urban Renaissance: Culture and Society in the Provincial Town, 1660–1770* (Oxford, 1989).

† *Reading Mercury*, 14 March 1770. Other local towns held assemblies and race meetings.

‡ Races were advertised in the *Reading Mercury*.

§ Robert Micklem was an alderman and a mercer. If this is the family with whom the Lybbe-Powys stayed, it provides an interesting insight into social relationships between gentry and trade. E. Climenson (ed.), *Passages from the Diary of Mrs Philip Lybbe Powys, passim.*

A print, South View of the Abbey Gate. Jane Austen attended a school here in the 1790s. (Man)

A print of the entrance to Thornton's theatre, 1804. (RL)

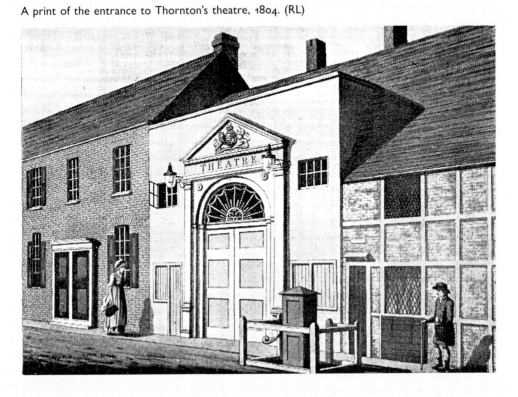

attraction, from a dancing master. In the *Reading Mercury* on 26 March 1770 Mr Dore, trained in London, offered tuition for ladies and gentlemen in the proper steps to perform cotillons, minuets, rigadoon and louvre, either at his house or to families at home.

Another feature of Race Week towards the end of the century was a theatrical performance, its late appearance probably the result of hostility from a strong Evangelical presence in the town. The theatre was a small building in Friar Street founded by Henry Thornton, theatrical entrepreneur who had already opened theatres in Newbury and Henley. It opened for a short summer season on 12 May 1788 and nightly performances during Race Week. In later years, London artists visited.*

Mrs Powys also attended the Music Festival in St Laurence's church on 9 August 1787. On Fridays during the year subscription concerts were organised, the subscription being 7s. 6d. for a series of three, a weekly wage for a Berkshire farm worker. At the fourth concert on Friday 2 October 1785 'a numerous and brilliant audience' heard a performance of a Corelli concerto. For ordinary folk the occasional charity concert was more affordable. On Tuesday 17 February 1785 the Musical Society of Reading charged sixpence for a concert and ball 'for the benefit of the poor', though even sixpence was beyond many pockets. Other amateur musicians enjoyed music at home. Lessons were given on the pianoforte and harpsichord, books of favourite songs and 'country dances' and newly published scores could be purchased. On 25 July 1785 the *Reading Mercury* advertised a second-hand Beck pianoforte for sixteen guineas.

The middle-class home acquired other possessions which contributed to a genteel lifestyle. In later years all the newest wallpaper patterns were available in Reading shops. Buying second-hand was a good way to furnish a home hence many advertisements for auction sales of bureaux, card tables, Wilton carpets, and china. Furniture could be also be bought new in the town; Charles Poulton, upholsterer, had a wide selection including book cases with glass doors and desks for the serious bibliophile.†

Reading was becoming a popular leisure pursuit; John Hocker had a bookshop in the Market Place. The *Reading Mercury* advertised the works of Shakespeare and Samuel Johnson and from at least the 1740s useful books for the ladies such as *The Accomplish'd Housewife*. The novel reached Reading in 1770 if not before when Carman's bookshop was selling copies of *Theodora*, an autobiographical novel published that year. By the 1790s several businesses combining bookselling, printing and selling stationery were established and Robert Snare also established a Circulating Library.‡

In the local press, shops advertised the latest 'must-have' fabrics from London – calicoes, dimity, striped cotton and muslin, farthingales and hoops to provide a fashionable profile, and the newest fashions in ready-made hats and gloves. A lacemaker, a 'chinaman', a gingerbread maker and a toyman were among the more esoteric Reading trades of the 1790s. Shops had to be as fashionable as their customers, bow-fronted shops appearing in King Street, a wide thoroughfare created in 1760.

---

* Lybbe Powys' diary: Daphne Phillips, *Reading theatres, cinemas and other entertainments, 1788–1978* (Reading, 1978).

† *Reading Mercury*, 15 August 1785.

‡ Diana R. Mackarill, *The Snares of Minster Street: the Printer and the Picture* (Reading, 2007), 3.

Appearance of the borough *c*.1830: gentrification and improvement

Despite population growth, the physical expansion of the borough was limited to only about 1,000 new houses in whole eighteenth century, the majority between 1780 and 1800, typical of the larger towns of south-east England though by 1831 a further 1,300 had been constructed.[41] Building was 'piecemeal and spasmodic', mostly in courts and gardens behind older houses in the main streets though there was some development of more fashionable properties along the main roads out of town: London Road to the east where leases of building land appear in the records in the 1780s and 1790s, and Castle Street to the west. Several Georgian houses survive on the south side of Castle Street especially the splendid Holybrook House (*c*.1750–60), now separated from the westward continuation of the street by the Inner Distribution Road (IDR). Adding to its classical air is St Mary's chapel with its fine façade of Corinthian columns and opposite a former Congregational/Independent chapel whose pediment and columns are at odds with its present function. Many of the houses on Castle Hill (mainly post-1800) are of Bath stone, transported via the Kennet and Avon Canal, although Ascham (later Castle Hill, then Yeomanry) House, now the Register Office, is earlier.

Bath stone was also used to provide stone-clad frontages to a few large houses on the north side of the King's Road, a new thoroughfare constructed by Commissioners of the Royal Forests following the sale of Crown land in 1832–33, and others in Eldon Road and Eldon Square.

A villa *c*.1800 on London Road, once the home of Mary Russell Mitford, author of *Belford Regis* and *Our Village*.

Georgian houses, Castle Hill.

Yeomanry House (late eighteenth century) Reading Register Office until 2018.

One or two brick houses on London Road including Acacias and a brick terrace, Portland Place, were constructed in 1818 and *c.*1830 opposite the classical stone-clad Albion Terrace of 12 houses with stables by Richard Billing II begun in 1825. Together they mirrored in the east the elegance of west Reading. Terraces of good middle-class houses were constructed elsewhere in the borough including Coley Hill (1809), Oxford Road (1813), Southampton Place (1813–18) and Conduit Close (1824). Some Crown land along London Road sold in 1833 was developed for middle-class housing and along the new Orts Road for artisan terraces.[42]

Houses were not the main reason why the town was described as 'considerably increased in rank, fashion and respectability' in the 1790s. This it owed, said an easily pleased observer, to 'the salubrity of the air and the pleasantness of situation',

Doorway of a house in Albion Place, now converted to apartments.

Albion Place by Richard Billing II, 1825–35.

though the town derived what little salubrity it possessed from a number of enterprises undertaken late in the century, mainly on private initiatives. Reading's charters, like those of boroughs generally, did not require the corporation to undertake improvements nor allow it to levy rates for the purpose. When in 1760 they wished to buy up properties between Sun Lane and Back Lane to create the wide thoroughfare of King Street, councillors had to reduce the mayor's allowance by £20 a year until the cost of £400 had been met.[43] Moreover, they showed little desire to keep the town clean; in April 1751 they refused to remove rubbish from Holy Brook 'except it be made appear they are obliged to'.[44] The extent of the corporation's failure to provide for an acceptable urban environment was remarked upon by 'A Lover of Useful and Elegant Improvements from Bath'. In a letter to the local newspaper published on 16 April 1770 he bemoaned 'streets so ill-paved, badly lighted' and the 'present incommodious state of Reading'. It was, he opined 'a disgrace to the town, inhabitants and magistrates'. He might also have noted that, unusually for a provincial town, Reading had no hospital; the People's Dispensary in Chain Street was not built until 1802 and then only through the generosity of local physicians.

It took another 25 years for concerned gentlemen in the borough to follow the example of other towns and sponsor a private Act of Parliament giving them powers to provide a better environment and levy a rate to meet the costs. This was Reading's first Improvement Act, 1785. A committee of 20 gentlemen to promote the Act was headed by the mayor, John Deane, and included seven other councillors. It gave limited powers to 62 commissioners, local politicians, tradesmen and solicitors, 'for paving the footways in the Borough of Reading ...; for better repairing cleaning lighting and watching the Streets, Lanes, Passages and Places ...; for removing Incroachments and Annoyances therefrom and preventing the like in the future.' All 62 were present at their first meeting at the Ship Inn on 4 July 1785 having subscribed varying sums to pump-prime the enterprise. The enthusiasm soon wore off, attendance frequently falling to single figures. Nevertheless, there were a few successes. The streets, but not the lanes, were paved with York stone with gutters and granite kerbs on the sides. The first paving stone was ceremonially laid by the mayor at the door of his house in Castle Street on 8 August 1785. The removal of overhanging signs and branches of trees extended the width of the main streets by four feet and others by three, while rules against parking waggons and carriages on the streets or riding horses on the footways (pavements) made for better traffic flow and relative safety. Improvements by the commission were paid for by a special rate, and loans up to £3,500 could be raised using this as security; a return of 5% on the loan made it a good investment.[45] Not everyone thought so. John Man complained that residents of Sivier

The Dispensary,
dated by Pevsner
to c.1840. (RL)

Coloured engraving by W.H. Tims of King Street, 1823, created by demolishing
Sun and Back Lanes. Several shops and old houses have been refronted in the new
fashionable style. (RL)

KING STREET, READING.

(Silver) Street were paying high rates but paving was very limited, that dung heaps sullied the elegant frontages of Castle Street and that pigs still wandered through the town, though the paving commission had forbidden both nuisances.[46]

Streets became safer at night in that from 1795 an increasing number of street lamps lit by oil were provided, although only between 1 September and 2 May and not on four days on either side of the full moon; there were 150 lamps the following year. By 1801 there were 174 lamps, said to be essential if cultural and intellectual activities were to take place in the evenings. Modernisation came in November 1819 when the first lamps were lit by gas from the Reading Gas Company's works set up in Gas Lane the previous year. However, more light did little to induce a sense of security since the streets were ineffectually patrolled by uniformed watchmen.

The corporation made its contribution to Reading's new image with two major building projects. Since 1560 the refectory of the former abbey guest house had served as schoolroom and town hall. It had become dilapidated after two centuries of use and, following complaints from the county gentry about the provision made for quarter sessions and assizes, the corporation agreed to rebuild the council chamber. In 1771–72 they

Engraving by Charles Tomkins of Blagrave's Piazza the west front of St Laurence, the vicarage and the new Town Hall, published 1802. (RL)

St. Lawrence's Church, Reading, 1802.

East view of the new High Bridge, published 1810–19. (RL)

spent at least £555 6s. 6d. on a new room with fine curtains and a lustre (chandelier) suspended by golden chains to add a touch of elegance,[47] but not until 1784 when several aldermen reported that the Town Hall itself needed a thorough repair did the corporation agree to rebuild it. The cost was not to exceed £1,600, part being met by a 30-year loan of £300. In a decision which smacked of jobbery they awarded the contract to Mr Charles Poulton, cabinet maker and upholsterer, assistant burgess and later alderman. The building nevertheless impressed Mrs Caroline Lybbe Powys. She wrote in her diary for 29 August 1786: 'The first opening of the new town hall, a fine room 74 by 36, not including the recesses at each end for the two judges.' However Coates wrote in 1802 that the Assembly Room was 'very handsome', 108 ft long, 32 wide and 24 high, and a few years later Man noted that the courts of justice met at either end of a long room, no doubt in these recesses. Here at last was a setting fit both for the county's courts and for assemblies and balls, essential to the social life of any self-respecting borough.[48]

A second major undertaking was completed in 1787: rebuilding the High Bridge in stone, replacing the wooden structure which had done service for 80 years. It still stands despite being crossed many times a day by some of the borough's fleet of double-decker buses. The architect was Robert Furze Brettingham who designed an elegant structure, said to

An obelisk with four lamps commissioned by Edward Simeon to improve the lighting and traffic flow in the Market Place, designed by Sir John Soane, 1804. (JD)

have had 'a classical air'. Constructed at a cost of £2,200, it was financed from the sale of 3,000 South Sea Company shares. The local newspaper reported,

> On Thursday last, the new stone bridge over the River Kennet in this town was so far completed as to be passable for horsemen and carriages. The first person who rode over on horseback was Mr Knight of Whitley, who gave half a guinea to the workmen to drink his health; observing at the same time 'that so long ago as the year 1707, when the late wooden bridge there was just finished, he recollected to have rode over it behind his father.'

A lamp was placed on the balustrades on either side, lit at the same times as others in the town; in 1819 these were gas lamps supplied by the Reading Gas Company.[49]

Lamps in the Market Place were supplemented in 1804 by a lighted monument in the centre, an obelisk surrounded by stout rails and curbs provided by Edward Simeon, not entirely for philanthropic reasons. It would, as well as extra light, create a 'regular line' for carts to follow, avoiding 'confusion' in the crowded space on market days. Four 'lamps' each with several 'lights' attached to it would be lit whenever existing ones were, the expense met by income from his gift to the borough of £1,000. Designed by Sir John Soane, it was erected by 7 January 1805. Mr Simeon was made a freeman of the borough, the grant being written on an illustrated scroll and presented in a gold box engraved with the borough arms. This had become a means by which the corporation rewarded such generosity or public service but also allowed them to ingratiate the town with local elites such as Henry Addington, high steward of the borough, Speaker of the Commons and future Prime Minister (1798).[50]

Need for reform

The 1830s saw the first of many reforms which affected both borough and national politics. The 1832 Parliamentary Reform Act increased the number of men able to vote and gave parliamentary represen-tation to many large towns. The next year the Municipal Corporation Commission into the state of the boroughs 'dealt out' to Reading 'the faint praise which damns'. 'They [the Corporation] had not squandered their trust in eating and drinking; … they did keep accounts [which they never published], they spent money in the public interest but the public to whom the corporation affairs were a "sealed book" continued to doubt their integrity.' A close grip on power by a few individuals allowed the same man to be Mayor, Town Clerk, [and] presiding magistrate at the Court of Record.[51] Desirable and inevitable reform followed in 1835 when, by the terms of the Municipal Corporations Act, Reading, along with all the other self-perpetuating corporations, acquired an elected borough council.

A disused water fountain on the south wall of St Laurence Church designed in 1860 by the architects, Poulton and Woodman.

West Street remains as wide as ever, allowing passengers to board buses on both sides despite a disused fountain and, on Wednesdays and Saturdays, market stalls in the centre.

The Sun Inn, Castle St, a seventeenth-century inn, later a departure point for carriers' carts and still a feature on the street.

9

From Belford Regis
to Biscuitopolis:
Reading, 1840–1911

I N half a century Reading was transformed from a market town of modest size to a substantial industrial and commercial centre. Growth brought problems of public health and housing but opportunities for large and small enterprises to thrive. In 1836 the borough had an elected council for the first time, an event of great significance for local democracy. By 1911 the built-up area and the borough boundary had extended into neighbouring parishes.

Population

From 1831 the town's population grew at a faster rate; by 1881 it stood at over 42,000 mainly through immigration. In 1851 all 13 heads of households in upper middle-class Eldon Square in east Reading were newcomers as were four in every five, almost all from Berkshire villages, in the adjacent artisan and working-class streets of St John's. Two-thirds

London Street looking north from the junction with Mill Lane towards High Bridge with St Laurence in the distance. On the left T.C. Williams, ironmonger and Kennet Brewery. (RL)

Reading
population,
1801–1911,
includes borough
boundary
extensions.

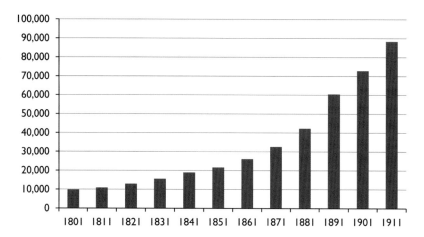

of the heads of household in the streets and courts of Coley, a mixed
working- and middle-class area, were not born in the town and nearby in
the wealthier and more salubrious Castle Street the figure reached three-
quarters, the same as in the whole of St Mary's parish ten years later.
The pattern continued through the century. The 1891 census showed
substantial migration from the capital and the West as well as from
Oxfordshire and Hampshire. Businessmen and the retired middle class of
independent means were attracted by the town's amenities and easy access
to the City; agricultural labourers, facing poor wages and fewer jobs as
agricultural depression and overseas competition hit the countryside, by
the prospect of employment. In 1911 Reading was named one of several
large towns with a significantly high number of immigrants, about half

One of the houses on Eldon
Square faced with Bath stone,
built by H. and N. Briant,
1835–39. (JD)

the population, though the rate of increase was slackening as both the birth rate and immigration declined.[1]

Expansion, housing and social class

To accommodate working-class newcomers, miserable dwellings, some built back-to-back, were crammed into narrow backyards creating courts behind street fronts. In St Laurence's parish, confined within the built-up area, such housing was the only option, but in St Giles' and St Mary's parishes beyond the crowded streets were fields and meadows ripe for less crowded development. As in other Victorian towns, much of this was piecemeal, with speculators buying small plots, building two or more houses to rent or less often to sell and using the profit for further investment. The Crown Estate north of King's Road from the 1840s and the Wheble and Cholmeley estates in the 1860s were developed in this way. Speculators with more capital could invest on a larger scale; the Morris and Stallwood partnership designed School Terrace in Newtown (1876) and the villas on the north side of London Road (1888) for George Palmer to house working- and lower-middle-class families.[2]

In the middle decades of the century Reading, like other market towns, was not large enough to have discrete suburbs. Instead, small 'integrated urban areas' housed homogenous social groups. In consequence for

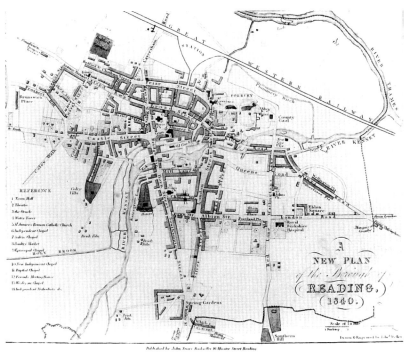

The expansion by 1840 of the built-up area to both east and west, middle-class villas and working-class terraces in close proximity. (RL)

Bath-stone
houses on the
King's Road,
c.1832–35
attributed to H.
and N. Briant,
now converted to
offices.

much of the period, and even later, the middle class, artisans and factory workers often lived within sight of each other. The former Crown Estate development was typical. On the north side of King's Road were detached and semi-detached Bath stone villas dating from the 1830s and 1840s. Farther east was Victoria Square, designed by John Billing in 1844–45. Around a pleasant green space were elegant villas, set well back from the thoroughfare, each with a long garden. In 1851 they housed retired business men, fund holders and professional families with up to six servants apiece. Behind the stables on the gardens' northern boundary ran Orts Road from which terraced streets, home to labourers and a few artisans, extended to Kennet Side and the canal. Victoria Square houses commanded a rent of £85 a year, those in Orts Road £8.

To the south, that part of the Crown Estate bounded by London Road, King's Road, Watlington Lane (later Street) and Eldon Road/Eldon Square also housed two disparate social groups. Employees of the biscuit factory and independent tradesmen paid £7 to £10 a year to rent houses in the respectable terraces of an area later described as 'the village in the town': St John's Street and Road, St John's Hill and Princes Street. The east end of St John's Road led into Eldon Road and Eldon Square where Bath stone houses built in the 1830s were occupied by professionals and fund holders

OS map, 1882, showing artisan terraces of St John's contrasting with the large semi-detached houses of Eldon Rd on the right.

A terrace of artisan houses in Princes Street, St John's c.1840. (JD)

Houses on Eldon Road, 1835–39, by H. and/or N. Briant faced with Bath stone. (JD)

whose rents ranged from £35 to £95 a year.[3] Entrepreneurs and professionals paid over £100 a year to rent large houses in Castle Street, five times more than the independent craftsmen and shopkeepers were charged for smaller properties. Stretching southwards from Castle Street was Pinkneys Lane, an ancient track which became Coley Street, the 'spine' around which grew the 'village' of Coley, an insalubrious district of courts and terraces on the slopes of the Kennet valley. In 1851 it was home to an eclectic mix of independent tradesmen, silk weavers, employees of the pottery, brewery and ironworks (unhealthily close to the houses) and large numbers of labourers of all kinds. Its crowded courts, some with deceptively rural names – Fir, Box, Elm, Holly and Willow – were crammed between Coley Street and Coley Place. It was one of the poorest areas of the borough, rents in the 1850s averaging between £4 and £5. Even so, a few families shared houses and others took in lodgers.[4] On rising ground to the west, the area between Coley Hill and Coley Avenue bordered by Coley Park to the south became a pleasant middle–class enclave.

During the next four decades more socially discrete areas emerged as the built-up area spread out in all directions. To the west, skilled working-class and lower-middle-class families occupied streets of terraced houses between Castle Street and Oxford Road and north to the railway line, and on either side of Caversham Road. Most houses were two-storey with two or three bedrooms, a back garden and a narrow forecourt. Villas for better-off middle-class professionals and business men lined both sides of the Bath Road. In the east between the King's Road and the canal, the terraces of Newtown, the borough's first true working-class suburb, reached the eastern boundary by the 1870s and intruded into Earley. Middle-class villas spread eastwards on the London Road from Eldon Square to the boundary and patchily up the Wokingham Road. In contrast a socially mixed suburb of Redlands was created by the 1880s on land south of London Road, sold by Lord Sidmouth in 1865, part to private individuals and developers for housing and the rest as the new site for Reading School. Biscuit factory workers in the terraces of Donnington and De Beauvoir Roads shared this Redlands Estate with the middle-class residents of semi-detached villas in Alexandra Road and Eastern Avenue. Wealthy townsmen who could afford to lease, buy or build property moved farther out, the favoured few like John Heelas into villas in Whiteknights Park, or into suburbs such as Southern Hill where Cintra Lodge was built for Martin Hope Sutton and Somerleaze designed by Waterhouse for William Silver Darter, a prosperous business man and former mayor. In the 1870s the nearby the Mount Estate, a picturesque development of semi-detached, polychrome-brick houses, was home to clerks, factory foremen, some professionals and other middle-class tenants who like most families rented their houses. By 1881 there were 8,027 houses in the borough and others beyond the boundary.[5]

PLAN
OF THE TOWN OF
READING

REFERENCE

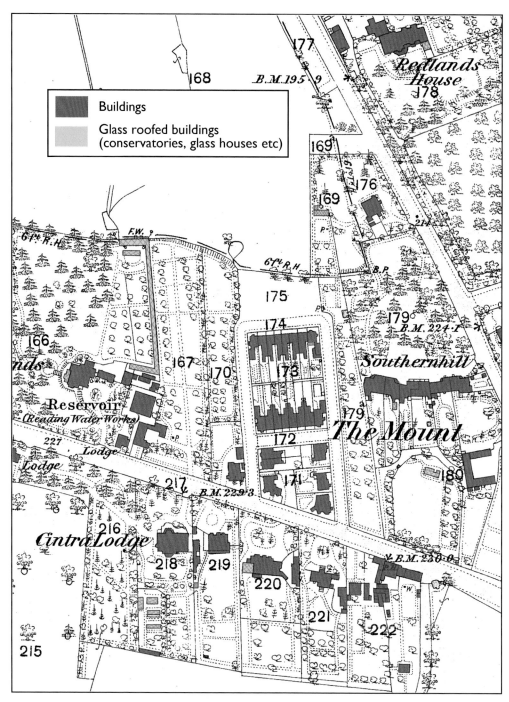

Some large houses on Southern Hill, later Christchurch Road, and the Mount Estate. Martin Hope Sutton lived in Cintra Lodge.

Part of a terrace in The Mount, *c.*1876. Decorative brickwork and terracotta window heads make for an attractive streetscape. (JD)

Consequences of growth: local government, poverty and public health

The Municipal Reform Act of 1835 provided for an elected council in Reading as in other ancient boroughs, ending government by an oligarchic corporation that had begun in 1542. In future councillors would be chosen for a three-year term, one third seeking re-election each year. They in turn would choose another six non-elected members as aldermen.[6] Though only 6 of the 22 members of Reading's unreformed corporation stood for election to the first 'democratically' elected council, the new members belonged to the same social and economic stratum as the old, middle-class industrialists and professionals, because until 1882 only men owning property worth £1,000 or with a rental of £30 a year were eligible for election, and voting remained limited to male ratepayers. Momentous as the change was for the future, the powers of the new council were limited to those of the old, except that it now had to provide a police force which it duly did in its first year. However, as an elected body it would eventually be subject to voter pressure for change.

Most reforms including that of the boroughs were preceded by an investigation by a parliamentary select committee or royal commission. One which had far-reaching consequences was the commission on the operation of the Poor Laws which reported in 1834. It judged that a system designed in 1598 for a predominantly rural population of 2 million was unfit to cope with an industrial society of almost 14 million.[7] Its proposals, embodied in the Poor Law Amendment Act (1834) determined that poor relief should still be administered and paid for locally but under a more uniform and centrally supervised system with government-appointed Poor Law Commissioners in London. Parish vestries were replaced by poor law unions, groups of parishes centred on a town, each union administered by an elected board of guardians employing paid officials. Poor relief was to be given only in a union workhouse where conditions would be less favourable than those of the poorest labourer outside, deterring claimants from applying. In theory this would force up wages and, by encouraging thrift and self reliance, improve the moral condition of the working poor.

Reading, the three borough parishes with Whitley and Southcote, was the smallest in area of the 12 Berkshire unions but one of the largest in population. Like some others in the county, Reading guardians did not immediately build a new workhouse, relying instead on the two existing parish poorhouses of St Mary and St Laurence. Annual expenditure on the poor had fallen in 1846–47 to £9,033 in total for the three parishes but if the data for the year 1848 are typical, provision was inadequate. On 1 July there were 273 'indoor' paupers and another 581, mostly the elderly, widows and the sick with their children, given 'outdoor relief' – two or three shillings in cash and one or more loaves each week – in their homes. In 1866 pressure from the commissioners resulted in the construction of a substantial workhouse on Oxford Road at the extreme western boundary of the borough, an area which centuries before had been part of Battle Manor. Designed by the borough surveyor, W.H. Woodman, and built and furnished at a cost of over £14,000, it met the standards commissioners required: separate accommodation for able-bodied men, able-bodied women with children under seven, and aged and infirm men and women with an infirmary and rooms for the master of the workhouse and his family. Pauper children aged seven and over were sent to a district school in the old Wargrave parish workhouse, jointly managed

A photograph c.1930s of Reading's Workhouse, at this date the Borough Public Assistance Institution. (BRO D/EX1638-65-60)

by Reading and Wokingham unions. The board employed the master and other workhouse officials, a relieving officer who referred paupers to the board and paid those receiving outdoor relief, and a medical officer (MOH) responsible for treating all the union's poor.[8]

The workhouse was well used as Reading guardians, in common with those of other unions, followed government policy in restricting outdoor relief to a decreasing number of paupers, just 30% of claimants in 1870 and in August 1892 just 86 compared with 324 in the workhouse and 132 children in the district school. Inmates were overwhelmingly the old of both sexes, many of whom had been labourers and some former domestic servants whose employers made no provision for their old age. One or two were young single women with illegitimate babies. These statistics do not give a true picture of poverty in the borough at this date. The workhouse was feared and entry to it avoided despite the dire poverty revealed by an inquest in 1892 on an old man, Henry Checkley. He died at the home of his married daughter, Annie King and her new baby. Her husband had been unemployed for six weeks. They had no poor relief 'and did not ask for it'; instead she pawned all their possessions including her wedding ring. The coroner's verdict was 'death by natural causes', that of the MOH either old age or 'want of nourishment'. On New Year's Eve 1904, poverty in Coley where 'people were starving for want of fuel and bread' moved a Mr C.F. Kite to anger at the churches' lack of charity. Unemployment brought real suffering. In 1888 William Silver Darter, a long-standing member of the Philanthropic Society which supported deserving workers who fell on bad times, expressed a wish that the guardians would 'adopt a judicious and extended system of outdoor relief' for the unemployed during the approaching winter though he did not comment on a major cause of poverty: Reading's low-wage economy, encouraged by the shortage of jobs in the county throughout the century and more particularly during the 'agricultural depression' of the 1870s and 1880s. Many employees were very poorly paid labourers – most of Huntley and Palmers' workers were unskilled – who lived close to the margins of poverty with no opportunity to save for inevitable family crises.[9]

The first signs of a radical change in attitudes to social welfare came with the reforms of the first Liberal government of the new century. A non-contributory pension of five shillings a week introduced in 1908 for those aged 70 and over who had not claimed poor relief was intended only to supplement existing income but was nonetheless a reform which accepted the reality of poverty for many in old age. In 1911 came compulsory National Insurance against sickness and unemployment paid for by contributions from employers, employees and the state. Winston Churchill at the Board of Trade had already set up a network of Labour Exchanges in 1909 where the needs of employer and potential employee

The dilapidated state of the original Vachel almshouses *c.*1860 necessitated their demolition and replacement. (RL)

could be met.[10] Since 1848 Reading families in steady work had been able to insure for sickness benefit with the Reading Friendly Society and after 1872 with the Berkshire Friendly Society which promoted 'providence among the industrial classes'.

For a fortunate few deserving poor, provision was made in almshouses. Nationally all existing endowments were transferred to local trustees in 1835 and placed under the supervision of charity commissioners in 1853. With their consent, all borough almshouse endowments including those of John a Larder, Thomas Vachel and William Kendrick were consolidated as the General Almshouse Charities of Reading in 1861. Four years later 32 almshouses to replace existing, dilapidated stock were built on the south side of Castle Street, funded by the charities, supplemented by public subscription.[11]

Reading also suffered from the problems common to great cities and many market towns: uncontrolled expansion, overcrowded and insanitary housing, a polluted water supply, and inadequate or non-existent drainage. The town lacked the requisite local government body to resolve them. Despite a new Improvement Act in 1826 the Improvement Commission remained largely ineffectual, lighting only the main streets by gas lamps and appointing watchmen to patrol by night. Otherwise, apart from clearing some congested areas including St Mary's Butts and King Street, it largely ignored its powers to cleanse and 'otherwise improve' the borough.[12] Much of the inertia came from disagreements between

economisers, commissioners and councillors reluctant to spend money, and the reformers. Prospects of improvement were hindered by the power of vested interests. Reading's utilities were supplied by private enterprise: the Reading Gas Company established in 1818 in Gas Lane (off Bridge Street) and the Reading Waterworks Company whose water tower was erected on Mill Lane, the site of the original 'engine'. The water company was the successor of the project begun in 1694, restored in 1818 and incorporated by Act of Parliament in 1826 though the quality and continuity of supply of its water had not improved in the interim. Neither body had much interest in promoting public utilities especially as some members of their boards were also councillors and commissioners.

A national outbreak of cholera, in 1831, the first of many, alarmed the authorities. The borough's response was to set up a Local Board of Health but, as elsewhere, interest soon waned. Nonetheless the medical men on the reformed council prompted the Sewers and Drains Committee to commission an enquiry into the dangers to public health in the borough by Mr John Billing, a local contractor, later the borough surveyor. The facts he revealed: half the houses without piped water, 75% without drainage; sewage discharging directly or indirectly into the Kennet streams used for the domestic water supply; 378 pigsties and 22 slaughter-houses in built-up areas; and a mortality rate double the national average amounted to an unanswerable demand for improvement. Though the

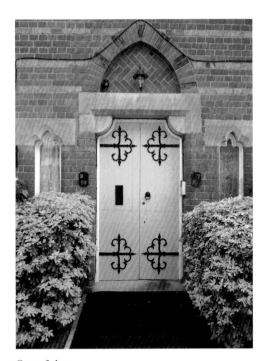

One of the rebuilt Vachel almshouses, Castle Street, showing the decorative brickwork typical of Victorian Reading. (JD)

all-encompassing Reading Improvement, Market, Waterworks, and Sewage Bill of 1847 aroused much local opposition and was rejected by a government enquiry as impracticable, reform could not be indefinitely delayed.[13]

Reading reformers supported by both local newspapers took advantage of the first Public Health Act of 1848 which followed reports showing high death rates in many towns. The Act established a General Board of Health in London whose inspectors would conduct a survey in any locality if requested, and allowed a local board of health to be set up following a petition from 10% of the ratepayers or if mortality rates exceeded 23 per 1,000. Local boards of health could levy a rate to provide sewerage and a pure water supply.[14] Reformers organised a petition for and obtained another enquiry, this one by an official of the General Board of Health, William Lee. His report in 1850 echoed that of Billing, with graphic detail supplied by clergy and parish medical officers confirming the appalling condition in areas inhabited by artisans, factory workers and paupers: back-to-back houses lacking ventilation; dwellings crammed into courts behind main streets with one privy to six or more families; several privies draining into a huge cesspool; open drains carrying 'night soil' down the street and many houses sharing one tap resulting in frequent 'epidemic, endemic and contagious diseases'. A second cholera outbreak in 1848–49 resulted in 17 deaths, most in Crown, Silver and Wynford streets, but Lee was insistent that the rising death rate, 30 per 1,000 in 1849, was not due to the disease. It was poor sanitation and drainage, resulting in outbreaks of typhoid, dysentery and diarrhoea and reducing average life expectancy in Reading to 26.3 years compared with almost 36 in Wokingham Union. Sickness also prevented men from working, took away their independence and self-respect and reduced them to pauperism.[15]

Among other improvements, Lee saw the provision of a constant supply of pure water to all houses as a necessary first stage before cesspits could be removed, water closets installed and a proper drainage system built, but since public health legislation was permissive not mandatory he could only recommend a local board of health (LBH) for the borough and for Whitley. Neither could the general board enforce change, so that improvement as in most towns and cities was hesitant or negligible. Even when Reading Council did become the LBH, its members were no more willing than before to initiate any improvements if they would increase the rates.

However, to enable it to function both as a corporation and a health authority, the council set up the beginning of a committee system which achieved some modest advances. Over the next two decades it eliminated or controlled several 'nuisances', a Victorian term for threats to health, provided no capital expenditure from council funds was required. Graveyards in the borough, condemned by Lee, were closed in 1851; a public abattoir was built (all other slaughter houses being closed); lodging houses regulated and street cleaning and removal of 'night soil' from privies put out to tender. In 1853 bye-laws were introduced allowing the council to regulate future development throughout the borough. In 1862 the LBH compulsorily purchased and demolished ten houses and shops in the slum which was Middle Row allowing Broad Street to live up to its name.[16]

The most urgent matters, clean water and effective sewerage, were sidelined for many years, partly because of a conflict of interest (councillors sat on the board of the Waterworks Company) and partly because such projects could only be financed through loans which required permission from the General Board or its successors. The need to seek such permission was seen by local government bodies of all kinds as unwarrantable interference with local autonomy. The council's hand

Photograph of a watercolour 'Mill Lane, Reading showing the mill and water tower' by Miss L.G. Parish probably *c*.1820: a somewhat romantic view. (RM)

was eventually forced by a combination of legislation and threat of legal action. In 1866 a Sanitary Act imposed on local boards of health the duty to remove nuisances and the Thames Conservancy threatened to petition parliament to prohibit the discharge of sewage into the Thames or its tributaries which Reading LBH permitted.

Action followed to improve both the water supply and drainage. The Waterworks Company had operated a pumping station at Southcote since 1850, with reservoirs there and at Spring Gardens, Whitley. However, in view of its proposal for a drainage system, the LBH applied for legislation, the Reading Local Board Waterworks Act of 1868, to acquire the company, take over its mortgage debt of £14,000 and borrow another £30,000 secured by the rates. In 1870 the Reading Local Board Waterworks, Sewerage, Drainage and Improvement Act empowered the LBH to acquire land outside its boundary at Manor Farm, Whitley, for a sewage works, set up a drainage and sewerage system for the borough, and lay more water pipes. The work took two successive surveyors several years to complete at an estimated cost of over £133,500, though new, improved waterworks at Fobney were soon needed to meet the demand from a growing population. The total debt eventually exceeded £285,000, more than a full year's income from the rates.[17]

Reading Corporation became the Urban Sanitary Authority (USA) in 1873 following the Public Health Act of the previous year which had made the provision of good public health measures and the appointment of a medically qualified Medical Officer of Health (MOH) compulsory, though his only specified duty was to report to the USA. Fortunately Reading appointed Dr John Shea, an exceptional individual. He insisted on the appointment of a sanitary committee of the council to which he reported monthly his investigations into poor water supplies, sewerage, and overcrowded housing, with detailed recommendations for changes on which he insisted. He did not spare the blushes of local dignitaries whose properties fell short of acceptable standards, insisting that no new houses should have cess pits, that owners should connect their tenants' houses to main drains and piped water, and that more houses should be built to relieve overcrowding. His reports, accompanied by statistics of progress or lack of it, make compulsive reading. He invoked the Artisans' Dwelling Act of 1868 to have some bad housing demolished, the shortage of alternative accommodation for the poor limiting progress. In 1881 the Reading Corporation Act gave the borough planning controls over minimum water and sewerage provision for all new dwellings. The first report after Dr Shea's death in 1886 by his successor, Dr Alfred Ashby, bore witness to his achievements: a small scarlet fever hospital, main sewers almost complete, 9,327 houses connected to them and 11,198 dwellings with piped water. There was still much to do. By 1902 infant mortality (under 12 months), 122 per 1,000 live births, was still

A drawing of the Royal Berkshire Hospital, *c*.1839, by the architect from an engraving by William Fletcher. (RL)

unacceptably high, but the overall mortality rate had fallen to 13.7 per 1000. The average for great towns in Britain was 17.4.[18]

The council should not be credited with all the advances towards a healthier borough though undoubtedly drains and pure water saved more lives than medicine during this period. Lagging far behind other towns of similar size and status, Reading finally gained a hospital through the generosity of Henry Addington, Lord Sidmouth, who donated the land, the determination of Mr Edward Oliver who canvassed support, and the governors of Reading Dispensary, the institution which since 1802 had provided a modicum of medical treatment for the 'industrious poor' of the town, who made a substantial donation. Public subscriptions of more than £12,000 supplemented by fund-raising events ensured that the building was completed, furnished and staffed ready to open in May 1839. It remained a voluntary hospital funded by bequests, donations, subscriptions from individuals and work groups, and charity events, in particular church collections on Hospital Sunday from 1886, the annual Hospital Saturday and Hospital Sunday parades.[19]

The other achievement of private enterprise was Reading Cemetery. In 1842 the Reading Cemetery Act incorporated the Reading Cemetery Company, empowering it to sell shares, purchase land in Sonning parish (Earley) immediately adjoining the borough boundary, and establish a

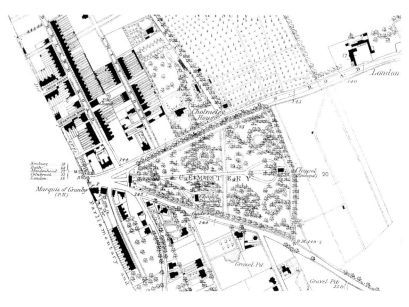

Reading cemetery in the OS map of 1875 showing its location in Earley on the borough boundary.

cemetery. Part of the area was consecrated with a chapel for Church of England burials, a similar area with its own chapel for nonconformist burials and a space set apart for those of paupers. The company had the exclusive right to sell and supervise burial plots which provided its profit, while fees for Anglican burial services were the perquisites of the vicars of the three Reading parishes who officiated in rotation. The first interment, that of Elizabeth Jacobs aged 22, took place on Monday, 1 May 1843 in the nonconformist area.[20]

Industry, commerce and transport

The coming of the railway was the catalyst for an expansion of existing industries which then attracted immigrants drawn by greater opportunities for employment. Reading was alerted to the coming of the Great Western Railway (GWR) by an invitation in the *Berkshire Chronicle* on 2 November 1833 to apply for shares. The following March the secretary, Charles Saunders, convinced a meeting of townspeople of the advantages of a railway from London to Bristol and Bath via Reading. Despite setbacks such as the difficulties of digging a cutting near Sonning and a strike by the navvies in June 1838 when their wages were not paid, the line from Paddington to Reading was complete in March 1840 and to Bristol the following year. The nearby Great Western Hotel was built in 1844 and twice extended. One line of the Berks and Hants Railway built in 1847 linked Reading to Bristol and beyond via the Kennet valley (a station at Reading West did not arrive until 1906), and another in 1848 ran south to Basingstoke to link with the London–Southampton line of the

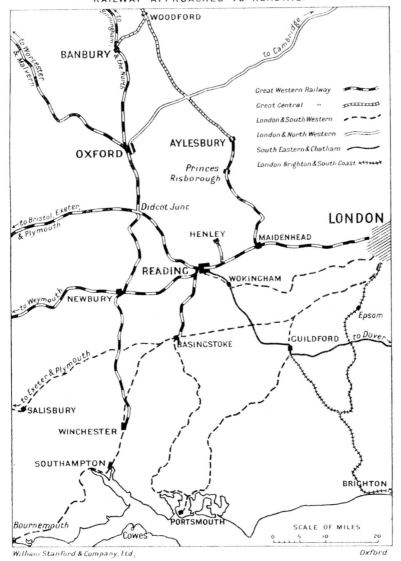

Reading, a transport hub on the railway network *c.*1900. (WMC)

Great Western Railway
Great Central   ,,
London & South Western
London & North Western
South Eastern & Chatham
London Brighton & South Coast

William Stanford & Company, Ltd.,   Oxford

South-Western Railway. A second line from Waterloo, the London and South Western Railway to Reading via Ascot joined the South Eastern and Chatham Railway from Guildford at Wokingham (1856) linking Reading to east Berkshire and much of south-east England. These lines used the Reading South Eastern Station adjacent to that of the GWR, a junction prevented by the latter's use of the broad-gauge track. Reading's status as the major transport hub of the region was enhanced.[21]

Within a few years the railway had strengthened the town's communications network and modified its occupational structure. The long–distance

A print by William Fletcher, published by Snare as 'View of Reading from the Railway near the Kennet's Mouth, 1840'. The water tower, three parish churches and St James Roman Catholic church are shown. (RL)

coach trade shrank; there were only two coaches a day from Reading to London in 1843, one in 1846 and none in 1849. Coaches operated to towns and villages but when these were connected to the line the services became uneconomic. Coaching inns reverted to mere inns or public houses. The great Cheese Fair, already in decline, disappeared as trade moved to the railway. In severe financial difficulties by the 1850s, turnpike trusts were gradually wound up with toll houses and other assets sold off. Some craftsmen involved in the coach trade were able to turn to other employment: coach builders, coachmen, blacksmiths, farriers and the like were still in demand since horses and horse-drawn vehicles remained an essential element of the transport infrastructure until well into the twentieth century. Not so the bargemen as trade on the Kennet and Avon declined. In 1851 the canal was bought by the GWR company subject to the navigation being maintained. The commercial role of the Thames had ceased long before 1885 when its value as a leisure resource was recognised.

However, the railway created more jobs than it destroyed. In 1891 at least 750 men worked on the trains, the track and at the station, but many

Example of journey from Great Western Railway timetable 1841

DOWN   Depart Reading 7.30 a.m. arrive Paddington 8.50 a.m.
UP   Depart Paddington 8.00 p.m. arrive Reading 9.25 p.m.

Fares   1st class 8s. 0d.; 2nd class 5s. 6d.; goods train (open trucks) 3s. 0d.

An aerial view of Simonds' Brewery *c.*1875 an advertisement in Smith's Reading Directory. (RL)

more in the industries it had fostered. Fondness for alliteration has led to Reading's Victorian industrial enterprises being summarised as three 'Bs' – biscuits, beer and bulbs (more correctly seeds) and the number should be at least four to include brick making, possibly five including the printing trade (books). A product which defies alliteration was Cock's Original Reading Sauce, claimed to be 'the best fish sauce ever made' though it would eventually lose out to Lea Perrins. The manufacturers had local raw materials to hand, wheat, malting barley and clay but as important was the entrepreneurial energy which drove the businesses. As ever, Reading's location, emphasised by its railway connections increased the town's ability to attract migrants: most of the town's leading industrialists and at least two of its important retailers were newcomers as were many workers.

The largest of Reading's industries during this century was created by two families, neither native to the town but both possessing the Quaker virtues of honesty, integrity and hard work who had the good fortune to arrive and build their businesses during the mid-Victorian boom years. Joseph Huntley and his sons, Thomas and Joseph, set up a biscuit bakery and shop in 1822. George Palmer, an experienced confectioner with an interest in engineering arrived in 1841. Huntley's business in London Street built on sales to passing coach passengers prospered, but had not Thomas Huntley and George Palmer become partners and

Aerial view of Huntley and Palmers' factory, 1889, from London Road. The Kennet flows through the factory from west to east and a branch line to the railway runs to the north. (RM)

The only surviving building of Huntley and Palmers' factory.

A collection of Huntley and Palmers' decorated biscuit tins, two shaped like their delivery vans, one an inlaid table and another an inlaid box, twentieth century. (RL)

moved to a new site between the Kennet and the railway, from which a branch line ran into the factory, it would have remained unremarkable. Their complementary skills resulted in a factory with modern machinery producing an enormous range of delicious biscuits, but it was the Palmers who controlled the firm from the death of Thomas Huntley in 1857 until 1921. In 1888 the site was described as 'a small town in itself'. An enterprise which in 1844 had employed just 17 men and boys, making a profit of about £200, became in 1900 the largest employer in the borough with 5,049 on the payroll, between one-fifth and a quarter of the town's workforce, of whom 10% were women. The profit that year was £158,500. Quaker values and strong paternalism prompted the provision of a range of benefits for employees: non-contributory pensions after 50 years' service; a sick fund, an annual paid excursion holiday, a Mutual Improvement Society and, from 1898, a multi-sport recreation club. Wages, however, were modest, men on average earning 16s. 9d. for a 58½ hour week in 1861.[22]

The Huntleys founded another business in 1832 which became essential for the biscuit trade and expanded in tandem with it, employing 800 workers by 1911. Joseph Huntley junior, an ironmonger, was persuaded by his father to make tins and tin-lined boxes which would keep biscuits fresh and undamaged. Boxes produced by his firm, Huntley, Boorne & Stevens, became the best known of their wide range of tin and iron products. Decorated tins were produced, especially for Christmas and national celebrations, becoming a selling point and later, collectors' items. More practically they ensured that their contents, exported all over the world, arrived in excellent condition.

Like the Huntley and Palmer families, James Dymore Brown was a newcomer, younger son of a Wiltshire farmer. The refusal of borough magistrates to grant fresh licences allowed existing firms which owned all the public houses to profit by selling poor-quality beer. Improvement came with Dymore Brown who arrived in 1831. From supplying just two outlets until in 1854 when he gained the contract to supply beer to the Royal Berkshire Hospital, he became the largest retail brewer in the town. The Simonds family had arrived in Reading in the previous century. William Blackall Simonds founded his brewery in 1789 but, unlike others, his firm produced a quality beer. His son, Blackall Simonds, increased production at his wholesale brewery to 15,000 barrels a year and was supplying 37 tied public houses by 1839. Both companies expanded from the 1860s using modern technology and energetic marketing. By the 1880s Dymore Brown's Royal Albert Brewery, Queen's Road, was producing 14,000 barrels of beer a year. Simonds' far greater annual output of 115,000 barrels was based on the sale of pale ale and their own SB beer to railway refreshment rooms in southern England and army barracks at home and abroad. The large site in Bridge Street purchased by William Blackall Simonds a century before now proved invaluable. In addition to these two, trade directories list ten more breweries including Weldale, Victoria and Lion breweries in the 1880s employing draymen, clerks and maltsters as well as brewers.[23]

The 1891 census recorded 558 gardeners and seedsmen, some working for G. Phippen, nursery man, seedsman and florist, with a shop in Broad Street and nurseries on Oxford Road. However, the firm which was the third of the Bs (as Bulbs) was Sutton's Royal Berkshire Seed Establishment, again developed by a second generation entrepreneur from the business begun by a newcomer to the town. John Sutton's seed and corn business was transformed by one of his sons, Martin Hope Sutton, through the same honest business practices, diligence, flair and ability to capitalise on the town's unique advantages, as obtained in the biscuit and brewing firms. He met a national demand for pure, viable seeds and quality plants, transporting them quickly and safely by rail. The introduction of the penny post in 1840 and the purchase of property in the centre of Reading for a retail shop, distribution centre and trial grounds were essential factors in the firm's success. In the later years

The jacket cover of a Sutton's book on growing vegetables and flowers, 1930–40. (RM)

The
CULTURE
of
VEGETABLES
and
FLOWERS

SUTTON

The
CULTURE OF
VEGETABLES
& FLOWERS
FROM SEEDS
AND ROOTS by

Sutton & Sons, Reading

CASH PRICE
8/6
NET
NINETEENTH EDITION

Seven Bridges House, Bridge Street, designed by Sir John Soane, 1790, the only surviving building of Simonds' Brewery. (JD)

of the century the offices and warehouses in the Market Place were extended and trial grounds acquired on London Road for scientific experiments by Martin Hope Sutton and his son to improve crop yields and disease resistance. There was a 'similar precision in organization and management' as at Huntley and Palmers but with a smaller number of employees, only 500 by the end of the century. National recognition of Sutton's achievements came with the granting of the royal warrant in 1871; the biscuit factory was similarly honoured in 1883.[24]

Though they began and grew as family firms, the combination of various factors induced all four to become limited companies. H. & G. Simonds was the first in 1885, then Huntley and Palmers (1898), Dymore Brown & Son (1902), and Sutton and Sons in 1931. In general the move proved successful though for another well-known firm, Barrett, Exall and Andrewes, once the largest supplier of agricultural machinery in England, incorporation as Reading Iron Works in 1864 was not sufficient to prevent closure. Despite innovative products, its lack of financial, managerial and commercial skills in the face of declining demand and strong competition resulted in its collapse in 1887. The trade depression which hit agriculture particularly hard made the 1880s and 1890s difficult for other local businesses. Reading's banks, notably Stephens, Blandy & Co., and Simonds (of brewery fame) despite remaining profitable throughout, lost their identities completely. The former amalgamated

with Lloyds in 1899 and the latter sold out to Barclays Bank in 1913. The Savings Bank established in 1817 under an Act of that year survived to attract the savings of working families able to put by small amounts from time to time. These savings banks – there were others in many towns – invested the small sums deposited by local savers into a special government fund at interest. No records survive for the Reading Bank, though the nature of its clientele is suggested by its opening hours: during workers' dinner hour three days a week and in the afternoon and evening on Saturdays.[25]

Bricks had been made in the borough almost as long as beer had been brewed; there is evidence of the craft in the twelfth century. From about 1800 several kilns were built and by the 1840s there were five, all in the Katesgrove and Castle Street areas. In 1851 there were 52 brick makers in the borough. By the 1870s kilns owned by three family firms, Coley Kiln (Wheeler Brothers), Katesgrove and Waterloo Kilns (William Poulton) and Avenue Works (S. & E. Collier) had opened to supply builders and developers though it was Collier who came to dominate, moving to his huge Grovelands complex in Tilehurst and later taking over Poultons. His speciality was 'Reading Red', though he and Poulton also produced grey-faced bricks, both used in creating the diaper patterned walls and terracotta mouldings which public buildings and many houses in the town still display, unless an unthinking owner has covered them with pebbledash. Reading brick was also used by architects outside the borough: Lutyens' house at Sonning is a famous example. Of the four Bs, brick making was probably the most arduous and unpleasant trade, despite mechanisation, but its products are still to be seen in every Reading street.[26]

Printing of books, newspapers and myriad ephemera had developed before 1835 and grew in importance. Histories of the town, Coates (1802), Man (1816) and others were published locally. The firm of F. & H. Cowslade continued to print the *Reading Mercury*, although their bookselling business was taken over by George Lovejoy in 1833. Later trade directories list 19 or so printing firms of varying size with 360 employees in 1901. Some newspapers, the *Berkshire Herald* (1868–70), *Telegraph* (1869–73) and the *Reading Express* (1879–84) were short-lived but the *Reading Mercury* (a Liberal paper) and *Berkshire Chronicle* (Conservative) continued, joined by the *Reading Observer* (1873–1924) and the *Reading Standard* (1887–1965).[27]

Describing it as a town dominated by three or even five trades is to

S. & E. COLLIER, LTD.,

MANUFACTURERS OF ALL KINDS OF BUILDING MATERIALS IN CLAY, LIME, AND CEMENT, AND OF PLAIN AND ORNAMENTAL POTTERY,

GROVELANDS, READING.

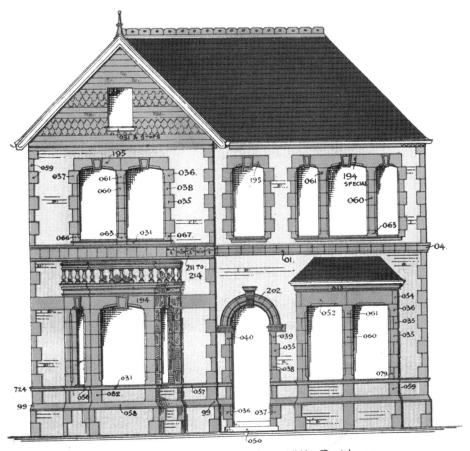

Terra Cotta Facings &c for a Villa Residence.
THE BLOCKS SHEWN ARE OF STANDARD DIMENSIONS
BUT THEY CAN BE MADE TO SUIT ANY BRICK GAUGE.
KEPT IN STOCK IN STANDARD DIMENSIONS.

SCALE OF FEET.

A page from a Collier trade catalogue, 1880–1908, displaying a range of terra cotta facing blocks. (RM)

paint a two- rather than the multi-dimensional portrait that was Victorian Reading, ignoring the many workers who catered for the day-to-day needs of a large town, those who still plied traditional crafts and the vast number of undifferentiated labourers. Despite the dominance of the biscuit factory, the town supported a very mixed economy. In the streets and lanes of Coley in 1851 were large numbers of male labourers, craftsmen including bricklayers, wood workers, suppliers of food including grocers, bakers and several women laundresses, washerwomen and charwomen. Thirty years later Chatham Street and the area south to the Oxford Road housed an eclectic range of shoemakers, tailors, beersellers and publicans, bakers, butchers, one or two shop workers and, drawn by proximity to the cattle market and the railway station, a few dealers in livestock and many railway workers. Most evident in an age of physical expansion were the building trades. In the Reading of 1891 builders, bricklayers, carpenters, joiners, plumbers, glaziers and others (not including labourers) made up almost 9% of the workforce. Family businesses, butchers' (182) grocers' (350) and bakers' shops were spread around the town, many streets having at least one general store; daily shopping was necessary in an age before domestic refrigerators. In Silver Street in 1888 between the White Horse at number 39 and the Rose and Crown at number 75 were three general shops, a grocer and a marine store dealer. Self-employed shoemakers, tailors, dressmakers and milliners (all women) competed with the few large stores, often called 'warehouses'. Public houses, about 130 of them, were mainly in the older parts of the town, but few residents were far from a hostelry or beer house.

A growing number of men (clerks were almost invariably men before 1900) were needed to deal with the paper work generated by large firms, as well as in local government departments, the offices of public utilities, banks and building societies. They formed the lowest tier of an expanding middle class. Higher in status, the middle middle class, were the professionals: Church of England and nonconformist clergy, medical men at the new hospital, chemists, and lawyers, auctioneers and valuers employed in an active property market as well as architects who designed houses for the élite business men who comprised the upper middle class. A sign of the changing times was the appearance in trade directories in the 1880s of several photographers, one or two electricians, and in the 1911 census, cycle manufacturers, electrical workers and even a few 'motor-car drivers', probably chauffeurs.

The majority of women were not in paid work and those who were tended to be in low-paid occupations. They appear in the 1850s as washerwomen and slightly superior laundresses, many still listed as such in the 1891–1911 censuses. However, by this date they were outnumbered by women in general domestic service, 3,238 in all in 1891. Mostly young and unmarried, servants were employed by middle-class families. Even commercial travellers and biscuit factory clerks living in The Mount could afford a solitary 'general servant'. Including 93 working in hotels and boarding houses, a total of 14% of Reading's women in 1891 were 'in service'. A few women entered more highly rewarded occupations, 1,013 as milliners, 593 teachers (outnumbering men), 176 nurses and 68 shopkeepers. Even fewer had broken into the world of commerce: 45 were commercial clerks and 32 worked in the printing trades.[28]

Wages remained low, many of the workers in the four major industries being unskilled or semi-skilled. A biscuit worker's average wage was 21 shillings for a 48-hour week in 1913. In contrast, skilled men in building, engineering and printing could earn from 25 to 41 shillings a week. Living standards improved in one important respect from the late 1870s: the availability of imported foodstuffs reduced the cost of some basic essentials. Unfortunately prices generally began to rise after about 1900 while wages remained static. In Reading in 1905 ¼lb tea cost 4d., sugar 2d. a lb, bread 5½d. a 4lb loaf and an egg a penny. 'Colonial' butter at 1s. 11d. or Irish at 1s. 0d. a lb, frozen mutton from New Zealand (5d.) and Danish pork (6d.) a pound were cheaper than English and were the preferred choice for many in Reading where food prices equalled those of London though wages were up to 20% lower. Rents absorbed between 4s. 6d. a week for a four-roomed and 7s. 6d. for a five-roomed house. The Reading Distress Committee, set up in 1905, dealt with hundreds of applications from men in irregular employment, those with large families or those unable to manage their meagre finances.[29]

The construction of the horse-drawn tram system by the Reading Tramways Company Ltd in 1878 provided transport for workers from the suburbs to town-centre factories. The first line stretched along

A posed photograph by Walton Adams of a horse-drawn double-decker tram in 1893 on Oxford Road en route from Palmer Park and Cemetery Junction. (RL)

A photograph of a Reading Corporation Belfast trolley bus going west along Oxford Rd, 1968, shortly before the system was abandoned. (RL)

Oxford Road from Brock Barracks via Broad Street and King's Road to Cemetery Junction. Passengers travelled for a penny a mile reduced by half for workers on services before 7 a.m. and after 5.30 p.m. In keeping with Victorian religious sensibilities, no trams ran on Good Friday, Christmas Day or between 11 a.m. and 1 p.m. on Sundays. At their furthest extent, the lines ran into town from Whitley, Caversham Bridge, Bath Road, Addington Road and Oxford Road. The corporation reserved powers to regulate the running of the system, and in 1899 and 1900 sought to extend the lines and build a generator in Mill Lane to provide electricity to drive the trams though electricity had been supplied to the town since 1893 by the Reading Electric Supply Company. The corporation acquired the tramway company in 1901, operating the first electric trams in 1903 on a slightly extended route. For a favoured few, the arrival of the automobile – the first Berkshire RAC annual general meeting was held in Reading in 1905 – heralded a new era in transport though its impact would come much later. Speedier oral communications came with the telephone. In 1894 there were 300 private, business and institutional subscribers, George W. and Walter Palmer being, respectively, Reading 2 and 3.[30]

Trade

Throughout the century Reading maintained its role as a centre for the exchange of agricultural produce with a still rural hinterland. Its major industries obtained the bulk of their raw materials from the locality until the latter years of the century. Better facilities ensured that farmers would make Reading their market of choice including a new cattle market in Great Knollys Street in 1850, financed as a commercial company. With more horses in work in the late nineteenth century than at any previous period, the horse market on the same site did good business. The most important market remained that for corn for which the borough sought legislation in 1853 to build a corn exchange as did many market towns. The Markets Act abolished existing tolls in kind on corn and payments for weighing other goods such as cheese but empowered the corporation to charge money tolls or an entry fee. These varied with the commodity (cheese, poultry, eggs, butter) and quantity sold. Pitched sales (bulk sales in the open air) were forbidden and all sample sales (small bags taken from a sack) had to be made in the Corn Exchange.

The entrance to the former Corn Exchange from the Market Place. (JD)

A photograph of Heelas shop, Minster Street *c*.1875. (RL)

The shops of independent traders and craftsmen, butchers, bakers, shoemakers and even an occasional hairdresser, crowded cheek by jowl along all the town-centre streets. They, their families, and sometimes unmarried employees lived behind and above the shop. Many employed a 'general domestic servant', often a teenager new to the town and doubtless overworked. By the 1880s directories and newspapers monitor the appearance of large retail shops with imposing frontages, and eventually the chain store. The largest occupied strategic corner sites: Jackson's on King's Road and High Street; McIlroy's, rebuilt in 1903–04 in palatial style on West Street, Oxford Street and Cheapside, was described as Reading's Crystal Palace. Heelas expanded from Minster Street through to Broad Street and Wellsteeds, drapers, occupied 126–132 Broad Street where four shop assistants still lived above the premises in the 1880s, the proprietors having abandoned the town centre.[31]

Reading's status as one of the most important markets in its region is also demonstrated by the number of carriers visiting the town, especially on market days. The country carrier was an essential link between village and market town, taking villagers' produce to sell, making purchases for them, and acting as a local 'bus service. As early as 1848, Reading ranked tenth in a national list of towns with most carriers' visits. By 1874 there were 67 carriers operating to or via 104 villages and eight towns, most within a radius of about ten miles but a few from farther afield. Almost all came on Wednesday and Saturday though others came more frequently to visit the many retail shops open daily. Nearby villages such as Arborfield, Theale and Pangbourne enjoyed one service a day, Tilehurst and Sonning two, and in the 1880s Caversham had an hourly service by horse-drawn omnibus. Carriers operated from the larger inns, each having his own preference, among them the Sun, the Broad Face, the Saracen's Head and the Duke's Head.[32]

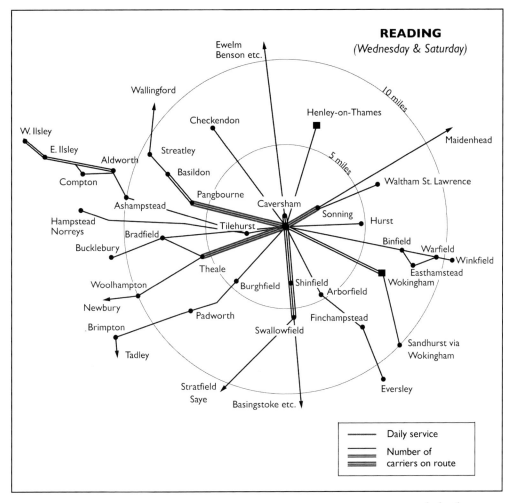

A sketch map showing villages and towns on the more important carriers' routes to and from Reading. Wednesdays and Saturdays were market days. (Trade directories 1887–88)

By the 1860s Reading's pre-eminence among the Berkshire towns was undeniable, confirmed in 1868 when it acquired the status of county town, Abingdon losing a role it had formerly shared.[33] Some 'county buildings' already existed; others were constructed. The County Gaol and House of Correction of 1793 was rebuilt in 1844 on the same site near the ruins of the abbey. Much of the county administration was located in the Forbury nearby: the Assize Courts in 1861 to house all future assizes and county quarter sessions and following the County Councils Act of 1888 and the election of the first Berkshire County Council the following year, Shire or County Hall, its administrative headquarters. In 1878 the newly named Berkshire Regiment occupied the newly built Barracks on Oxford Road. The corporation had already provided civic buildings to reflect its status and to house its expanded administration. In 1874 they commissioned one of the outstanding architects of the age, Alfred

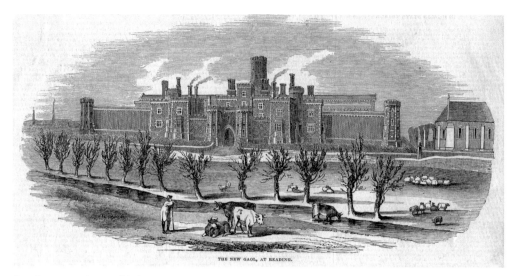

An 1844 engraving, entitled New Gaol at Reading from the railway embankment. It also shows St James' Roman Catholic Church. (RL)

An engraving from 'The Building News' 15 July 1910, with the caption 'Berkshire County Hall', Reading. Built in 1858–61 it also housed the Assize Courts. (RL)

The Town
Hall designed
by Alfred
Waterhouse and
others, 1872-97,
and the entrance
to it by Alfred
Waterhouse,
1875. (JD)

Waterhouse, to design a new Town Hall 'encasing' the old. Within a few years a substantial extension was needed.[34]

The Act of 1888 also designated as county boroughs all towns with over 50,000 inhabitants. Reading, with a population increased to almost 60,000 as a consequence of the boundary extension of 1887, became the only county borough in Berkshire. As such it became a 'multi-purpose authority' responsible for all aspects of local administration independent of the county: highways in 1889, education in 1902, and the poor law in 1929. Boroughs had been public health authorities since 1875.

The extension had not been universally popular. Among other dignitaries, George Palmer voiced his opposition at a public meeting held to discuss the necessary legislation. The proposal was mainly driven by public health concerns. Absorbing Southcote and Whitley seemed logical since they belonged to borough parishes for poor law purposes. However, though Newtown was mostly in the borough, it extended into Earley Liberty, then part of Wokingham Poor Law Union and Rural Sanitary Authority (RSA), centred on Wokingham, seven miles away. Wokingham RSA had failed lamentably to provide drainage and sewers for Newtown, whose sewage emptied directly into the Kennet and which relied on Reading for its water. The Education Act of 1870 had allowed the establishment of board schools, one of which was in

Earley but run jointly by the borough and the Liberty. 'To all intents and purposes,' said the mayor, 'they [Newtown residents] are Reading people.' He might have added that most of them worked in the factories and workshops of the borough, especially at Huntley & Palmers at the western end of the suburb. Some middle-class families had migrated to more salubrious areas in Earley where large semi-detached villas were being built close to the tram terminus. To a lesser extent the built-up area had also extended into Tilehurst parish in Bradfield Union and RSA. The Reading Corporation Act of 1887 incorporated parts of both liberty and parish into the borough and extended its boundaries for sewerage and drainage purposes well beyond its immediate needs since, as its supporters correctly surmised, further population growth would extend the built-up area. Tilehurst and Earley School Board districts were transferred to Reading School Board, parts of Earley and Tilehurst removed from their respective RSAs became part of Reading RSA but the poor law jurisdictions remained unchanged. A new entrance to Reading workhouse and more accommodation was needed in 1894 and again in 1911.[35]

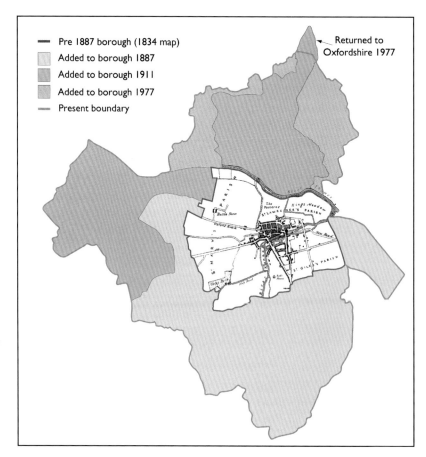

A map showing the expansion of Reading from 1887 to 1977. (Originally drawn by Margaret Simons and published in *Atlas*.)

Adjoining the borough's northern boundary on the far side of the Thames, Caversham had become to all intents and purposes a suburb of Reading. By 1909 it had a socially mixed population of 9,785 and a diverse economy. Caversham Bridge, the only crossing for wheeled traffic, had been rebuilt and widened by the corporation in 1869, which now controlled and managed it. The bridge with one tram terminus situated on its southern approach provided a direct route to the Reading Station for passengers and railway workers in Caversham village. Those from Lower Caversham, developed from the 1880s into a distinct neighbourhood of terraced streets, had a pedestrian bridge, the Clappers, which led directly to the biscuit factory. In several respects Caversham was dependent on the borough: at least half of its wage-earners worked there; some children attended Reading schools; and the community relied on Reading Waterworks to supply the clean water its Medical Officer of Health demanded. The sewerage works, constructed in 1896 by its new Urban District Council (UDC) were not coping and there was little hope of improvement. Although Caversham was in Oxfordshire, Reading was best placed to supply its local government provision such as education, a fire and police service as well as drainage, sewerage and water, but would only do so if it became part of the borough. Again, an expanding residential area with attendant public health issues was driving administrative change, though Reading was accused of 'earth hunger'. But Caversham was not Earley: it lay in another county. A bitter and protracted attempt locally and in parliament by Oxfordshire County Council and the UDC to prevent the loss of Caversham's separate status ended in July 1911 when the Reading Extension Act was passed bringing the developed and developing area along the Thames into the borough. Caversham Park Estate and the rural north of the parish remained outside. The same Act incorporated another tranche of Tilehurst parish into Reading, creating a boundary that survived for just sixty years.[36]

Successive borough extensions required a larger council, 39 councillors and 13 aldermen representing the 13 wards into which the five medieval wards were now divided. Modest political change was also underway. For most of the period since 1835 contested council elections had been few, most councillors belonging to a small group of leading business men and lawyers – Palmers, Suttons, Simonds, Blandy – and mostly Liberals. However, the abolition of the property qualification for councillors in 1882 had resulted in some contested elections coinciding with the arrival of a new political movement, the Social Democratic Federation in 1891 whose extremely small membership belied the future significance of socialism in the borough. Only five Socialist councillors were elected between 1894 and 1906 and election to the aldermanic bench would take several decades.[37]

However, Reading's greater population did not warrant additional

A marble statue of Queen Victoria by George Simonds at the east end of Friar Street erected by the borough to commemorate her golden jubilee, 1887. (JD)

MPs. The Great Reform Act of 1832 abolished most 'rotten boroughs' and gave a vote to all men paying £10 a year rent, the majority of the existing borough electorate, which hardly changed. It began to increase with later parliamentary reform. The Act of 1867, enfranchising all male occupiers of a dwelling house and lodgers paying £10 annual rent, resulted in a borough electorate of 3,228, rising to over 6,000 in 1884 and over 11,000 by 1913. Until the secret ballot was introduced in 1872, corruption was as bad as ever, though the larger number of voters made it more expensive; as early as 1841 Charles Dickens declined to stand because of the cost. Organised political parties emerged, first Whig and Tory and after the 1840s, Conservative and later Liberal, the latter two setting up local organisations. Thomas Noon Talfourd sat as a Whig in the 1830s and 1840s, Sir F.H. Goldsmid, George Palmer, G.W. Palmer and Rufus Isaacs as Liberals, the party which, with the exception of three elections 1885, 1886 and 1895, represented Reading from 1868 to the First World War, even when Reading became a single-member constituency in 1884. Signs of change began in the 1890s with the emergence of working-class politics in the borough. An 'Independent Labour' councillor was elected for Battle Ward in 1894 and two members of the Social Democratic Federation (SDF), formed in the borough in 1891, won seats on the School Board in 1895. Though Harry Quelch (SDF) stood unsuccessfully in the 1898 parliamentary election, the newly formed Labour Representation Committee, forerunner of the Labour Party was represented on the council from 1900. The formation in 1911 of a branch of the National Union of General Workers, the majority of whose members worked at Huntley and Palmers further strengthened the socialist movement which would be increasingly influential in borough politics in coming decades.[38]

10

Religion, education and culture
c.1892: retrospect and prospect

B Y THE 1890s organised religion had reached a peak of influence in secular as well as spiritual concerns. Modest provision of leisure pursuits and education provided by voluntary effort before 1840 blossomed into an eclectic range of elite and popular cultural activities with opportunities for learning from elementary to further education. Clubs and amateur societies supported by local business men attempted to wean the working classes from drink, and the churches provided practical as well as moral and spiritual support. Before the end of the century localism and church/chapel membership were both challenged by national institutions and professional entertainment.

A tinted postcard of Caversham Lock and lock keeper's house, 1906, when the Thames provided leisure facilities such as boating, swimming and fishing. (RL)

Caversham Lock.   M.J.R. B.2964.

A photograph of Holy Trinity church, Oxford Road, originally a chapel-of-ease from St Mary's.

Church and chapel

The 1851 Religious Census, the only one of its kind before 2001, demonstrated that the three ancient parish churches and St Mary in Castle Street and the several nonconformist chapels were no longer alone in meeting the spiritual needs of the growing population. The three attracted large congregations, at least 2,800 at one or other service on Sunday, 30 March 1851.[1] About 1,100 parishioners worshipped at new churches built to serve the new residential areas: Holy Trinity, Oxford Road (1825), a chapel-of-ease in St Mary's parish with full autonomy in 1875 and St John in Watlington Street (1837) serving a parish carved out of St Giles. However, the Church of England was shaken by the strength of nonconformity revealed in the census for though at least 66% of the townsfolk attended a church service on 30 March, over 48% of them were nonconformists.[2]

This partly explains the determination to provide for potential parishioners. The energetic evangelism of Samuel Wilberforce, Bishop of Oxford, to whose diocese Berkshire was transferred in 1836, contributed powerfully to the formation of new parishes and churches in the 1860s: Christ Church (from St Giles' parish); a reconstruction of Greyfriars in St Laurence's parish and All Saints, Downshire Square.[3] St Luke in Erleigh Road and St Stephen in Newtown (both from St Giles' parish), St Saviour, Berkeley Avenue and St George in Tilehurst (both from St Mary's parish) were built in the 1870s and 1880s. Outside the borough when the church was built in 1877–80, St Bartholomew's parish was carved out of St Peter's, Earley, itself formed from Sonning as recently as 1854.[4]

The nonconformists were equally energetic. To the chapels of 1851 – Congregational, Baptist, Methodist both Wesleyan and Primitive and the Quaker Meeting in Church Street – were added others. The confidence of the Methodists was displayed in their Watlington Street Chapel, its spire matching in height and splendour that of the rebuilt St John's church opposite, and in the elegant Primitive Methodist Chapel in London Street, formerly the New Public Rooms. Enthusiastic evangelisation spurred some individuals and congregations to build other centres, including the imposing Free Church in Gosbrook Road, designed by Waterhouse and partly financed by a large donation from Ebenezer West (1877) replacing a smaller Baptist Free Church (1865), the Unitarian Chapel (1878) and the new Wycliffe Baptist Chapel both in London Road (1881). Growing congregations built Methodist chapels in Lower Caversham and Caversham Heights matching the new Anglican churches there. Roman Catholics, with one church, St James in 1851, built St Anne, Caversham (1902) and St William of York (1904). The synagogue dates from 1900. The result was a profusion of religious buildings with 'the means of grace more visible than the means of production'.[5]

The cost of building was high, at St John met by the incumbent; others were funded from donations of land and money from the wealthy as well as the pennies of the less well-off. Support was not confined by confessional allegiance. Though the Palmers were Quakers, their friendship and the Liberal politics they shared with its first vicar procured George Palmer's gift of the land and financial support for a mission church and later for the parish church of St Bartholomew. Charles Stephens, a

By 1890 Reading's ancient parishes had been sub-divided to provide new parishes and churches and Greyfriars' church restored for worship.

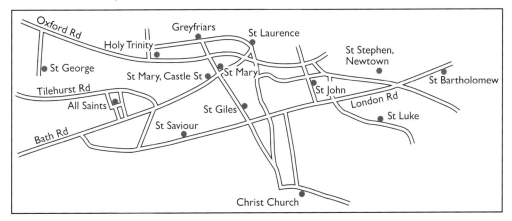

New Public Hall, London Street, Reading.

The New Public Hall in London Street opened in 1843 for lectures, concerts and other 'improving' events.

banker of Woodley Hill House, Earley, and many parishioners and other well wishers also contributed. St Luke's congregation on the Redlands estate made do, as did several other congregations, with an iron church, replaced by a brick building when gifts of land and money by wealthy patrons and local fund-raising permitted. Maintenance costs left most congregations with little to spare and caused concern as congregations dwindled at the century's end.[6]

Education

Most new congregations and the ancient parishes established schools or Sunday schools, all too few as the Education Census of 1851 showed. In addition to five small endowed schools, there were nine Church of England schools and one nonconformist, the British School. Including the 85 boys at the Ragged School and 98 pupils at the prison school, there were 2,132 children in elementary education in 1851, fewer than half of the under ten-year-olds in the borough. Even so, by the 1860s 73% of Reading men and 76% of women were literate, although a report in 1861 would show that most English children attended school for less than six years. Greater national provision came slowly, partly the result of a small but increasing annual grant from central government begun in 1833 and shared by the two societies, National and British, at first just to build schools. Running costs were to be met by parochial fund-raising and until 1891 by one or two pennies a week from the pupils (school pence). So began the bi-partite system, schooling supported locally by religious bodies and centrally by the state. Government influence grew: an inspectorate, Her Majesty's Inspectors (HMI) was set up in 1839 and a scheme for training teachers in 1846.[7]

Determination to ensure value for money resulted in 1862 in a new system of funding schools, the Revised Code popularly known as 'payment by results'. The award of a government grant to a school depended on each pupil's record of attendance and attainment in standardised tests in the '3Rs' conducted by HMIs. In time additional subjects such as history and geography attracted funding. From 1864 head teachers were required to keep log books recording information on attendance and test results. Many of them included far more, providing us with a graphic picture of Victorian school life. In 1892 infants at Newtown School, sitting on tiered benches, had a series of 'object lessons', each on a single subject – the cat, the dog, coal and an orange – while in music lessons older children learned five songs that year including 'Home, Sweet Home'. Among the staple fare were mind-numbing recitations and spellings learned and tested, short and long division sums worked *ad nauseam* and tedious needlework lessons producing garments the school could sell to raise funds. There were lighter moments. Church school pupils enjoyed Sunday School outings and holidays on patronal feast days. Older children from all schools took part in a Children's Concert at the Town Hall in 1892. Though schools had to open for a minimum number of days, the timing of the school year was determined by each school. Since a good attendance record for each pupil was essential to secure his or her government grant, the head would close a school in periods of severe weather or epidemics to avoid absenteeism, adding extra days in lieu at the end of term. In January 1892 measles and scarlet fever closed six schools for several weeks.[8]

By the 1860s it was clear that the provision of school places was beyond the capacity of religious bodies, especially in large towns. William Forster's Education Act of 1870 aimed to 'fill up gaps' with schools built and administered by locally elected, voluntary school boards and funded by the rates, supplemented by the government grant and school pence. Full responsibility for organising the school system was under local control: managing the budget, providing books and equipment, determining the dates of school terms, appointing and deciding the salaries of teachers and enforcing attendance, although government determined the school-leaving age: 10 in 1880, 11 in 1893 and 12 in 1899. As in the provision of poor relief and road repairs, the parish was losing out to larger, democratic bodies and ultimately to central government.

Reading was one of ten School Board Districts in Berkshire. By far the largest, it took its place with the Poor Law Board and the Local Board of Health as one more local authority in a crowded field. The printed, neatly bound copies of the annual reports of Reading School Board testify to the commitment of its members, some like J.H. Wilson (chairman 1871–96) and Alfred Sutton (1871–83), serving for almost the whole period. Election for three-year terms helped to ensure continuity, and membership of the borough council provided political experience. Both Anglicans and nonconformists were represented but, as the law required, religious education was non-denominational even though the school day began with a hymn and a prayer as it did in parish, now called voluntary, schools. By 1876 when the government allowed school boards to enforce school attendance in their own and in the voluntary schools in the district, there were board schools at Coley Street, Katesgrove, Silver Street and a joint Reading–Earley school in Newtown, the buildings financed by loans guaranteed by the rates. Year on year the board continued to build as the borough population grew. Grovelands eased the strain on Oxford Road schools, overcrowded with 1,000 pupils in 1888 though Newtown with 1486 was even more pressured. That year the six board schools provided for 5,465 pupils, the thirteen voluntary schools only 4,899. Average attendance was almost 80%, enforced by attendance officers with fines on recalcitrant parents. Generally excellent reports in attendance, the 3Rs, needlework and music from HMIs ensured high levels of government funding with higher grants for the few older pupils learning English, geography, cookery (girls) or drawing (boys).[9]

The Reading School Board filmed at its last meeting in 1903 with E.P. Collier, Chairman, Miss Edith Mary Sutton and Miss Daisy Jane Ridley, both elected in 1901. (RL)

The 1892 report noted a new school, Battle, a new infant school at Redlands and most significant, a Central School in Dorothy Street for boys staying on beyond the statutory leaving age, encouraged by a government ruling of 1889 which allowed the establishment of technical education on the rates. The syllabus had been broadened in some schools to include English, geography, drawing, animal physiology, botany and chemistry. Board schools accommodated 6,423 pupils, voluntary schools 5,613 with 85% average attendance. In 1902 with E.P. Collier in the chair, and with two woman members present, Miss Daisy Jane Ridley, the first woman elected to the board, and Miss Edith May Sutton, the first woman elected to the borough council in 1907, the board drew up a balance sheet of its achievements on the eve of its dissolution: 12 schools, the latest in Swansea Road, E.P. Collier School, serving the community near Caversham Bridge, and a new junior mixed (boys and girls) in that part of Earley absorbed by the borough, later Alfred Sutton School. All had been designed by local architects, notably Joseph Morris and S.S. Stallwood.[10] In 1901 the first class for disabled children in the borough was set up in Oxford Road School. In hand were proposals for the John Henry Wilson School, built in 1904, and a 'higher elementary school' in Finch's Buildings. Wilson had served as chairman from 1871 with 'marked distinction and eminent ability' until a few weeks before his death. The board schools were filled to capacity: 9,326 children on the registers, taught by 273 teachers and 71 pupil-teachers with 169 boys and 179 girls staying on beyond the school leaving age to Standard VII. The Borough Free Library had supplied school libraries with books, 22,354 loans being recorded. Senior scholars visited the Art Gallery and the Abbey Ruins. There were evening classes at Central, Battle, Oxford Road and Redlands where 870 scholars were taught a range of subjects from composition and arithmetic to shorthand, book-keeping, ambulance /home nursing and French. These classes had been established through pressure from Socialist members of the Board and would after 1902, the board recognised, be classified as Higher Education. The legality of the provision of free higher grade and evening schools by bodies, elected to provide elementary education only, had been challenged in the courts in 1899 and declared illegal by the Cockerton Judgement. However, the board could be satisfied with its achievement, much though later generations might quarrel with the Victorian view of what constituted education.

By 1902 the government 'block grant' to the board amounted to £11,325 14s. 0d. The cost to the rates was higher, at £15,952 7s. 8d., a six-fold increase since 1875. The highest expense, £21,180 10s. 4d., was teachers' salaries, locally agreed and ranging from £150 a year for the head of Newtown, Miss Jones, who had a training-college certificate, to £50 for an assistant teacher, untrained but qualified through service in school. Though the board met running costs from income, they had borrowed heavily for building especially in the previous few years, resulting in a debt of £117,419 10s. 8d., including over £51,000 to Reading Corporation.[11]

The board had recently taken over one voluntary school, Southampton Street British School with 801 pupils, which later became the George Palmer School, Basingstoke Road. Southampton Street's experience was not unusual. Many voluntary schools, including eleven in Reading, had found it difficult to repair and rebuild after government funding for building was removed in 1870, and consequently provided fewer than half of the places of the board schools. Several schools administered by the ancient parishes were in the town centre, in overcrowded, slum or potentially slum areas whereas population growth was on the periphery.[12]

In 1902 the Balfour Education Act took advantage of the creation of county councils and county boroughs to re-organise the education system. Local control of schools was transferred to county, county borough or borough councils, the local education authorities (LEAs). Board schools were re-named council schools, and though the managers of voluntary (church) schools remained responsible for the buildings, running costs were to be met from the rates. Reading's status now proved significant since county boroughs, unlike municipal boroughs such as Newbury and Maidenhead, were given control over both elementary and secondary education. Reading Corporation added one more committee, the Education Committee to the borough administration. Almost immediately it faced problems: a 'ratepayers' strike', a feature of many urban areas with large nonconformist congregations who objected to supporting church schools from the rates.[13] In 1906 the Liberal government allowed LEAs to provide school meals and, from 1907, a school medical service.

Reading School and other schools

The Municipal Corporations Reform Act of 1835 removed from the corporation its responsibilities for municipal charities which had been carried out with varying levels of care and integrity for over 250 years, assigning them to bodies of trustees nominated by the council. Among the charities were two which circumstances threw together in the 1870s. Reading Free (Grammar) School had experienced a chequered history reaching its nadir in 1866 when with just three scholars and the lease on the schoolhouse about to expire, the headmaster abruptly left. The second was the Kendrick bequest of 1624, partly used to build the Oracle which had long since lost its original purpose, being occupied by a number of small tradesmen and manufacturers of rope, sacking and pins. It was demolished following a final and successful legal challenge to Reading's right to the endowment by the Governors of Christ's Hospital. In 1849 they took from the borough the remains of the bequest except some land including the Portland Place estate, bought with the £500 bequeathed

THE NEW GRAMMAR SCHOOL AT READING.

New buildings,
Reading School,
1871.

to support poor clothiers which had been faithfully administered. This remainder became the 'Kendrick Loan Charity'. In 1867 following negotiations between the trustees of the charity and those of the grammar school, and with the approval of the Charity Commissioners, the Reading School Act received royal assent. This provided for the rebuilding on a new site of the grammar school to be a fee-paying institution administered by 13 trustees including borough councillors. Land on part of the Redlands estate was purchased, a contract to design the school placed with Alfred Waterhouse, subscriptions invited and a contractor agreed. The new buildings opened on 11 September 1871.

The cost, far exceeding the sum raised by public subscription, was met by a huge mortgage, partly secured on the Portland Place estate. A series of crises – inability to service the loan; insufficient fee income to meet running costs and salaries; conflicting views between successive headmasters and the council and within the borough as to the character of the school – came to a head in 1882. The previous year the Reading Corporation Act enabled the borough to issue corporation stock through the Bank of England and use the income to liquidate debts. From the half a million pounds subscribed, the corporation settled many outstanding debts (for drainage schemes, the new Town Hall etc.), including paying off the school's mortgage. The school was to repay this loan over 70 years but when in 1908 it became clear that it could not, the site and buildings were handed in trust to Reading Corporation which took over

Kendrick Boy's School, Queen's Road.

the administration and effectively guaranteed the debt in return for free places being offered to Reading day scholars.

The transfer of the remainder of John Kendrick's bequest, 73 acres at North Farm, Tilehurst, and land in Waltham St Lawrence from Mary Kendrick's Charity, had been accepted by the Endowed Schools Commission in 1875 into the Kendrick Schools Scheme. This empowered ten governors, one a woman, to build two fee-paying day schools, one each for 100 boys and 100 girls admitted by entrance examination with a small number of free places, awarded on merit. Each taught a grammar-school syllabus. Watlington House became the girls' school with new buildings on Queen's Road for the boys. Both were soon over-crowded.

In 1904 the council's proposal to use its powers over secondary education under the 1902 Education Act to solve the accommodation needs of the Kendrick Boys' School and the financial shortcomings of Reading School by amalgamating the two generated bitter argument. Should an institution originally intended to benefit the town's scholars be funded from the rates as a public boarding school? 'Amalgamation' was delayed but eventually took place in 1916 However, since 208 Kendrick boys but only one member of staff transferred to Reading School, a 'take-over' would be a more accurate description. It retained a small boarding element but in essence became a fee-paying grammar school controlled by the borough which awarded free places to 25% of the 500 or so day scholars. In 1909 Kendrick Girls' School became a separate foundation, eventually relocated to a new building on London Road. The existence of these two fee-paying schools would complicate attempts by

The Green Girls' School in Broad Street until 1884 when it moved to Russell Street. (RL)

future councils to meet the very different educational requirements of the twentieth century.[14]

The Blue School, now known the Blue Coat School, continued its role of educating boys to be craftsmen. It was administered by trustees, mostly tradesmen who in 1853 transferred the school from its cramped and unhealthy site in Silver Street to Brunswick House next to Reading Waterworks on Bath Road. It remained a free residential school for 42 poor boys aged 11–14 or 15 from the three ancient parishes, and after 1887 from the extended borough. The three-year curriculum, including science and mathematics, aimed 'to qualify [them] for trade, superior mechanical employment or a professional clerkship'. The Green School continued to train students for domestic service well into the next century.[15] Among new foundations was Leighton Park, a Quaker public school which opened in 1890.

Libraries, private and public

The 1851 Education Census recorded two other quasi-educational institutions, in Reading. The Athenaeum in Friar Street, the only one in the county, was founded in 1841. Members, all male save for six women, paid a guinea a year to use a library of 1,253 volumes and a reading room and to attend literary and scientific lectures. Similar provision was made by the Literary, Scientific Society and Mechanics' Institute. In return for a subscription of twenty shillings a year, half price for mechanics, it provided a library with over 2,000 volumes and weekly lectures on a variety of subjects.

Photograph of the New Public Hall, London Street, built 1843.

From 1843 to 1861 it held meetings in a suite of rooms in the New Hall, an imposing building in London Street, built as a venue for public lectures, concerts and balls. It was succeeded in 1881 by the Reading Literary and Scientific Society which began as a local organisation in the Redlands area.[16]

The concept of lending libraries was not new – its origins are traceable back to the eighteenth century – but always on a subscription basis. The largest in Reading was begun by Edmund Havell at his shop in London Street, taken over by George Lovejoy in 1833 and developed to become the Southern Counties Circulating Library of 70,000–80,000 volumes 'not surpassed by any library in the South of England' by the 1880s.

In 1855 the stamp tax on newspapers was abolished and in the same year the Public Libraries Act authorised local authorities to provide library buildings and books. Reading needed a museum to house Mr Horatio Bland's collection, bequeathed to the borough in 1877, but it was pressure from some townsmen especially Thomas Rogers, a former Town Clerk, and William Isaac Palmer which resulted in Reading gaining both a museum and a library. Public support for William Isaac's existing free library in West Street, set up at his own expense, was partly the reason why the council agreed to build not only a free library but also a museum, a reading room, accommodation for the Schools of Science and Art and a concert hall in which a Willis organ was installed.[17] The problems involved in acquiring the land, organising a public subscription to defray the cost, persuading ratepayers to meet the substantial shortfall in donations, and organising a competition for the design, delayed the opening to May 1882. William Isaac, who contributed £25,000 to the cost of the buildings and donated all his West Street books to the new library, chaired the Library Committee of the Council until his death the next year. In 1897 an extension in Valpy St provided a newspaper reading room and an art gallery (now the Majedski Gallery). Meanwhile the museum acquired the finds from the archaeological excavations at Silchester (*Calleva*), which attracted 1,570 visitors on Bank Holiday Monday, 1892.[18]

Other public-spirited individuals were responsible for branch libraries in two expanding suburbs: in Caversham, Dr Jamieson B. Hurry and

The terracotta entrance to West Street Hall, 1887. In 1899 an extension to the Hall was built called the William Isaac Memorial Building.

Caversham Library, a prize-winning design by William Lewton, 1907. (JD)

W.B. Williams and in West Reading a Voluntary Committee chaired by E.P. Collier. The sites were purchased or donated by private individuals with grants to the tune of £4,000 and £2,575 respectively from the Carnegie Trust for buildings and equipment. Once the libraries were built, Reading Borough and Caversham UDC took over their maintenance. Caversham Library became a borough responsibility in 1911.[19]

Churches and chapels also took seriously the need to provide the means of education and improvement, with many providing reading rooms. St Peter's Church, Caversham, and St John's Mission Room had reading rooms. St John's, equipped with a library of 600 volumes and daily newspapers, was for working men. At an AGM in March 1892 it was agreed they should provide a bible class, the chairman stating that it was 'no use learning until the age of 13 or 14 and then dropping it'. Continuing education was a 'necessity'.

Adult Education, the Extension College and the WEA

Such a belief was already being demonstrated. Public libraries, open until 10 p.m., were usually full in the evenings with 2,000 readers daily in 1898, and 207,674 loans made annually by 1912. Adjoining the library with their own entrance on Valpy Street were the Schools of Science and Art, which had begun as separate institutions in Reading in 1860 and 1870. They amalgamated in 1882 under a scheme funded by the government Department of Science and Art, South Kensington with additional income from the borough. Effectively providing secondary and adult education, they taught teenage students, a few of whom progressed to university, and arranged lectures for the 'industrial classes' on a range of subjects from book-keeping to natural sciences, 'likely to be of practical use to the working man'.[20]

Other lectures proved to be of lasting significance. On 20 August 1892 the *Berkshire Chronicle* reported, 'What was last year little more than a dream is now an accomplished fact'. The first University Extension College had been founded, it declared, 'due to the Governing Board of Christ Church College, [Oxford] and the citizens of Reading.' The lecture series which had this happy outcome was an initiative of the Oxford University Extension Movement which brought the expertise and learning of the university to a wider public. Since 1885 the University Extension Association in Reading, the oldest and most important in the Oxford District, had been organising series of lectures. The fee for twelve Saturday lectures on Shakespeare in the academic year 1891–92 was five shillings, but more accessible and more popular were the Tuesday evening lectures at the Town Hall by Mr H.J. Mackinder of the University of Oxford on *Revolutions in Commerce*. Costing just a penny a time, they were intended to enable working men and women 'to widen their knowledge and generally improve themselves'. Some of 1,500 who attended the autumn series in 1892 wrote essays, much praised by the visiting academics who corrected them. The students' achievement was in part due to the support of the Students' Association presided over by the vicar of St Laurence, Rev. J.M. Guilding, and the book supply of the public library. That the local press reported the text of the lectures indicated that adult education was newsworthy.

The enterprise of the Extension Association and the great appetite for learning shown by the townspeople explain Christ Church College's choice of Reading for a great experiment, the creation of a local college affiliated to the University of Oxford. H.J. Mackinder, elected to a studentship by Christ Church, relieved of his Oxford duties but retaining his salary, became head and eventually principal of the college to which the borough council transferred the management of the Schools of Science and Art and the use of their accommodation both in Valpy Street and in the Hospitium of the Abbey. Additional teaching rooms and a library were built creating a hotch-potch of make-do to which the British Dairy Institute transferred in 1896. In this cramped space 658 students, young and old, attended day or evening classes on all manner of subjects from the classics to agriculture, the latter attracting some full-time scholars. In 1896 a court of governors and an academic board was established, Mackinder remaining as principal until succeeded by William Macbride Childs in 1903. With 55 teaching staff in five departments, Letters and Science, Agriculture, Horticulture, Fine Art and Music, the pattern was set for decades to come. The initiative had come from Oxford but the finance and effort from townspeople, Mackinder, and the University Extension College's first Vice-Chancellor, Childs.

The Hospitium of the abbey from St Laurence's churchyard which housed the Schools of Science and Art and then the University College. (RL)

Honouring a Victorian philanthropist

Reading's many benefactors have been honoured in various ways. Beginning in the eighteenth century a donor might be made an honorary freeman of the borough during his lifetime. After death the names of streets (Blagrave and Sidmouth), institutions such as schools (Kendrick and Wilson), baths (Arthur Hill) and green spaces (Palmer) perpetuated their memory. Uniquely in the last decades of Victoria's reign, public demonstrations of gratitude and affection marked the passing of particularly generous townsmen.

One such was the great and sombre gathering to pay last respects to William Isaac Palmer (1824–93). A younger brother of George and like him a migrant to Reading where he served an apprenticeship, he later returned here to become a partner in the firm where he was factory manager. He never married and at the time of his death in January 1893 he was living in a house, Hillside, in Allcroft Road designed for him by the firm of Morris & Stallwood, well cared for by his four indoor servants, his coachman and gardener. On Saturday, 30 December, in apparent good health he presided over the usual entertainments and next day, despite the inclement weather, walked to the Quaker meeting. That evening he was taken ill with an abdominal aneurism and died on Wednesday 4 January, aged 69. As the news spread, the bell of St Laurence tolled and flags flew at half mast.

Unlike some other businessmen, he never sought public office and though he did become a magistrate in his later years it was as 'the life and soul' of the Temperance Movement and a great benefactor to the borough that he was revered. A genuinely religious man who was active in the Reading Quaker Meeting, his philanthropy was anchored in and driven by his Christian faith. It was said of him that his 'life was entirely devoted to the good of others'. He was an active president of several local temperance societies, one of which, the Help Myself Society, he had founded, and regularly attended the Saturday evening entertainments in the West Street Hall and elsewhere. In addition to substantial donations to major projects such as the new municipal buildings, he is said to have given £10,000 a year 'on good works' to needy individuals and worthy causes.

As a member of the Palmer family, it was inevitable that he would be given a high-profile funeral; in fact it was virtually a civic occasion. All shops were asked to close during the proceedings and despite the rain and cold of Monday, 9 January 1893, huge crowds lined the route of the cortege as it moved slowly from his home to the Meeting House in Church Street via Kendrick Road, London Road and London Street, including many of the 'poor and needy' to whom he had been 'the truest friend'. Preceded by 2,000 biscuit factory workers walking six abreast, an open hearse carried the coffin, covered in flowers from the family. Behind came 55 carriages carrying family members, his servants, representatives of borough organisations, county gentry and delegates from national temperance societies. The procession took twenty minutes to pass, men raising their hats and caps as it did so.

In contrast to this great demonstration of public grief and respect, the burial service followed traditional Quaker practice of silent worship occasionally interrupted by prayers and quotations from scripture from individuals moved by the Spirit. William Isaac was then buried in the burial ground near his mother and sister. Since the Meeting House could accommodate only 300 worshippers, a service in St Laurence was held at the same time attended by many councillors and local dignitaries. His favourite hymn, *Rock of Ages*, was sung as it would be at memorial services held over the coming days in other churches and chapels in the borough and at Grazeley where William Isaac owned a farm. Perhaps some of the tributes verged on hyperbole but there is no mistaking the impression that his life of service made on the community. In 1899 an extension to the West Street Hall to be called the William Isaac Memorial Building was erected in his memory, paid for by public subscription. He is now little known in the borough where others have been awarded higher recognition. He deserves better, if only as an example of a life of devoted service to others.

Sources: Reading Mercury 30 December 1892 and 7 January 1893; T.A.B. Corley, *A Quaker Enterprise*, 120–2; Census returns, Reading District 23, 1893; Gold, 121.

Portrait of
W.I. Palmer, JP,
by Frank Holt, 1885.
(RM)

Generous financial grants allowed the college to survive and then prosper: from Lord Wantage and Walter Palmer in the 1890s to liquidate its debts; from the Sutton family towards new buildings and from the brothers George William and Alfred Palmer £50,000 as its endowment. With the gift by Alfred Palmer of Acacias, the family's house on London Road with the six acres on which it stood, and the option to buy Portland Terrace fronting the street, Childs was able to move in 1904 to the site on London Road that would be the college's home for the next sixty or so years, though most of its teaching accommodation had still to be built. The number of full-time students rose as 'hostels' were built, the first being Wantage Hall for men largely funded by Lady Wantage after her husband's death. The pre-eminence of agricultural studies was confirmed by the establishment of the National Institute for Research in Dairying in Shinfield in 1909.[21] The college's aims were noble: 'to bring education of a university type within reach of those who cannot go to the university … to stimulate the desire for intellectual life, to diffuse both "liberal" and technical education, to train good citizens and to erect a ladder by which the chosen intellects of all classes may climb to the universities themselves.' The last of these proved difficult to achieve.

An important feature of its early history was the college's involvement in adult education, offering in-service training in academic subjects to teachers and pupil teachers, later in its School of Education, and co-operating with the Workers' Educational Association, the WEA. In 1904 a meeting to form the first WEA branch in Reading was attended by Albert Mansbridge, a part-time clerk with the Co-operative Wholesale Society in London who had founded the movement the previous year. The WEA's maxim that students should not be mere recipients of

The Library, University College, London Road, 1923. (JD)

learning but share in its delivery and organisation was a belief shared by Childs. The links between the WEA and the college developed, especially as tutorial classes became an important part of the WEA's work, though whether such classes should help a few working men into higher education or provide 'liberal studies' for the many became a contentious issue. Nevertheless, the joint committee of the two bodies, formed to organise tutorial classes in 1910, played an important role in adult education in the borough until the late twentieth century.[22]

Leisure activities: improving and popular

Many other self-improvement organisations which could be found even in small towns flourished in Reading, appealing to all manner of social classes and interests.[23] Among the more intellectual organisations were the Berkshire Archaeological and Architectural Society whose members included local architects and clergy, the Reading Natural History Society formed in 1881 'to promote the natural history of the Reading area', and the Literary and Scientific Society dating from 1887 whose president was the early historian of Reading Abbey, Jamieson B. Hurry. For those with practical skills the Gardeners' Mutual Improvement Association and the Beekeepers' Association provided support and advice. Opportunities to make amateur music, serious and light, could be found with a number of orchestral and choral societies which gave concerts at several venues in the town including the Town Hall, and by the early years of the new century the University College Department of Music was giving public performances. The well-established series of subscription concerts featuring works by classical composers remained firm fixtures of the winter months. Perhaps less melodious were the vocal renderings which formed part of the annual dinner, soirée or smoker of every sporting, trade or intellectual society, many held in public houses or inns. In 1892 the Waltonian Angling Society chose the ironically named *Moderation* in Caversham Road, the Quoits Club the *Duke of Edinburgh* in the same street.

Less morally acceptable yet easily accessible was alcohol, for some the 'demon drink'. Public houses were ubiquitous. A trade directory for the 1888 lists at least 113 licensed premises in the borough with 13 in Broad Street, 4 in the Market Place and 11 in Friar Street. Of more concern to moral crusaders were the many public houses and beer shops in working-class districts. Despite the presence of a powerful brewing fraternity, the Temperance Movement whose origins in the borough date from the 1830s became a prominent feature of town life as it was in very many urban communities. The Methodists and other nonconformist congregations took the lead in forming Bands of Hope in Reading in the mid-1850s, and by 1878 the *Reading Mercury* could report that 'the adherents to the cause have rapidly increased in numbers, and the temperance platform now

A postcard of Broad Street with a statue of George Palmer and an electric tram.
The archway on the right leads to the Market Hall. (RL)

forms a common ground on which all parties and members of religious communities can unite'.[24] Temperance societies, of which there were 12 by the 1880s, numbered their members in hundreds, and Temperance hotels and cafes appeared in the town centre. In 1892 George Palmer chaired some of the popular Sunday afternoon meetings of the oldest of these organisations, the Reading Temperance Society, in the Town Hall. More attractive were the free Saturday evening entertainments begun in 1872 by George's brother, William Isaac, especially in the 1890s when moralising speeches were curtailed in favour of songs, recitations and other musical interludes. This simple diet was popular, partly because it was free. In 1892 the Reading Lads' Temperance Association offered the audience of 300–400 youngsters aged 10 to 18 an illustrated lecture, *A Temperance Voyage Round the World*, still somewhat heavy fare though they were promised models including one of an entire working railway the following week.

There were lighter moments, one such being the annual Temperance Festival. In 1892 it was held on 27 June with transport from Reading by special train to Padworth Park. Swings and roundabouts were provided for the children, refreshments and entertainment for the adults. In 1894 the same event at Coley was attended by a crowd of 14,000 including 4,000 members of temperance societies.[25]

Other organisations unashamedly displaying a moral, even religious purpose were founded or supported by the middle class whose sense of social obligation was inspired by religious conviction. An historian of the borough has commented on the 'purity of its middleclassness', unsullied by any 'lordly influence', and to judge from an 1880 tax assessment its middle classes either formed a larger social group or collectively enjoyed more wealth than did those in other parliamentary boroughs such as Bath, Salisbury and Oxford.[26] In addition to serving on a range of public bodies from the corporation to the Hospital and Dispensary Committees, the Palmers, Suttons and others gave their time and not a little money to 'improving' societies of one sort and another, mainly for the artisan and working class. They saw active leisure as a way to promote individual moral improvement and eventually a society based on sound moral principles; members of all classes should be actively involved in at least one organisation or leisure pursuit.[27] It was a pious hope given that many working–class men earned too little to spare either time or money to indulge in much leisure.

A very different organisation, the Pleasant Sunday Afternoon Society, a national inter-denomination movement, came to Reading in 1892 where it was closely associated with the Broad Street Congregational Chapel. Four hundred men attended its first meeting in February. Prizes for regular attendance, clothing and sick clubs were also offered. Significantly it was a working-class movement, not beholden to paternalism or piety; several future local Labour Party politicians were among its members.[28]

Physical activity was also considered important in creating a moral society. This required space which, as development in the centre became denser and the fields near the town succumbed to housing, was provided by public bodies and private individuals. The first, unintentionally, was the cemetery, founded in 1843 and described in directories of the 1880s as 'an interesting resort for the townspeople who find pleasure in loitering amid the pleasant natural pictures of this secluded spot'. Altogether more cheerful were the Forbury Gardens, acquired by the corporation in stages between 1854 and 1861. Designed as pleasure gardens with a bandstand to provide entertainment, a gigantic iron statue of a lion to marvel at (commemorating the men of the Berkshire regiment who fell at the Battle of Maiwand in Afghanistan), and with access to the abbey ruins for a romantic stroll, they attracted large crowds. In 1875 King's Meadow, used from 1814 to 1874 for race meetings, became a public recreation ground partly through the generosity of George Palmer. In 1901 the corporation bought Prospect Park on the border with Tilehurst, a welcome green space amid the advancing terraces of west Reading, and in 1907 laid out the Thames Promenade. One great advantage of all these places was that access was free, an important consideration for poorer townspeople.[29]

An 1865 engraving of Reading Cemetery with the two chapels, Church of England (centre) and Nonconformist (right).

They also provided opportunities to engage in sport, one of the active leisure pursuits encouraged by Reading's middle class and religious organisations. To judge by the number of amateur clubs, football was the most popular. These clubs proliferated especially after the introduction of bank holidays in 1871 and half-day Saturday working. Fixture lists of matches between local clubs, the Post Office, the Royal Seed Establishment, Reading East End and Christchurch among them, appeared in the press. Huntley & Palmers' huge workforce could field a number of teams drawn from various departments, rejoicing in 1892 in such names as the Madeleine Rovers and the Sugar Wafer Swifts. Appropriately they played in Palmer Park which had opened the previous year on a 49-acre site between St Bartholomew's church, the railway line and Wokingham Road given to the borough by George Palmer and where his

The Maiwand Lion in the Forbury Gardens by George Simonds (1886) commemorating the Berkshire Regiment's role in the 1880 Afghan Campaign.

A statue of George Palmer in the park which he gave to the borough in 1891.

statue, erected in Broad Street during his lifetime, now stands. The Park was large enough to accommodate a cinder track where Reading Athletic Club and the Cycling Club could train and hold competitions.

Sport of all descriptions was a year-round activity. Swimmers used the indoor pool at South Street in winter and moved outdoors to the rivers or segregated bathing places for men (1879) and women (1903) in King's Meadow in summer. Reading Athletic Harriers turned out in all weathers for cross-country runs and the Angling Association's devotees frequented the banks of local streams and rivers. In summer cricket, tennis, bowls and quoits clubs resumed activities, athletes moved on to running tracks and rowers practised for the Amateur Regatta on the Thames, held on Bank Holiday Monday. Indoors, members of boxing and billiards clubs were just as keen though the 'smokers', lavish teas and annual dinners in which every club indulged reduced their members' physical fitness.[30] It is doubtful whether all these activities were accessible to all townspeople. Many were beyond the reach of many poorer workers since they required specialist clothing and equipment to say nothing of club fees.

A drawing *c.*1920 of the Vaudeville Electric Theatre. It was enlarged in 1921, called 'The Vaudeville', still showing silent films. (RL)

The Royal County Theatre, Friar St, *c.*1908. (RL)

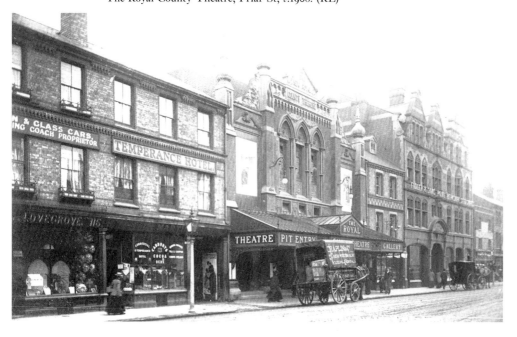

The Reading Establishment: a posed photograph *c*.1846 of W.H. Fox Talbot and members of the photographic studio set up by Talbot (possibly standing centre-left) and Nicolaas Henneman (third from the right) in Russell Terrace. (RL)

Those with money to spare might be seduced into less energetic pursuits. After a long period of being unfashionable, theatre-going made a come-back towards the latter part of the century. The theatrical venture begun by Henry Thornton could not be sustained after 1817 despite several attempts by his successors. In early Victorian Reading, occasional celebrity performances such as those given by Charles Dickens in the 1850s or spectaculars of a pseudo-scientific kind were what drew the crowds. The slow return of theatre began in 1868 in a building in Friar Street which operated 'with fair success' for two years as the Assembly Rooms. It was damaged by fire in 1870, restored and converted into the Theatre Royal and refurbished in 1887 to become the Royal County Theatre. Its varied programme and wide range of seat prices attracted some big audiences in the early 1890s; the pantomime *Dick Whittington and his Cat* was so popular in February 1892 that many people were unable to get tickets. The theatre's success was short-lived. In August 1894 it burned down, its place being taken by the Princes Theatre, originally a chapel in Friar Street. Magnificently refurbished in 1895 with elaborate plaster ceilings, velvet-covered seats and electric light, it was re-named, with singular lack of originality, the New Royal County Theatre. For the rest of the period it enjoyed great success offering drama from Charley's Aunt to plays by Bernard Shaw with occasional pantomimes and musicals. Music hall and variety shows filled the Palace Theatre in Cheapside, built in 1907. The Vaudeville Electric Theatre offered an exciting new art form: moving pictures. More successful than similar pre-war venues, it flourished as cinema became the entertainment of choice.[31]

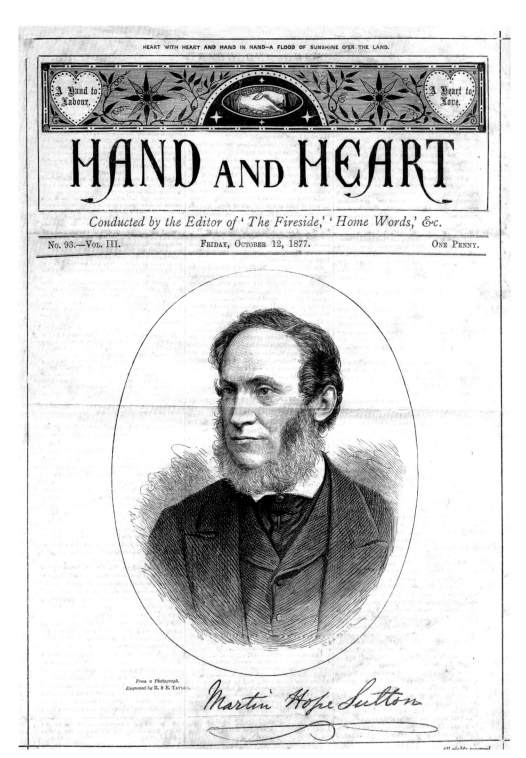

Front cover of Hand and Heart magazine with a portrait of Martin Hope Sutton, 12 October 1877. (RL)

Theatre and cinema were alien to the active leisure promoted by the moral and religious leaders of Victorian Reading in that both were passive and undemanding. Football was beginning to follow suit. From its formation in 1871 Reading Football Club had been an amateur side playing at the Recreation Ground, King's Meadow, but like all such clubs felt compelled to adapt to circumstances. The employment of professionals in some northern teams opened up an unacceptably wide gap between their standard of play and that of amateurs. In 1894 Reading FC joined the Southern League and the next year signed its first professional player, becoming mainly professional by about 1900, by which time the club had been settled at Elm Park in Norfolk Road, Tilehurst, for four years. The ground held 10,000, the largest venue in and around the borough with an entrance fee of 6d. (half price for boys and ladies). In Reading as elsewhere, though amateur clubs still flourished, football was increasingly becoming a spectator sport.[32]

Other leisure pursuits organised by commercial enterprises such as boat trips on the Thames and excursions by rail or char-a-banc were also something to be paid and budgeted for like any other commodity, competing with churches and local societies for people's time and money. Sunday remained sacrosanct – shops, theatres and public houses (open only for short periods at lunch and tea time) – were closed, but even so, towards the end of the century, attendance at church and chapel declined, Roman Catholics excepted. The decline in Reading has been attributed partly to the conflicting demands of God and Mammon, partly to the discomfort felt by many workers at being unable to contribute to parish funds, partly to the snobbishness of some congregations. There is no evidence of a falling-off from Christianity's moral standards or a rejection of its core beliefs, but attendance at a Sunday service had become a matter of choice rather than of obligation.[33] Even so, this was a matter of degree; 34% of the population had been absent from church in March 1851 in an altogether more deferential age, so arguably it was the religious revival of the intervening years that was exceptional.

Certainly there were perceptible alterations in the character of provincial towns to which Reading was not immune. Social solidarity was still evident in the huge crowds assembling to witness the unveiling of George Palmer's statue (1891) and the funeral processions of local benefactors such as William Isaac Palmer (1893) and Martin Hope Sutton (1901). But societies as well as religious organisations were finding it harder to recruit members especially among the working class, many of whom could not afford the contributions. Upper-middle-class supporters of voluntary movements such as the Palmers and Suttons were either dead (George died in 1897) or no longer resident in the borough. Like many successful businessmen they invested in land, becoming gentry. Their sons, products of public school and university, were remote from the world of business and of social

Postcard showing McIlroy's department store, Oxford Road *c*.1905. It later expanded to occupy the corner with West St. (RL)

obligation. If Reading was losing active participation in parish and chapel and 'the purity of its middleclassness', it was also losing something of its localism. The town's banks were taken over by larger national organisations, several having branches in the borough by 1911. Local businesses including McIlroys, Heelas and Jacksons still dominated the High Street though national chain stores were evident, including the Co-operative Society, Boots, the Chemist and Smiths, the stationers. With the abolition of the stamp duty on newspapers, mass-circulation national daily papers were available in libraries and reading rooms and at ½*d.* a copy *The Evening News* and the *Daily Mail* (1881) were even affordable for the lower middle class and some 'respectable' working men.

The unveiling of a statue of Edward VII in 1902 by the latest generation of the Palmer and Sutton families marked not only the beginning of a new era but also the passing of an age during which a few committed, civic-minded Christian businessmen had been responsible not only for the borough's commercial prosperity but had contributed substantially to the spiritual, mental and physical well-being of its inhabitants.

11

Survivals and arrivals:
Reading, 1912–1960

MUCH of its Victorian past was still evident in early twentieth-century Reading, not least its poverty and insalubrious working-class housing. Both would be addressed by local and national government, though neither was eliminated. Meanwhile, a new economy was beginning to evolve, a development that would be well advanced by mid-century, with traditional industry giving way to a growing service sector. Access to new technology, especially cinema, radio and eventually television, continued to dilute local popular culture.

Reading before the First World War

Attractions in the shape of the silent cinema, the bicycle and the motor car were there to enjoy in what has been called the 'Edwardian summer', although a substantial number in Reading, as elsewhere, could not afford

A plan of the main roads and features of the town after the boundary expansion of 1887 and including much of Caversham. (WMC)

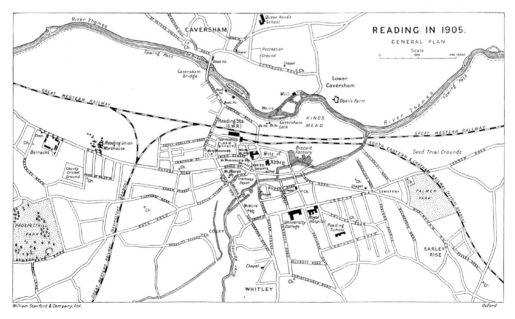

them. Rising prices, stagnant wages and unresponsive employers resulted in a period of widespread industrial unrest in the immediate pre-war years. At Huntley & Palmers where the paternalism of the first generation had been replaced by a less considerate management, the first ever strike took place in 1911 over wages and trade-union recognition, resulting in a modest wage rise and eventually, after government threats, improvements in pay and working conditions in both the biscuit and tin factories. It was not an auspicious beginning to a new century.

The struggles of the less fortunate, the working poor, were described by A.L. Bowley in 1912. His survey showed that the level of poverty experienced in Reading was largely for reasons persisting since the previous century: one dominant employer offering many low-waged, unskilled jobs and a pool of labour from the surrounding area where rates of pay were even lower. With no 'considerable group' of highly paid workers, the town's wage-rates were 'abnormally low' by the standards of south-east England, over half of wage earners subsisting on 20–25 shillings a week. Bowley estimated that from 25–30% of working-class families (19% of the whole population) in Reading lived below the poverty line. This had been defined in a study of York by Seebohm Rowntree: having the minimum needed to provide the essentials for life, eating a largely vegetarian diet and spending nothing on medicine or luxuries such as beer or tobacco. Almost half the children in Reading's elementary schools lived in poverty; in the survey year free meals (authorised by an Act of 1906) were provided for 1,407 children from 512 families by the Borough Education Committee. At some stage before they reached 14, more than half the working-class children in the borough would belong to households living below the poverty line or, put another way, wages of unskilled workers were insufficient to maintain a family of three or more children. The same report itemised the weekly wages of young workers. At 14 a lad could expect 6s. 6d. in a factory or trade and 5s. or more as a clerk; a girl of 14 would earn 5s. 6d. in a factory, 2s. or 3s. in service and 1s. 6d. as apprentice with a dressmaker. These earnings, increasing with age, provided the family with basic essentials while the young ones lived at home, and they help explain why so many left school as soon as possible.[1]

The First World War

The coming of war on 4 August 1914 was viewed with foreboding by some, but the mayor and 'an immense crowd of cheering well-wishers' assembled as the first young volunteers from the borough and the county to serve in the Royal Berkshire Regiment left from Reading station. Over the next four years local newspapers faithfully recorded the names of the many dead and wounded and those winning honours for gallantry,

The memorial in Abbey Walk to Trooper Fred Potts, awarded the Victoria Cross for rescuing a wounded companion though injured himself. It shows him dragging the man on a shovel. (JD)

the highest being the Victoria Cross, awarded to Trooper Fred Potts of Reading for rescuing a wounded comrade though wounded himself.[2]

Large numbers of casualties were treated at the Royal Berkshire Hospital or at branch war hospitals in the workhouse, its infirmary and in five schools handed over by the borough: Battle, Central Boys, Katesgrove, Redlands and Wilson. Grovelands housed the sick poor from the workhouse. The RBH was staffed by Red Cross nurses and VADs with many retired doctors returning to fill the gaps left by those recruited for war service. By 1917 the hospitals had over 2,000 patients, including some from Canada.

They added to the large concentration of troops in the town throughout the war. Reading was a major recruiting centre with mass rallies held in the Town Hall, reservists enlisting at the Barracks and by 1915 'alive with troops' billeted in schools, private houses and empty buildings. An influx of between 300 and 400 Belgian refugees put further pressure on

Ambulances outside Reading War Hospital, formerly the Union Workhouse, 1916. (RL)

accommodation. In 1917 the threat of air raids on London prompted some families to flee, many coming to Reading. The result was severe overcrowding for many local families. The education of Reading children was disrupted as pupils displaced from schools given over to the military were allocated to others, attending either the morning or afternoon session of the school day. Catholic Belgian children went to St James' School and others to schools in the borough once they were proficient in English.

Nationally, food and fuel prices began to rise in August 1914 and continued to escalate, the situation in the borough being exacerbated by its swollen population. As early as summer 1915 less meat was provided in the workhouse where, in line with the national average, food costs had risen by a third. Harvest failure and a drop in imported foodstuffs as supply ships fell victim to submarine warfare meant serious national shortages of bread flour, sugar, meat and even potatoes by 1917, the local situation exacerbated by the concentration of troops in the town. Lengthy queues formed daily in all Reading shops, with police controlling the crowds, the local press writing dramatically of a 'Fight for Food'. One response, a communal kitchen set up as part of a national scheme to save food, proved very popular, especially with working mothers. A Food Control Committee, set up on government orders, controlled prices, but the rationing of essentials – butter, tea and bacon among them – became inevitable. Introduced locally early in 1918, it became national policy in April.

Volunteers helped the war effort in various ways. A Reading Citizens Defence Force was organised early in 1915. The Chamber of Commerce set up a Hospital Supplies Depot to make and supply bandages, splints and the like. The Reading Care and Comfort Committee and local organisations provided entertainment for convalescing troops at the theatre, town hall, or on river cruisers. Flag days brought in funds for war charities, Belgian refugees and our ally, Russia. As well as volunteering as nurses, women took over jobs such as 'postmen' and tramcar conductors, especially

One of the stalls selling favours in Belgium's colours on Belgian day, 1915, raising £551 for refugee relief. From *Reading Standard Pictorial Record* vol. 1 1916. (RL)

Official welcome of the 2nd Battalion, Royal Berks. Regiment on its return from the war, 17 May 1919 (RL).

after conscription in 1916, or moved into war production. Huntley & Palmers' engineers made gun parts, shells and aircraft engines, not quite consistent with Quaker pacifism.

Despite the restrictions on street lighting, theatres and the cinema remained open, and in summer time, excursions by rail and char-a-banc were popular with troops and townspeople. These pleasures were totalled eclipsed by the celebrations on 11 November 1918 with thanksgiving services in all churches and chapels and 'mafficking pure and simple' in the streets though rationing continued and the 'flu epidemic raged.[3]

Reading between the wars

Even discounting the losses resulting from the war, the growth in Reading's population had slowed, the local press claiming in 1913 that it was in absolute decline. This it attributed to emigration encouraged by advertisements proclaiming the delights of 'Australia, the Land of Sunshine' and the wide open spaces of Canada. Censuses confirmed the situation: a mere 5.2% growth between 1911 and 1921 and the same by 1931, the last count before the Second World War. A more plausible explanation may lie in the high mortality rate during the 'very severe epidemic of influenza' and the 'quite unusual number of deaths' from pneumonia and bronchitis in 1918, and a declining birth rate recorded in all sectors of society and all religious denominations nationally in the 1911 census, though particularly apparent in towns in the South, including Reading, with a substantial middle class.[4] The borough's low birth-rate noted in the 1921 census was later confirmed by Reading's Medical Officer of Health. In 1929–30 it was the lowest ever recorded, 14.9 per 1,000, and the death-rate, again due to bronchial infections, the highest since 1918. Reading also shared the experience of other urban communities in attracting fewer immigrants; the 1931 census recorded a decline in numbers moving into the borough and rising numbers leaving, especially to Wokingham UD which was the fastest growing area in the county in the 1920s.[5]

Party politics

The balance of political control in parliamentary representation and borough politics changed during the inter-war period. Nationally the split in the Liberal Party in 1916 slowly reduced its chances of electoral success. In Reading, the candidate of the Labour Party, constituted here in 1918, came second in the parliamentary election of that year and in 1923 the borough elected its first Labour MP, Dr Somerville Hastings, who was again returned in 1929 though in neither instance with an overall majority. On the council, Labour representation increased in the 1920s despite electoral pacts between Liberals and Conservatives. Local politics became increasingly partisan as a better organised Labour group challenged middle-class domination of the aldermanic bench and mayoralty. In 1926 Labour contested the established procedure: that the choice of mayor be decided by seniority. They failed, but the following year John Rabson and in 1933 and 1936 Labour members, Edith Sutton (of Suttons Seeds) and Alice Jenkins, the first women to hold the office, were elected.[6]

Housing and council housing

Arguably the greatest social need both nationally and locally was decent, affordable housing, not a new situation in the borough. In the tradition of forceful Medical Officers of Health, H.J. Milligan condemned the state of Reading's working-class houses, most over a century old, many built back-to-back, and at least 600 'deficient' yet attracting exorbitant rents. Belatedly, Reading Council set up a Housing and Town Planning Committee in 1917, whose Labour members were at the forefront in the drive to take advantage of government legislation. The first of these, Addison's Housing and Town Planning Act, 1919, required local authorities to assess housing need and provide houses, the cost above that of a penny rate to be met by the first-ever government subsidy for housing. Reading's response was to build over 200 two- and three-bedroom dwellings grouped in short terraces or as semi-detached houses with gardens, the Shinfield Road estate. Following the Housing Acts of 1923 and 1924 offering subsidies per house, building accelerated, including a substantial development around Oxford Road and flats in Silver Street, but it still fell far short of demand. Resulting changes in the distribution of population within the borough were already apparent in

A drawing of council houses on the Shinfield Estate where construction of the first 162 dwellings began in January 1920. The architect was S. Paton, Housing Architect for Reading County Borough. Rents ranged from 8s. 6d. to 12s. 6d. a week. (RL)

the 1931 census as central areas were cleared of slums and council estates begun in the west and south of the borough. The 1930 Housing Act offering subsidies for re-housing residents displaced by slum-clearance accelerated the process of removing many of the worst areas, mainly the courts in Coley and others near the town centre, displaced residents being allocated council houses or flats. In the process the town centre ceased to be a residential area as new working- and lower-middle-class suburbs were created. Despite the withdrawal in 1933 of some housing subsidies, 35 slum areas were cleared, more planned and a total of 3,140 council houses, maisonettes and flats built in Reading by 1939, 2,017 of them in Whitley. The provision of one million erected nationally has been described as 'one of the most obvious expressions of expanding welfare provision' in the twentieth century but was later criticised as creating a dependency culture.[7]

The attack on sub-standard privately rented properties, begun by Reading's first MOHs in the 1880s, continued throughout the period with legal action against recalcitrant landlords. Nevertheless, there was still a shortage of good-quality housing on the eve of the Second World War. Reading's Borough Architect reported in 1938 that there were 683 families on the waiting list and more council houses were needed to eliminate overcrowding and slums, although some of their elderly residents would be unable to afford council house rents. Already on the Whitley estate, though all houses had a bathroom and indoor toilet, over half had just a single living room and two bedrooms, all many families could afford. The result was some overcrowding especially where, in contravention of the by-laws, families took in lodgers. This was overlooked by the authorities if it helped tenants to pay the rent. Even so, life for Whitley residents was superior in every respect to that in the slums though not until the late 1930s and only after pressure from residents, local clergy and the

WEA did the estate acquire a recreation ground (1936), a clinic (1937), a community centre and a Church of England church (1938).[8]

Between the wars more than twice as many houses for sale were built nationwide by private developers as council houses for rent; in Reading it was about 30% more. In the 1930s it was possible to buy a house in the borough for £450 with £25 deposit and a 21-year mortgage, making house-ownership possible for someone earning £3 10s. a week. Half the mortgages were taken out on houses costing less than £600. There was considerable development in the green areas outside the boundary, especially after the sale of three large estates on the periphery of the borough in Wokingham UD: the Wheble family's Bulmershe estate (sold 1926) stretching two miles into Woodley; the Maiden Erlegh estate extending east and south into Earley (sold in 1932 after Solomon Joel's death); and the land belonging to Erleigh Court on the north-eastern border, auctioned in 1932. In 1939 a middle-class family could aspire to a semi-detached house on the Maiden Erlegh estate, advertised by James T. Cook for upwards of £825 and a detached house for £1,025.[9]

An advertisement for a detached house on the Maiden Erlegh Estate built by Cooks the Builders. (*Reading Review* July 1936)

Standard II, eight–nine year old girls in St John's C of E Junior School, Queens Road in the 1930s. (RL)

Education

To provide school places for the children on the new council estates was the responsibility of the Education Committee, new schools being built for the children of Whitley, Basingstoke Road and Caversham, with additional places at Norcot and Battle. The committee seems to have had great ambitions for young people in this period within the limits imposed by financial constraints; it has been described as one of the most progressive in the country. In all schools there were opportunities for sport, especially football as well as netball and swimming, though with inadequate playground space these activities took place in public recreation grounds or baths. In 1937 'wireless' sets (radios) were provided on which BBC schools programmes could be received. For a few children, opportunities were widening further. The four Central Schools, Wilson, E.P. Collier, George Palmer and Alfred Sutton and two Junior Evening Institutes continued to offer post-14 education with free places for the most able at evening classes at the university. Clothing allowances were paid to some of the 126 boys and girls annually winning scholarship places at Kendrick and Reading schools. These grammar schools prepared pupils for the Oxford School Certificate Examination (forerunner of 'O' levels and GCE) but so did the Central Schools while others took the Royal Society of Arts Examination in Commercial Subjects including shorthand. Although over a thousand pupils attended the Central Schools, such success was limited to the few whose parents were willing and able to keep them at school until 16. 'Poor girls' were also eligible for grants from the endowment of the Green School to train in domestic subjects or other skilled trades, the school having closed in

Reading University degree day, 1927 with the Vice-Chancellor W.M. Childs (right) and honorary graduands Alfred Palmer (centre) and H.J. Benyon, Lord Lieutenant of Berkshire.

Reading University Memorial Tower commemorating College and University members fallen in war (1914–18 and 1939–45), and the Friendship Gates and Peace Garden sponsored by the University and Gyosei College, Reading, 1992. (JD)

1922 because of falling numbers, a symptom of the declining attraction of domestic service. Adult education was provided by the WEA, and the Joint Committee of the Association and the borough, with funding from the Education Committee. The borough also shared in the success of the University College which in 1926 was granted a charter conferring university status, the only such promotion in Britain in the inter-war period.[10]

Poverty, health and welfare

There was less poverty in Reading by the mid-1920s when Bowley repeated his 1912 survey, partly because of higher rates of pay. To meet increased food costs during the war, wages had been supplemented in some firms by a war bonus. A one-day strike at the biscuit factory on 23 June 1916 by 'many comrades' over the dismissal of one girl for leaving work early and the 15 women who supported her was quickly resolved when the management not only reinstated them but offered to increase the war bonus. Pressure from the Reading branch of the Gas Workers and General Labourers' Union, formed in 1911 (later the GMB), most of whom were Huntley & Palmers' employees, persuaded the directors to replace the bonus by a rise in wages for all their workers.[11]

Increased wages, smaller families and a decline in food prices after 1922 reduced to 8% the proportion of poor families, mostly concentrated in a few areas, but the number of children in poverty, their poor health and lack of physical fitness still gave concern. Reports of the Borough School Medical Officer from the late 1920s give some indication of the state of children's health and the measures being taken to improve it. As well as providing opportunities for sport, the Public Health Committee employed school nurses who by visiting problem homes, examining thousands of heads and bathing a few 'dirty' children successfully reduced the incidence of 'unclean' heads and bodies. Given the almost total absence of bathrooms in borough houses, this was a creditable achievement, though the provision of hot baths at the Arthur Hill's Swimming Baths must have contributed. School dentists provided free dental care. Milk in ⅓ pint bottles was provided in school to increasing numbers of children, free to those in need, and meals for 'necessitous children' at six feeding centres in the centre, east and west of the borough. Their 'necessity' was mainly the result of parental unemployment or low wages.[12]

Dealing with poverty and health generally became the borough's responsibility in 1929 when the Local Government Act transferred to the Public Assistance Committees (PACs) of local authorities the work of the poor law guardians along with new duties relating to public health. The workhouse system was abolished, its buildings being converted to new uses. As with many other towns, Reading's workhouse with its infirmary became the Municipal Hospital, administered by the Borough Health Committee, maintained from the rates and renamed Battle Hospital in 1930. In future, vagrants would be put into 'casual wards' intended for an overnight stay only. By 1931 a replacement for the one in the old workhouse had been built in Woodley, the census that year recording its 31 occupants. PACs were also responsible for those with the right to claim poor relief under the settlement laws of the 1660s and 1690s which were not abolished until 1948.[13]

Nationally the extent of poverty was exacerbated in the late 1920s and early 1930s by unemployment, which rose as a result of the depression in trade and manufacture. At its highest in 1933 there were 2.4 million workers out of work. The great industrial towns of the West Midlands and the North suffered disproportionally, the South East less so. In Reading where there was no heavy industry, unemployment was comparatively low, although that was not much comfort to those who lost their jobs. Biscuit factory workers, subject to periodic short-time employment, found difficulty in balancing their budgets. In 1929 the PAC noted a request to 'put in hand' any outstanding painting work to employ the many out-of-work painters in the borough, and the Highways Committee placed a few men on other projects. Workers with fully paid-up unemployment insurance under the 1911 Act – 'insured workers' – could 'of right' claim 15 weeks' benefit followed by a 'Transitional Benefit', popularly called the 'dole', for a maximum of 26 weeks, but only after a tough means test (introduced in 1931) by which all possible sources of potential family income were investigated before relief would reluctantly be granted. Those temporarily off work through sickness could claim benefit and free medical treatment, but not medicine, from a GP as a 'panel patient' but dependants were not covered. All others in need, except widows and the over-70s with a pension, depended on poor relief.[14] The 1931 census recorded a male unemployment rate of 8% in Reading. This rose until 1933 before falling by 1936. In some areas including Coley unemployment was probably much higher and more protracted.[15]

Industry, commerce and occupations

The picture of industrial Reading between the wars would have been familiar to a Victorian visitor, though he would have noticed important changes. In 1911 about 40% of male workers were employed in industry. Huntley & Palmers, with the town's largest workforce, Simonds' brewery and Cock's Reading Sauce factory in King's Road were responsible for Berkshire being singled out in the 1921 census as the county with the highest number of food producers. The establishment of the Co-operative Wholesale Society's Preserves Factory in 1919 further strengthened the food sector. Suttons was the other nationally recognisable Reading firm. However, the largest occupational group in 1921, over 9%, were 'metal workers', some at traditional firms like Huntley, Bourne & Stevens and Wilders but others at the Pulsometer Engineering Company or as motor mechanics at garages and car showrooms. Road transport employed more men, as tram, bus and lorry drivers, than did the railway, but clerical workers outnumbered both road and rail employees. By 1931 the building trade, doubtless buoyed by the council house building programme, employed more than all these combined. Gas fitters and electricians were also in demand as some council and private houses acquired modern methods of heating, lighting and cooking. Established firms such as Collier's brickmakers and several printing firms flourished, as did Elliots of Caversham who supplied modern fittings to shops and businesses.

The service sector increased its share of the job market. Locally owned department stores continued to dominate the High Street, selling everything from ladies' fashion to bedroom suites. Smaller local shops of all kinds employed over 2,000 male and female shop assistants, but apart from the Reading Savings Bank, the only financial institutions were branches of national firms such as Barclays and Lloyds. The situation for women had changed little, the vast majority of married women not being in paid employment. Of those women in work in 1921, over 3,000 were in domestic service (one in four of the female workforce) compared with about 600 in teaching. Just 33 were telephone operators. Ten years later there were 555 typists and over 1,100 clerks, although domestic servants still numbered over 3,100. This economic diversity and expanding white-collar and skilled job sector helped to sustain the improved wage rates that had begun during the war.[16] Amid these changes, Reading's traditional role as a market for agricultural produce was restated by the opening in 1936 of the New Corn Exchange in Caversham Road next to the Cattle Market.[17]

Trams and buses

After the war electric tram routes extended into the newly absorbed suburbs and council estates, carrying thousands of passengers and earning substantial profits. In 1919 the first motor buses began operating on two routes, from Tilehurst to Caversham Heights and from Shinfield Road to Caversham. Logistics such as low bridges would make them the better option for these journeys when in 1936 the latest in transport systems, the trolley bus, was chosen to replace trams on the Tilehurst to Three Tuns, Earley route and to supplement the 'bus from Whitley to Caversham Bridge, though other trams remained in service until May 1939.[18] Transport continued to make an important contribution to the

Reading Bridge, constructed in 1923. Steam traction engines were driven onto the bridge to test its strength. (RL)

changing urban landscape, convenient means of travel to work and places of entertainment allowing townspeople to live in more distant suburbs, and separating industrial from residential space. The opening of Reading Bridge in 1923 and a new Caversham Bridge three years later tied the growing suburb closer to the borough.

Leisure

Undoubtedly the most popular leisure pursuit of the inter-war period was going to the cinema – 'the pictures' – rivalled only for the younger and more energetic by ballroom dancing and roller skating. In the 1930s twenty million cinema tickets were sold in the UK. Huge cinemas showed musicals and romances, many made in the USA in technicolor. Reading eventually had seven 'picture houses' including the 1936 art-deco Savoy where admission cost from 6*d*. to 1*s*. 10*d*., and light refreshments were offered to patrons in their seats. With music hall at the Palace Theatre, plays and light opera at the County Theatre and occasional celebrity concerts at the Town Hall, those with spare cash need never be bored. Second Division football at Elm Road drew several thousand on Saturday afternoons; rather fewer patronised the Greyhound Stadium on the Basingstoke Road. Amateur football and cricket in the parks, including Sol Joel Playing Fields in Earley and Christchurch Playing Fields in Caversham were still popular. In summer the mecca for anglers, bathers and rowers was the Thames in competition with punts, motor launches and steamers. Stay-at-homes had the wireless; McIlroys sold sets for 6½ guineas (£6 16s. 6d.), somewhat expensive given that a bedroom suite cost nine guineas. Borrowing books from the growing collection at the library was free, a new branch library in Palmer Park improving access for Newtown residents. When life in Reading became dull there were works' outings by coach or train to resorts and beauty spots which the affluent middle class could visit by car, a Ford ex-works costing £100 in 1935. The really wealthy could book a two-week winter sports holiday at Heelas' Travel Bureau for £20.[19]

Reading in the Second World War

Council minutes show that by June 1938 preparations for war were well advanced: Air Raid Precaution (ARP) wardens had been appointed; trench and underground shelters dug in local parks; and first-aid posts and air-raid sirens set up. By early the following year the Southern Region Civil Defence Headquarters, the Control Centre for Civil Defence, was established in the basement of Shire Hall.[20] The borough became home to several government departments including the Ministry of Works in 'temporary' buildings in Whiteknights and the RBH joined a local group of hospitals under an Emergency Hospital Scheme to treat civilian and military casualties.

As a 'safe area' Reading and the county were designated as reception areas for evacuees. The council organised a survey of potential accommodation though a leader in the *Reading Mercury* probably echoed middle-class apprehension at 'receiving children from the slums', the problem of 'the housewife with inadequate help … unable to give proper supervision to mischievous children'. In the event 25,000 evacuees, of whom 12,000 were children, began arriving on 1 September 1939, two days before war was declared. When 39 London schools and their teachers were allocated to borough and private schools to share the schools' day, both education and discipline suffered, caused it was claimed by a lack of parental supervision, fathers being at war and mothers at work. A further 1,600 evacuees arrived in mid-1940 and although some soon returned home, new arrivals, servicemen and government officials increased pressure on accommodation, especially for working-class residents in private- and council-rented housing. [21]

Many national and local initiatives were based on the experiences of the First World War. Food and petrol rationing began in 1940, clothing,

During the Second World War women were encouraged to take up work outside the home as in this advertisement in the *Berkshire Chronicle* 8 August 1941.

"*Show what Reading women can do*"

There are jobs waiting for *all* in the women's services, and in local industries. It doesn't matter whether you have previous experience or not. You can soon be trained for a really useful job — and be paid while training.

READING WOMEN'S WAR WORK WEEK
AUGUST 9TH TO AUGUST 16TH

During this week a special office will be open for recruitment and advice at Great Western Motors, Station Road, Reading, or your local office of the Ministry of Labour will gladly help you.

YOUR DUTY NOW IS WAR WORK

ISSUED BY THE MINISTRY OF LABOUR & NATIONAL SERVICE

In cold winter light, the three-times life-size Lion looks impressively fierce. Made of cast-iron, he weighs over 16 tons.

Gas mask drill at Huntley & Palmers, 1939. Gas masks had to be carried throughout the war years but were never needed. (RC)

meat, bacon, milk, all fats, cheese, eggs (one a week), sugar and preserves following in 1941.[22] The council let all 4,000 allotments for vegetable and fruit growing, the Co-op Preserve Factory bought the fruit grown there and McIlroys set up a fruit preserving centre. From 1941 the Education Committee provided thousands of school meals for children whose mothers were on war work and from 1943 a residential nursery for the very young. After 1941, basic nourishing meals were available 'off-ration' at British Restaurants, the one in Reading, The People's Pantry, feeding about 800 a day.

Peacetime commerce continued including the weekly market and cattle market. Some factories were engaged in war work: Phillips & Powys at Woodley made the Miles Master aircraft fitted with Rolls Royce engines; Vickers Armstrong at Caversham made aircraft, and Elliotts made parts for bombers and fighter planes, and the gliders used for the Normandy landings. Women, many literally wearing the trousers in the form of 'siren suits', did men's work: the younger ones drove vans, ambulances and troop transports while their elders kept production going at Huntley & Palmers.

People found light relief in entertainment on the river and the Thames Promenade. Cinemas, closed for a few weeks in 1939, soon re-opened including on Sunday evenings. Performances at the theatres and dances at the Central Ballroom attracted large crowds despite the absence of buses after 9.30 p.m., although the introduction of Double British Summer Time in April 1943 made for very light evenings. Outdoor sports, both professional and amateur, were encouraged as were evening classes at the university attended by many service personnel. ARP wardens and United States troops organised Christmas parties for children.

Damage to the west front of St Laurence, Blandy's offices and the Town Hall following the air raid, 10 February 1943. (RL)

Reading was not an obvious target for enemy attack and suffered few civilian casualties and little property destruction. To avoid giving comfort to the enemy it was only in 1945 that full details of bomb damage at Caversham, Coley and Minster Street were revealed. Far worse was the bombing on 10 February 1943 of the People's Pantry, St Laurence and Blandy's offices: 41 killed and 200 injured. Local servicemen were killed in action: at Scapa Flow in October 1939, at Dunkirk in 1940, and later in far-flung theatres of war.

Post-war Reading

The end of war in Europe, VE Day on 5 May 1945, was celebrated in Reading with two days' holiday, street parties, a victory parade and service at St Laurence. Despite the peace which followed the end of the war with Japan in August 1945, better times were slow to arrive. Rationing, food and fuel shortages continuing until 1954, even bread being rationed in 1946–48, the bitter winter of 1946–47 adding to the gloom. The task of post-war reconstruction nationally fell to the Labour government led by Clement Attlee; in Reading the first Labour-controlled council was led by the redoubtable Phoebe Cusden who became mayor in 1946. The following year she established the borough's close links with the German city of Dusseldorf which remain strong. True to its reputation as a bell-wether constituency, Reading returned a Labour MP, Ian Mikardo, in 1945 and 1950 and though he survived in 1951 and 1955 when the country went Conservative, he was ousted in 1959. Even so, Labour controlled the borough council for most of the 1940s and 1950s.[23] By 1957 the national situation had so far changed that it was said Britain had 'never had it so good' with near full employment, a greater supply of better quality housing and increased spending on household goods, clothes and entertainment.[24]

Population

In the absence of a census in 1941, all we have is a population estimate of 124,000, falling rapidly to about 109,000 in 1945 as wartime visitors returned home. The 1951 census recorded 114,196 residents, an unexpected 11% increase on the pre-war figure, partly explained by the twenty-year gap between censuses but more so by the large number of babies born after 1945, the so-called 'Bulge' or 'Baby Boom'. Nationally this produced about an extra million babies each year.

However, as in the Victorian period, most growth was the result of immigration. Over 16% of the population originated from London and the South East, some no doubt having decided to stay after the war, and 4% from the South West, Reading's traditional recruiting ground. Overall almost 37% came from outside the county including almost 2,000 from outside the UK. Among these were refugees from Germany

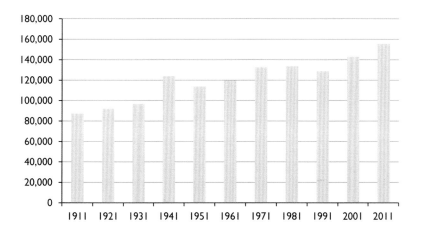

Reading population, 1911–2011.

and Poland in the 1930s. Some of the latter who had come to Britain to fight with the Allies stayed after the war and began to move into towns, including Reading, in the late 1940s. The Introduction to the 1951 Census considered the population increase small, especially compared with larger growth in areas adjoining the borough, attributing the difference to the 'tendency of people working in Reading to seek dormitory accommodation in the surrounding area'. Over the period 1939–48 Reading's growth was the lowest in the county whose population grew by 22%, mostly in the Wokingham Urban District.[25]

These two features of population change, immigration into the borough and a growing population on its eastern border, were even more pronounced in the 1961 census and would accelerate in the future. In 1961 almost 7,000 Reading residents were recorded as having been born outside the UK, the majority from the Commonwealth and Colonies and the Irish Republic. Whereas Ireland had long sent emigrants to work in England, in the 1950s newcomers came from farther afield, especially from the Caribbean, invited by the British government to provide much needed labour, including in Reading's traditional industries. In Reading most settled in Newtown and the Oxford Road.[26]

Housing

For the borough, as for the country, housing was a major concern with local authority housing for rent given priority by government. About 1¼ million dwellings were needed to meet the needs of a growing national population and to replace war-damaged, sub-standard and slum houses. Consequently, the decade 1945–55, first under a Labour and then a Conservative administration, saw the second great age of council-house provision, private-house building being halted in 1947 by the Housing Ministry to concentrate scarce resources on rented accommodation. Subsidies were provided by the 1946 Housing Act at £22 per house a year for 60 years, 75% from government and 25% from the rates. Some larger houses were intended for lower-middle as well as working-class families though rents were considerably higher. To relieve immediate needs the government commissioned 125,000 modern, compact pre-fabricated houses, modular structures assembled on site; Reading had 200 by 1948. The council continued its pre-war policy of 'minimising and eventually eliminating the housing shortage'.[27] Building permanent houses began in 1946 by private firms employing some German POWs and Polish workers and continued into the 1950s including over 1,300 dwellings in Tilehurst, Calcot and Southcote, nearly 200 in Whitley Wood and over 250 in Emmer Green. By 1955 just over 3,000 dwellings had been completed, concentrated in these estates. Pressure on building land, improved building techniques, and the Conservative government's increased subsidy in 1956 for high-rise dwellings linked to slum clearance may explain the council's decision to include an eight- and a five-storey block of flats in the Southcote estate and one of 15 storeys in Coley. These solved an immediate housing crisis and were cheaper to build but they were to prove less attractive as places to live. By 1963 there were over 8,300 families occupying council accommodation concentrated in four or five large estates including one of 500 houses in Woodley, released by Wokingham UD for Reading 'overspill'. Even so, the waiting list for council houses remained stubbornly high. Over 10,000 properties were rented from private landlords where some facilities were still lacking: a quarter of all households had no fixed bath.

To serve the new estates within the borough, Reading Transport belatedly opened more trolley- and motor-bus routes. Successive town guides highlighted the town's good transport system with its early-morning and late-evening services for workers (on special workmen's

A map of trolley bus and motor bus routes in the 1950s from a map in the *Reading Official Town Guide,* *1953.*

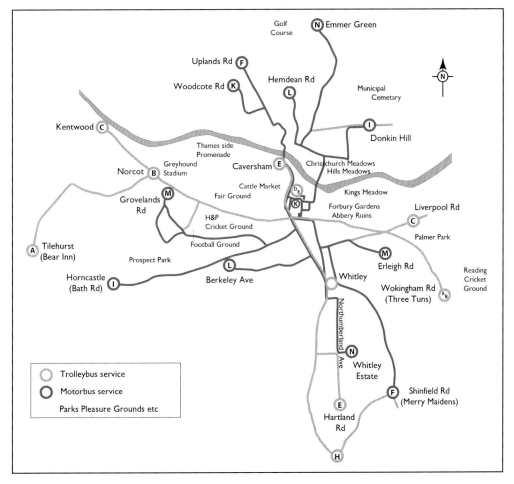

fares) and leisure seekers. Forty-million passengers used these services in the 1950s paying from 1½d. to 6d. per journey. Beyond the boundary council and private developments resulted in at least 75% more houses in the Wokingham District in 1963 than in 1931.[28]

Social security and health

Providing decent housing was only one aspect of a major programme of social reform, much of it implementing the Beveridge Report of 1942, commissioned by the wartime coalition government. Beveridge proposed a comprehensive scheme for state provision of social welfare which would eliminate want, disease, ignorance, squalor and idleness. In 1946 a series of measures introduced by the Attlee government, accepted by all political parties to a greater or lesser extent, provided such a scheme, funded from general taxation. It came to be known as the Welfare State. Among its provisions were compulsory government, employer, and employee contributions to a National Insurance scheme, National Assistance (replacing the dole) and the National Health Service. In addition, under the Family Allowance Act of 1945, mothers received 5s. a week for every child after the first. All Reading families gained from these reforms to some degree, many by the improvements in housing and the poorest from a small boost in income. Organisations and individuals providing health care were profoundly affected. When the National Health Service (NHS) came into operation in 1948 both the Royal Berkshire Hospital (RBH), Battle Infirmary and the Dispensary ceased to be voluntary organisations, coming instead under the control of the Reading and District Management Committee, the first of a succession of such bodies. The following year the two hospitals amalgamated, dividing the provision of medical services between them.[29]

Education

While engaged in a world war, the wartime coalition gave parliamentary time in 1944 to introduce the Butler Education Act with profound implications for a generation of schoolchildren. It proposed secondary education for all up to age 15, pupils being assigned on the basis of age, aptitude and ability to one of three types of school: secondary grammar for the more academic; secondary technical for those with practical skills, and secondary modern for the rest. Selection was by the 11-plus examination, with the possibility of transfer from a secondary modern to a grammar school at 13-plus. Free places in private grammar schools, funded by local authorities, would supplement LEA grammars. Reading already had its two single-sex grammar schools, Reading and Kendrick, providing an academic education for a small proportion of

the children able to profit from it. A few extra places for girls were offered at the private Abbey School under a direct grant scheme by which the LEA paid the fees of some successful 11-plus scholars. For the rest, the Borough Chief Education Officer, Percy Taylor, devised a plan of single-sex paired bi-lateral schools, secondary moderns but with grammar-school streams. In the event only three pairs were built, in the south, east and west of the borough: Ashmead (boys) and Southlands (girls); Alfred Sutton Boys and Alfred Sutton Girls; Stoneham (boys) and Westwood (girls). The remaining five senior departments of the council schools, Battle, Caversham, Cintra, The Grove and Wilson became secondary moderns, but they were eventually closed or amalgamated. Hugh Faringdon School which opened in 1958 served the Roman Catholic population. Unfortunately neither Reading nor the country generally ever developed a clear idea of the educational purpose of the secondary modern school. In another variation, E.P. Collier Mixed School offered engineering and commercial subjects, the only secondary technical institution in the borough until 1955. Taylor 'transformed the school system of the town', at best allowing easy movement between differing types of secondary education and at worst scattering resources through too many institutions. One is left with a feeling that maintaining the two grammar schools dominated policy. Until 1955 when the Technical College opened on the former Victoria Square site providing 8,500 students with courses in engineering, science, commerce and catering to O and A level, Reading was the only borough in the county without such provision. Practical education provided by the Blue Coat School was lost to the borough with its move to Holme Park, Sonning, in 1947. It eventually became an independent public school based on Christian principles. All its endowments were consolidated and used to fund the move and, in keeping with the intentions of its founders, to offer bursaries and scholarships to boys from the borough and Sonning.[30]

The Faculty of Letters, the first building on the University's Whiteknights Campus in the 1950s. This later extension displays the University crest with the scallop shells which once featured on that of the abbey. (JD)

After negotiations begun in 1946, the foresight of the Vice Chancellor, Sir Frank Stenton and the negotiating skills of the Bursar, E.H. Carpenter finally secured the Whiteknights Park estate for the university 'the single most important event in [its] history'. The London Road campus was attractive but confined. Whiteknights would allow expansion to accommodate greater numbers of working- and middle-class students from the new grammar schools. The first buildings there did not open until 1957, by which time John (later Lord) Wolfenden had become Vice Chancellor, and major developments came only in the 1960s and after. Meanwhile in 1951 another far-sighted academic, realising that mechanised farming was leading to the destruction of traditional tools and vehicles, began a collection which became the basis of the Museum of English Rural Life. The university's association with the WEA to provide adult education, continuing the connection begun by Childs, also added to its involvement in the town.[31]

Trade and industry before 1960

The last town guide before the Second World War was perceptive: 'Big business is moving south, and Reading is willing to receive it.' Reading, it claimed, 'is a place with a future', but the future would be very different from the past as industry diversified in this era of full employment, with increasing numbers of skilled workers. Brewing by the Courage, Barclay and Simonds' Group continued at Seven Bridges and Suttons traded in the Market Place. Huntley & Palmers remained the largest single employer in the 1950s with Huntley Boorne and Stevens making its biscuit tins. However, as in some other southern towns, engineering had become the largest branch of industry with such important enterprises as Pulsometer Pumps, Gascoigne (dairying equipment) and the Precision Engineering Company with other firms building motor-bodies. The tradition of practical research continued but now in centres such as the National Institute for Research in Dairying at Shinfield, allied closely to the university's strong agricultural departments. Printing remained important and Elliots profited from the demand for fitting out new shops. However, in terms of its share of employment, industry had given way to a variety of non-industrial occupations, including the service sector. The 1951 census showed over 65% of male workers were in such occupations. In particular the borough's retail trade prospered, reputedly worth £30 million a year by 1963. National chains including Marks & Spencer and Boots expanded on Broad Street and local retailers were absorbed by larger enterprises – Heelas by the John Lewis Partnership in 1953 (though the family name on the shop front gave an illusion of localism for many years) and Wellsteeds by Debenhams. The borough was reverting to its earlier role as a commercial and service centre, the main limit on further expansion being a labour shortage which even immigration did not solve.[32]

Leisure

Despite 'mass purchasing' of television sets early in 1953, only 2.5 million British households possessed one in time for the Coronation in June but thereafter sales boomed with ten million owned by 1960. The impact of the small screen increased with the arrival of ITV in 1955 when up to half the country's households tuned in to BBC or its rival. Nationally cinema audiences began to decline; five of Reading's nine cinemas closed before 1961. The three dance halls; the Majestic, the Oxford and the Olympia remained popular, attracting up to 2,500 on Saturdays energetically responding to the new sound, rock-and-roll, as the music of Bill Haley and Elvis Presley spread from screen to juke-box. The big bands and ballroom dancing were under siege.[33]

For devotees of classical music there were the occasional concerts by visiting orchestras, the Reading Symphony Orchestra, the Reading Youth Orchestra and several good amateur choirs, and for lovers of light music the varied performances at The Palace Theatre. Amateur societies provided the only serious drama in the town. Traditional amateur sports, especially football, athletics and swimming remained popular, though local support was not enough to push professional football into a higher league. Most of these activities would survive, others would appear, but some would disappear in the new age of the 1960s and beyond.

A photograph of the Forbury Gardens, unusually quiet and deserted in the snow, captured through the impressive wrought–iron Victoria Gate.

In 2017 after the Gaol closed it was used for an exhibition of art and writing celebrating prisoners of conscience and in particular Oscar Wilde.

12

The latest transformation: Reading since 1960

HAVING SURVIVED the troubled decades of the early twentieth century, Reading finally cast off the legacy of Victorian industry to become home to many high-tech, commercial and insurance companies, to consolidate its role as a major transport hub, shopping and leisure centre, to attract an ever larger number of migrants and to build houses within and beyond its borders for its growing population, many of whom worked on the periphery of or outside the borough. The position of Greater Reading as the most important urban centre of the region was and is unchallenged, though growth continues to produce its own problems. Lasting judgements on the long-term significance of these developments must await studies by future historians.

What is contemporary Reading?

A television series in the 1970s featured the Wilkins, a 'typical' British family in Reading a 'typical' British town, however unlikely that description might now appear. A survey in the 1980s suggested that Reading was 'as pleasant a place to live and work as anywhere in the country'. More prosaically, a survey in 1994 suggested several definitions of contemporary Reading: the borough confined in its 1911 boundary; the Reading Travel to Work Area (TTWA), the area within which most trips to work are made, covering much of Wokingham District, part of Newbury District and of South Oxfordshire; and Reading Functional Urban Region (FUR) extending even further. Despite the boundary extension of 1977 bringing Caversham Park Village and Mapledurham into the borough, there remains a discrepancy between Reading as a unit of local government, a residential area, and an economic entity. In consequence, Reading politicians are unable to take the necessary 'strategic infrastructure decisions' in transport, housing and education for a region whose population far exceeds that of the borough. Yet another unit was used in the published census data of 2001: the Reading Urban Area including the borough, Earley, Purley, Shinfield, Winnersh and Woodley (population 232,662), an area it is useful to call Greater

Reading. It is clear that Reading has far outgrown its ancient boundaries, labelled 'anachronistic' in 2005, although none of its neighbouring local authorities wishes to relinquish its historic identity. In what follows, 'Reading' will continue to apply to the borough.[1]

Population and migration

In terms of population the period falls into two halves: decline until 1991 and growth afterwards. The 1961 census showed only a small increase over ten years to 119,937, evidence of a slowing population growth. A larger increase by 1971 took the total to 132,939 but despite the boundary extension of 1977, only 1,600 more in 1981. Numbers actually fell to 128,877 by 1991. There are several possible explanations: the demolition of overcrowded slums; some council tenants being housed outside the borough, and substantial numbers leaving to settle in the TTWA. In some decades more people were leaving than were entering the borough.[2]

The trend then reversed, the population rising to 143,096 in 2001 and to 155,698 in 2011. Much of this is due to an increasing number of migrants in the recent past, Reading proving to be as much a magnet in the early years of the twenty-first century as it had been in the middle decades of the nineteenth. Its new residents now came from farther afield, changing the ethnic balance of the community. Until the 1950s Reading was a 'multi-British' community with immigrants from all over the British Isles but with few foreigners. Change began in the 1950s, as we have seen, with workers from the Caribbean although overall, overseas migrants were a tiny minority in the 1960s. As late as 1991 over 90% of the townspeople considered themselves White British, down to 87% in the next census. In 2011 only 75% claimed to have been born in the UK. With borough electors in 2012 belonging to 80 different nationalities, Reading, with Slough, is the most ethnically diverse of Berkshire's unitary authorities. The Caribbean community has ceased to be the largest ethnic group, narrowly overtaken by newcomers from the Indian subcontinent. In addition to refugees fleeing conflicts in Somalia, the Balkans and elsewhere, a growing number of economic migrants have come from West Africa, Asia and those countries of eastern Europe which joined the EU in 2004, the greatest number, about 10,000, from Poland. There is also a significant Nepalese community. About 70 languages are spoken by the 15% of the population for whom English is not their mother tongue, the proportion varying across the borough in relation to the ethnic composition of the area. Newcomers from overseas mainly settled near the centre, predominantly in areas of Victorian terraced houses, particularly Abbey and Park Wards (which include Newtown), Redlands, Battle (especially around the Oxford Road) and Katesgrove. New arrivals from Poland mostly settled near the Oxford Road and in Caversham. Some of these wards, notably Park, are among the most densely populated in the borough. Migrants have brought with them much of the richness of their own cultures, not least in the many ethnic restaurants and shops which have sprung up in the centre and suburbs.[3]

Throughout the period the population tended to be young. In 1971 about 40% were under 24 years of age; in 1991 the borough had the largest proportion of young adults aged 16–24 in the county. In 2001 over one in five were in their twenties and in 2011

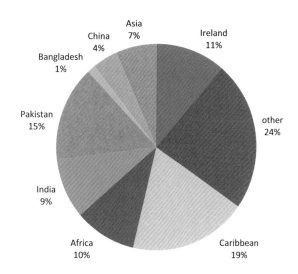

National origin of non-UK-born residents in Reading 2001.

the age-group 20–24 comprised almost 10% of the borough population, way above the national average. This is possibly explained by immigration, which also accounts for the high proportion of unmarried people, although there is a larger number of over 65s, many living alone, in the borough than in Greater Reading.[4]

Religion

One important result of immigration from overseas has been an increased variety of religious allegiance. Victorian Reading had a diversity of Christian belief; contemporary Reading has a diversity of religions. Since 1991, when for the first time since 1851 religious affiliation was included in the census, it has been possible to chart this phenomenon with some assurance. In 2011 only half of respondents claimed to be Christians, though arguably the most striking feature has been the growing number of those with no religion, about two in ten in 2001 and almost three in ten in 2011, higher than the national average. The claim may not imply the absence of some kind of belief in the transcendent, yet is highly significant. Without access to the detailed returns, any explanation must be largely an educated guess though a connection with the large proportion of young adults in the community seems possible. In contrast, adherence to Islam has almost doubled since 2001.

Changing religious allegiance and population distribution have affected the fortunes of places of worship in the borough. Ancient parish churches in the town centre have lost their local congregations but have found other purposes or attracted worshippers beyond their boundaries: St Laurence with its refashioned interior is a mission centre for young people; St Mary is the civic church with a successful youth choir; and

St John's Church, Watlington Street, now the Polish Church.

St Giles remains the epitome of 'high church' worship. St Mary Castle Street services are 'low church'. St John, Watlington Street, is now resplendent as a traditional Polish Roman Catholic church. Roman Catholics in the outer suburbs have built new churches and welcomed co-religionists from many countries. Nonconformist chapels have had mixed fortunes. Many have continued a Christian ministry from the original building, but Abbey Road Baptist Chapel and St Andrews United Reformed, London Road were rebuilt. Broad Street Congregational Chapel has become Waterstone's bookshop, though many reminders of its original purpose have been sympathetically retained in the structure. The Methodist chapel in Whitley was adapted as a Hindu temple in 2010. Muslims in Tilehurst have a purpose-built mosque; another is planned for east Reading. A Jewish congregation has worshipped in the Goldsmid Road Synagogue since 1900.

Housing

Any rise in population exacerbated Reading's perennial housing problem though the council continued to build, adding 3,000 dwellings to the 8,000 it had owned in 1963. About 600 were added to Whitley but the largest number, about 900, were on the Dee Road estate (later Dee Park) completed in 1969, mainly to accommodate 3,500 people evicted from the slums of the Hope Street area, demolished to make way for the Butts Centre. Lessons had been learned about the need to provide for a community. Dee Park's mixture of houses, flats, maisonettes and bungalows, some with garages, meant that one- or two-person households as well as families were accommodated. Shops and a health centre were among the amenities. In 1979 the council owned 11,000 rented dwellings, the vast majority built since the war, but even so there were 3,000 families on the waiting list and possibly 7,000 people still effectively homeless in 1987. The sale of council houses, which began in 1980 under the Thatcher government, increased the demand for social housing especially as councils were given very little opportunity to replace those sold. By 1990 at least 1,700 council tenants had bought their houses and by 2010 the council owned a mere 7,500 dwellings. In contrast 69% of householders were owner occupiers by 2001. Several blocks of flats were constructed in the next three decades, including those on London Road and King's Road but taking to heart the lessons of high-rise developments, none was above six or seven storeys. A major achievement of the period beginning in 1976 was the gradual redevelopment of the western section of Newtown from Orts Road to Rupert Street with flats and houses, including some on Kennet Side, an attractive riverside location. The first phases were built by the council but subsequently housing associations have provided affordable properties to buy or rent. A new parish church and centre, St John and St Stephen, serves a community which has developed strong supportive networks.[5]

A photograph, 2016, of the end of a terrace of four council houses on the Shinfield Road Estate. Compare with the drawing on p. 186. Some of these houses have been bought by their council tenants.

Rennie's Cut on the Kennet with modern housing development of Kennetside (Newtown)

Despite its building programme, private rented accommodation continued to exceed that of the council, the gap increasing significantly after 1991, as demand grew, especially from newcomers. Some of this was met by privately built up-market apartment blocks, several near the town centre, but mostly by older properties being converted for multi-occupation. Some of the latter were poorly maintained with considerable overcrowding, particularly in streets of Victorian terraces. Periodic attempts were made by the Council Housing Committee to 'crack down' on unlicensed multi-occupation, excessive rents and unsatisfactory conditions, but demand from young people and the poorer members of the community sustained the high demand even for sub-standard accommodation. The extent of the problem was revealed by successive censuses which from 1991 included questions on housing quality. In one respect this improved over the next two decades: in 1991 Reading had the largest proportion of households in the county sharing the use of bathroom and toilet and lacking central heating, 2.5% and 17.5% respectively; by 2001 fewer households were without central heating though the number sharing facilities reduced only slightly.[6]

Some pressure on accommodation was relieved by private house building in the Greater Reading Area, the largest development of the 1970s and 1980s being in Earley, the same ancient parish which a hundred years earlier had seen the expansion of Newtown. The huge Lower Earley estate took shape in the 1970s and 1980s. By 1985 its 11,000 residents included both those moving from nearby districts and newcomers to the county. More housing was also built in Woodley and Winnersh, further reducing the green space between the borough and Wokingham. The

The south bank
of Rennie's Cut
on the Kennet
houses, the
re-development
of Rupert Street
and other old
properties. The
only remaining
building of
Huntley and
Palmers' offices
lies isolated on
the King's Road.

closing of the National Institute for Research in Dairying in 1985 was the prelude to the emergence of another estate in Shinfield. In 2013 plans were announced for several thousand dwellings in Wokingham Unitary Authority, many south of the M4, once regarded as a barrier to development. In the south of the borough the construction of Green Park Village with over 700 houses and flats was begun in 2016, part of the development of the area adjoining Green Park Business Park.

Education

Secondary educators have rarely been allowed time to consolidate one re-organisation before governments have determined on another. Before the 1944 Act came of age, its founding principle of selection was challenged, especially within the Labour Party and by some educationalists. In 1957 the Labour group on Reading Borough Council, followed in 1962 by the Labour Party, pledged to abolish the 11-plus and replace it by the neighbourhood comprehensive school, either mixed or single-sex, which would educate all pupils from 11 to 16, some having a sixth-form for those staying on to 18. Circumstances conspired to delay implementation until the 1970s: a split on the Council between Labour (pro-comprehensive schools) and the Conservatives (pro-grammar schools) and Conservative control of the council from 1967 to 1972 and of government after the 1970 election. Selection was maintained in the borough despite the creation of mixed comprehensives, Highdown in Caversham, formed in 1970 from E.P. Collier and Grove schools and the Meadway in Tilehurst, a result of a merger of Battle and Wilson secondary moderns in 1972.

In the local government re-organisation of 1974, control of education in the borough passed from Reading Borough to Berkshire County Council and was not regained until 1998. The county determined on converting its secondary schools to comprehensives but in the borough these were comprehensive in name only since selection to the two grammar schools continued. Ironically, given later population growth, some schools with falling numbers closed in the 1980s and others merged. Westwood and Stoneham became Prospect School in 1983 though Southlands resisted a merger with Ashmead, choosing to become a grant maintained school for girls in 1990. Pupils living in that part of South Oxfordshire annexed to Reading in 1977 could attend Chiltern Edge, a comprehensive school in Sonning Common. By 1998 the borough had three large mixed comprehensive schools: Highdown, Meadway and Ashmead; four grant-maintained: Prospect (by then Prospect Technical College), the bilateral Reading Girls' School (formerly Southlands) and the two grammar schools, as well as the Roman Catholic Hugh Faringdon School.

Between 1974 and 1998 some Reading pupils had attended schools in neighbouring districts where the catchment areas for Maiden Erlegh, Bulmershe, Denefield and Little Heath comprehensive schools extended deep into the borough. Former secondary modern school buildings were gradually adapted to accommodate growing numbers of primary school children, but no new comprehensives were built.

Education change continued. In the borough problems arose after 1998 as the County Council was dissolved with its administrative duties, including education, devolved to six unitary authorities. Reading regained its former borough status and with it responsibility for education, the borough's comprehensive schools being renamed 'community schools'. More changes followed in the new century. Meadway closed in 2001 as Prospect College was enlarged and another, Ashmead, renamed Thamesbridge College in 2000, closed five years later. Legislation by the Blair government encouraged schools to opt out of local government control, seek private sponsorship and become academies, depriving education authorities of income and influence over policy. The first of these in Reading in 2005 was the John Majedski Academy built on the Thamesbridge site and largely sponsored by Sir John. By 2013 almost all secondary schools including the two grammars had become academies. Even so, many Reading students opted to attend popular schools in neighbouring authorities, causing excessive demand for places and prompting the redrawing of their catchment areas. In response a new secondary school, Maiden Erlegh School, Reading opened in autumn 2015 with 180 students in its first year (Year 7) and the borough plans to expand its primary school provision with 2,500 more places for growing numbers of younger children.[7]

Reading Technical College (now Reading College) after a short-lived merger with Thames Valley University 2004–10, reverted to what it did best, providing a wide range of practical and academic courses in old and new buildings. Another choice for students aged 14–19 wishing to specialise in engineering and computing is Reading University Technical College, sponsored by some educational institutions, a number of high-tech companies and those employing workers with these skills. Not to be outdone, Reading University closed its Bulmershe Campus, the land sold for private housing, modernised many of the buildings on its London Road campus and in 2012 returned the Institute of Education to its original home. The London Road site also continued to house adult education classes although since the university axed its School of Continuing Education in 2009, these were provided by Oxford University Department for Continuing Education until 2018.[8]

The library service became a county responsibility after 1974, so it was Berkshire County Council which commissioned the new Central Library building in Abbey Square in 1985, administered by the borough since 1998. Built over the culverted Holy Brook, it now houses a lending, children's, reference and local studies library, with one floor and part of another leased to other users. The borough continues to host the Berkshire Record Office which moved out to Shire Hall, Shinfield Park, in 1980 and returned to a new building on Coley Avenue in 2000.[9]

Commerce

Though the Market Place, the covered Market and the Corn Exchange no longer serve their original purposes, and most of the small, independent retail shops are long gone, the town centre retains its traditional role as a market in the widest sense, more especially since shopping has become a leisure activity rather than a household chore. The Harris Arcade, an esoteric collection of businesses constructed in 1929 between Friar and Station streets continues to provide a modicum of under-cover shopping, but perhaps inevitably as more ambitious retail centres were pioneered in large cities, smaller towns such as Reading followed suit. The Butts Centre of 1972, part of a major redevelopment of the run-down area south of Oxford Road was later given a major refurbishment. Broad Street became more inviting after becoming a pedestrian zone in 1998; a small attractive arcade, King's Walk, came two years later. The more ambitious Oracle shopping and leisure centre, 'an urban response to the mammoth out-of-town shopping mall initiated in the 1980s by Gateshead's Metro Centre' was planned as early as 1989 but not opened until September 1999.[10] The irony of its name goes unnoticed by visitors to its shops, riverside restaurants and multiplex cinema. The original Oracle cloth workhouse was a charitable foundation to provide the poor with work; its successor is a monument to leisure, providing employment for sales

The Oracle which extends from the Kennet north to Broad Street takes its name from Kendrick's Workhouse formerly on part of this site. Now there are shops and cafes.

assistants and restaurant staff. The Kennet which once supplied water for industrial and domestic use still flows serenely past shoppers and diners carrying tourists on canal boats or cabin-cruisers. In an interesting parallel with its predecessor, the shopping centre has drawn trade away from some streets on the margins of the central area, just as the Kendrick Workhouse once threatened small-scale cloth workers.

As befits this new Reading, banks and building societies maintain a powerful presence in the centre. Marks & Spencer and John Lewis stores which remain outside the Oracle have ensured that, for the present, Broad

Festivities in 2012 on the Kennet side of the Oracle. The shopping centre extends to Minster Street, across the site of the former Oracle workhouse.

Jackson's Department Store was Reading's oldest family-owned business. It gave its name to the site it occupied from 1875 until its closure soon after this photograph was taken in December 2013. (JD)

Surviving red brick and terracotta fronts in Queen Victoria Street from 1900–1901.

Street retains an important commercial function. Waterstone's is here, the town's one remaining bookshop (apart from a well-patronised Oxfam version). A few persistent survivals, such as Hickie's music shop, still remind passers-by of what shopping used to be like, although Jackson's drapery store closed in December 2013, and Vicars, the butcher in West Street, a few months later. Above the shop fronts, decorated brick and terracotta tenaciously reflect an earlier streetscape. Overall the borough has made itself an attractive market centre for the twenty-first century as it did in the past, but whether it will see off the dual challenge from long-established out-of-town hyper- and supermarkets and more recent internet shopping, lies in the future.

Manufacture and industry

Old and new. The Blade, among the latest of Reading's high-rise office blocks soars above the flint core of the abbey's walls, now preserved for posterity. (JD)

Commercial developments proceeded alongside periodic slum clearance and the end of traditional manufacturing in the centre as factories moved to the periphery of the borough, beyond to the Greater Reading Area or out of the region completely, allowing a major transformation both in the town centre's appearance and its function. They also reflected national economic developments as large-scale industry gave way to knowledge-based enterprise. Huntley & Palmers, part of Associated Biscuits, stopped production in Reading in 1976 though the group's headquarters remained here until 1991. Following its merger in 1960 to become Courage, Barclay & Simonds Ltd, Simonds/Courage transferred its brewing to Worton Grange just inside the borough boundary in 1973 when its central site

The Prudential building on part of the former Huntley and Palmers' factory site, 1991–93. (JD)

proved too restrictive, but ended production there in 2010. The area was developed for housing. In 1969 Huntley, Bourne & Stevens moved to the Woodley Industrial Area, part of the former airfield. Suttons transferred its whole operation to Torquay in 1974 freeing for development an area extending south and east as far as Abbey Square.[11]

Victorian factories were replaced by ever taller high-rise office blocks of mixed architectural worth housing the town's new banking, financial, insurance and high-tech enterprises. After the Prudential's first building in 1962 came the Western Tower and Market Place House (1965). From the 1970s buildings sported an array of colours, the white Queen's House, the home of Metal Box (1974), dwarfed by the pinkish Apex Plaza built in the following decade which in turn gave best to The Blade of 2009 whose upswept sail-like peak is its most intriguing feature. The second Prudential Building, built in the early 1990s on part of the site of Huntley & Palmers' factory, is more reassuringly solid. Most were built in what have been called 'obsolete and unattractive' areas, and in an age when little attention was paid to aesthetics. Later planners and developers continued to be more concerned to attract tenants than to beautify the town though there were 'significant townscape benefits'.[12] Plus ça change!

The arrival of office blocks confirmed the changes whose beginnings had been evident in the 1951 census. Over the following decades engineering, insurance, service and high-tech companies as Foster-Wheeler, Hewlett Packard, Oracle, Digital and Thames Water moved their head offices to Reading. The 1971 census showed the main occupations for men resident

Reading since 1960   291

Reading Gaol seen from the Blade and part of the Abbey Ruins showing the conservation of the walls.

in the borough to be engineering, transport and communications, clerical and sales, and scientific research. Fewer than 2% were in food and drink production. Unemployment, at 3.76%, was low. Women were predominantly employed as clerks and sales assistants, in the caring professions, or as teachers and nurses. More than half of all married women were in paid employment. By 1989 almost 80% of the workforce was in the service sector: distribution, finance, insurance and health. The 1991 census analysis showed almost one man in three belonged to the professional, managerial or technician class, more than four in ten were skilled workers, and barely 20% were partly or unskilled. In 2001 the largest occupational groups were dealing in property (21%), car sales and repairs (16%) followed by transport and communications, manufacturing, health and social work, construction and financial services. Ten years later public administration (19%), retail and transport (both 15%) and health and social care (11%) employed most workers.[13] What the census did not

reveal was the extent to which residents worked in the borough. Traffic densities on road and rail at peak times and the small numbers cycling or walking to work suggests that many work in the TTWA and beyond, and that workers from the TTWA travel either to the town centre or to one of the business parks such as those on or near the Basingstoke Road and the A33 Relief Road.[14]

The largest employers, Reading Borough Council, the Royal Berkshire Hospital (RBH) and the University of Reading all have large numbers of graduate and similarly qualified staff, while some small research enterprises are housed on the University's Whiteknights campus.[15] Indeed most occupations in the borough and the Reading TTWA demand a highly skilled workforce. In 2011 over 35% of borough residents had either a university degree or similar qualification such as qualified medical or dental status, a Higher National Diploma or their equivalent. Another 13% had 'A' levels making Reading the 12th best qualified community in the South East. Not surprisingly, an analysis of 56 urban economies by The Work Foundation in 2008 placed Reading among ten 'Enterprise powerhouses', highly productive economies with a strong private sector, though whether the borough or Greater Reading was the unit surveyed is not clear. This judgement was confirmed by the decision of Scottish and Southern Energy (SSE) to rent the new office block, No 1, The Forbury, in September 2015, bringing 1000 more staff to its headquarters there.[16]

Wealth and social structure

The shift in the town's economy was not to everyone's advantage, inequalities in earning power resulting in great disparities of wealth. The divide which Breheny noted in the 1990s between well-qualified professionals and skilled workers and those without skills as regards job opportunities and satisfaction, and the consequent disparity in wealth, has persisted and if anything, intensified. Highly paid employment has allowed some families to move to desirable areas within the borough, to the new suburbs on its borders, or to one of many attractive villages in the county and beyond to enjoy a comfortable lifestyle in a pleasant environment. But such good fortune is not for those adults, almost one in five, who have no academic qualifications or skills and so are employed at best in routine jobs or at worst in labouring or other insecure work or none at all. Most live in the more densely populated central areas in rented accommodation and are likely to suffer from a range of social problems. Fewer than half of these families have cars, sometimes a necessity for travelling to work especially to firms which have moved to business parks on the periphery or outside the borough. In 2001 almost one in five borough residents walked or cycled to work. The absence of traditional industries providing consistent employment for semi- and unskilled workers explains why earnings are on average lower in the borough than in Greater Reading. Poverty persists, less harsh than a century ago, though with similar causes – a low-wage sector, low skills, unemployment, single-parent households, large families, and poor health. Child poverty was not eradicated with the slums, and in 2011 fuel poverty affected 10% of borough households. In 2000 Reading had one of the most deprived wards in England, Whitley, judged on an index of factors including unemployed- and single-parent households. Despite these grave statistics, studies of the latest census have suggested that overall the population is healthier and more prosperous than ever before.[17]

Transport

The axing of branch railway lines in the 1960s was hardly noticed in Reading and the loss of the Coley branch in 1983 came after the demise of the industries it had served. Conversely the high-speed trains of 1976 reducing journey times especially to London, and extra traffic generated on several cross-country routes from competing train operators since the privatisation of the railways have emphasised the town's role as a major route centre, necessitating improvements to the station. An extension in 1989 provided a car park, shops and cafes. A 'transformation' was completed in 2013 with two new entrances and, to remove a bottleneck on the line, five new platforms accessible from a wide upper concourse. More than 6% of borough commuters travel to work by train and many more come into Reading by this means. Cross Rail will eventually allow Reading commuters to travel direct to Canary Wharf and other east London destinations. The Railair coach link from Reading to Heathrow and a direct train service to Gatwick have attracted more passengers in transit through Reading. More will follow when the GWR line from Reading to Paddington is eventually electrified and a direct connection to Heathrow made via Slough.[18]

If changes to the railway network in the 1960s had little effect on Reading, those on the road system certainly did. The M4 London–South Wales motorway reached Reading in 1971, temporarily reducing the traffic flow on an overcrowded A4 and creating space on the town's roads by allowing travellers to avoid Reading altogether. Unfortunately traffic abhors a vacuum and as car ownership increased, overcrowding returned. An urban motorway, the Inner Distribution Road (IDR), more than twenty years in the making, was intended to relieve congestion but financial pressures left it half-finished though not before planners had authorised the demolition of some medieval houses in London Street and a splendid Georgian pile in the Forbury which stood in its path. Even

A cyclist/pedestrian bridge connecting between Caversham and Reading
(north entrance to the railway station) opened.
(J McM)

the Town Hall was threatened by an orgy of corporate vandalism which threatened more of the borough's built heritage. More positively, a large area of poor housing in Coley was demolished for the road which cuts through historic Castle Street, forever destroying a streetscape which had matured over centuries. Later, dual-carriageway connections from two motor-way junctions, the A329M from the east and the A33 Relief Road from the south improved the flow of traffic into the borough though queues still build up as vehicles converge onto narrower town-centre roads.[19]

Developments in both road and rail have not eliminated the problems resulting from the expanding economies of the town and county and the pressure of numbers. For the 50% of borough residents travelling to work by car, the choice lies between lengthy traffic jams either at motorway junctions and on cross-town roads, ever earlier journeys to and later returns from work, or finding a circuitous route: a 'rat-run'. A much-needed third Thames crossing to the east of the town has not

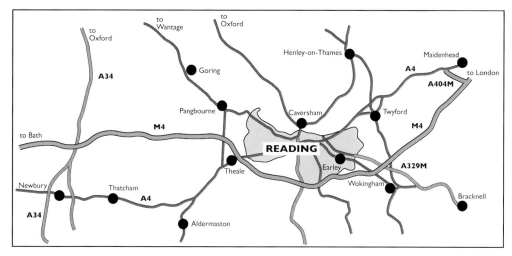

yet materialised despite more hopeful discussions since 2014, leaving frustrated motorists funnelled onto the two existing bridges. However in 2015 a pedestrian/cycle bridge across the river from Caversham to Reading was opened, encouraging healthier and environmentally sympathetic travel. The provision of multi-storey car parks, two of them adjoining shopping malls, makes the car the preferred option for shoppers as well as workers, reducing the need to walk to an unhealthy minimum. A substantial number of travellers, though only one worker in eight, uses the borough's colour-coded buses or those of private companies. One major artery of the bus network is the original horse-drawn, west–east tram route from Tilehurst to Cemetery Junction extended at both original termini, and others cross the town from north to south and other compass points on the boundary and beyond with commendable frequency.

Local and national politics

The second half of the twentieth century witnessed the most far-reaching changes in local government since 1835. In 1974 Reading lost its county borough status and the powers of an all-purpose authority, becoming a mere borough within a much-reduced Berkshire. It was supremely ironic that the new Civic Centre, planned since 1960, should be completed only after much of the administration it was designed to house had been transferred to the county. The site chosen was on the western edge of the town, where some property had already been demolished in readiness for a major redevelopment. In the process ancient thoroughfares such as Hosier Street were lost. As if to add to the borough's discomfiture, Berkshire County Council determined on a new Shire Hall. In 1980 it left the building in the Forbury, its home since 1904, for Shinfield Park, a striking new multi-million pound headquarters. The former County Hall was later converted into an elegant addition to the town's hotels and conference centres.

Berkshire suffered from further local government re-organisation in 1998 which abolished the County Council and restored both Reading Borough's independence and its pride, though it ranked only as one, albeit the largest, of the six unitary authorities which replaced the county administration. Shire Hall was sold at a loss to Foster Wheeler. In December 2014 the borough moved its civic offices to Plaza West, modest accommodation more suited to the reduced budgets and powers of twenty-first-century local government. For much of the period, Liberals, Labour and Conservatives shared control of the Borough Council, 'no overall control' being the frequent election result especially after 1998. However, as in the past, parliamentary election results have followed the national trend: Conservatives held both seats throughout the Thatcher and Major eras but Labour regained them when Tony Bair took office in 1997. Both went Conservative in 2010.[20]

Popular culture

For most of the year Reading shares in the monoculture which has increasingly pervaded British towns and cities. The occasional coffee bars with glittering espresso machines which arrived in the 1950s have self-seeded as coffee shops throughout the town centre. More substantial fare is provided by an eclectic mix of ethnic restaurants. Ballrooms are long gone, replaced by night clubs, of which the town has more than its fair share, magnets for the young, especially on Saturday nights. Licensing hours have steadily lengthened and now extend far into the wee small hours. Just a couple of multiplex cinemas cater for comparatively small numbers, devotees preferring such venues as Reading Film Theatre.

Summer in the borough is punctuated by outdoor events, some old, some new. The revived Reading Amateur Regatta on the Thames was joined in 1990 by the Waterfest celebrating the Kennet and Avon Canal. West Reading's colourful Community Carnival celebrates the vibrant culture of the borough's ethnic communities as visibly as Corpus Christi processions were once witness to the depth of medieval devotion. Following the departure of WOMAD which from 1990 to 2006 was at Reading, bringing music, dance and the arts from round the world to the delight of hundreds of British and foreign visitors, there has been only one national/international festival here: Reading Festival. One of the largest rock festivals in the country, it has, since 1971, drawn thousands of fans to camp near the Thames and enjoy leading rock bands and singers during August Bank Holiday weekend.

Reading's tradition of more formal music-making still flourishes all the year round. Several amateur choirs and orchestras give concerts ranging from Bach to Gospel and everything in between. The magnificent Victorian Concert Hall in the Town Hall is the venue for annual series of performances from the classical repertoire by world-class British and international soloists and orchestras. Since 1977 the Hexagon, a multi-purpose venue, has provided an eclectic programme of leading professional and local amateur music, dance and drama to suit all tastes and an annual pantomime. A new theatre/concert hall has been proposed for the site after the departure of the civic administration. Serious dramatic performances are rare; instead the Progress Theatre in which the young Kenneth Branagh honed his craft, provides a few high-quality productions each season, and although there is no permanent professional theatre in the borough, good transport links facilitate journeys to London and Oxford.

Sport, too, is seasonal. Football still attracts the largest following, especially since 1998 when Reading FC moved to a palatial new stadium through the generosity of its then chairman, Sir John Madjeski. For two glorious seasons (2006–08) the club played in the Premier League and again in 2011/12. The stadium also plays host to Rugby Union's London Irish. Reading's amateurs practise a wide range of sports, indoors and out, summer and winter, on dry land and on the rivers. Splendid new facilities such as the Redgrave Pinsent Rowing Lake near Sonning and the athletic track and velodrome at Palmer Park enable serious sportsmen and women to achieve ever higher standards while other local parks make ample provision for the less ambitious. Waterways and lakes are busy with both local rowers and anglers, and tourists in narrow boats and launches, the Thames and Kennet paths with walkers and cyclists.[21]

In keeping with its up-market and secular image, the borough's bingo halls have been replaced by casinos, two of its nonconformist chapels converted to night-clubs and vacant premises to betting shops. St Mary's vicarage is now a pleasant restaurant though the elegant Dispensary which was once its neighbour is no more. The former Lovejoy Library and Bookshop later the London Street Bookshop is now the Reading International Solidarity Centre, RISC. As is fitting for a multi-cultural, multi-national, Fairtrade town, RISC supplements its 'ethnic' shop and restaurant with activities campaigning on issues of human rights, world poverty and injustice. Several more high-status buildings have fared equally well. Caversham Park, owned by the Crawshays, ironmasters until 1918, has housed the BBC since 1941, hovever, the Monitoring Centre is moving to London. The same could be said of Prospect House, Coley House and Calcot Court which have also survived by acquiring new functions. Reading Prison whose most famous inmate was Oscar Wilde, closed on 31 December 2013. A Grade II listed building, it lies within the

The north front of Caversham Park built in 1850 for William Crawshay to replace the mansion destroyed by fire. From 1943 to 2018 it was the home of the BBC Monitoring Service which is now returning to offices in London. BBC Radio Berkshire shared the site. (JD)

historic Abbey Quarter which includes St James RC church designed by Pugin, the Forbury Gardens and the Abbey Ruins. In September 2014 the council launched Reading Abbey Revealed, a project to preserve the ruins and enhance the Quarter's appeal for residents and visitors. Funded jointly by the borough and a grant from the Heritage Lottery Fund, it was successfully completed in 2018 when the Abbey Ruins re-opened to the public. The prison is the property of HM Government which is proposing to sell the site. Reading Borough Council is vigorously attempting to preserve both it and the ruins, both important in the town's history. How central government reacts will indicate what value, if any, it places on the borough's heritage.[22]

The west door of St James' Roman Catholic Church built within what is now called the Abbey Quarter, an area within the ancient abbey precinct.

Into the future

Reading in the early twenty-first century is the creation of the two factors which have dominated its development for a thousand years: location and migration, both magnified by recent changes at national and international levels. Commerce and service industries again dominate the economy as they have for much of the past. Only in the late Tudor and the Victorian eras did Reading's prosperity rely primarily on manufacturing goods for export. The town is among the most affluent in the South East but still suffers from social and environmental problems, some the result of its attraction as a place to live and work. The most serious concern is housing, or rather the lack of it. There is still a formidable queue of families, nearly 5,000 in 2010, for council houses, conditions in many privately rented properties are far from ideal and the possibility of 'getting on the housing ladder' recedes as prices continue to rise faster than incomes. They were already twelve times average incomes in the borough in 2010.[23] There is widespread and possibly endemic poverty among the many low-paid workers, relieved to some extent by food banks and other charitable organisations in which Christian and other religious groups are prominent. School places are in short supply and crowded roads still pollute the town centre.

However, an enlarged and modernised railway station and projected improvement to the lines to London will enhance Reading's traditional role as a transport hub and provide access to well-paid jobs in the town – Reading is a net importer of labour – the region and the capital. In the borough schools are being built or enlarged, and houses constructed. Businesses have been created by entrepreneurs among whom, as in the past, immigrants are well represented.[24] The university has an enviable reputation, attracting growing numbers of both home and overseas students, some of whom choose to stay after graduation. Visitors come for shopping and entertainment and townspeople can escape to the green and pleasant areas which still surround the town. Both council and townspeople are increasingly aware of the town's architectural heritage and determined to preserve it. Described in 2013 as among the best places to provide a 'good life-work balance', how this balance plays out in the twenty-first century will determine whether Reading continues to be a desirable place to live and a magnet for newcomers.

Bibliographical essay

Dates

Until 1752 England followed the Julian Calendar, beginning each year on 25 March. For example, documents from 1 January to 24 March would be dated 1710 and 25 March 1711 (Old Style). To avoid confusion, I have treated all dates from 1 January as beginning a new year so in the example above, 1 January has been written 1 January 1711. In September 1752 England adopted the Gregorian Calendar, beginning each year on 1 January (New Style).

Currency

The basic unit was a silver penny, 240 weighing one pound (lb). Twelve pennies (12*d*.) equalled one shilling (1*s*.) and 20*s*. equalled one pound (£1). From the thirteenth century coins to a fractions of a penny: a half penny (½*d*.) and a farthing (¼*d*.) were minted, and later a groat (4*d*.), a shilling and a noble (6*s*. 8*d*.) and others of greater value.

A mark (13*s*. 4*d*.) was a unit of account, not a coin. Fractions 6*s*. 8*d*. (½ mark) and 3*s*. 4*d*. (¼ mark) were frequently used in the middle ages. See Lionel Munby, *How Much is That Worth?* (Phillimore, 1989), 9. In 1971 a decimal currency of pounds (£) equal to 100 new pence (p) replaced the traditional coinage so 1*s*. = 5p.

Abbreviations

Aspinall	A. Aspinall, Barbara Dodwell, M.D. Lambert, C.F. Slade, E.A. Smith, *Parliament Through Seven Centuries: Reading and its MPs* (1962)	BRS	Berkshire Record Society
		CUH1	D.M. Palliser (ed.), *The Cambridge Urban History of Britain, vol. I, 600–1540* (2000)
Alexander	Alan Alexander, *Borough Government and Politics: Reading 1835–1985* (1985)	*CUH III*	Martin Daunton (ed.), *The Cambridge Urban History of Britain, vol. III, 1840–1950* (2000)
Atlas	Joan Dils and Margaret Yates (eds), *An Historical Atlas of Berkshire* (2012)	Childs	W.M. Childs, *The Town of Reading during the Early Part of the Nineteenth Century* (1910)
BAJ	*Berkshire Archaeological Journal*	Coates	Charles Coates, *The History and Antiquities of Reading* (1802)
Belson, Diary	Account book /diary of Edward Belson, 1707–1722 BRO, D/EZ12/1–3	Diary	unpublished volumes of the Diary of Reading Corporation in BRO
B.O. and N.	*Berkshire Old and New*, journal of the Berkshire Local History Association	*Diary*	J.M. Guilding (ed.), *Reading Records: Diary of the*
BRO	Berkshire Record Office		

303

	Corporation, 1431–1654, 4 vols (Reading and London, 1892–96)
DNB	*Oxford Dictionary of National Biography*
Ford	Ben M. Ford, Daniel Poore, Ruth Shaffery and David R.P. Wilkinson, *Under the Oracle* (Oxford, 2013)
Gold	Sidney M. Gold, *A Biographical Dictionary of Architects at Reading* (privately published, 1999)
Kemp, *Cartularies*	B.R. Kemp (ed.), *Reading Abbey Cartularies*, 2 vols, Camden Fourth Series, 33 (1987)
Man	John Man, *The History and Antiquities of the Borough of Reading in the County of Berks* (Reading, 1816)
Petyt	Malcolm Petyt (ed.), *The Growth of Reading* (Stroud, 1993)
Pritchard	C.F. Pritchard (ed.), *Reading Charters, Acts and Orders, 1253–1911* (1913)
RLSL	Reading Local Studies Library
Slade, 'Reading'	Cecil Slade, 'Reading in Saxon and Danish Times' in Malcolm Petyt (ed.), *The Growth of Reading* (Stroud, 1993)
Slade, *The Town of Reading*	Cecil Slade, *The Town of Reading and its abbey* (Reading, 2001)
Slade, *Accounts*	Cecil Slade (ed.), *Reading Gild Accounts, 1357–1516*, BRS 6 and 7 (2002)
Spurrier, *Registrations*	Lisa Spurrier (ed.), *Berkshire Nonconformist Meeting House Registrations, 1689–1852*, BRS, 9 and 10 (2005)
TNA	The National Archives (formerly the Public Record Office)
Tyack	Geoffrey Tyack, Simon Bradley and Nikolaus Pevsner, *The Buildings of England: Berkshire* (2010)
Yeo	Stephen Yeo, *Religion and Voluntary Organisations in Crisis* (1976)

General works

Outstanding in its national coverage of urban history from the Roman period to 1950 is the three-volume *Cambridge Urban History of Britain* (2000), with contributions from specialists throughout. On Reading, the *Victoria County History of Berkshire*, vol. iii (*VCH*) has a detailed account of the history and topography of the borough up to c.1900. A useful general work is Daphne Phillips, *The Story of Reading* (revised edition, Newbury, 1990). Two early studies, Charles Coates, *The History and Antiquities of Reading* (1802) and John Man, *The History and Antiquities of the Borough of Reading in the County of Berks* (Reading, 1816) contain useful information but should be approached with care over interpretation. C.F. Pritchard, *Reading Charters, Acts and Orders* (1913) contains all Reading's charters up to 1911. A full and reliable discussion of the borough's parliamentary history up to about 1900 is A Aspinall *et al.*, *Parliament*

Through Seven Centuries: Reading and its MPs (1962) and for biographies of MPs consult the relevant volumes of *History of Parliament. The Commons.* For buildings throughout rely on Geoffrey Tyack, Simon Bradley and Nikolaus Pevsner, *The Buildings of England: Berkshire* (2010) and also from about 1800, Sidney M. Gold, *A Biographical Dictionary of Architects at Reading* (privately published, 1999). *An Historical Atlas of Berkshire* (2nd edn, 2012), edited by Joan Dils and Margaret Yates, has several articles on or including the borough. Reading Local Studies Library (RLSL) has an unrivalled collection of almost everything written on the borough, both general and specialised. Reading's archives are kept at the Berkshire Record Office which has an on-line catalogue accessible at www.berkshirerecordoffice.org.uk/search-archives

Chapter 1: Beginnings and the early medieval town to c.1350

General works on medieval towns abound; Colin Platt, *The English Medieval Town* (1976) remains one of the most useful. Indispensable for Reading during the whole medieval period are the works of Cecil Slade especially 'Reading' in M.L. Lobel (ed.), *Historic Towns*, vol. I (1969), 'Reading in Saxon and Danish Times' in Malcolm Petyt (ed.), *The Growth of Reading* (Stroud, 1993), and numerous articles in *The Berkshire Archaeological Journal*. Grenville Astill, *Historic Towns in Berkshire: an archaeological appraisal* (Reading, 1978) includes an important article and several maps on the borough. Philip Morgan (ed.),

Domesday Book, 5, Berkshire (Chichester, 1979) prints the text and translation of the entries for Reading, also found in *VCH*, vol ii. Ben M. Ford *et al.*, *Under the Oracle, Excavations at the Oracle Shopping Centre* (Thames Valley Landscapes Monograph, 2013) is a most useful discussion of the buildings and economy of the area now occupied by the Oracle shopping mall. In the RLSL is a copy of Peter Rixon, 'The Town of Reading c.1200–c.1542', unpublished D.Phil thesis, University of Oxford (1998), an in-depth study of the town's economy.

Chapter 2: Abbey, borough and urban government, 1121–1529

Essential reading is the work of Reading's two leading medieval historians, Brian R. Kemp, *Reading Abbey 2: an introduction to the history of the abbey* (Reading, 1968) and his two-volume edition of the abbey cartularies, and Cecil Slade, *The Town of Reading and its Abbey* (Reading, 2001). Ron Baxter, *The Royal Abbey of Reading* (2016) is the first full-length survey of the abbey's architecture. Jamieson B. Hurry, *The Rise and Fall of Reading Abbey* (1906) remains a useful detailed description of the abbey and its monks. Alan Coates, *English Medieval Books: the Reading Abbey collection from foundation to*

dispersal (Oxford, 1999) is well worth consulting for its detailed studies of the abbey library and monastic scholarship. The *VCH*, vol. iii, has a good introduction to the history of the abbey, the friary and abbey–town relations. Cecil Slade (ed.), *Reading Gild Accounts, 1357–1516*, BRS 6 and 7 (2002) and vol. 1 of J.M. Guilding (ed.), *Reading Records: Diary of the Corporation, 1431–1654*, 4 vols (Reading and London, 1892–96) are the best sources for borough government. Small monographs by Leslie Cram of Reading Museum include the results of excavations of the abbey waterfront.

Chapter 3: Prosperity and piety, c.1350–1540

There is little published work on this period of Reading's history apart from Slade, *Accounts*. The most comprehensive national study of medieval religious practice is Eamon Duffy, *The Stripping of the Altars* (2nd edn, 2005). For heresy see J.A.F. Thomson, *The Later Lollards, 1414–1520* (Oxford, 1965) which includes a short piece on Reading as does the *VCH*, vol. iii. Charles Kerry, *A History of the Municipal Church of St Lawrence, Reading* (Reading, 1883) is a useful if limited introduction to parish life. More detailed is Joan Dils, *Reading St Laurence Churchwardens'*

Accounts 1498–1570, BRS, 19 and 20 (2013). An excellent general study of popular culture, Ronald Hutton, *The Rise and Fall of Merry England* (1994) includes some Reading material. See also Rixon, thesis, and Ben Ford, *Under the Oracle* for the economy, Tyack for buildings and P.J.P. Goldberg, *Women in England, c.1275–1525* (Manchester, 1995) for a very detailed account of women's work in towns with fuller records than Reading.

Chapter 4: The years of crisis, 1529–1600

Serious and popular works on the period of the English Reformation are almost too numerous to list. A recent, accessible yet scholarly account is Eric Ives, *The Reformation Experience: living through the turbulent 16th century* (2012). Ronald Hutton, 'The local impact of the Tudor Reformations' in Peter Marshall (ed.), *The Impact of the English Reformation, 1500–1640* (1997) discusses events in many communities including Reading while Patrick Collinson and John Craig (eds), *The Reformation in English Towns, 1540–1600* (Basingstoke, 1998) includes Jeanette Martin's study of Reading. Robert Tittler, *The Reformation and the Towns in England: politics and political culture, c.1540–1640* (Oxford, 1998) provides useful comparisons with other towns. Reading is also discussed in the *VCH*, vol. iii, and the Introduction to Joan Dils (ed.), *Reading St Laurence Churchwardens' Accounts, 1498–1570*.

Chapter 5: Borough society and economy, *c.*1540–1640

The Cambridge Urban History, vol II, covers the development of towns for the wider period 1540 to 1840. For a general survey of towns before 1700 see Sybil M. Jack, *Towns in Tudor and Stuart Britain* (Basingstoke, 1996). A useful short local study is Joan Dils, *Redding 1540–1640* (Reading, 1980) and Joan Dils 'Reading in the Sixteenth and Seventeenth Centuries' in M Petyt (ed.), *The Growth of Reading* (Stroud, 1993). *Under the Oracle* includes a chapter on the crafts of the borough.

Chapter 6: A troubled and divided community 1600–1660

Among the many books on the period before, during and after the Civil War, arguably the best is Barry Coward, *The Stuart Age* (2nd edn, 1994). For Berkshire see D.S. Disbury, *The Civil War in Berkshire* (1978*)*. Politics in Reading are best discussed in M. Brod, *The Case of Reading: Urban governance in troubled times, 1640–1690* (Peterborough, 2006). See also Aspinall for parliamentary affairs, the *DNB* for important local and national individuals and Brod's article in *Atlas*. For the 1643 epidemic see Joan A. Dils, 'Epidemics, Mortality and the Civil War in Berkshire 1642–6', *Southern History*, 11 (1989), 40–52. For tables of prices and the cost of living index see C.G.A. Clay, *Economic expansion and social change: England, 1500–1700* (1984) vol. I, 49–51, and for a discussion of the general crisis in the English cloth trade see B.E. Supple, *Commercial Crisis and Change in England, 1600–1642* (Cambridge, 1959)

Chapter 7: A changed society and economy, 1660–1740

Aspinall, Brod and Coward are again the most useful for political developments. On economic change generally see *Cambridge Urban History, vol II*. For Reading see N.R. Goose, 'Decay and regeneration in seventeenth-century Reading: A study in a changing economy', *Southern History*, 6 (1984). General developments in transport are covered in Charles Hadfield, *Canals of Southern England* (1955) and William Albert *The Turnpike Road System in England, 1663–1840* (2007). The works on religion listed below for Chapter Eight are also relevant here.

Chapter 8: Politics, commerce and improvement, 1740–1835

For a general study of towns at this period Rosemary Sweet, *The English Town, 1680–1840. Government, Society and Culture* (Harlow, 1999) is useful. There has been very little written on Reading between 1700 and 1800 and virtually nothing on borough politics with the exception of

W.M. Childs' *The Town of Reading in the Early Part of the Nineteenth Century* (1910) on latter years of the period based mainly on newspapers but none the worse for that. Charles Coates and John Man provide valuable material on the borough as they knew it about 1800 and Mary Mitford for the years immediately following. Man, *A Stranger in Reading*, edited by Adam Stout (2005) provides an idiosyncratic viewpoint. On religion, Lisa Spurrier's introduction to her *Berkshire Nonconformist Meeting Houses*, BRS, 9 and 10 (2005) is concise and informative. For a good short account of religion in this period see Geoffrey Holmes and Daniel Szechi, *Age of Oligarchy: Pre-industrial Britain, 1722–1783* (1993), 101–33. For the Church of England, J. Walsh, C. Haydon and S. Taylor (eds), *The Church of England c.1689–c.1833: From Toleration to Tractarianism* (Cambridge, 1993), 1–64. For the Evangelical Revival see Ben Fulford, 'The Effect of the Great Awakening on Reading', *B.O. and N.*, 15 (1998). There are several excellent pamphlets on local enterprises by T.A.B. (Tony) Corley including *The Road to Worton Grange: Simonds' and Courage's Brewery at Reading, 1785–1980*. Corley also wrote a number of articles on local banks, breweries and industries for the *BAJ* in vols 66 and 68.

Chapter 9: From Belford Regis to Biscuitopolis: Reading 1840–1911

There is almost too much literature on this period. For the national picture try Martin Daunton (ed.), *The Cambridge Urban History of Britain, vol. III, 1840–1950* (Cambridge, 2000) or P.J. Waller, *Town, City and Nation: England 1850–1914* (1983). Poor Law literature is interminable; try A. Digby, *British Welfare Policy: Workhouse to Workfare* (1989). T.A.B. (Tony) Corley is unsurpassed as the historian of Reading business enterprises and entrepreneurs. See his *Quaker Enterprise in Biscuits: Huntley & Palmers of Reading 1822–1972* (1972). Alan Alexander's expertise as a lecturer in politics and a local politician gives added depth to his discussion of public health and education in relation to borough politics in his *Borough Government and Politics: Reading 1835–1985* (1985). The history of the Royal Berkshire Hospital is admirably covered in Margaret Railton and Marshall Barr, *The Royal Berkshire Hospital, 1839–1989* (Reading, 1989). The *DNB* includes short but informative studies of leading figures such as George Palmer, Martin Hope Sutton and Thomas Talfourd. Otherwise most material is to be found in general collections or short, locally published books and pamphlets. RLSL has a wealth of short works on specialist subjects such as transport, local industries and societies. For early photography in Reading see Martin Andrews, *Fox Talbot & the Reading Establishment* (Two Rivers Press, 2014). For researchers there is a complete run of trade directories, a large collection of sale catalogues and digitised photographs as well as local newspapers and census data on microfilm.

Chapter 10: Religion, education and culture, *c.*1892: retrospect and prospect

Some aspects of this chapter will be covered by general studies of towns such as the *Cambridge Urban History* and Alexander's volume on Reading. Among many works on education is J. Lawson and H. Silver, *A Social History of Education in England* (1973). There are numerous histories of local schools, of varying quality. Stephen Yeo's study, *Religion and Voluntary Organisations in Crisis* (1976) is not an easy read but is indispensable. Important for a study of domestic, public and religious buildings in addition to Tyack is Sidney Gold, *A Biographical Dictionary of Architects at Reading* (privately published, 1999). Still valuable is the work of W.M. Childs, Reading's first vice-chancellor and a pioneer in making local history available to the community. His *The Making of a University* is the best study of the university's early years and J.C. Holt, *The University of Reading: the first fifty years* (1977) for later developments. Numerous works on aspects of local recreation include Gillian Clark, *Down by the River: the Thames and Kennet in Reading* (Reading, 2009) and Nigel Sutcliffe, *Reading: A Horse-racing Town* (Reading, 2010).

Chapter 11: Survivals and Arrivals: Reading, 1912–1960

The national background is covered in numerous works easily accessible in local libraries and bookshops. Locally, Alexander remains the best read on local politics and social reform and Phillips for the changes in the borough's appearance. Mark Clapson's study of the Whitley estate, *Working-class Suburb* (2012) has many perceptive comments on social problems in the borough generally. Relevant chapters in books on Huntley & Palmers and other Victorian enterprises relate their departure from the town. A variety of works large and small on specialist subjects such as migration, local communities, public libraries, transport and football is available in RLSL as are census data and newspapers on microfilm. Books depicting the period in photographs vary in usefulness, and though based solely on material in local newspapers, those by Stuart Hylton are worth consulting particularly his *Reading at War* (Stroud, 1996). Sadly many lack references. The *DNB* includes articles on a number of local individuals of national significance whilst the biographies of many more are available in local libraries. Among local publications on World War I are David Bilton, *Reading in the Great War* (2016) and a study by Margaret Simons on Reading's wartime experiences (forthcoming).

Chapter 12: The latest transformation: Reading since 1960

Most subjects are covered by the books listed for Chapter 11. In addition, Michael Breheny and Douglas Hart, *Reading in Profile: a survey of key economic issues for the Greater Reading Area in the 1990s* (Reading, 1994), Ann Westgarth, *Routes to Reading* (Reading, 2006) and Adam Stout's *Risc: of books, stones, friends and visions: nos 35–39 London Street, Reading* (Reading, 1997) have important things to say about the economy, migration and culture of contemporary Reading.

References

Foreword

1　*BAJ* 59, (1961), 43–46.
2　In 1977 Cecil kindly gave me a copy of his unpublished transcripts of the Court Leet records and the Elizabethan Cofferers' accounts, and found in a cupboard a long-neglected map based on a 1552 manuscript survey in The National Archives which he allowed me to copy.

3　B.R. Kemp, ed., *Reading Abbey Cartularies* (2 vols Camden Fourth Series, 31 and 33 (1986–7); Cecil Slade, ed., *Reading Gild Accounts, 1357–1516* (2 vols BRS 6 and 7, 2002). The chief promoter and first chairman of the BRS was Donald Matthew, then the University's Professor of Medieval History.

Chapter 1: Beginnings and the early medieval town to c.1350

1　Cecil Slade, 'Reading', in M.L. Lobel (ed.), *Historic Towns*, vol. 1 (1969), 1–2.
2　Maps 9 and 10 in Joan Dils and Margaret Yates (eds), *An Historical Atlas of Berkshire* (2nd edn, 2012); Andrew Hutt, Paul Goodenough, Valerie Pyne, 'Living in the Iron Age in and around Berkshire', *Berkshire Archaeological Journal*, 78 (2009), 150–4. Borough sites are in Katesgrove Lane, Addington Road and Northcourt Avenue. There were rural settlements at Three Mile Cross, Pingewood and Shinfield. Steve Preston, ed., *Archaeological Investigations to the south of Reading, 2002–2008* (Thames Valley Archaeological Services Monograph 13, 2010), 1–2; 58–9.
3　Cecil Slade, 'Reading in Saxon and Danish Times' in Malcolm Petyt (ed.), *The Growth of Reading* (Stroud, 1993), 1; Jill Greenaway, 'Roman Berkshire' in *Atlas*, 21. In 2010 a 'logboat' coffin and the skeleton of a woman dating from *c.*AD 50–*c.*150 were discovered at Smallmead Farm: *Get Reading*, 30 July 2010.
4　Slade,'Reading', 3. This chapter by Reading's foremost medieval historian provides both an erudite account of the town's early development and a sympathetic description of

its social life.
5　Margaret Gelling, *The Place-names of Berkshire*, 3 vols (English Place Name Society, Cambridge, 1973), 170, 1–2. She quotes Asser (AD 893): 'which district is so called from *Berroc*, a wood where box grows abundantly'. Grenville Astill, *Historic Towns in Berkshire: an archaeological appraisal* (Reading, 1978), 75–7; Grenville Astill, 'The Towns of Berkshire' in J. Haslam (ed.), *Anglo-Saxon Towns in Southern England* (Chichester, 1984), 55.
6　Catherine Edwards, 'Saxon Archaeology and Medieval Archaeology at Forbury House, 10–12 the Forbury' (*BAJ*, 77, 2004–08), 39–45; Peter Rixon 'The Town of Reading *c.*1200–*c.*1542', unpublished D.Phil. thesis, University of Oxford (1999), 4; Astill, *Historic Towns*.
7　*The* historian of minsters is John Blair on whose work this paragraph is based. John Blair 'The Minsters of the Thames' in John Blair and Brian Golding (eds), *The Cloister and the World* (1996), 5–28. See also his article in Dils and Yates, *An Historical Atlas*. Some minsters were on rivers (Sonning, Cookham etc.), others not (Childrey, Thatcham etc.).
8　Astill, *Historic Towns*, figure 23, Astill, 'The

Towns of Berkshire', 58–60. The properties in Old Street (*in veteri vico)* and New Street (*in novo vico)* occur in a lease of 1165–73. B.R. Kemp (ed.), *Reading Abbey Cartularies*, 2 vols (Camden Fourth Series, 33, 1987), ii, number 887. A cartulary is a collection of official records.

9 For a very succinct account of these events see John Blair, 'The Anglo-Saxon Period (*c.*440–1066)' in Kenneth O Morgan (ed.), *The Oxford Illustrated History of Britain* (Oxford, 1984).

10 Blair, 'The Anglo-Saxon Period', *passim*; Michael Swanton (ed. and trans.), *The Anglo-Saxon Chronicles* (paperback edn, 2000), 71–2, 136–7. Commentators interpret 'ignite their beacons' as meaning they burned the settlements after plunder.

11 Anthony Freeman, Michael Swanton (ed. and trans.), *The Anglo-Saxon Chronicles* (paperback edn, 2000), 71–2; 'Reading; its status and standing as a minor late Anglo-Saxon Mint' *BAJ*, 72 (1983–85), 53–6; Slade, 'Reading', 23–4. However, a more recent source suggests Oxford produced only five coins in this reign and Winchester 15. Derek Keane, 'The south-east' in D.M. Palliser (ed.), *The Cambridge Urban History of Britain*, vol. 1 (2000), 578.

12 Slade, 'Reading' in M.L. Lobel (ed.), 29.

13 Philip Morgan (ed.), *Domesday Book, 5, Berkshire* (Chichester, 1979), introduction. The hundred was an administrative, judicial and financial division of the shire. Reading was in Reading Hundred which covered the whole of central Berkshire from Woolhampton to Whitley. See Slade, 'Reading', 6.

14 This may have meant four separate mill buildings or a cluster of wheels on a single site. The most likely site is the one later occupied by St Giles' Mill though this appears to have been outside the Saxon borough. The two mills/mill wheels were probably on or near the site of the future Minster Mill.

15 As a royal borough, Reading would have possessed at least the basic aspects of local government known to have existed elsewhere. Cecil Slade (ed.), *Reading Gild Accounts, 1357–1516* (Berkshire Record Society, 6 & 7 (2002), Part 1, xiii.

16 The income from these was farmed, possibly to the sheriff who made his account to the king. He lost on the bargain; the 28 plots paid £4 3*s.* but he paid £5: H.R. Loyn, *Anglo-Saxon England and the Norman Conquest* (1962), 382.

17 There were 545 properties listed in Wallingford, 477 in Oxford, 95 in Windsor and 59 in Reading. *CUH 1*, 752.

18 Morgan, *Domesday*, 1, 41; 42. 15, 2. 1, 21. 'Villager', 'smallholder' etc. are the translations of the Latin terms *villani* and *bordarii* used in Morgan's edition of the Domesday Book. There is considerable debate among historians about these translations. Slade, 'Reading', 3; Astill, *Historic Towns*, 79. The history of the area of St Mary's and the origins of Reading are discussed above.

19 Rixon, thesis, 31.

20 The deed mentions three stalls next to the wall of the abbey between two others and a stall in the middle of the market place of Reading between the wall and another stall. Kemp, *Cartularies*, ii, number 844. Unless otherwise stated, the description of the town *c.*1350 is based on the abbey cartularies, Reading borough deeds and Slade, *Accounts.*

21 Astill, *Historic Towns*, 78. Astill also suggested that the layout of the Market Place and New Street was a deliberate attempt by the abbey to create a new street pattern as happened in other planned towns..

22 Slade locates the medieval Fish and Butchers' Shambles in King Street (*Accounts*, Part I, lxxii) and Fish Row and Butcher Row in modern Broad Street C.F. Slade, 'Reading', in M.D. Lobel, *Historic Towns* (1969) where they also appear on Speed's map of 1611. The New Shambles seems to have replaced the 'King Street' Shambles by 1534. See my chapter 4. Rixon attaches the name High Street to modern Broad Street, Slade to the street from the Market Place over High Bridge. King Street and the eastern end of what became Broad Street was almost certainly known as High Street at least from Gutter Lane before turning south to High Bridge. A deed of *c.*1250 refers to a lane (*venella*) leading from the High Street to New Street. BRO, R/AT1/4 and Thomas Carpenter's will, 1520 (PROB 11/20/3) talks of his properties 'in the Highe Strete in Redyng in a place there called the Chese Rew. As late as 1706 it is called 'High Street alias Broad Street'. BRO, Will of Richard Piggott, 1706 D/P110/25/16.

23 TNA· Survey of Reading, 1552, Misc Bks Land Rev 187, 314–17; Kemp, *Cartularies*, ii, 944. The other crosses were High Cross near the gild hall and Gerards Cross in High Street. P.H. Ditchfield, *An Ecclesiastical History of Reading* (Reading, 1883), 93, claims the chapel was deconsecrated.

24 For a discussion of all medieval taxes, see M. Jurkovski, C.L. Smith and D. Crook, *Lay Taxes in England and Wales, 1188–1688* (Public Record Office, 1998), xxx–xxxi. Barbara Dodwell (ed. and trans.), 'Taxation Roll, 1297', *BAJ*, 60 (1962), 106–12. Basic essentials were untaxed, in particular one garment each for a man and his wife, their bed, a buckle, girdle and drinking cup of precious materials if in daily use. All other goods valued at nine shillings or over were taxed including food surplus to requirements and stored grain. M. Jurkovski, *Lay Taxes*. TNA, Lay subsidy, 1327, E179/73/6. The population estimate is based on an assumed taxpaying household size of 4.5; Edward Miller and John Hatcher, *Medieval England: towns, commerce and crafts, 1086–1348* (1995), 393–4, 419–20; Rixon estimated only about half the property owners paid, and another 20–25% of the population were too poor to be taxed. Rixon, thesis, 32–5.

25 Kemp, *Cartularies*, ii, numbers 845–6, 935–6, 973, 1014 and others; Dodwell, 1297 Tax; TNA, lay subsidy, 1327 (see note 32 below); Rixon, thesis, 43–50; Doris Mary Stenton, *English Society in the Early Middle Ages, 1066–1307* (3rd edn, 1962), 261, 191–2.

26 Kemp, *Cartularies*, ii, numbers 841, 850, 909; Slade, 'Reading', 29.

27 H.R. Loyn, *Anglo-Saxon England and the Norman Conquest* (1962), 371. Domesday Book mentions markets in Wallingford and Cookham and traders in Abingdon.

28 Kemp, *Cartularies*, ii, numbers 962, 975; BRO, Calendar of Reading Deeds R/AT1/35, 36 and 83.

29 The only record of this official is in the Gild Accounts after 1373. He seems to have visited the town but not lived there. Slade, *Gild Accounts*, i, xcvi–ii.

30 Bruce M.S. Campbell, J. Galloway, D. Keene and M. Murphy, *A Medieval Capital and its Grain Supply: agrarian production and distribution in the London region c.1300*

(Historical Geography Research Series, 30, 1993), 139.

31 Brian Kemp, 'Reading Abbey and the Medieval Town' in Petyt, *The Growth of Reading*, 48; Cecil Slade, *The Town of Reading and its Abbey, 1121–1997* (Reading, 2001), 8–9; many varieties of English pottery were found at the Oracle site, some possibly used as containers. Ben M. Ford *et al.*, *Under the Oracle* (Oxford, 2013), 165. St Laurence fair 'fell out of use' in the early fourteenth century.

32 Charles Gross, *The Gild Merchant*, 2 vols (1890) i, 15; Slade, *Accounts*, i, xiii; Kemp, *Cartularies*, ii, number 824. The activities of the gild will be discussed in the next two chapters.

33 For the significance of the term 'potter' see D. and R. Cromarty (eds), *The Wealth of Shrewsbury in the Early Fourteenth Century* (Shropshire Archaeological and Historical Society, Stroud, 1993), 41. For pottery found at the Oracle site see Ford, 163–7.

34 Kemp, *Cartularies*, ii, *passim*.

35 The word 'spicer', comes from the French 'épicier', which becomes 'grocer' in English; Cartularies nos 875, 969, 897, 956; BRO, Calendar of Medieval Deeds, c.1240–70, R/AT1/2,11,12; *Reading Post*, 24 April 2013; Ford, 200.

36 Compare the entry 'Adam le Polyter has all kinds of merchandise goods worth 12s.' with 'William le Conynger has in the tannery goods worth 19s.; also goods for shoemaking worth 9s.'

37 Kemp, *Cartularies*, nos 869, 891, 959, 971, 1016; Slade, 'Reading'. In the middle ages, drapers produced as well as sold cloth.

38 Miller and Hatcher, 257–8.

39 Kemp, *Cartularies*, ii, nos 855, 839, 981, 1160.

40 A quarter, equal to eight bushels, was a measure of volume, not weight so no exact quantity can be given, and additionally there was no nationally agreed weight per bushel. Miller and Hatcher (page xii) suggest approximately 291 litres.

41 Kemp, *Cartularies*, ii, nos 868, 872, 948, 865, 850, 910.

42 Slade, 'Reading'; David Lewis, 'Windsor and the oldest profession, 1300–1850', *B.O. and N.*, 30 (2013), 17.

43 Leslie Harman, *The parish of S. Giles-in-Reading* (1946), 8; C. F. Slade 'Reading' in

M. L. Lobel (ed.), *Historic Towns*, vol. I (1969).

44 Kemp, *Cartularies*, ii, nos 909, 913, 958, 934.

45 Margaret Yates, *Town and Countryside in Western Berkshire, c.1327–c.1600* (Woodbridge, 2007), 72–3. My calculations on Reading's wealth are based on Dr Yates' transcript of the 1327 lay subsidy (TNA, E/179/73/6) which she kindly gave me and for which I am most grateful. This subsidy was levied at a twentieth of the assessment.

46 Keene, 'The south-east', 557, 567; R. Glasscock, *The Lay Subsidy of 1334* (British Academy, Records of Social and Economic History, new series, 2, 1975), 14. Lay subsidies were occasional taxes on the personal property of the laity (non-clergy) granted by parliament to the king, usually to wage war. Reading as a taxation borough paid a tenth of its assessment and Newbury as a town paid a fifteenth, hence Newbury was assessed more highly than Reading. Assessment calculated from tax paid as quoted by Glasscock.

47 James Masschaele, 'Town, country and law: royal courts and regional mobility in medieval England', in R. Goddard *et al.* (eds), *Survival and Discord in Medieval Society* (Turnhout, Belgium, 2010) 143–4; Daniel and Samuel Lysons, *Magna Britannia: Berkshire* (Ilkley, 1806/1978), 339, say the gaol was moved following a petition and complaint in 1314 that Windsor was too remote.

Chapter 2: Abbey, borough and urban government, 1121–1529

1 The section on the founding and early years of the abbey is from Brian R. Kemp, *Reading Abbey 2: an introduction to the history of the abbey* (Reading, 1968), 1–10; Cecil Slade, *The Town of Reading and its abbey* (Reading, 2001), 1–4. In fact future kings were buried elsewhere, notably at Fontevraud in Normandy and Westminster abbey.

2 For full details of all Reading's endowments see Kemp, *Reading Abbey*, 13–23; for its architecture see Tyack, 441–3. In 2011 the then Archbishop of Canterbury, Dr Rowan Williams, blessed the new library at Douai Abbey, a modern Benedictine house near Reading. Hurry states that the abbey's income at the Dissolution was £2,042 9s. 4½d., the smaller sum of £1,938 14s. ¾d. quoted in the text above being the clear annual value. Jamieson B. Hurry, *Reading Abbey* (1901), 91.

3 Jamieson B. Hurry, *The Rise and Fall of Reading Abbey* (1906), 105–23; Alan Coates, *The Reading Abbey Collection from Foundation to Dispersal* (Oxford, 1999), *passim*.

4 In 1539 these amounted to almost £60 a year. Charles Coates, *The History and Antiquities of Reading* (1802), 294; Rixon, thesis, 64.

5 Slade, *The Town of Reading*, 8–9. St Laurence's fair died out before 1300.

6 For more about miracles attributed to the hand of St James see Brian Kemp, 'The miracles of the hand of St James', *BAJ*, 65 (1970), 1–20. A hand discovered in the abbey during excavations is now in the RC church of Marlow. It was not the hand of St James but may have belonged to Adeliza, wife of Henry I.

7 Leslie Cram, *Reading Abbey* (Reading Museum and Art Gallery, n.d.); Wessex Archaeology Trust and Reading Museum and Art Gallery, *Reading Abbey Rediscovered* and *Reading Abbey Waterfront* (Reading, 1983 and 1986). Caen stone to build the abbey was transported via the Thames and Kennet.

8 Ben Ford *et al.*, *Under the Oracle* (2013), 284–7, 291; Slade, *The Town of Reading*, 10; Hurry, *The Rise and Fall of Reading Abbey*, 48–9. In a cartulary of 1313–14 William Bartram is named as the cook of the abbot and several abbey servants were listed in the 1381 poll tax; Winifred A. Harwood, *The Southampton Brokage Book, 1447–48* (University of Southampton, 2008), 148.

9 Hurry, 20–6. The word *hospitium* means hospital/almshouse, hospice or guest house. Reading's Hospitium served as guest house and almshouse. Only its dormitory has survived. Recent research has suggested that the leper hospital/almshouse may have stood at or near modern Cemetery Junction. An enquiry of 1479 said it was 'in the est side of the towne': *VCH*, ii, 98–9.

10 *VCH*, ii, 245–7; Michael Naxton, *The History of Reading School* (Reading, n.d.), 6–12.

11 Burgage tenure and the right to form a Merchant Gild often went together. Susan Reynolds, *An Introduction to the History of English Medieval Towns* (Oxford, 1977), 102.

Other aspects of the gild are assumed since they appear in later documents. For the gild's income see Cecil Slade (ed.), *Reading Gild Accounts, 1357–1516*, BRS, 6 and 7 (2002), i, xxxiii–lvii. For swans see *Diary*, 144 and *passim*.

12 Slade, *The Town of Reading*, 4–6. The following discussion on abbey–town relations is taken from this source or from the *VCH*, iii, 344–9 unless otherwise stated. Details of all Reading's charters are printed in C.F. Pritchard, *Reading Charters, Acts and Orders* (1913).

13 *VCH*, iii, 344–5; Slade, *The Town of Reading*, 4–6. Details of abbey–town relations are limited by the paucity of the records. Few abbey records survived the Dissolution; gild accounts begin only in 1357, and 'minutes' of gild meetings in 1431.

14 R.B. Dobson (ed.), *The Peasants' Revolt of 1381* (1983), 41, 314; Slade, *The Town of Reading*, 14. The order imposing a fine for non-attendance was made in 1442 and lateness in 1463, but was collected from at least 1440, Slade, *Accounts*, i, lvi; *Diary*, i, 151.

15 *VCH*, iii, 346, 352; B.R. Kemp (ed.), *Reading Abbey Cartularies*, 2 vols (Camden Fourth Series, 33, 1987), i, number 117. The incapacity of Henry VI was a major factor in the political instability of the period. It is just possible that the king or his advisers were seeking political support, though the pious king may have been unwilling to offend a churchman, especially one as powerful as the Abbot of Reading; *Diary*, i, 48.

16 The abbot did not receive any thing from the payment for breakfast. Meals may have been provided by the mayor for most of the period. Slade, *Accounts*, lxxxviii–xc.

17 *Diary*, i, *passim*.

18 There is no better discussion of the finances of the gild than the Introduction to the edited accounts, Slade, *Accounts*, i, xxii–civ. It also contains much information on the history of the period.

19 *Diary*, i, 18, 21, 57.

20 For a full account see Slade, *The Town of Reading*. For documents (only one of which was dated) detailing the issues see C.F. Slade (ed.), 'Reading Records, 4', *BAJ*, 61 (1963–64). The final agreement is printed in *Diary*, i, 105–9.

21 A. Aspinall, Barbara Dodwell, M.D. Lambert, C.F. Slade and E.A. Smith, *Parliament through Seven Centuries: Reading and its MPs* (1962), 3–5; J.S. Roskell (ed.), *History of Parliament: The Commons, 1386–1421* (Stroud, 1992) i, 266–9 and ii, *passim*; S.T. Bindoff (ed.), *History of Parliament: The Commons, 1509–1558* (1992), i, 34.

22 For a detailed account of Reading's MPs see Aspinall, 1–34; *Calendar of Patent Rolls Henry VII, 1485–94*, 115; *Calendar of Patent Rolls Henry VII, 1494–1509*, 351, 452, 484; *Letters & Papers Henry VIII, 1509–13*, II, 1122; TNA, Will of Richard Smyth, 1516, PROB 11/18/22; will of Henry Kelsall printed in C. Kerry, *A History of the Municipal Church of St Lawrence, Reading* (1883), 169.

Chapter 3: Prosperity and piety, *c.*1350–1540

1 P.J.P. Goldberg's suggestion that the elite were more vulnerable to later outbreaks is interesting in that Abbot Henry of Reading died in 1361: *Medieval England: a social history, 1250–1550* (2004), 84–5.

2 Alien subsidy TNA E179/236/84; C.C. Fenwick (ed.), *The Poll Taxes, Part 1* (Oxford, 1998), 39–41.

3 A tax on the very wealthy was levied in 1523 and 1527. TNA, Lay Subsidy Returns, 1524/25, E179/73/133, 135, 138. The total in the 1524 list is probably 514; towns and the tax are discussed in John Sheail edited by R.W. Hoyle, *The Regional Distribution of Wealth in England*

as Indicated in the 1524/5 Lay Subsidy Returns (List & Index Society Special Series 2, 28 (2 vols, 1998), i, 50–2 and ii, 17; W.G. Hoskins, *The Age of Plunder: The England of Henry VIII* (1986), 39–42. In Coventry, Norwich and Great Yarmouth 25–50% of the population were below the tax threshold. Some demographers suggest a multiplier of 6.5 will provide a rough estimate of population.

4 John Hatcher, *Plague, Population and the English Economy, 1348–1530* (1977), 68–71.

5 Wills of John Kent TNA, PROB 11/27/1; William Justice, 20/6; Thomas Carpenter, 20/2; Thomas Coxwell, 22/32.

6 Cecil Slade, *The Town of Reading*, 5–6; Charles Gross, *The Gild Merchant*, 2 vols (Oxford, 1890), i, 16; ii, 202–4. Chapter 2 has more details about this agreement.

7 *VCH*, iii, 347.

8 The document in medieval French is printed in Gross, ii, 205–9 and some translated extracts in i, 45–6. He dates the document in the abbey cartulary to the fourteenth century. Court leets were usually bi-annual but Slade suggests this may not have been so in Reading.

9 *VCH*, iii, 350; *Diary*, 58, 36, 103. The feast of Corpus Christi falls on the Thursday after Trinity Sunday.

10 Slade, *The Town of Reading*, 14; Slade, *Accounts*, ii, 164.

11 *Puncta Gilde*. Terce (third) was the monastic service held at the third hour after the first service at 6 a.m.

12 William Catour and John Kent paid 6s. 8d. aulnage for 18 whole cloths between July 1394 and January 1395. TNA, Aulnage Accounts Berks E101/343/24 m.4; J.S. Roskell (ed.), *History of Parliament: The Commons, 1386–1421*, 2 vols (Stroud, 1992), vol. i, 266; vol. ii, *passim*. Exports of cloths from Oxfordshire and Berkshire leapt from 252 in 1356–58 to 2,128 in 1394–95. A.R. Bridbury, *Medieval English Clothmaking* (1982), 114.

13 Slade, *Accounts*, Part I, xlvi, and *passim*; *Diary*, *passim*. At this time drapers produced cloth as well as selling it; Richard Aman, draper, had the lease of a dyehouse (will 1538, TNA, PROB 11/27/29). It is possible that 'callemaker' was intended for maker of cauls, a kind of cap.

14 *Diary*, i, 119–20.

15 All exports paid a duty of 4d. per 'cloth of assize' and were checked for quality by a royal official. Kent and Catour paid 6s. 8d. aulnage for 18 whole cloths between July 1394 and January 1395. TNA, Aulnage Accounts Berks, E101/343/24 m.4; J.S. Roskell (ed.), *History of Parliament*, i, 266; ii, *passim*. Reading's share of Berkshire cloths paying aulnage was 16%, 20%, 20%, 14%, 14.8%, 13.5% in successive years 1468–69 to 1473–74. It fell to 2.4% 1476–78. I owe the material on the Reading aulnage payers to Dr Margaret Yates who kindly loaned me her data from the accounts.

16 Pritchard; Charter of 2 Henry VII, 1487; S.T. Bindoff (ed.), *History of Parliament: The Commons, 1509–1558* (1982), 649.

17 TNA, Will of William Knight of Reading made 5 May 1525 PROB 11/26/1. A probate inventory itemised and valued a deceased's estate for probate in a church court.

18 *Diary*, i, 18. For occupations see *Diary, passim* and Slade, *Accounts, passim*; Ford, 284–7. This building may have been *le Kychene* in a lease of 1370 (Ford, 286). Southampton trade details from edited volumes of the Brokage Books of Southampton, 1439–40, 1443–44, 1477–78, 1448–49 and 1527–28 published between 1941 and 2008 by the Southampton Record Society or the University of Southampton.

19 Slade, *Accounts, passim*; *Diary*, i, 119–20; Brokage Book, 1439–40..

20 Slade, *Accounts*, Part I, xlvi. After 1507 there are no entries since the rents were paid to the abbey from that date.

21 TNA, Wills of Thomas Glover, 1509, and Alys Adams, widow, 1537, PROB 11/16/17 and 27/11; Gross, 207; B.W. Clapp, H.E.S. Fisher and A.R.J. Jurica (eds), *Documents in English Economic History* (1977), 183. I owe this reference to Dr Margaret Yates.

22 The document is damaged, a large section at the end having been torn off. Of 583 taxpayers, 442 names are legible but only 418 tax payments. A typical Reading entry is '*Richardus Godewynde, Margaret uxor 5s od* Richard Godwind, [his] wife Margaret 5s'.

23 Goldberg has exploited this feature of the poll tax for a number of towns. P.J. Goldberg, 'Urban identity and the poll taxes of 1377, 1379 and 1381', *Economic History Review*, 43 (1990). The returns for Oxford are particularly rewarding. The proportion of married people in his calculations varied from 68% in suburban Oxford to 38% in Coventry and servants 14% to 54%. The suggested figures for Reading are 62% and up to 28%.

24 The subsidy returns are by parish, one for each payment in 1524 and 1525. While both returns are extant for St Mary and St Giles the 1524 nominal list for St Laurence is missing though the total tax collected is given. There are minor discrepancies between total tax take in the summary returns and some of the parish totals. Where the number of taxpayers varied slightly between the two payments, the larger has been used.

25 Wills up to 1550 have been consulted on the grounds that will-makers would have lived

most of their lives in the late middle ages. TNA, Wills of William Justice, mercer, 1520, PROB 11/20/6; Thomas Everard, chandler,1542, 29/4; William Knight, 1536, 26/1.

26 TNA, Wills of Christian Nicholas, 1508, PROB 11/16/12; Robert Bennett,1515, 18/14; Nicholas Hyde, 1528, 22/35; Walter Barton's will is printed in Charles Kerry, *A History of the Municipal Church of St Lawrence, Reading* (Reading, 1883), 179–84.

27 BRO, Reading Borough Records, Calendar of Medieval Deeds, R/AT1/121, 163, 169; 1433–78; TNA, Wills of Thomas Glover, 1509, PROB11/16/17; William Wrottesley, 1513, 17/10; George Hyde, 1535, 25/28; Nicholas Hyde, mercer, 1527, 22/35 and Nicholas Parker, 1527, 22/22.

28 Jeanette Martin, 'The People of Reading and the Reformation, 1520–1570', unpublished Ph.D. thesis, University of Reading (1987), 278; *VCH*, iii, 343; *Feudal Aids, 1284–1431* (HMSO, 1899), i, 71; *Valor Ecclesiasticus*, 1535.

29 Those for St Giles date from 1518, BRO, D/P96/5/1, part of which was published as *The Church-Wardens' Account Book for the Parish of St Giles, Reading*, part 1, *1518–46*, ed. W.L. Nash (Reading 1881); Joan Dils, *Reading St Laurence Churchwardens' Accounts, 1498–1570* (Berkshire Record Society, 19 and 20, 2013).

30 TNA, Wills of Richard Smythe, 1516, PROB 11/18/22; Thomas Glover, 1509, 16/17; Nicholas Nicholas, 1514, 18/1; BRO, Will of Julian Bye, 1520, D/A1/1/33; J.M. Horne, *Register Hallam*, no. 739 and Appendix II.

31 TNA, Wills of William Justice, 1520, PROB 11 20/6 ; John Pownsar, 1517, 19/1; William Bowyer, 1536, 25/36; N.E. Fox (ed.), *Chantry Certificates for Berkshire* (privately published, 1994), 38.

32 TNA, Wills of Thomas Everard 1527 PROB 11/22/32, Christian Nicholas 1508, 16/12;

William Justice 1520, 20/6. A noble was a gold coin worth 6*s* 8*d*.

33 TNA, Wills of John Love, 1503, PROB 11/13/26; Thomas Pantry, 1537, 27/6; William Knyght, 1536, 19/10.

34 J.T. Rosenthal, *The Purchase of Paradise: Gift Giving and the Aristocracy* (1972). For other chantries in Berkshire see Andrew D. Brown, 'Perpetual chantries in late medieval Berkshire', in J. Dils (ed.), *An Historical Atlas of Berkshire* (Reading, 1998), 30, and the same author in the new edition. The will is printed in Man, Appendix B; BRO, Calendar of Medieval deeds R/AT/1/169.

35 TNA, Wills of Christian Nicholas PROB 11/16/12; William Trewe, 20/19; Nicholas Hyde, 22/35; Edith Chester, 25/9, John Stanshawe 18/19. BRO, Will of Robert Stanshawe, 1549, D/A1/114/115.

36 TNA, Will of William Knight PROB 11/26/1.

37 J.M. Horn (ed.), *The Register of Robert Hallam, Bishop of Salisbury, 1407–17* (Canterbury and York Society, 72, 1982), no. 1133; J.A.F. Thomson, *The Later Lollards, 1414–1520* (Oxford, 1965); Jeanette Martin, 'The People of Reading and the Reformation, 1520–1570', unpublished Ph.D. thesis, University of Reading (1987), 22–9. Attributing nicknames to unorthodox religious groups is a typically English practice; cf. Papists, Quakers, Methodists. See also R. Rex, *The Lollards* (Basingstoke, 2002).

38 Slade, *Accounts*, Part II, 146; *Southampton Brokage Book, 1448–49*, 146.

39 The description of social activities is taken from the churchwardens' accounts, especially of St Laurence, the most detailed. These activities do not appear in the accounts every year, perhaps only when there was expenditure or income. This is especially true of the plays. Robin Hood fell out of favour nationally after about 1510. See Ronald Hutton, *The Rise and Fall of Merry England* (1994).

Chapter 4: The years of crisis, 1529–1600

1 Christine Jackson, 'The Berkshire Woollen Industry, 1500–1650', unpublished Ph.D. thesis, University of Reading (1993), 144; Alan R.G. Smith, *The Emergence of a Nation State, 1529–1660* (1984), 433; BRO, St Laurence churchwardens' accounts (D/P97/5/2), 185,

193, 195; Letters and Papers Henry VIII, v, 1531–56, nos 686, 1003, 1451; M. St Clare Byrne (ed.), *The Lisle Letters* (Penguin edn, 1985), 144–6.

2 There is no simple or accurate way to equate this with modern values. One way is to relate

it to wages. In 1535 a Reading craftsman earned 7*d*. or 8*d*. a day. The abbey's income could amount to several million pounds at today's prices and wages.

3 Letters and Papers Henry VIII, 13 (1538) part I, 367, part II, 377; BRO, Will of Thomas Stanshawe, 1549, D/A1/114/115; and see chapter 3 note 35.

4 Jeanette Martin, 'The People of Reading and the Reformation, 1520–1570', unpublished Ph.D. thesis, University of Reading (1987), 144, 136–52 and 376–90 has a detailed discussion of Crown grants. Despite Cromwell's intention to build up Crown lands, Henry's and his successors' need for ready cash resulted in the sale of much monastic land.

5 L and P Henry VIII, 14 (1539), part II, 399. The steward of the borough had been an abbey official, appointed to maintain its interests, including financial ones, in the town. He usually had legal training. The last incumbent had been William Edmonds/Edmunds.

6 Jeanette Martin, 'Leadership and Priorities in Reading during the Reformation', in Patrick Collinson and John Craig (eds), *The Reformation in English Towns, 1540–1600* (Basingstoke, 1998), 122–4; Robert Tittler, *The Reformation and the Towns in England: politics and political culture, c.1540–1640* (Oxford, 1998), 345; C.F. Pritchard (ed.), *Reading Charters, Acts and Orders* (1913), 5–14.

7 *Diary*, i, 213, 228, 230, 243, 249.

8 The grant in Letters and Papers Henry VIII, vol xx, part II, is printed in Ernest W. Dormer, *Gray of Reading* (Reading, 1923), 143–5.

9 Roger Amyce was one of the chief officials of the Court of Augmentations which administered the property of dissolved religious houses and Surveyor General of Glastonbury and Reading abbeys.

10 Arthur Preston, 'The Demolition Accounts of Reading Abbey', *Berkshire Archaeological Journal*, 39 (1935).

11 For this and the future of the abbey site see Slade, *The Town of Reading*, 29 ff.

12 Churchwardens' accounts record parish income and expenditure, revealing patterns of religious, social and economic life. Reading is very fortunate in having two extant volumes of churchwardens' accounts for the whole period, St Giles and St Laurence and from *c*.1522

F. and A. Garry (eds), *The Churchwardens' Accounts of the Parish of St Mary's, Reading* (Reading, 1893) and see chapter 3, note 29. The advowson was the right to present a clergyman to a benefice. The patronage of the two parishes returned to the Crown after Sir Francis Englefield left England. In 1640 the patronage of St Laurence was granted to St John's College, Oxford.

13 The Act of Uniformity of 1549 imposed the use of the First Book of Common Prayer (BCP), The Second BCP imposed in 1552 embodied more radical Protestant doctrines.

14 He began his will by leaving his soul to God 'trustyng and having full confidence the same will be savid by the merites of the passion of his most glorious sonne, our saviour Christ'. TNA, Will of Stephen Cawett, PROB 11/29/18.

15 The high steward was usually a high-ranking gentleman or noble who could use his influence at court for the town's benefit but expected to have some borough offices in his gift.

16 BRO, Will of John Hethe, 1556, D/A1/7/13; W.M. Childs, *The Story of the Town of Reading* (Reading, 1905), 109–11. The full story of Julin's martyrdom is told by John Foxe in what became known as *The Book of Martyrs*.

17 BRO, Will of William Boxwell, 1573 (D/A1/40/22).

18 P.W. Hasler, *The History of Parliament: the Commons, 1558–1603* (1981), 116.

19 M.I. Connolly, 'The Godly in Berkshire from the reign of Elizabeth to *c*.1642', unpublished Ph.D. thesis, University of Reading (1977), chap. 5; BRO, Will of John Richer, haberdasher of St Laurence, 1578, D/A1/111/52. Connolly says Sir Christopher Hatton supported the moderates.

20 Pritchard, 15–53. Charters were granted to petitioners usually the town's elite and almost always the men named in the charter as the first corporation. Tittler, *The Reformation and the Towns*, 90.

21 Four of the capital burgesses named were aldermen but it is not clear why the other five were chosen. Of 26 burgesses attending meetings in the preceding years, all but two became members of the corporation.

22 In the early seventeenth century there was

a true election for the mayor, the votes for each nominee recorded. From 1621 he was elected unopposed. About the same date, newly promoted capital burgesses became mayor within a year or two, for example Roger Knight promoted and elected mayor 1616; Walter Bateman promoted 1618, mayor 1620. *Diary*, ii, *passim*.

23 Sources disagree about whether the council met in an upper storey or in half of a single-storey hall. It was large enough, 120 by 20–30 feet, to be divided. Michael Naxton, *The History of Reading School* (Reading, 1986), 23.

24 *Diary*, i, *passim*.

25 *Diary*, i, *passim*; BRO, Regulations and Ordinances of the Reading Gilds c.1570, R/HMC/LVI; TNA, Wills of Thomas Aldworth, clothier, 1577 and Thomas Turner,1570 mercer, PROB 11/59/73 and /52/295. Richard Johnson, mercer, and Bernard Harrison, brewer, were also capital burgesses.

26 BRO, Reading Cofferers' Accounts *passim*. Entries in the volume 3 of the *Diary* seem to confirm Coates' judgement that Reading was the assize town, at least until the Civil War. Coates, 461.

27 BRO, Parish registers of St Giles and St Mary D/P 96/1/1 and D/P98/1/1; *A Midsummer Night's Dream*, Act 2, scene 1.

28 N.E. Fox (ed.), *Chantry Certificates for Berkshire* (privately published, 1994), 38. Most demographers assume that over-sixteens made up two-thirds of the population; TNA, Survey of Reading, 1552, Misc. Bks. Land Rev. vol 187, ff. 314–47.

29 The map of Reading has been reproduced in a number of publications including Petyt. Among many modern editions of the whole atlas is Nigel Nicolson and Alasdair Hawkyard, *The Counties of Britain: A Tudor Atlas by John Speed* (1988).

30 The gild accounts for 1496–97 include the purchase of building materials and 23 shillings

spent 'for the new shambles in all things': Slade, *Accounts*, Part II, 144. This may be the New Shambles of 1534 though Slade does not make the connection and Peyton does not mark it on his map. The Cofferers' accounts for 1585–86 state that the lofts over the New Shambles were converted to a Wool Hall with a beam for weighing. It was rented that year for 46s. 8d. (BRO, R/FA2/74); leases of the Woolhall, 1636–72, R/AT3/1/7/1–5.

31 BRO, Lease of the Weighing House, 1534 R/AT3/1/1/1–2. The east end of the street which Speed called Broad Street was called High Street earlier. See Chapter 1, note 22. King Street and the east end of Broad Street were later called Browne's Hill. See chapter 7.

32 One or two larger houses have survived in Castle Street and one in the Market Place. These details appear in probate inventories, lists of possessions of the deceased whose wills were proved in the church courts. They relate only to the richer 20–25% of the population but are invaluable in providing details of everyday life. See Pat Naylor, *Berkshire Archdeaconry Probate Records, 1480–1652* (Berkshire Record Society 3 vols, 2011). *Diary*, i, 394. All those paying the subsidy were required to keep at least two buckets ready to fight fires. No major fire was recorded in Reading.

33 TNA, A General Certificate of the Number of Taverns, Inns and Alehouses within the County of Berkshire, 1577 SP/12/119.

34 BRO, Reading Borough Court Leet, 1563–1587 R/JL1/1–16, *passim*. Several undated records list the matters which the court would deal with. The Commission of Sewers, 1575 (BRO, R/Z1/4/1–2), laid down the duties of the riverines. Offences were reported to the court leet. Commissions of Sewers (watercourses, not urban sewers) were established by a law of 1531 to protect low-lying land.

Chapter 5: Borough society and economy, *c*.1540–1640

1 Population totals for 1547 are based on those in the Chantry Certificates. See above. Those for 1640 are deduced from parish register baptisms, assuming a birth rate of about 33 per 1,000. The register for St Mary survives from 1538, St Giles from 1564 and St Laurence

from 1606. For details on natural population growth see J. Dils (ed.), *Redding, 1540–1640* (Reading, 1980), 11. However, only 1,210 men signed the Protestation Returns in 1642, a figure which would suggest a much smaller population. BRO, T/A160.

2 Two-thirds of Reading witnesses in the church courts, 1558–1620, were migrants. BRO, Berkshire Archdeaconry Deposition Books, 1558–1620, general reference D/A2/c; Peter Clark, Migration in England during the late seventeenth and early eighteenth centuries', *Past and Present*, 83 (1979).

3 BRO, St Laurence seating plan, 1607 D/P97/5/3. The plan contains about 350 names.

4 *Diary*, iii, 43; BRO, St Giles' Overseers' Accounts, 1634–35, D/P96/12/1. The total population of the parish was about 1,500 based on parish register evidence..

5 BRO, Ordinances and list of members of the Clothiers' and Clothworkers' Company, c.1560, R/AG1/1. The other three sets of ordinances are catalogued at R/AG1/2–4. Though five books were compiled, only four now survive. Slade, 'Reading'.

6 Toulmin Smith (ed.), *The Itinerary of John Leland, 1535–43, Part I* (1907) 109, 111. Shuttles were used by weavers and ash produced an alkaline solution used in washing wool.

7 *Diary*, i, 398. The cloth trade has given many phrases to the language, including 'dyed in the wool' and 'to be on tenterhooks'.

8 A petition to the Crown in c.1623 stated that one coloured cloth needed as much work and yielded as much profit as six white. BRO, R/Z3/24.

9 BRO, Inventory of Walter Bateman, 1631, D/A1/16/269; Christine Jackson, 'The Berkshire Woollen Industry, 1500–1640', unpublished Ph.D. thesis, University of Reading (1997), 106.

10 TNA, Inventory of Walter Bye of St Giles, clothier 1579 PROB 2/411; BRO, Inventory of William Lawde, clothworker, D/A1/201/188.

11 That mercers and drapers belonged to the same company is significant; drapers had become retailers rather than producers of cloth.

12 BRO, inventories of Richard Johnson, mercer, 1628 D/A1/86/103 and John Beele, mercer, linen draper, 1638, D/A1/177/76. Chapmen were travelling salesmen, though in Reading they also had shops. The council was ordered by the Privy Council to provide a list of licensed tobacco sellers since many complaints had been made to the king that tobacco was 'causing many intolerable inconveniences, and abuses'. BRO, Reading tobacco sales, April

1633 and return sent to the Privy Council, November 1633 R/Z3/19/1, 2, 3.

13 BRO, Will and inventory of William Knight, 1587, D/A1/89/9 and Henry Knight, 1623, D/A1/89/113.

14 BRO, Inventories and accounts of John Sharpe, 1591, D/A1/212/158 and Francis Duke, 1597, D/A1/186/65; inventory of Richard Blackman, 1617, D/A1/42/135.

15 John Man, *The History and Antiquities of the Borough of Reading in the County of Berks* (Reading, 1816), 352–3, listed 301 craftsmen in 42 different trades.

16 BRO, Reading Court Leet Records begin in 1563: general reference R/JL1.

17 BRO, Apprenticeship Register, 1603–1700, R/HMC V3 IIC; Reading Court Leet Records, Michaelmas Law Day, 1584. R/JL1/1/10; evidence in cases in the Archdeaconry Court Deposition Books.

18 Pritchard, *Reading Charters*. Fair days were the eve, day and days following 2 February (Candlemas), 1 May (feast of SS Philip and James), 25 July (feast of St James) and 21 September (feast of St Matthew)..

19 BRO, Lease of Reading market tolls 1639 (R/FZ1/1); Henley was Loder's preferred market. C.S. Fussell (ed.), *Robert Loder's Farm Accounts, 1610–1620*, Camden Society, 3rd series (1936). Newbury leather sellers were allowed only on fair days and were prosecuted in the same way as were Reading men for bad quality goods.

20 See, for example, wills of Richard Aldworth, 1623 (in Charles Kerry, *A History of the Municipal Church of St Lawrence, Reading* (Reading, 1883), 459, John Bagley, 1630 BRO, D/A1/43/80 and Edward Butler, 1584 TNA, PROB 11/67/17.

21 John Taylor, *The Carrier's Cosmography*, 1637; BRO, will and inventory of Abraham Edwards D/A1/65/163.

22 BRO, admons., accounts and inventories of John Sone, 1593, D/A1/212/163 and Benjamin Turner, 1597, D/A1/217/74; probate accounts of Robert Johnson, 1608, D/A1/86/103 and 104; deposition book, 1590–94, D/A2 c.154, fol. 125.

23 TNA, Wills of Nicholas Gunter 1635, Robert Johnson, 1611, John Gateley, 1577, Thomas Aldworth, 1577 PROB 11/167/437, 117/551, 59/571, 59/73.

24 BRO, Wills and inventories of Humphrey Dewell, 1611 D/A1/61/246; Francis Duell/ Dewell, 1616, D/A1/186/108; William Sampson, D/A1/119/108.

25 TNA, Will of Hugh Tewe, 1582 PROB 11/64/46; BRO, deposition book, 1594–1600, D/A2 c.155 f. 161; BRO, Register of admission of freemen, 1603–1700, R/RF1/1.

26 Population calculated from parish registers; BRO, deposition book, 1557–72, D/A2 c. 151, fol. 211.

27 *Diary*, iii, 150. *Diary*, ii, 112–13; The corporation dispensed these charities meticulously throughout the centuries.

28 BRO, Will of Robert Reve, clothier, 1620, D/ A1/212/37; Records of Reading Court Leet, February 1587, R/JL1/15; deposition book, 1597–1601, D/A2 c 40, f. 166v; inventory of Elizabeth Kent, widow, 1550, D/A1/88/10. For a valuable account of women in Reading at this period see Mary Fellgett, 'Daily and domestic life in 17th century Reading', *Berkshire Old and New*, iii (1986), 10–17.

29 Surveys of alehouses, disorderly conduct and the consequent removal of licences occur throughout the *Diary*. Observance of Lent by 'victualler' and butchers was ordered by the Crown in the 1620s. Ruth Spalding, *The Improbable Puritan* (1976), A coney was a rabbit, easily trapped.

30 *Diary*, iii, 119; BRO, Reading borough records; list of persons licensed to sell tobacco in Reading, 1632–34, R/Z3/19/2 and 3; BRO, inventories of James Shylard, 1630, D/ A1/118/142, Matthew Jackson, 1627, 86/149, Thomas Gatley, 1617, 71/207. See also, Joan Dils (ed.), *Redding, 1540–1540* (Reading, 1980).

31 Joan Dils, 'The books of the clergy in Elizabethan and early Stuart Berkshire', *The Local Historian*, 36 (2) (2006), 92–105. In 1642 Parliament ordered all men to take an oath in their parishes to support the Protestant religion and the privileges of Parliament. For Reading only the list of 86 men in St Laurence parish survives. Repairs to the schoolhouse occur throughout the cofferers' accounts. Appointments of schoolmasters are recorded in the Corporation *Diary*.

32 BRO, Reading Cofferers' Accounts, 1618/19, 1619/20, 1621/2, 1627/8. R/FA3/4, 5, 6, 9; *Diary*, iii, 79. There may have been more visits since detailed expenses were not recorded every year.

Chapter 6: A troubled and divided community, 1600–1660

1 *Diary*, iii, 459; BRO, Parish registers of St Giles, D/P96/1/1, St Laurence, D/P97/1/1, St Mary, D/P98/1/1

2 *Diary*, iii, *passim*. The amounts collected are not given but an estimate based on the 1638 poor rate suggests well over £250.

3 Acts of the Privy Council, Charles I, June 1630–June 1631 (HMSO, 1964), 329, 363; Calendar of State Papers Domestic (CSPD), Charles I, 1629–31, 486–7; W.G. Hoskins, 'Harvest Fluctuations and English Economic History, 1620–1759', *Agricultural History Review*, 16 (1968); *Diary*, iii, 379. There was a similar disturbance in 1633. Such riots in a later century prompted E.P. Thompson to coin the phrase 'moral economy of the English crowd'.

4 BRO, R/Z3/18 and R/Z3/20.

5 *Diary*, iii, 94, 153, 321, 400; BRO, Reading Chamberlains' Accounts, 1633–34, R/FA3/12.

6 BRO, Copy of petition from the corporation to the Privy Council, c.1623, R/Z3/24; Jackson, thesis, 148ff; BRO, R/Z3/24; BRO, Inventory of Walter Bateman, 1631, D/A1/16/269; *Diary*, iv, 238–65. The cloth staple moved to Reading during 1625 to ensure cloth sales continued.

7 The borough archives contain a small, undated collection of petitions to the Corporation for relief. BRO, Petitions by the poor, early seventeenth century R/AZ3/9/52–66.

8 Paupers in St Laurence's, c.1630–40, and St Mary's parishes, 1620–30, BRO, R/ AP2/1and R/AP3/5, 1620–30; St Giles' Overseers' accounts, 1634–35, D/P96/12/1. Petitions for relief show that many were workers fallen on hard times. BRO, Reading Borough Records. Petitions, undated, R/ AZ3/9/52–66.

9 In or before 1802 Charles Coates saw a record of 21 children and 41 old people in the Hospital in 1578, the costs met from parish poor boxes and donations. This record has not survived. Coates, 308; *Diary*, ii, 59.

10 *Diary*, iii, 187, 175, 223. The box still survives

near the west door of the church. Craftsmen earned at most £5 a year.

11 BRO, Wills of Joan Dewell, widow, D/A1/16/380;William Brackston, tanner, 16/363; Richard Johnson, mercer, 16/226; Thomas Deane, 1623, D/P97/5/2; Man, 402, 407–8; *Diary*, iii, 273, 426, 502.

12 Acts of the Privy Council, 1630–31, 889, 1060; Christine A. Jackson, 'The Berkshire Woollen Industry, 1500–1650', unpublished Ph.D. thesis, University of Reading (1993), 203–9, 213–19; H.M. Appleby, *The Kendrick Book* (Reading, 1948). 68–70, 101–4. For further discussion of the later history of the bequest see below, chapters 7 and 10.

13 *Diary*, ii, 264 and *passim*.

14 *Diary*, ii, 305–6, 384ff, 480.

15 BRO, Order to the mayor 1631, R/Z3/17/1–2; CSPD, Charles I, 1636–37, 251. Reading's assessment was the highest of the county's boroughs, Newbury paying £120, Abingdon and Windsor £100, Wokingham £50 and Wallingford £20. Reading's assessment in 1635 and 1636 was £260, *Diary*, iii, 288.

16 CSPD, Charles I, 1639, 54; *Diary*, iii, 327, 343, 351, 403, 496; letter from George Purefoy to Edward Nicholas quoted in C.F. Durston, 'Berkshire and its county gentry, 1625–1649', unpublished Ph.D. thesis, University of Reading (1977).

17 No financial records between 1600–1605 and 1608–11 survive. Many, especially in the 1630s, do not give details on income or expenditure. The large increase in rents must have come from generally higher entry fees for leases and for rents on houses and shops but there is no documentary proof. *Diary*, ii, 96, 99.

18 *Diary*, ii and iii *passim*; BRO, Reading cofferers' accounts, R/FA3/2–12. Some rent arrears were written off; 1624–25, over £35 in 'rents and other things whiche will never be haulf paid'. The text of the 1638 charter says the borough did not pay a fine (fee) for it so the £60 noted in the accounts was presumably legal and drafting fees. Dates of the assizes from *Diary*, iii, *passim* and Lysons, *Magna Britannia*, 339.

19 Pritchard.

20 Laud's concern to improve clerical standards and income led him to include in his bequest to Reading in 1640 a stipend of £20 a year to the vicar of St Laurence. For a description of Laud's Arminian views and for the whole of this period see Barry Coward, *The Stuart Age* (1994), 112–13, 172–6 and *passim*.

21 *Diary*, ii, 250, 406; M. Connolly, 'The godly in Berkshire from the reign of Elizabeth I to c.1642', unpublished M.Phil. thesis, University of Reading (1977). Sermons were preached at Sunday service and at the distribution of several charities, the installation of a new mayor and the burials of leading townspeople.

22 The discussion on elections 1640–60 is based on Aspinall, 48–62 and M. Brod, *The Case of Reading: urban governance in troubled times, 1640–1690* (Peterborough, 2006), *passim*.

23 G. Philip (ed.), *Journal of Sir Samuel Luke*, Oxford Record Society, vol. 29 (1947), i, 12.

24 There are several accounts of Reading's experiences during the Civil War and Commonwealth including that by Brod. Documentary sources include the *Diary*, iv, 1640–54, and those in the BRO catalogue under R/Z3 (letters, petitions, demands etc.). My account uses all these.

25 Joan A. Dils, 'Epidemics, mortality and the Civil War in Berkshire, 1642–46, *Southern History*, vol. 11 (1989), 40–52.

26 Brod, 37–9; Aspinall, 53–4.

27 Petition from Reading to Parliament, December 1644, HMC 11th Report Appendix vii, 51; BRO, St Laurence churchwarden's accounts D/P97/5/3; calendar of petitions to mayor and burgesses, 1625–54, R/AZ3/9/6, 23.

28 W.G. Hoskins, 'Harvest Fluctuations and English Economic History, 1620–1759', *Agricultural History Review*, 16 (1968), 20.

29 M.A.E. Green (ed.), *Calendar of the Committee for Compounding, 1643–1660*, 5 vols (1890), ii, 1565.

30 Coward, 227, 266–7; *Diary*, iv, *passim*; BRO, St Laurence churchwardens' accounts, D/P97/5/3. For more about Fowler, Pordage and borough politics see Brod.

31 Michael Naxton, *The History of Reading School* (Reading, 1986), 33–9; Brod, 61–5.

32 For this and elections up to 1660 see Aspinall, 56–60.

33 BRO, Diary, 1657–58, R/AC1/1/7, pp. 47, 89; 1657–58, R/AC1/1/8, p. 116; 1658–59, R/AC1/1/9, pp. 1, 2, 5v, 11, 13, 16; Aspinall, 59–60.

34 BRO, Diary, 1647–55 and 1655–59, R/AC1/1/5 and /6–9, *passim*.

35 BRO, Diary, 1658–59, R/AC1/1/9, *passim*; Diary, 1659–60, R/AC1/1/10, *passim*.

36 See Brod, 62–5, for a discussion of the factional quarrels surrounding Garrard's appointment. The process of removing him can be found in the Diary in 1659–60.

Chapter 7: A changed economy and society, 1660–1740

1 N.R. Goose, 'Decay and regeneration in Seventeenth-century Reading: a study in a changing economy', *Southern History*, 6 (1984). The Compton Census of 1676 (on religious affiliation) gives 3,000 (communicants, adults aged 16 and over) for two parishes. St Giles is missing. Based on this survey, the total population could have been about 6,000. The 1740 totals are from baptismal records. All are approximate.

2 Diary, 1715–26, R/AC1/1/20, first pages of volume, no pagination; BRO, St Mary's overseers' papers: 487 settlement certificates, 1698–1786, D/P98/13/1/1–487, as calendared by the Berkshire Family History Overseers' Project. These provided evidence of an individual's right to claim poor relief.

3 All three parish registers; *Reading Mercury*, 25 April and 13 June 1785; M.J. Dobson, *A Chronology of Epidemic Disease and Mortality in South-east England, 1601–1800*, Historical Geography Research Series, 19 (November 1987), 75–6. In this context, south-east England means Essex, Kent and East Sussex; S. Markham (ed.), *John Loveday of Caversham, 1711–89* (Salisbury, 1984), 47–8; BRO, Account book/diary of Edward Belson, 1707–22, D/EZ12/1–3. An edition of the book will be published by the Berkshire Record Society at a future date. I owe this and several later references to Dr Skidmore who lent me his transcript. I will refer to it as a diary though in fact Belson used it mainly for his accounts. For more on smallpox in Reading and Berkshire see Gillian Clark, 'Eighteenth-century mortality crises' in *Atlas*, article 43.

4 Hoskins, *Ag. Hist. Rev.*, 18, 23,29; Belson, *Diary*, 20.

5 The administration of the Hearth Tax was amended several times. Tom Arkell, 'Printed instructions for administering the Hearth Tax', in Kevin Schurer and Tom Arkell, *Surveying the People* (Oxford, 1992), 38–41. The tax was abolished in 1689.

6 The only returns to survive for Reading are one for St Laurence, 1662–63, and one of 1663–64 for the other two parishes (TNA, E179/76/460). In 1913 Edgar Powell made a transcript of the returns (RLSL). Historians suggest a figure of about 4.5 persons per household. Goose, 'Decay and Regeneration' estimates two-thirds of the townspeople were poor. Nationally only a third of the expected yield of 1662–63 was collected.

7 Goose, 'Decay and regeneration', 64–5; BRO, wills and inventories of Peter Horne, junior, 1663, D/A1/80/122, Robert James, 1662, D/A1/87/6, will of Stephen Attwater, 1673, D/A1/37/63.

8 BRO, Register of admission of freemen, 1603–1700, R/RF1/1. The book was hardly used after 1680.

9 Goose, 'Decay and Regeneration', 65.

10 Will Simon Dee, D/A1/63/10; Goose, 64; Diary, 1665–67, R/AC1/1/13 p. 2; 1694–1712, R/AC1/1/19 pp. 6, 75; 1715–26, R/AC1/1/20; BRO, Reading Borough leases, 1672–1741, R/FZ1/2/1–8.

11 Diary, 1715–26, R/AC1/1/20, p. 1.

12 Diary, 1694–1712, R/AC1/1/19, pp. 116–17, 122, and 1715–26, R/AC1/1/20, 22 April 1721; Kenneth R. Clew, *The Kennet and Avon Canal: An Illustrated History* (Newton Abbot, 1968), 24–7; Fred S. Thacker, *Kennet Country* (Oxford, 1932), 309–12; data from 135 wills in the BRO.

13 Data from 118 wills in the BRO from 1700 to 1730 and 135 from 1731 to 1760.

14 Aspinall, 46–7. For more about the candidates and elections see Basil Duke Henning, *The History of Parliament. The Commons, 1660–1690* (1983), 132–3.

15 Diary, 1659–60, R/AC1/1/10, 19, 22, 24; Diary, 1660–62, R/AC1/1/11; Aspinall, 62–3.

16 Coward, 294; Diary, 1660–62. The houses of new councillors had between 3 and 12 hearths. For a detailed discussion of this and other council changes see Brod, 75–89.

17 Diary, 1662–64, R/AC1/1/12, pp. 8, 16, 17, 24; Diary, 1665–67, R/AC1/1/13, pp. 2, 17, 25, 44; Diary, 1668–72, R/AC1/1/14, 10, 27; Diary, 1688–94, R/AC1/1/18, 1694, no date,

no pagination; Diary, 1694–1713, R/AC1/1/19, p. 5v.

18 Coward, 332; Brod, 80–7; Aspinall, 64–5, Diary, 1682–86, R/AC1/1/16, p. 16.

19 Coward, 339–41; Brod, 94–5.

20 BRO, Chamberlains' Accounts, 1688–89, R/FA3/50; Brod, 98–9; *VCH*, iii, 361–2; Coward, 336–43; Diary, 1688–94, R/AC1/1/18, p. 67; Coates, 46–7. The accounts of the events of December 1688 by Brod, 99 and Phillips, 73–4 differ in some details, including the date, 9 or 10 December.

21 Diary, 1688–94, *passim*; Receiver's Account, 1742–43, R/FA4/6; H.F. Burgess, *A History of the Reading Blue Coat School* (published by the school, 1977), 19–27. Hall's School merged with the Blue Coat in 1796, the building becoming Reading Dispensary.

22 Diary, 1668–72, R/AC1/1/14 pp. 27, 46; Diary, 1672–85, R/AC1/1/15 p. 97, 254; Diary, 1682–94, R/AC1/1/18 p. 57; Diary, 1694–1712, R/AC1/1/19 p. 3.

23 D.W. Hayton (ed.), *The History of Parliament. The House of Commons, 1690–1715*, 4 vols (Cambridge, 2002), i, 113. He was made a freeman in 1694 (Diary, 1694–1712, p. 32.

24 Reading Chamberlains' Accounts: Rent Roll. 1701–02, R/FA8/71; Receiver's Account, 1740–41, R/FA4/4. In 1737 the corporation appointed a receiver to collect all borough and charity income and disburse it to the chamberlains as necessary.

25 Diary, 1665–67, R/AC1/1/13, p. 5; Diary, 1668–72, R/AC1/1/14, p. 1; Diary, 1672–82, R/AC1/15, p. 128. Houses were tiled but not outhouses.

26 Diary, 1694–1712, R/AC1/1/19, p. 2; lease of land at Browne's Hill 1696, R/AT7/25/1 and St Giles' Mill, 1697, R/AT7/39/1; RLSL O Kean, *A Brief History and Development of Reading Waterworks* (1950), Browne's Hill was formerly High/Broad Street.

27 Aspinall, 68–75. Hayton (see note 27) calls Reading a 'potwalloper' borough before 1708, effectively voters being all males not receiving poor relief.

28 The discussion of Reading nonconformists is based on W.H. Summers, *History of the Berkshire, South Bucks and South Oxon Congregational Churches* (Newbury, 1905); Leslie Harman, *The History of Christianity in Reading* (Reading, 1952).

29 Episcopal Returns, 1669, printed in G. Lyon Turner, *Original Records of Early Nonconformity*, 3 vols (1911), i, 112–13; A. Whiteman, *The Compton Census of 1676: a critical edition* (1986), 115. Charles II issued a Declaration of Indulgence of 1672 suspending the penal laws, so allowing Catholics to worship at home and offering licences to dissenters to worship publicly until the Declaration lapsed in 1675.

30 A noble was worth 80 silver pence or 6s. 8d., or half a mark. The fine was therefore £6 13s. 4d. A craftsman's daily wage was one shilling. BRO, Reading Quarter Sessions Diary, 1682–83 and 1687–88, R/JQ1/1.

31 The attempted sale of corn is recorded in Reading Quarter Sessions Diary, 5 May 1682. The document referenced in note 34 is the sole survivor of Reading quarter session records before 1835. Most early information on Reading comes from dissenting or other sources. All references to Lisa Spurrier (ed.), *Berkshire Nonconformist Meeting House Registrations, 1689–1852* (BRS, 9 and 10, 2005) unless otherwise stated; A. Gordon, *Freedom After Ejection* (1911), 6.

32 Joseph Besse, *A Collection of the Sufferings of the People called Quakers, 1650–1689* (published London, 1753; photocopy of Berkshire section in BRO); Beatrice Saxon Snell, 'The character of early Friends as illustrated by Berkshire Records in possession of the Reading Monthly Meeting of the Society of Friends', unpublished typescript in BRO; Chris Skidmore 'The Old Quaker Burial Place in Reading, 1660–1833', *BLHA Newsletter*, 104 (September 2012).

33 Diary, 1672–85, R/AC1/1/15 p. 70; BRO, St Giles' Overseers' accounts, 1663–85, D/P96/12/1–16. Goose suggests that 13.8% of Reading households were permanently dependent on relief.

34 Diary, 1688–94, R/AC1/15, *passim*; Reading Quarter Sessions Diary. A person's place of legal settlement was the parish responsible for their poor relief.

35 *Reading Mercury*, 14 March, 1738; Belson, diary, 61. In the previous two centuries St Mary's parish register had occasionally recorded the burial of executed felons. In this period the assizes were usually held alternately in Reading in spring and Abingdon

in summer. Diary, *passim* and J.S. Cockburn, *A History of English Assizes, 1558–1714* (CUP, 1972), 34.

36 Lorna Weatherill, *Consumer Behaviour and Material Culture in Britain, 1660–1760* (1988).

37 BRO, will James Cowdrey, maltster, 1666, D/A1/56/86; inventory of Richard Plummer, jeweller, 1593, D/A1/209/101; inventories of John Chandler, 1679, and Francis Tassell, 1684, D/A1/184/15 and 128/140.

38 Worcester had a newspaper in 1690, Stamford in 1795 and Oxford in 1753, John West, *Town Records* (1983), 225; K.G. Burton, 'The early

newspaper press in Berkshire, 1723–1855', unpublished MA thesis, University of Reading (1950).

39 Calendar of State Papers Domestic, Charles II, 1680–81 (HMSO, 1921), 136; Belson, diary, 1 and *passim*. *Reading Mercury*, 1 April, 1745; Sarah Markham, *John Loveday of Caversham, 1711–89* (Guildford, 1984), 27, 37, 435.

40 The wills of ten councillors of 1700 were proved in the PCC, five of whom were gentlemen and in 1710, six of ten; BRO, R/AL4.

Chapter 8: Politics, commerce and improvement, 1740–1835

1 The 1740 Reading total is deduced from baptismal totals, the 1801 and later population totals from table of population *VCH*, ii, 236–43; national totals from Holmes and Szechi, 345; Rocque's map of Berkshire, 1761.

2 Diary, 1758–86, R/AC1/1/23, p. 207.

3 The occupations of 9 of 21 councillors in the 1750s have been traced, three gentlemen, two brewers and two merchants, one dealing in timber. Four brewers and several retailers appear in the *Universal Directory*, 1796. Length of service by 1796 from BRO, Record of admission of freemen 1700 – R/RF1/2.

4 Diary, 1715–26 and 1737–58, R/AC1/1/20 and 22, *passim*. The properties insured in 1752 were the Oracle for £400, the Town Hall £500 and the Blue School £400. (ibid, p. 154). In the 1774 parliamentary by-election, for Berkshire, the meeting to nominate candidates was held at Reading and the election at Abingdon.

5 Diary, *passim*.

6 Diary, 1758–86 and 1786–1809 (R/A1/1/23 and 24), *passim*; Michael Naxton, *The History of Reading School* (Reading, n.d.), 43, 49–50.

7 Diary, 1786–1809, p. 195; Reading Borough miscellaneous bills 1813/14 R/FZ2/40/29 and R/FZ2/40/44.

8 Chamberlains' Accounts 1742/3–1821/35 (R/FA3/76–128); Receivers' Accounts, 1737–1822 (R/FA41–41) and Rent Rolls, 1766–1820 (incomplete) (R/FA8/92–94).

9 Chamberlains' Accounts, 1721–23 (R/FA3/71) and Receiver's Account, 1760–61 (R/FA4/29); Diary, 1758–86, p. 81. Between 1737 and 1822 rental income was recorded in the receiver's accounts. Annesley became a councillor in 1771.

10 To meet the huge costs of the French wars, in 1799 Pitt's government changed the old tax on land dating from 1693, landowners being encouraged to redeem the charge for a one-off payment. Eric J. Evans, *The Forging of the Modern State, 1783–1870* (3rd edn, 2001), 101; Diary, 1786–1809, pp. 102, 105, 119. Land Tax was abolished in 1963.

11 Diary, 1786–1809, pp. 184–5; Chamberlains' Accounts, 1821–35 (R/FA3/128); Report of the Municipal Corporations Commission: the Corporation of Reading, 1833.

12 Sir Lewis Namier and J. Brooke, *The History of Parliament: The Commons, 1754–1790* (1964), 212; Aspinall, 78, 80–1.

13 Diary, 1737–58, p. 236.

14 Daniel and Samuel Lysons, *Magna Britannia: Berkshire* (1806), 340; Kenneth R. Clew, *The Kennet and Avon Canal: an illustrated history* (Newton Abbot, 1968), 24–7; Diary, 1694–1712 (R/AC1/1/19), pp. 116, 117, 122; Man, 163. The waterway was named for its engineer, James Rennie.

15 Diary, 1758–86, p. 156; *Reading Mercury*, 12 November, 1791; Jeremy Sims (ed.), *Thames Navigation Commission Minutes, 1771–1790* (BRS, 11 and 12, 2008–09), i, vii, xv–xxiv. The corporation had 1,000 handbills printed advertising a public meeting, a technique adopted on several occasions.

16 Charles Hadfield, *The Canals of Southern England* (1955), *passim*; Clewer, 79; Reading Quarter Sessions, 1768–77 (R/JQ8/2).

17 Brian Boulter, 'The roads of Berkshire' in Joan Dils (ed.), *An Historical Atlas of Berkshire* (Reading, 1998), 68–9; *Reading Mercury*, 26

May, 1762, 16 May 1785; *Universal Directory,*
*c.*1796; *Horniman's Reading Directory,* 1826.
For turnpikes generally see W.I. Albert, *The*
Turnpike Road System in England, 1663–1840
(1972).

18 C.W. Chalklin, 'South East', in P. Clark (ed.),
Cambridge Urban History, 2 (2000), 56, 65.
Archaeological evidence suggests that St Giles'
Mill was substantially extended in this period,
confirmation of the importance of the grain
trade (Ford, 298).

19 Chamberlains' Accounts (R/FA3/28); Man,
166; BRO, Market Account Book, 1800–13
(R/FA14/16); Diary, 1737–58, p. 155 and
1786–1809, pp. 79, 109, 184; Pat Smart, 'The
covered market, the forgotten archway and the
Arcade at Reading', *B.O. and N.,* 28 (2011),
37–41. A quarter was a measure of volume not
weight, equal to eight bushels. A quarter of
wheat weighed over 500 lbs.

20 Chamberlains' Accounts, general reference
R/FA3; Coates, 456; Diary, 1758–58, p. 281;
Lysons, *Britannia,* 340; William Clift,
Reminiscences of William Clift of Bramley
(Basingstoke, n.d.), 25.

21 Coates, 456; BRO, Windsor Forest Turnpike
Trust Account Book (D/EGL/01) for 24
September 1759.

22 They and five others reclaimed excise duty
because the barge sank. Borough Quarter
sessions R/JQ1/7; Childs, 23; T.A.B. Corley,
The Road to Worton Grange: Simonds' and
Courage's Brewery at Reading, 1785–1980
(Reading, n.d.).

23 T.A.B. Corley, 'Reading in the Eighteenth
Century and Victorian Times' Petyt (ed.),
90–2; Diana Mackarill, 'Early Nineteenth-
century Printers in Reading' *B.O. and N.,* 25
(2008).

24 Borough Miscellaneous Receipts (R/
FZ2/33/8).

25 Account of Several Workhouses, 1732
quoted in Paul Slack, *The English Poor Law,*
1531–1782 (Basingstoke, 1990), 42. Pigot's
Directory, 1830 located St Giles' workhouse in
Southampton Street, St Mary's in Coley Street
and St Laurence's in Friar Street.

26 Reading Quarter Sessions, 1768–1777 (R/
JQ8/2); St Giles' Overseers' accounts (D/
P96/16/3/2). The totals and analysis are of
the examinants only, not counting wives
and dependent children. The total number

claiming poor relief is therefore much higher
though it is difficult to say many of the
children were dependants.

27 Abstract of Returns Relative to the State of the
Poor, 1802–03 (Parliamentary Paper 175, 1804).

28 BRO, St Giles' Vestry Minutes, 1815–36, D/
P96/8/4, no pagination. For national food
prices see Lionel Munby, *How Much is That*
Worth? (British Association for Local History,
1989), 28.

29 Diary, 1737–58, R/AC1/1/22, p. 236; BRO,
Reading Miscellaneous receipts, February
1766/67, R/FZ33/1–3.

30 Man, 413–20; Chamberlains' Accounts
throughout.

31 Diary, 1737–58 (R/AC1/1/22); Diary 1758–86
(R/AC1/1/23), pp. 346–7; Diary, 1786–95
(R/AC1/1/24), p. 27; Reading Borough,
Miscellaneous Bills, February 1767 (R/
FZ33/1, 2, 3) and 1814 (R/FZ2/40/8 and 9).
Quarter Sessions transportation orders (R/
JG1/2/1–110. In the parish of Barkham, the
weekly income of farm labourers averaged
between eight and nine shillings. Pamela
Horn, *A Georgian Parson and his Village*
(Abingdon, 1981), 63–9.

32 BRO, Childrey Churchwardens' Accounts 1594
(D/P35/5/1); Peter Southerton, *Reading Gaol*
*by Reading Town (*Stroud, 1993), ch. 2; Diary,
1758–86, pp. 60, 70, 89, 383. The *Reading*
Mercury regularly reported trials and sentences
at the Epiphany assizes.

33 BRO, Churchwardens' presentments of
St Laurence, 1688–1837, p. 167; St Giles,
1688–1837, p. 96 and St Mary, 1666–1837,
p. 343 D/A2 c.130.

34 St Laurence churchwarden's presentments,
pp. 161, 188.

35 In October 1792 Coates asked to borrow
historic corporation documents to write a
history which was published in 1802. Diary,
1786–1809, p. 47; St Laurence churchwardens'
presentments, 1688–1837, p. 161.

36 John Dearing, *The Church that Would Not Die*
(Reading, 1993), 11–42; Leslie Harman, *The*
History of Christianity in Reading (Reading,
1952), 54–69; Leslie Harman, *The Parish of St*
Giles in Reading (Reading, 1946), 76–7.

37 Spurrier, Part 1, xxxv–xxxviii,13,15, 40, 106,
180; Summers, *Congregational Church,* 3–9,
157–67, 178–80. Broad Street Chapel is now
Waterstone's bookshop.

38 *The Works of John Wesley* (Michigan, 1872, reprinted London, n.d.), vols 1, 2, 4, *passim*; Spurrier, Part 1, 75. The building disappeared from the record before 1851.

39 John and Lindsay Mullaney, *Catholic Reading* (Reading, 2013), 11–14; Gerard Dwyer, *Diocese of Portsmouth, Past and Present* (Portsmouth, 1981), 35. Mrs Carman inherited and managed the firm which published the *Reading Mercury*. Her daughter married Thomas Cowslade who took over the business.

40 BRO, St Giles' Vestry Minutes, 1781–90 (D/P96/8/2); F.C. Parry, An account of the charitable donations to places within the County of Berks, 1818 (D/QR3/5); Man, 208–10. Man mistakenly dates the school to 1779.

41 C.W. Chalklin, *The Provincial Towns of Georgian England: a study of the building process, 1740–1820* (1974), 53–4. Reading had a total of 1,751 houses in 1801 and 3,081 by 1831.

42 Diary, 1786–1809, 1809–27 and 1827–35 (R/AC1/1/24, 25 and 26) gives details of leases, many to Richard Billing, the borough surveyor; Geoffrey Tyack, Simon Bradley and Nikolaus Pevsner *Berkshire* (Yale and London, 2010), 470–1, 475–7; Gold, 16; sale particulars of Crown Lands, 1833. There were two Richard Billings, father and son, both architects. See Gold, 15–17. Uniquely 2 Eldon Road was not merely faced but built of Bath stone.

43 *Universal Directory*, c.1796; Diary, 1758–1786, p. 25.

44 Diary, 1737–58, p. 142.

45 BRO, Paving Commissioners' Minute Book, 1785–1822 (R/AS1/1/1), no pagination.

46 John Man, *The Stranger in Reading*, ed. Adam Sowan (Reading, 2005), 6, 10–11.

47 Chamberlain's Accounts Michaelmas–Michaelmas 1771–72 (BRO, R/FA3/94).

48 Diary, 1758–86, pp. 164, 353, 354, 358, 381, 387; *The Universal Directory*; E Climenson (ed.), *Passages from the diary of Mrs Philip Lybbe Powys*; Coates, 455; Man, 14–15. Part of the building includes the Victoria Room and is now enclosed within the Victorian town hall.

49 Sidney M. Gold, *A Biographical Dictionary of Architects at Reading* (privately published, Reading, 1999), 20; Diary, 1786–95, p. 9v; *Reading Mercury*, 3 December 1787, p. 3; Chamberlains' Accounts, 1821–35 (R/FA3/28).

50 Diary, 1786–1809, pp. 138, 147, 149; BRO, Register of admission of freemen, 1700–1879, R/RF1/2.

51 Childs, 30.

Chapter 9: From Belford Regis to Biscuitopolis: Reading, 1840–1911

1 Census enumerator's books, St Giles' parish, 1851 and 1881, and Coley 1851 TNA, HO 107/1692 and RG.11/1306 on microfilm RLSL; S.T. Blake, 'The physical expansion of the Borough of Reading', unpublished Ph.D. thesis, University of Reading (1976); Census of England and Wales 1911, vol. vi (HMSO, 1913) and 1891, vol. ii (HMSO, 1893). The census abstracts give birthplaces outside the county, not outside the borough.

2 Crown Estate sale catalogue, RLSL; talk by Mlle D Bloch-Rive to the History of Reading Society, 1996; Blake, thesis; Gold, 120–1.

3 An unpublished analysis of the 1851 census by an extramural class at the University of Reading in 1992.

4 Census Enumerators' books, 1851; BRO, Reading Local Board of Health General Rate Book, 1850. R/FR2/1.

5 Census of England and Wales 1831 (HMSO, 1833). St Mary's parish occupied over half the land in the borough, 1,260 acres to St Laurence 340. St Giles had 480 acres; OS Map 6 inches to mile, 1st edn, 1881–87; Wm R. Nichols, Register of Properties 1890, RLSL; 1881 census enumerator's return for St Giles, Southern Hill.; Gold, *passim*. For the Redlands Estate see Redlands Local History Group, *Old Redlands* (Reading, 1990). The middle class was defined in 1860 as all employers, all non-manual employees and all those living on unearned income. Upper middle-classes were large industrialists, leading businessmen; middle middle-class, 'middling' manufacturers, managers, substantial dealers and professionals; lower middle-class, white collar employees, small retailers and craftsmen with employees. *CUH III*, 674, 686.

6 Report of the Municipal Commissioners into the state of the Corporations in England and Wales, 24 October 1833: The Corporation of Reading. RLSL R/FA 1985.

7 Ursula Henriques, *Before the Welfare State* (1979), 246–50.

8 BRO, Reading Board of Guardians' Minute Book, 1845–46, G/R1/7; Return of the Number of Paupers in Receipt of relief in the several Unions of England and Wales on 1st day of July, 1848, Appendix to the Fourteenth Report of the Poor Law Commissioners, 1848; Peter Durrant, 'Workhouses under the Old and New Poor Law' in *Atlas*, 104; Patricia Preece, 'A new workhouse for Reading', *B.O. and N.*, vol. 3 (1986), 32–8; Gold, 217–19.

9 Marguerite Dupree, 'The provision of social services' in *CUH*, 367; 1881 Census of Reading; *Berkshire Chronicle* 20 August 1892; 2 January 1904; Yeo, 108–114; Daphne Phillips (ed.), *Reminiscences of Reading: An Octogenarian* (Newbury, 1985), 92–3.

10 Michael Lynch, *An Introduction to Modern British History, 1900–1999* (2001), 10–11.

11 W.E.M. Blandy, *A History of Reading Municipal Charities* (no date or place of publication).

12 Alexander, 2–5; Pritchard, Reading Improvement Act, 1826. The Act specified properties the commissioners could compulsorily purchase and improve.

13 John Billing, Second Report on Reading drainage etc., printed in Report of the Commission into the Reading Improvement, Markets, Waterworks and Sewage Bill, 1847 (RLSL, qR/FJ).

14 Alexander, 18; Henriques, 117–32. Reports of Royal Commissions on Public Health and the Registrar General's Annual Abstracts of Statistics were published as parliamentary papers (PP). The legislation was permissive not mandatory.

15 William Lee, A Report to the General Board of Health on a preliminary enquiry into the Sewerage, Drainage and Supply of Water, and the Sanitary Condition of the Inhabitants of the Borough of Reading in the County of Berks (London, 1850). Alexander suggests men with interests in the Water Company supported reform as their business would profit from providing an improved water supply for which the council lacked the finance.

16 The application to Reading of the Public Health Act and other powers needed for public health improvements were acquired by Orders from the General Board of Health, other powers by private or local Acts of Parliament. See Pritchard; Alexander, *passim*; Gold, 86.

17 The Act is printed in Pritchard. It also empowered the LBH to buy St Giles' Mill and fill in the Minster Stream, a health hazard; Gold, 104, 218, 131. See also O. Kean, *A Brief History and Development of Reading Waterworks* (1950). The Fobney Works was enlarged in 1890–93 and a new reservoir built at Tilehurst, 1902.

18 BRO, Reading Urban Sanitary Authority, Minutes of the Sanitary Committee, 1873–1893, R/AC2/10/1–6; Report of the Royal Commission on the Cost of Living of the Working Classes, PP Cd 3864, 1908.

19 Margaret Railton and Marshall Barr, *The Royal Berkshire Hospital, 1839–1989* (Reading, 1989), *passim*. A controversial proposal to sell the original hospital site for a 'Free School' was made and abandoned in 2013.

20 Pritchard; Patricia Smart, 'Reading Cemetery: A Private Enterprise, *B.O. and N.*, vol. 5 (1988). The land belonged to Francis Cholmeley after whom a local street is named. The cemetery was closed to new burials and a new cemetery and crematorium established in Caversham in 1927.

21 *Berkshire Chronicle*, 2 June 1838, 2 November 1833, 6 March 1834; Brian Boulter, 'The railways of Berkshire', *Atlas*, 106–7; Phillips, 113; Tyack, 468.

22 T.A.B. Corley, *Quaker Enterprise in Biscuits; Huntley and Palmers of Reading, 1822–1972* (1972), *passim*; Stevens' Directory of Reading, 1888. The 'mid-Victorian boom' lasted from *c*.1857–*c*.1873 Arthur Marwick, *Britain in our Century* (1984), 16.

23 T.A.B. Corley, *The Road to Worton Grange: Simonds' and Courage's Brewery at Reading, 1785–1980* (Reading, n.d.); T.A.B. Corley, 'A Small Berkshire Enterprise: J. Dymore Brown & Son, 1831–1944', *BAJ*, 69 (1977–78); Jonathan Brown, 'Malting and Brewing', in *Atlas*, 168–9.

24 Stevens' *Directory of Reading, 1888;* Earley Local History Group, *Suttons Seeds: A History, 1806–2006* (Reading, 2006), 13–16; articles on the Sutton family in the *Dictionary of National Biography* (2004); Kelly's *Directory of Reading*, 1911 and 1931.

25 T.A.B. Corley, 'The Reading Iron Works

in Decline 1864–1887' in Roy Green and Jonathan Brown, *Barrett, Exall & Andrewes The Reading Iron Works: The Firm and its Products* (2010), 44–8; T.A.B. Corley, 'Banks' in J. Dils (ed.), *An Historical Atlas of Berkshire* (BRS, 1998), 100.

26 James Ford 'Brickmaking', in *Atlas*, 134–5; Stevens' *Directory*; Jane Wight, *Patterns in brick: the making and use of brick in Reading* (Catalogue notes for an exhibition at Reading Museum, 1977). Thomas Hardy in *Jude the Obscure* called Reading *Aldbrickham*.

27 Census enumerators' books, 1851; Stevens' *Directory*, 1888; Martin Andrews, *George Lovejoy: a man of book and print*, unpublished typescript intended for future publication (2012); James Smart (ed.), *London Street Described* (privately published, 2007), 25; Report on the Cost of Living of the Working Classes P P Cd.3864, 1908.

28 1891 Census Abstracts, vol. x, Occupations and Industries (HMSO, 1913, Cd 7019), 29–3; census enumerator's returns 1881.

29 Report on the Cost of Living, 386–90; Stevens' *Directory* 1888; Yeo, 356.

30 Report on the Cost of Living; Reading Tramway Order 1878 and Reading Corporation (Tramways Act), 1900, printed in Pritchard. The generator and tram depot was in Mill Lane; *Berkshire Chronicle*, 2 May 1913.

31 Pritchard, Reading Corporation Markets Act, 1853; Gold, 38; John Dearing (ed.), *Reading Book of Days* (2013); 1881 census. The Corn Market entrance survives but the main building is reduced to a passageway.

32 Barrie Trinder, 'Country carriers revisited', *LH*, vol. 42, no. 2 (2012), 140; Joan Dils, 'Nineteenth-century country carriers', *Atlas*, 126–7; Directories (Kelly, Billing, Stevens) 1840, 1847, 1854, 1878, 1888. Kelly lists more carriers than do local directories of a similar date.

33 Order in Council dated 14 September 1868; Kelly's *Directory of Berkshire*, 1869, refers to Reading as the county town.

34 For all buildings see Gold, especially 103 and 198. Peter Southerton, *Reading Gaol by Reading Town* (Stroud, 1993), 12–19, 24–30. Until 1868 Berkshire had two county towns. Judith Hunter suggested that Abingdon built its County Hall in 1678 to further its claim to the title though it was only able to share the honour with Reading. Judith Hunter, *A History of Berkshire* (Chichester, 1995), 80–1, 103. Alfred Waterhouse was a Liverpool man who had built his own house, Foxhill, at Whiteknights.

35 Meeting reported in the *Berkshire Chronicle* 20 November 1886; Alexander, 90–102; Wm R, Nichols, Register of Properties, 1890 RLSL; Pritchard.

36 Joan A Dils, 'From Village to Suburb: Caversham, 1840–1911 *Oxoniensia*, vol. lxiv (1999); Alexander, 102–24. As part of the 1911 extension, Reading agreed to widen or reconstruct the bridge and make a substantial footbridge at the Clappers. A new Caversham Bridge was built in 1926 and Reading (road) Bridge in 1923.

37 Alexander, 174–5; Yeo, 253–62. Socialists gained seats on the School Board and Board of Guardians.

38 Aspinall, 94–97, 114–15; Alexander, 174–5; Lorenzo Quelch, *An Old-Fashioned Socialist: An Autobiography* (Lorenzo Quelch Memorial Group, Reading, n.d.).

Chapter 10: Religion, education and culture *c.*1892: retrospect and prospect

1 Kate Tiller (ed.), *Berkshire Religious Census, 1851* (BRS, 14, 2010), 67–9.

2 Tiller, xxxvi; Yeo suggests 68.5%, but he does not allow for those attending two services.

3 There is a small memorial tablet to him in St Mary's church.

4 Gold *passim*, Tyack, *passim*.

5 The Religious Census did not record all the chapels known from other sources. Gold, *passim*; Tyack, *passim*; Stephen Yeo, *Religion and Voluntary Organisations in Crisis* (1976), 53 and *passim*; H.G. Arnold, *Victorian Architecture in Reading* (1976). Ebenezer West was the initiator of the Baptist Free Church, later called the West Memorial Institute, now converted to apartments.

6 St Bartholomew, apart from the chancel and porch, was designed by Waterhouse who came from a Quaker background. Later worshippers wrote church and chapel histories, many available in RLSL. They include

St Bartholomew, St Luke and Caversham Heights Methodist Church.

7 The Newcastle Commission on Popular Education reported in 1861.

8 See chapter 9 for schools before 1840; 1851 Census on Education, England and Wales P P, 1852–53, vol. xc. Literacy is defined as the ability to make a signature in a register – W.B. Stephens, *Education, Literacy and Society, 1830–70* (1987). See Joan Dils, 'Elementary education, 1819–1902', in *Atlas*, 118–9. Most school log books are now in the BRO.

9 Reading School Board Annual Reports, 1874–1902, RLSL R/GB/12856.

10 Most of these schools are still in use.

11 Reading School Board Annual Reports. Pupil-teachers were apprentices, learning on the job with subject teaching from the principal. They were eligible for entry to training college if successful in the Queen's Scholarship Examination where they could become certificated teachers. See Alexander, ch. 5, for the relationship between borough council and school board.

12 The 1902 report did not mention St James RC School which had more than 150 pupils.

13 Yeo, 60.

14 Michael Naxton, *The History of Reading School* (Reading, 1986), *passim*; Pritchard, Reading School Act, 1867 and Kendrick Schools Scheme, 1875, 1908, 1910; Alexander, 132–7; OS map, 1st edn, 1882; J.L. Hobbs, *Kendrick Boys' School, Reading, 1877–1916*, unpublished typescript, RLSL (1965). Mary Kendrick (1691–1713) was the last of the family to live in Reading.

15 H.F. Burgess, *A History of the Reading Blue Coat School, 1660–1960* (Reading, 1977). See Chapter 8 for the Green School.

16 Directories; Redlands Local History group, *Old Redlands* (Reading, 1990), 17.

17 The Willis organ, presented to the council in 1864, was moved from the Small Town Hall, enlarged and placed in what is now called the Concert Hall. Phillips, 134

18 Alexander, 81–2; Gold, 103; Martin Andrews, *George Lovejoy, a man of book and print*, typescript in preparation for publication (2012).

19 Directories; David Cliffe, *Roots and Branches: The Centenary History of Battle and Caversham Libraries, Reading* (Reading, 2007), *passim*; Alan Rogers, *Approaches to Local History* (1977), 211–13. The Carnegie Trust was set up by Andrew Carnegie, a Scots immigrant to the USA turned iron and steel millionaire, to build and equip public libraries in Britain provided that local authorities provided the sites and guaranteed maintenance.

20 Yeo, 299; Gold, 103; *Reading Observer*, 3 January 1891.

21 Local press 1892. For the early years of the college see William Macbride Childs, *Making a University* (1933), *passim*. Sir Robert Loyd-Lindsay, Lord Wantage owned an estate near Wantage.

22 Mel Doyle, *A Very Special Adventure: the illustrated history of the Workers' Educational Association* (2003); Childs, *passim*.

23 1851 Census of Education; Reading Directories, 1840–1900; Yeo, especially chs 6 and 7.

24 Yeo, 63.

25 For all details on the Temperance Movement see Yeo, *passim*; for meetings see local press and directories.

26 Yeo, 34. Reading, ranked 14th of 63 towns was assessed for Schedule D income tax at £11.87 per head of population. Richard Trainor, 'The middle class' in *CUH III*, Table 21.1, 690.

27 Yeo, 34, 36.

28 Yeo, 291–2.

29 For earlier accounts of horse-racing see Chapter 8.

30 All these were advertised in the local press or listed in directories. For water sports see Gillian Clark, *Down by the Rivers: the Thames and Kennet in Reading* (Reading, 2009).

31 Daphne Phillips, *Reading Theatres, Cinemas and Other Entertainments, 1788–1978* (Reading, 1978); *Reading Chronicle* advertisements throughout the period. Since the theatre burned down in 1937 the borough has lacked a permanent location for serious drama.

32 David Downs, *Biscuits and Royals: A History of Reading Football Club, 1871–1986* (Reading, 1986).

33 Yeo, especially ch. 6.

Chapter 11: Survivals and arrivals: Reading, 1912–1960

1 Corley in Petyt (ed.), 106; A.L. Bowley, 'Reading', in A.L. Bowley and A.R. Burnett-Hurst, *Livelihood and Poverty: a study in the economic condition of working-class households in Northampton, Warrington, Stanley and Reading* (1915), *passim*. Bowley, a professor at the University College, considered that income should be sufficient to allow some expenditure on more than bare necessities, such as a few pence on meat. He used the techniques and criteria pioneered by Charles Booth's and Seebohm Rowntree's investigations of working-class families in respectively London 1903 and York 1901.

2 C. Fox *et al.*, *Responding to the Call: the Kitchener Battalions of the Royal Berkshire Regiment at the Battle of Loos, 1915* (Reading, n.d.). A bronze memorial to Trooper Potts in Abbey Walk was unveiled on 2 October 2015.

3 *Reading Standard, Reading Observer* and *Berkshire Chronicle*, 1914–19; Minutes of Reading Borough Council, 1913–14, 1915–16, 1917–19; Railton, ch. 6; Phillips, 149–50; RLSL exhibition, November 2013. The government's official cost-of-living index, July 1914 = 100 was 203 by 1918. Lionel Munby, *How Much is That Worth?* (Chichester, 1989), 38.

4 MOH reports to Reading Borough Health Committee, 1918–19 (RLSL, R/FA); Simon Szreter and Anne Hardy, 'Urban fertility and mortality patterns' in Martin Daunton (ed.), *CUH III*, 649, 652.

5 *Reading Chronicle*, 2 May 1913; MOH Report in Reading Borough Council Minutes, 1929–30 and 1930–31, BRO, R/AC1/3/45 and 47. Population in census 1921: 92,278, 1931: 97,153. The Second World War prevented a census in 1941, the only gap between 1801 and the present.

6 Aspinall, 115–16; Alexander, 179–82, 192–6. Payment for MPs, introduced in 1911, allowed politicians without private means to serve in parliament.

7 BRO, Reading Borough Council Minutes: Housing Committees 1929–30, 1930–31, 1937–38, R/AC1/3/45, 48, 69; Alexander, 195–8; Margaret Simons, 'Local Authority Housing in Berkshire, 1919–1938', in *Atlas*; Colin G. Pooley, *Local Authority Housing: origins and development* (Historical Association,

1996).

8 BRO, Reading Borough Council Minutes: Housing Committee, 1937–38, R/AC1/3/69; Mark Clapson, *Working-class Suburb: Social Change on an English Council Estate, 1930–2010* (Manchester, 2012), 21–73; Colin G. Pooley, *Local Authority Housing: origins and development*.

9 Sale catalogues in RLSL; Reading Official Town Guide, 1939; Mary French, *The Housing of Reading* (reprint from *Reading Standard*, 1948).

10 Alexander, 152; BRO, Education Committee Minutes, 1929–30, 1930–31, 1937–38 R/AC1/3/45, 48, 68; W.E.M. Blandy, *A History of Reading Municipal Charities* (n.d.).

11 Reports in the *Reading Mercury* and *Reading Standard*, 1 and 8 July 1916. My thanks to Keith Jerome for alerting me to these reports.

12 A.L. Bowley and M. Hogg, *Has Poverty Diminished? A Sequel to 'Livelihood and Poverty'* (1925); BRO, Reports of the MOH 1929 and 1931 R/AC1/45 and 48; Lionel Munby, *How much is that worth?*, 38–9.

13 BRO, Reading Borough Council Minutes, Public Assistance Committee Minutes, 1930–31, R/AC1/3/48; Railton and Barr, 212–14. The Health Committee also administered Park Hospital, Whitley Smallpox Hospital and Dellwood Maternity Home.

14 Arthur Marwick, *Britain in our Century; Images and Controversies* (1984), 97; BRO, Reading Borough Council Minutes: Public Assistance Committee, 1930–31, R/AC1/3/48.

15 BRO, Reading Borough Council Minutes: Public Assistance Committee, 1929–30, R/AC1/3/45; Group Project, *The South Street Labour Exchange* (Reading, 2011), 2; letter to *Reading Midweek*, 16 April 1984; Coley Local History Group, *Talking of Coley* (Reading, 1990), 28.

16 Census 1921 (HMSO, 1924) and 1931 (HMSO, 1933); advertisements in the *Reading Review* 1930s and 1940s.

17 Pat Smart, 'Corn for sale! The markets and corn exchanges in Reading and Wokingham', *B.O. and N.*, 30 (2013).

18 D.A. Hall, *Reading Trolley Buses, 1936–1968* (Reading, 1991) 11–37; *Reading Town Guide*, 1957.

19 Anon, *Airs and Places: People and Music in Berkshire* (Reading, 1999); *Reading Review*, monthly, 1935 and 1936; *Reading Town Guide*, 1927 and 1939. There was roller skating at the New Corn Exchange. See note 15.

20 BRO, Reading Borough Defence Committee Minutes, 1938–39. Since much of Reading's war-time history replicates what other towns of its size and significance experienced, I have merely sketched an outline with a few details of local significance. I have used advertisements and reports in the *Reading Mercury* extensively but have not referenced them except by a date in the text. See also Joan Dils, 'Berkshire in World War II', in *Atlas*, 146–7.

21 Railton, 235; M.I. Parsons, *I'll Take That One: Dispelling the Myths of Civilian Evacuation, 1939–45* (Peterborough, 1998), 189. See Clapson for social conditions revealed in the Whitley Survey 1943.

22 Allowances for children were more generous. The resulting diet was one of the healthiest on record.

23 Aspinall, 116. Reading returned two members in 1950 and 1951, Mikardo for Reading South. In 1955 the borough was again a single-member constituency.

24 Prime Minister, Harold Macmillan in 1957, quoted by Peter Hennessy, *Having it So Good: Britain in the Fifties* (2006), 1.

25 1951 Census of England and Wales (HMSO, 1954), xiii–xv; talk at History of Reading Society: Poles in Reading (2012).

26 1961 Census of England and Wales vol. 1 (HMSO, 1964); *The South Street Labour Exchange* (2011), 11–13; Ann Westgarth (ed.), *Routes to Reading* (2006), 189–92, 197–203. The period of West Indian immigration is

known as the Windrush era from the name of the first immigrant ship.

27 Clapson, 118.

28 Pooley, 19–20; Mary French, *The Housing of Reading* (reprint from *Reading Standard*, 1948); Borough Treasurer's Report to Housing Committee 1955; 1963 *Town Guide.*

29 Railton, 283–4. For a succinct summary of the Report and the reforms of the 1940s see Michael Lynch, *An Introduction to Modern British History, 1900–1999* (2001), 203–6, 133–5. The Dispensary was demolished in 1976 to make way for an expansion of John Lewis' store though the firm offered to rebuild it on another site.

30 *Reading Town Guide*, 1947 and 1963; Alexander, 154–8. Alexander discusses the political problems resulting from this re-organisation. I am more critical of the scheme than he in terms of its educational and social value. 'O' and 'A' (Ordinary and Advanced level) examinations replaced School Certificate in 1951. For the Blue Coat School see H.F. Burgess, *A History of Reading Blue Coat School*, 132–48.

31 J.C. Holt, *The University of Reading: the first fifty years* (Reading, 1977), 137–154; Reading Town Guide, 1963. The Whiteknights Park estate was bought for £105,000, financed by a grant from the University Grants Committee in London.

32 David Gilbert and Humphrey Southall, 'The urban labour market' in *CUH*, 623; David Reeder and Richard Rodger, 'Industrialisation and the city economy', in *CUH*, 570; 1841 and 1951 census abstracts. In 1947 there were 2800 job vacancies and only 400 unemployed. Earley Local History Group, *Suttons Seeds: a History, 1806–2006* (Reading, 2006), 26.

33 Hennessy, *Having it So Good*, 245, 537, 491.

Chapter 12: The latest transformation: Reading since 1960

1 Michael Breheny and Douglas Hart, *Reading in Profile: a survey of key economic issues for the Greater Reading Area in the 1990s* (Reading, 1994), 2, 5; evidence on the borough in the Report of the Housing, Planning, Local Government and the Regions Committee (Stationery Office, 2006)

2 1971 Census (HMSO, 1976); 1981 and 1991 Censuses (HMSO, 1982 and 1993).

3 Censuses, 1991–2011; *Reading Midweek*, 14 November 2012; Reading *Evening Post*, 2 January 2013; *An Analysis of the Main Languages in Reading* (for Reading Borough Council, 2013); Ann Westgarth, *Routes to Reading* (Reading, 2006). The Oxford Road area was described in 2012 as 'A World in One Place'.

4 Censuses, 1971–2001; *1991 Census* (Berkshire

Office of Population Census and Surveys, 1992); 2001 Census: Key Statistics by Local Authority KS01: Reading (HMSO, 2003); *Reading in the 2011 Census; data analysis by students of the University of Reading* (Reading, 2013); Caroline Hancock *Reading Borough Profile in 2001 census* (2003).

5 Dee Road Official Opening Souvenir 4 November 1969; *Reading Official Town Guide*, 1980, RLSL; Clapson, 153; *Revealing Reading's Hidden History: Orts Road and Newtown* (Reading Museum, 2013); local press reports since 1976.

6 Censuses, 1991–2011; Key Statistics for local authorities: Reading Urban Authority; Reading Borough Consultation Paper on Multiple Occupancy November, 1987; *Reading Midweek* 22 May 2013.

7 All information on schools from the county and borough guides on parental choice of school since 1998 and from local newspapers.

8 Alexander, 159–164; Reading East Parliamentary Report, Spring, 2013. Bulmershe College of Higher Education became part of Reading University in 1989.

9 Souvenir Guide to Reading's new Central Library, July, 1985; Joan Dils, *A 100 Years of Public Service; a History of Berkshire County Council* (Reading, 2000), 12.

10 Tyack, 472.

11 Corley, *passim*; S.H. Pitman, *Huntley, Boorne and Stevens of Reading and Woodley, 1832–1985* (Reading, n.d.), 26–7.

12 John V. Punter, *Office Development in the Borough of Reading, 1954–1984: a case study of the role of aesthetic control within the planning process* (Working paper, Reading University, 1985); Tyack, 467, 474.

13 10% sample of occupations, 1971 Census of England and Wales, Economic Activity (HMSO, 1976); Breheny, 5; 1991 Census Table 93 10% Sample by social class and economic position; 2001 census; *Reading in the 2011 Census: data analysed by students from the University of Reading.*(Reading, 2013).

14 Caroline Hancock, *Reading Borough Profile: the 2001 Census* (Reading, 2003) shows over two-thirds of borough workers travel to work by train, bus or car.

15 The services provided by Battle Hospital were transferred to a much enlarged RBH from 1993 to 1995.

16 Caroline Hancock, *Reading Borough Profile*; *The Guardian*, 16 July 2008.

17 Clapson, 158; Caroline Hancock, *Reading Borough Profile: the 2001 census*; *Reading Midweek*, 12 June 2013; Census 2011 data analysed by Reading University students.

18 Brian Boulter, 'The railways of Berkshire', in *Atlas*, 106–7; *Reading Official Guide*, 1980.

19 Census data, 1971–2011; Reading Borough Guides. Simon Bradley admired the Victorian station though he regarded the extension of 1985–89 as 'ungainly': Tyack, 457. The Civic Society was founded in 1961 in response to the threat to Reading's architectural heritage. It has had mixed success.

20 Reading had two MPs, representing Reading North and South after 1971 and Reading East and West since 1984.

21 Gillian Clark, *Down by the River: the Thames and Kennet in Reading* (Reading, 2009), 190–195.

22 Adam Stout (ed.), *Risc: of books, stones, friends and visions: nos 35–39 London Street, Reading* (Reading, 1997); Tyack, *passim*.

23 *Evening Post*, 13 October 2010; *Guardian*, 12 June 2013.

24 *Migrant Entrepreneurs: Building Our Business Creating Our Jobs* reported over 7,000 firms in Reading set up by migrants. *Evening Post*, 12 March 2014.

Index

Index of Places